MONGOLIA

COUNTRY STUDY GUIDE

VOLUME 1

STRATEGIC INFORMATION AND DEVELOPMENTS

International Business Publications, USA
Washington DC, USA - Mongolia

MONGOLIA

COUNTRY STUDY GUIDE

VOLUME 1 STRATEGIC INFORMATION AND DEVELOPMENTS

UPDATED ANNUALLY

We express our sincere gratitude to all government agencies and international organizations which provided information and other materials for this guide

Cover Design: International Business Publications, USA

2018 Edition Updated Reprint International Business Publications, USA
ISBN 0-7397-4382-1

For additional analytical, business and investment opportunities information,
please contact Global Investment & Business Center, USA
at (703) 370-8082. Fax: (703) 370-8083. E-mail: ibpusa3@gmail.com
Global Business and Investment Info Databank - www.ibpus.com

Printed in the USA

MONGOLIA

COUNTRY STUDY GUIDE

VOLUME 1

STRATEGIC INFORMATION AND DEVELOPMENTS

TABLE OF CONTENTS

STRATEGIC AND DEVELOPMENT PROFILES

BASIC INFORMATION

Capital and largest city	Ulaanbaatar Coordinates: 47°55′N 106°53′E
Official languages	Mongolian
Official scripts	Mongolian Cyrillic Mongolian script
Ethnic groups	• 96% Mongols • 4% Kazakhs
Religion	Buddhism (53%) Islam (3%) Shamanism (2.9%) Christianity (2.2%)
Demonym	• Mongolian • Mongol
Government	Unitary semi-presidential republic
• President	Khaltmaagiin Battulga
• Prime Minister	Ukhnaagiin Khürelsükh
Legislature	State Great Khural
Formation	
• Xiongnu Empire	formed 209 BC
• Mongol Empire	formed 1206
• Declaration of independence from Qing dynasty, China	December 29, 1911
• Mongolian People's Republic was established	November 26, 1924
• Independence was recognized by Republic of China	January 5, 1946
• Current Constitution	February 13, 1992
Area	
• Total	1,566,000 km^2 (605,000 sq mi) (18th)
• Water (%)	0.43
Population	
• 2016 estimate	3,081,677 (134th)
• Density	1.97 km^2 (5.1/sq mi) (238th)
GDP (PPP)	2018estimate
• Total	$40.1 billion
• Per capita	$12,925
GDP (nominal)	2018 estimate
• Total	$11.5 billion
• Per capita	$3,720
Gini	36.5 medium
HDI (2014)	▲ 0.727 high · 90th
Currency	Tögrög (MNT)
Time zone	(UTC+7/+8

• Summer (DST)	(UTC+8/+9
Date format	yyyy.mm.dd (CE)
Drives on the	right
Calling code	+976
ISO 3166 code	MN
Internet TLD	.mn, .мон

Mongolia literally *Mongol country/nation*) is a landlocked country in East and Central Asia. It is bordered by Russia to the north and the People's Republic of China to the south, east and west. Although Mongolia does not share a border with Kazakhstan, its western-most point is only 38 kilometres (24 mi) from Kazakhstan's eastern tip. Ulaanbaatar, the capital and largest city, is home to about 38% of the population. Mongolia's political system is a parliamentary republic.

The area of what is now Mongolia has been ruled by various nomadic empires, including the Xiongnu, the Xianbei, the Rouran, the Gökturks and others. The Mongol Empire was founded by Genghis Khan in 1206. After the collapse of the Yuan Dynasty, the Mongols returned to their earlier pattern of constant internal conflict and occasional raids on the Chinese borderlands. In the 16th and 17th centuries, Mongolia came under the influence of Tibetan Buddhism. At the end of the 17th century, most of Mongolia had been incorporated into the area ruled by the Qing Dynasty. During the collapse of the Qing Dynasty in 1911, Mongolia declared independence, but had to struggle until 1921 to firmly establish *de facto* independence from the Republic of China, and until 1945 to gain international recognition.

As a consequence, it came under strong Russian and Soviet influence; in 1924, the Mongolian People's Republic was declared, and Mongolian politics began to follow the same patterns as the Soviet politics of the time. After the breakdown of communist regimes in Eastern Europe in late 1989, Mongolia saw its own Democratic Revolution in early 1990, which led to a multi-party system, a new constitution in 1992, and transition to a market economy.

At 1,564,116 square kilometres (603,909 sq mi), Mongolia is the 19th largest and the most sparsely populated independent country in the world, with a population of around 2.9 million people. It is also the world's second-largest landlocked country after Kazakhstan. The country contains very little arable land, as much of its area is covered by steppes, with mountains to the north and west and the Gobi Desert to the south. Approximately 30% of the population are nomadic or semi-nomadic. The predominant religion in Mongolia is Tibetan Buddhism, and the majority of the state's citizens are of the Mongol ethnicity, though Kazakhs, Tuvans, and other minorities also live in the country, especially in the west. About 20% of the population live on less than US$1.25 per day. Analysts have predicted that Mongolia can become one of fastest-growing economies of the 2010s, as well as a key investment target for global mining corporations

STRATEGIC PROFILE

Background: Long a province of China, Mongolia won its independence in 1921 with Soviet backing. A communist regime was installed in 1924. During the early 1990s, the ex-communist Mongolian People's Revolutionary Party (MPRP) gradually yielded its monopoly on power. In 1996, the Democratic Union Coalition (DUC) defeated the MPRP in a national election and has attempted to establish a number of reforms to modernize the economy. However, many former communists retain key posts and implementation has been difficult.

GEOGRAPHY

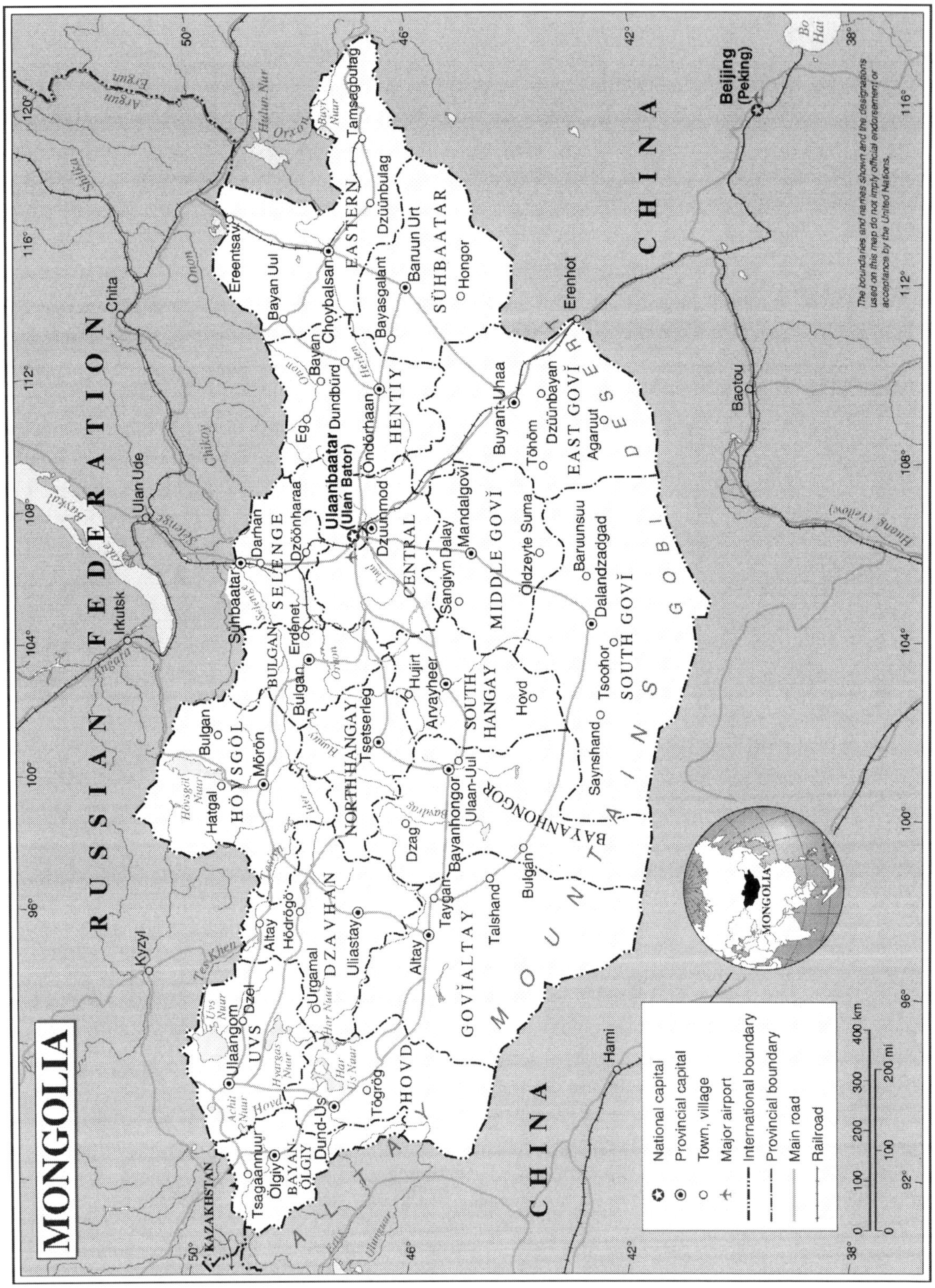

Location: Northern Asia, between China and Russia

Geographic coordinates: 46 00 N, 105 00 E

Map references: Asia

Area:
total: 1.565 million sq km
land: 1.565 million sq km
water: 0 sq km

Area - comparative: slightly smaller than Alaska

Land boundaries:
total: 8,114 km
border countries: China 4,673 km, Russia 3,441 km

Coastline: 0 km (landlocked)

Maritime claims: none (landlocked)

Climate: desert; continental (large daily and seasonal temperature ranges)

Terrain: vast semidesert and desert plains; mountains in west and southwest; Gobi Desert in southeast

Elevation extremes:
lowest point: Hoh Nuur 518 m *highest point:* Tavan Bogd Uul 4,374 m

Natural resources: oil, coal, copper, molybdenum, tungsten, phosphates, tin, nickel, zinc, wolfram, fluorspar, gold

Land use:
arable land: 1% *permanent crops:* 0% *permanent pastures:* 80%
forests and woodland: 9% *other:* 10%

Irrigated land: 800 sq km
Natural hazards: dust storms can occur in the spring; grassland fires
Environment - current issues: limited natural fresh water resources; policies of the former communist regime promoting rapid urbanization and industrial growth have raised concerns about their negative effects on the environment; the burning of soft coal in power plants and the lack of enforcement of environmental laws have severely polluted the air in Ulaanbaatar; deforestation, overgrazing, the converting of virgin land to agricultural production have increased soil erosion from wind and rain; desertification and mining activities have also had a deleterious effect on the environment

Environment - international agreements:
party to: Biodiversity, Climate Change, Climate Change-Kyoto Protocol, Desertification, Endangered Species, Environmental Modification, Hazardous Wastes, Law of the Sea, Nuclear Test Ban, Ozone Layer Protection, Wetlands
signed, but not ratified: none of the selected agreements

Geography - note: landlocked; strategic location between China and Russia

ADMINISTRATIVE DIVISIONS

Mongolia is divided in 21 *Aimags* (provinces) and three municipalities/cities (*khot*): Arkhangai, Bayan-Ölgii, Bayankhongor, Bulgan, Darkhan-Uul, Dornod, Dornogovi, Dundgovi, Govi-Altai, Govisümber, Khentii, Khovd, Khövsgöl, Ömnögovi, Orkhon, Övörkhangai, Selenge, Sükhbaatar, Töv, Uvs, Zavkhan.

Local *khurals* (parliaments) are elected in the 21 aimags plus the capital, Ulaanbaatar. On the next lower administrative level, they are elected in provincial subdivisions and urban sub-districts in Ulaanbaatar.

PEOPLE

Population: 2,650,952

Age structure:
0-14 years: 34% (male 461,719; female 447,426)
15-64 years: 62% (male 816,851; female 816,651)
65 years and over: 4% (male 46,682; female 61,623)

Population growth rate: 1.54%
Birth rate: 21.53 births/1,000 population
Death rate: 6.14 deaths/1,000 population
Net migration rate: 0 migrant(s)/1,000 population

Sex ratio:
at birth: 1.05 male(s)/female
under 15 years: 1.03 male(s)/female
15-64 years: 1 male(s)/female
65 years and over: 0.76 male(s)/female
total population: 1 male(s)/female

Infant mortality rate: 41.22 deaths/1,000 live births

Life expectancy at birth:
total population: 67.25 years
male: 64.98 years
female: 69.64 years

Total fertility rate: 2.4 children born/woman

Nationality:
noun: Mongolian(s)
adjective: Mongolian

Ethnic groups: Mongol 90%, Kazakh 4%, other 6%
Religions: predominantly Tibetan Buddhist, Muslim 4%
note: previously limited religious activity because of communist regime
Languages: Khalkha Mongol 90%, Turkic, Russian

Literacy:
definition: age 15 and over can read and write
total population: 82.9%
male: 88.6%
female: 77.2% (1988 est.)

GOVERNMENT

Country name:
conventional long form: none
conventional short form: Mongolia
local long form: none
local short form: Mongol Uls
former: Outer Mongolia

Data code: MG
Government type: republic
Capital: Ulaanbaatar

Administrative divisions: 18 provinces (aymguud, singular - aymag) and 3 municipalities* (hotuud, singular - hot); Arhangay, Bayanhongor, Bayan-Olgiy, Bulgan, Darhan*, Dornod, Dornogovi, Dundgovi, Dzavhan, Erdenet*, Govi-Altay, Hentiy, Hovd, Hovsgol, Omnogovi, Ovorhangay, Selenge, Suhbaatar, Tov, Ulaanbaatar*, Uvs

Independence: 13 March 1921 (from China)
National holiday: National Day, 11 July (1921)
Constitution: 12 February 1992

Legal system: blend of Russian, Chinese, Turkish, and Western systems of law that combines aspects of a parliamentary and presidential system; constitution ambiguous on judicial review of legislative acts; has not accepted compulsory ICJ jurisdiction

Suffrage: 18 years of age; universal

Executive branch:

chief of state: President Khaltmaa BATTULGA (since 10 July 2017)
head of government: Prime Minister Ukhnaa KHURELSUKH (since 4 October 2017); Deputy Prime Minister Ulziisaikhan ENKHTUVSHUN (since 18 October 2017); note - Prime Minister Jargaltulga ERDENEBAT (since 8 July 2016) was voted out of office by the Parliament on 7 September 2017

cabinet: Cabinet nominated by the prime minister in consultation with the president, confirmed by the State Great Hural (parliament)

elections/appointments: presidential candidates nominated by political parties represented in the State Great Hural and directly elected by simple majority popular vote for a 4-year term (eligible for a second term); election last held on 26 June 2017 with a runoff held 7 July 2017 (next to be held in 2021); following legislative elections, the leader of the majority party or majority coalition usually elected prime minister by the State Great Hural
election results: Khaltmaa BATTULGA elected president in second round; percent of vote in first round - Khaltmaa BATTULGA (DP) 38.1%, Miyegombo ENKHBOLD (MPP) 30.3%,

Sainkhuu GANBAATAR (MPRP) 30.2%, invalid 1.4%; percent of vote in second round Khaltmaa BATTULGA 55.2%, Miyegombo ENKHBOLD 44.8%

Legislative branch:
description: unicameral State Great Hural or Ulsyn Ikh Khural (76 seats; members directly elected in single-seat constituencies by simple majority vote; each constituency requires at least 50% voter participation for the poll to be valid; members serve 4-year terms)
elections: last held on 29 June 2016 (next to be held in June 2020)
election results: percent of vote by party - MPP 45.1%, DP 33.1%, MPRP 8.0%, independent 4.8%, other 9.0%; seats by party - MPP 65, DP 9, MPRP 1, independent 1

Judicial branch:
highest court(s): Supreme Court (consists of the Chief Justice and 24 judges organized into civil, criminal, and administrative chambers); Constitutional Court or Tsets (consists of a chairman and 8 members)
judge selection and term of office: Supreme Court chief justice and judges appointed by the president upon recommendation to the State Great Hural by the General Council of Courts, a 14-member body of judges and judicial officials; term of appointment is for life; chairman of the Constitutional Court elected from among its members; members appointed by the State Great Hural upon nominations - 3 each by the president, the State Great Hural, and the Supreme Court; term of appointment is 6 years; chairmanship limited to a single renewable 3-year term

subordinate courts: aimag (provincial) and capital city appellate courts; soum, inter-soum, and district courts; Administrative Cases Courts

Political parties and leaders:
Democratic Party or DP [Sodnomzundui ERDENE]
Mongolian National Democratic Party or MNDP [Bayanjargal TSOGTGEREL]
Mongolian People's Party or MPP [Miyegombo ENKHBOLD]
Mongolian People's Revolutionary Party or MPRP [Nambar ENKHBAYAR]

Political pressure groups and leaders:
human rights groups; women's rights groups; disability rights groups

International organization participation:
ADB, ARF, CD, CICA, CP, EBRD, EITI (compliant country), FAO, G-77, IAEA, IBRD, ICAO, ICC (NGOs), ICCt, ICRM, IDA, IFAD, IFC, IFRCS, ILO, IMF, IMO, IMSO, Interpol, IOC, IOM, IPU, ISO, ITSO, ITU, ITUC, MIGA, MINURSO, MONUSCO, NAM, OPCW, OSCE, SCO (observer), UN, UNAMID, UNCTAD, UNESCO, UNIDO, UNISFA, UNMISS, UNWTO, UPU, WCO, WHO, WIPO, WMO, WTO

Diplomatic representation in the US:
chief of mission: Ambassador Yondon OTGONBAYAR (since 28 March 2018)
chancery: 2833 M Street NW, Washington, DC 20007
telephone: [1] (202) 333-7117
FAX: [1] (202) 298-9227
consulate(s) general: New York, San Francisco

Diplomatic representation from the US:
chief of mission: Chargé d'Affaires a.i. Manuel P. Micaller
embassy: Denver Street
mailing address: P.O. Box 341, Ulaanbaatar 14192
telephone: [976] 7007-6001

FAX: [976] 7007-6016

Flag description: three equal, vertical bands of red (hoist side), blue, and red; centered on the hoist-side red band in yellow is the national emblem ("soyombo" - a columnar arrangement of abstract and geometric representation for fire, sun, moon, earth, water, and the yin-yang symbol)

ECONOMY

Foreign direct investment in Mongolia's extractive industries – which are based on extensive deposits of copper, gold, coal, molybdenum, fluorspar, uranium, tin, and tungsten - has transformed Mongolia's landlocked economy from its traditional dependence on herding and agriculture. Exports now account for more than 40% of GDP. Mongolia depends on China for more than 60% of its external trade - China receives some 90% of Mongolia's exports and supplies Mongolia with more than one-third of its imports. Mongolia also relies on Russia for 90% of its energy supplies, leaving it vulnerable to price increases. Remittances from Mongolians working abroad, particularly in South Korea, are significant.

Soviet assistance, at its height one-third of GDP, disappeared almost overnight in 1990 and 1991 at the time of the dismantlement of the USSR. The following decade saw Mongolia endure both deep recession, because of political inaction, and natural disasters, as well as strong economic growth, because of market reforms and extensive privatization of the formerly state-run economy. The country opened a fledgling stock exchange in 1991. Mongolia joined the WTO in 1997 and seeks to expand its participation in regional economic and trade regimes.

Growth averaged nearly 9% per year in 2004-08 largely because of high copper prices globally and new gold production. By late 2008, Mongolia was hit by the global financial crisis and Mongolia's real economy contracted 1.3% in 2009. In early 2009, the IMF reached a $236 million Stand-by Arrangement with Mongolia and it emerged from the crisis with a stronger banking sector and better fiscal management. In October 2009, Mongolia passed long-awaited legislation on an investment agreement to develop the Oyu Tolgoi (OT) mine, among the world's largest untapped copper-gold deposits. However, a dispute with foreign investors developing OT called into question the attractiveness of Mongolia as a destination for foreign investment. This caused a severe drop in FDI, and a slowing economy, leading to the dismissal of Prime Minister Norovyn ALTANKHUYAG in November 2014. The economy had grown more than 10% per year between 2011 and 2013 - largely on the strength of commodity exports and high government spending - before slowing to 7.8% in 2014, and falling to the 2% level in 2015. Growth rebounded from a brief 1.6% contraction in the third quarter of 2016 to 5.8% during the first three quarters of 2017, largely due to rising commodity prices.

The May 2015 agreement with Rio Tinto to restart the OT mine and the subsequent $4.4 billion finance package signing in December 2015 stemmed the loss of investor confidence. The current government has made restoring investor trust and reviving the economy its top priority, but has failed to invigorate the economy in the face of the large drop-off in foreign direct investment, mounting external debt, and a sizeable budget deficit. Mongolia secured a $5.5 billion financial assistance package from the IMF and a host of international creditors in May 2017, which is expected to improve Mongolia's long-term fiscal and economic stability as long as Ulaanbaatar can advance the agreement's difficult contingent reforms, such as consolidating the government's off-balance sheet liabilities and rehabilitating the Mongolian banking sector.

GDP (purchasing power parity):

$38.4 billion (2017 est.)
$37.63 billion (2016 est.)
$37.27 billion (est.)
note: data are in 2017 dollars
country comparison to the world: 122

GDP (official exchange rate):
$10.87 billion (2017 est.)

GDP - real growth rate:
2% (2017 est.)
1% (2016 est.)
2.4% (est.)
country comparison to the world: 156

GDP - per capita (PPP):
$12,600 (2017 est.)
$12,500 (2016 est.)
$12,600 (est.)
note: data are in 2017 dollars
country comparison to the world: 121

Gross national saving:
29.3% of GDP (2017 est.)
25.9% of GDP (2016 est.)
21.1% of GDP (est.)
country comparison to the world: 27

GDP - composition, by end use:
household consumption: 51.9%
government consumption: 13.7%
investment in fixed capital: 21.7%
investment in inventories: 4.1%
exports of goods and services: 70.8%
imports of goods and services: -62.1% (2017 est.)

GDP - composition, by sector of origin:
agriculture: 13.2%
industry: 36.1%
services: 50.7% (2017 est.)

Agriculture - products:
wheat, barley, vegetables, forage crops; sheep, goats, cattle, camels, horses
Industries:
construction and construction materials; mining (coal, copper, molybdenum, fluorspar, tin, tungsten, gold); oil; food and beverages; processing of animal products, cashmere and natural fiber manufacturing

Industrial production growth rate:
6.1% (2017 est.)
country comparison to the world: 33

Labor force:
1.24 million (2016 est.)
country comparison to the world: 138

Labor force - by occupation:
agriculture: 31.1%
industry: 18.5%
services: 50.5% (2016 est.)

Unemployment rate:
8% (2017 est.)
7.9% (2016 est.)
country comparison to the world: 107

Population below poverty line:
21.6% (2014 est.)

Household income or consumption by percentage share:
lowest 10%: 13.8%
highest 10%: 8.8% (2016 est.)

Distribution of family income - Gini index:
36.5 (2008 est.)
32.8 (2002 est.)
country comparison to the world: 90
Budget:
revenues: $2.623 billion
expenditures: $3.711 billion (2017 est.)

Taxes and other revenues:
24.1% of GDP (2017 est.)
country comparison to the world: 121

Budget surplus (+) or deficit (-):
-10% of GDP (2017 est.)
country comparison to the world: 207

Public debt:
91.4% of GDP (2017 est.)
90% of GDP (2016 est.)
country comparison to the world: 25

Fiscal year:
calendar year

Inflation rate (consumer prices):
4.4% (2017 est.)
0.6% (2016 est.)
country comparison to the world: 165

Central bank discount rate:
12% (14 January 2016 est.)
13% (15 January 2015 est.)
country comparison to the world: 15

Commercial bank prime lending rate:
19.9% (31 December 2017 est.)
19.74% (31 December 2016 est.)
country comparison to the world: 17

Stock of narrow money:
$1.109 billion (31 December 2017 est.)
$839.6 million (31 December 2016 est.)
country comparison to the world: 154

Stock of broad money:
$6.257 billion (31 December 2017 est.)
$4.851 billion (31 December 2016 est.)
country comparison to the world: 124

Stock of domestic credit:
$9.406 billion (31 December 2017 est.)
$7.326 billion (31 December 2016 est.)
country comparison to the world: 112

Market value of publicly traded shares:
$632.6 million (31 December 2015 est.)
$766.1 million (31 December 2014 est.)
$1.095 billion (31 December 2013 est.)
country comparison to the world: 110

Current account balance:
$-532 million (2017 est.)
$-700 million (2016 est.)
country comparison to the world: 106

Exports:
$5.676 billion (2017 est.)
$4.804 billion (2016 est.)
country comparison to the world: 104

Exports - commodities:
copper, apparel, livestock, animal products, cashmere, wool, hides, fluorspar, other nonferrous metals, coal, crude oil

Exports - partners:
China 84.1%, UK 6.8%

Imports:
$4.196 billion (2017 est.)
$3.466 billion (2016 est.)
country comparison to the world: 131

Imports - commodities:
machinery and equipment, fuel, cars, food products, industrial consumer goods, chemicals, building materials, cigarettes and tobacco, appliances, soap and detergent

Imports - partners:

China 33.2%, Russia 25.6%, South Korea 8.6%, Japan 7%

Debt - external:
$22.28 billion (31 December 2017 est.)
$19.79 billion (31 December 2016 est.)
country comparison to the world: 91

Stock of direct foreign investment - at home:
$19.42 billion (31 December 2017 est.)
$16.28 billion (31 December 2016 est.)
country comparison to the world: 79

Stock of direct foreign investment - abroad:
$475.2 million (31 December 2017 est.)
$455.2 million (31 December 2016 est.)
country comparison to the world: 93

Exchange rates:
togrog/tugriks (MNT) per US dollar -
2,378.1 (2017 est.)
2,140.3 (2016 est.)
2,140.3 (est.)
1,970.3 (2014 est.)
1,817.9 (2013 est.)

ENERGY

Electricity access:
population without electricity: 300,000
electrification - total population: 90%
electrification - urban areas: 98%
electrification - rural areas: 73%

Electricity - production:
5.192 billion kWh (est.)
country comparison to the world: 121

Electricity - consumption:
5.785 billion kWh (est.)
country comparison to the world: 116

Electricity - exports:
51 million kWh (est.)
country comparison to the world: 86

Electricity - imports:
1.427 billion kWh (est.)
country comparison to the world: 61

Electricity - installed generating capacity:
1.106 million kW
country comparison to the world: 126

Electricity - from fossil fuels:
94.9% of total installed capacity

country comparison to the world: 54

Electricity - from nuclear fuels:
0% of total installed capacity (est.)
country comparison to the world: 136

Electricity - from hydroelectric plants:
0% of total installed capacity (est.)
country comparison to the world: 186

Electricity - from other renewable sources:
5.1% of total installed capacity (est.)
country comparison to the world: 97

Crude oil - production:
23,430 bbl/day (2016 est.)
country comparison to the world: 65

Crude oil - exports:
14,360 bbl/day (2014 est.)
country comparison to the world: 56

Crude oil - imports:
0 bbl/day (2014 est.)
country comparison to the world: 155
Crude oil - proved reserves:
0 bbl (1 January 2017 est.)
country comparison to the world: 163

Refined petroleum products - production:
0 bbl/day (2014 est.)
country comparison to the world: 169

Refined petroleum products - consumption:
26,000 bbl/day (est.)
country comparison to the world: 127

Refined petroleum products - exports:
0 bbl/day (2014 est.)
country comparison to the world: 176

Refined petroleum products - imports:
24,380 bbl/day (2014 est.)
country comparison to the world: 109

Natural gas - production:
0 cu m (2013 est.)
country comparison to the world: 164

Natural gas - consumption:
0 cu m (2013 est.)
country comparison to the world: 204

Natural gas - exports:

0 cu m (2013 est.)
country comparison to the world: 144

Natural gas - imports:
0 cu m (2013 est.)
country comparison to the world: 151

Natural gas - proved reserves:
0 cu m (1 January 2014 est.)
country comparison to the world: 167

Carbon dioxide emissions from consumption of energy:
14 million Mt (2013 est.)
country comparison to the world: 94

COMMUNICATIONS

Telephones - fixed lines:
total subscriptions: 225,287
subscriptions per 100 inhabitants: 7 (July 2016 est.)
country comparison to the world: 125

Telephones - mobile cellular:
total: 3,367,573
subscriptions per 100 inhabitants: 110
country comparison to the world: 137

Telephone system:
general assessment: network is improving with international direct dialing available in many areas; a fiber-optic network has been installed that is improving broadband and communication services between major urban centers with multiple companies providing inter-city fiber-optic cable services

domestic: very low fixed-line teledensity; there are four mobile-cellular providers and subscribership is increasing

international: country code - 976; satellite earth stations - 7

Broadcast media:
following a law passed in 2005, Mongolia's state-run radio and TV provider converted to a public service provider; also available are 69 radio and 131 TV stations, including multi-channel satellite and cable TV providers; transmissions of multiple international broadcasters are available (2017)

Internet country code:
.mn

Internet users:
total: 674,949
percent of population: 22.3% (July 2016 est.)
country comparison to the world: 144

TRANSPORTATION

Railways:
total: 1,928 km
broad gauge: 1,928 km 1.524-m gauge

Highways:
total: 49,250 km
paved: 1,674 km
unpaved: 47,576 km
note: much of the unpaved rural road system consists of rough cross-country tracks

Waterways: 400 km of principal routes
Ports and harbors: none
Airports: 34
Airports - with paved runways:
total: 8
2,438 to 3,047 m: 7
under 914 m: 1

Airports - with unpaved runways:
total: 26
over 3,047 m: 3
2,438 to 3,047 m: 5
1,524 to 2,437 m: 10
914 to 1,523 m: 3
under 914 m: 5

MILITARY

Military expenditures:
0.92% of GDP (2016)
0.87% of GDP (2015)
0.86% of GDP (2014)
0.82% of GDP (2013)
0.92% of GDP (2012)
country comparison to the world: 120

Military branches:
Mongolian Armed Forces (Mongol ulsyn zevsegt huchin): Mongolian Army, Mongolian Air Force (2016)

Military service age and obligation:
18-27 years of age for compulsory and voluntary military service; 1-year conscript service obligation in army or air forces or police for males only; after conscription, soldiers can contract into military service for 2 or 4 years; citizens can also voluntarily join the armed forces (2017)

TRANSNATIONAL ISSUES

Disputes - international: none

Refugees and internally displaced persons:
stateless persons: 14

IMPORTANT INFORMATION FOR UNDERSTANDING MONGOLIA

Official Name: Mongolia

PROFILE

Geography
Area: 1,566,500 sq. km. (604,103 sq. mi.); slightly larger than Alaska (land boundaries 8,114 km.).
Terrain: Almost 90% of land area is pasture or desert, of varying usefulness; 1% arable; 9% forested.
Climate: Continental, with little precipitation and sharp seasonal fluctuations.

People
Nationality: *Noun and adjective*--Mongolian(s).
Population (2009): 2.735 million.
Annual population growth rate (2009): 1.4%.
Health: *Infant mortality rate* (under 1 year)--19.4/1,000 (2008); 20/1,000 (2009). *Life expectancy*--67 yrs. (2008); 67.9 yrs. (2009).
Ethnic groups (2004): About 95% Mongol (predominantly Khalkha); 5% Turkic (largest group, Kazakh); Buriat.
Language: Mongolian.
Religions (2004): Buddhist Lamaism 50%, Muslim 4% (primarily in the southwest), shamanist and Christian 6%, and none 40%.
Education: *Years compulsory*--9 (provided free by the government). *Literacy*--98%.

Government
Type: Mixed parliamentary/presidential.
Independence: gained in 1921; in 1990, democratic reform begun and shift from dependence on the former Soviet Union declared.
Constitutions: 1960 and February 12, 1992.
Branches: *Executive*--power is divided between a president (elected by a popular election in May 2009) and prime minister (current cabinet nominated by the prime minister was approved in November 2009 following the appointment of a new prime minister; most cabinet members remained in place from the September 2008 government of the previous prime minister, who stepped aside due to health problems). *Legislative*--State Great Hural (parliament; 76 members elected in June 2008). *Judicial*--Constitutional Court is empowered to supervise the implementation of the constitution, makes judgment on the violation of its provisions, and solves disputes. Legal code based on Continental and Russian law. Legal education at Mongolian State University and private universities. Mongolia accepts International Court of Justice jurisdiction.
Political parties (2010): 17 registered political parties.
Suffrage: Universal at 18.
Administrative subdivisions: 21 aimags (provinces) and one city (Ulaanbaatar).

Economy
GDP (2010 est.): 8.25 trillion Mongolian Tugruks/MNT (U.S. $6.8 billion at current exchange rates).
GDP growth (2010): 7%.
Per capita GDP (2010): approx. $2,008.
Natural resources: Coal (thermal and metallurgical), copper, molybdenum, silver, iron, phosphates, tin, nickel, zinc, wolfram, fluorspar, gold, uranium, and petroleum.
Agriculture (15% of 2010 GDP, livelihood for about 40% of population): *Products*--livestock and byproducts, hay fodder, vegetables.

Industry (31% of 2009 GDP, composed of mining 21.8%, manufacturing 6.4%, and utilities (electricity, gas, and water) 2.4%: *Types*--minerals (primarily copper and gold), animal-derived products, building materials, food/beverage.
Trade: Total turnover of foreign trade for 2010 was $6.2 billion. *Exports*--$2.9 billion (U.S. dollar (USD) figures based on current USD/MNT exchange rate): minerals, livestock, animal products, and textiles. *Markets*--Asian countries (approx. 87.4%), European countries (approx. 4.5%), and countries of American continent (approx. 5.1%). *Imports*--$3.3 billion: machinery and equipment, fuels, food products, industrial consumer goods, chemicals, building equipment, vehicles, textiles. *Suppliers*--91 countries account for 93.2% of total imports, of which European countries (46.5%) and Asian countries (47.3%).
Aid received: From 1991-2009, official development assistance to Mongolia from bilateral and multilateral donors totaled over $4.056 billion. Received $357.47 million in official development assistance in 2009.
Fiscal year: Calendar year.

PEOPLE

Life in sparsely populated Mongolia has recently become more urbanized. Nearly half of the people live in urban centers, including the capital, Ulaanbaatar. Semi-nomadic life still predominates in the countryside, but settled agricultural communities are becoming more common. Mongolia's birth rate is estimated at 25.1 births per 1,000 people (2009 est.). About 58% of the total population is under age 30, 47.8% of whom are under 14.

Ethnic Mongols account for about 95% of Mongolia's population and consist of Khalkha and other groups, all distinguished primarily by dialects of the Mongol language. Mongol is an Altaic language--from the Altaic Mountains of Central Asia, a language family comprising the Turkic, Tungusic, and Mongolic subfamilies--and is related to Turkic (Uzbek, Turkish, and Kazakh), Korean, and, possibly, Japanese. Among ethnic Mongols, the Khalkha comprise 90% and the remaining 10% include Dorvod, Tuvan, and Buriat Mongols in the north and Dariganga Mongols in the east. Turkic speakers (Kazakhs, Turvins, and Khotans) constitute 5% of Mongolia's population, and the rest are Tungusic-speakers. Most Russians left the country following the withdrawal of economic aid and collapse of the Soviet Union in 1991.

Traditionally, Buddhist Lamaism was the predominant religion. However, it was suppressed under the communist regime until 1990, with only one showcase monastery allowed to remain. Since 1990, as liberalization began, Buddhism has enjoyed a resurgence. About 4 million ethnic Mongols live outside Mongolia; about 3.4 million live in China, mainly in the Inner Mongolia Autonomous Region, and some 500,000 live in Russia, primarily in Buryatia and Kalmykia.

HISTORY

In 1206 AD, a single Mongolian state was formed based on nomadic tribal groupings under the leadership of Chinggis ("Genghis") Khan. He and his immediate successors conquered nearly all of Asia and European Russia and sent armies as far as central Europe and Southeast Asia. Chinggis Khan's grandson Kublai Khan, who conquered China and established the Yuan dynasty (1279-1368 AD), gained fame in Europe through the writings of Marco Polo.

Although Mongol-led confederations sometimes exercised wide political power over their conquered territories, their strength declined rapidly after the Mongol dynasty in China was overthrown in 1368. The Manchus, a tribal group which conquered China in 1644 and formed the Qing dynasty, were able to bring Mongolia under Manchu control in 1691 as Outer Mongolia when the Khalkha Mongol nobles swore an oath of allegiance to the Manchu emperor. The Mongol rulers of Outer Mongolia enjoyed considerable autonomy under the Manchus, and all Chinese claims to Outer Mongolia following the establishment of the republic have rested on this oath. In 1727, Russia and Manchu China concluded the Treaty of Khiakta, delimiting the border between China and Mongolia that exists in large part today.

Outer Mongolia was a Chinese province (1691-1911), an autonomous state under Russian protection (1912-19), and again a Chinese province (1919-21). As Manchu authority in China waned, and as Russia and Japan confronted each other, Russia gave arms and diplomatic support to nationalists among the Mongol religious leaders and nobles. The Mongols accepted Russian aid and proclaimed their independence of Chinese rule in 1911, shortly after a successful Chinese revolt against the Manchus. By agreements signed in 1913 and 1915, the Russian Government forced the new Chinese Republican Government to accept Mongolian autonomy under continued Chinese control, presumably to discourage other foreign powers from approaching a newly independent Mongolian state that might seek support from as many foreign sources as possible.

The Russian revolution and civil war afforded Chinese warlords an opportunity to re-establish their rule in Outer Mongolia, and Chinese troops were dispatched there in 1919. Following Soviet military victories over White Russian forces in the early 1920s and the occupation of the Mongolian capital Urgoo in July 1921, Moscow again became the major outside influence on Mongolia. The Mongolian People's Republic was proclaimed on November 25, 1924.

Between 1925 and 1928, power under the communist regime was consolidated by the Mongolian People's Revolutionary Party (MPRP). The MPRP left gradually undermined rightist elements, seizing control of the party and the government. Several factors characterized the country during this period: The society was basically nomadic and illiterate; there was no industrial proletariat; the aristocracy and the religious establishment shared the country's wealth; there was widespread popular obedience to traditional authorities; the party lacked grassroots support; and the government had little organization or experience.

In an effort at swift socioeconomic reform, the leftist government applied extreme measures that attacked the two most dominant institutions in the country--the aristocracy and the religious establishment. Between 1932 and 1945, their excess zeal, intolerance, and inexperience led to anti-communist uprisings. In the late 1930s, purges directed at the religious institution resulted in the desecration of hundreds of Buddhist institutions and imprisonment of more than 10,000 people.

During World War II, because of a growing Japanese threat over the Mongolian-Manchurian border, the Soviet Union reversed the course of Mongolian socialism in favor of a new policy of economic gradualism and buildup of the national defense. The Soviet-Mongolian army defeated Japanese forces that had invaded eastern Mongolia in the summer of 1939, and a truce was signed setting up a commission to define the Mongolian-Manchurian border in the autumn of that year.

Following the war, the Soviet Union reasserted its influence in Mongolia. Secure in its relations with Moscow, the Mongolian Government shifted to postwar development, focusing on civilian enterprise. International ties were expanded, and Mongolia established relations with North Korea and the new communist governments in Eastern Europe. It also increased its participation in communist-sponsored conferences and international organizations. Mongolia became a member of the United Nations in 1961.

In the early 1960s, Mongolia attempted to maintain a neutral position amidst increasingly contentious Sino-Soviet polemics; this orientation changed in the middle of the decade. Mongolia and the Soviet Union signed an agreement in 1966 that introduced large-scale Soviet ground forces as part of Moscow's general buildup along the Sino-Soviet frontier.

During the period of Sino-Soviet tensions, relations between Mongolia and China deteriorated. In 1983, Mongolia systematically began expelling some of the 7,000 ethnic Chinese in Mongolia to China. Many of them had lived in Mongolia since the 1950s, when they were sent there to assist in construction projects.

Chronology of Mongolian History 1921-Present

March 13, 1921: Provisional People's Government declared independence of Mongolia.
May 31, 1924: U.S.S.R. signed agreement with Peking government, referring to Outer Mongolia as an "integral part of the Republic of China," whose "sovereignty" therein the Soviet Union promised to respect.
May-September 16, 1939: Large scale fighting took place between Japanese and Soviet-Mongolian forces along Khalkhyn Gol on Mongolia-Manchuria border, ending in defeat of the Japanese expeditionary force. Truce negotiated between U.S.S.R. and Japan.
October 6, 1949: Newly established People's Republic of China accepted recognition accorded Mongolia and agreed to establish diplomatic relations.
October 1961: Mongolia became a member of the United Nations.
January 27, 1987: Diplomatic relations established with the United States.
December 1989: First popular reform demonstrations. Mongolian Democratic Association organized.
January 1990: Large-scale demonstrations demanding democracy held in sub-zero weather.
March 2, 1990: Soviets and Mongolians announced that all Soviet troops would be withdrawn from Mongolia by 1992.
May 1990: Constitution amended to provide for multi-party system and new elections.
July 29, 1990: First democratic elections held.
September 3, 1990: First democratically elected People's Great Hural took office.
February 12, 1992: New constitution went into effect.
April 8, 1992: New election law passed.
June 28, 1992: Election for the first unicameral legislature (State Great Hural).
June 6, 1993: First direct presidential election.
June 30, 1996: Election resulted in peaceful transition of power from former communist party to coalition of democratic parties. From 1998-2000, four prime ministers and a series of cabinet changes. In early 2000, Democratic Coalition dissolved.
July 2, 2000: Election resulted in victory for the former communist Mongolian People's Revolutionary Party (MPRP); first-past-the-post electoral system enabled MPRP, with 52% of the popular vote, to win 95% of the parliamentary seats; formation of new government by Prime Minister N. Enkhbayar.
June 27, 2004: Motherland-Democracy Coalition formed in early 2004 to contest the parliamentary election. Election resulted in roughly 50/50 split of parliamentary seats between former communist party and democratic opposition and formation of new government by Prime Minister Ts. Elbegdorj (Democratic Party).
January 2006: MPRP ministers resigned from the government, and the government dissolved. A new coalition government was formed, led by the MPRP with the participation of four smaller parties.
October 2007: MPRP ousted its leader, Prime Minister M. Enkhbold, who resigned as Prime Minister. The new leader of the MPRP, Sanjaagiin Bayar, became Prime Minister and formed a new cabinet.
December 2007: Bayar's cabinet was approved.
July 1, 2008: Two days after parliamentary elections, and 1 day after the ruling MPRP claimed a landslide victory, a sizeable protest outside the MPRP headquarters turned violent. The MPRP headquarters was burned beyond repair and clashes between civilians and security forces left at least five people dead, 13 missing, hundreds injured and hundreds in police detention. President N. Enkhbayar declared a 4-day state of emergency, imposing a curfew, a ban on public gatherings, and a broadcast-news blackout (apart from the state broadcaster).
July and August 2008: Newly elected members of parliament from the opposition Democratic

Party refused to take the oath of office, demanding, among other things, that the nine-member General Election Commission resign for alleged electoral irregularities.
May 2009: Former Prime Minister and Democratic Party legislator Tsakhiagiin Elbegdorj was elected as President of Mongolia in free and fair elections.
October-November 2009: Prime Minister Sanjaagiin Bayar resigned for health reasons, and Foreign Minister Sukhbaatariin Batbold was selected as Prime Minister. Prime Minister Batbold largely retained former Prime Minister Bayar's cabinet, with only a few changes.
December 2010: The MPRP changed its name to the Mongolian People's Party.

GOVERNMENT AND POLITICAL CONDITIONS

Until 1990, the Mongolian Government was modeled on the Soviet system; only the communist party--the MPRP--officially was permitted to function. After some instability during the first 2 decades of communist rule in Mongolia, there was no significant popular unrest until December 1989. Collectivization of animal husbandry, introduction of agriculture, and the extension of fixed abodes were all carried out without perceptible popular opposition.

The birth of perestroika in the former Soviet Union and the democracy movement in Eastern Europe were mirrored in Mongolia. The dramatic shift toward reform started in early 1990 when the first organized opposition group, the Mongolian Democratic Union, appeared. In the face of extended street protests in subzero weather and popular demands for faster reform, the politburo of the MPRP resigned in March 1990. In May, the constitution was amended, deleting reference to the MPRP's role as the guiding force in the country, legalizing opposition parties, creating a standing legislative body, and establishing the office of president.

Mongolia's first multi-party elections for a People's Great Hural were held on July 29, 1990. The MPRP won 85% of the seats. The People's Great Hural first met on September 3 and elected a president (MPRP), vice president (SDP--Social Democrats), prime minister (MPRP), and 50 members to the Baga Hural (small Hural). The vice president also was chairman of the Baga Hural. In November 1991, the People's Great Hural began discussion on a new constitution, which entered into force February 12. In addition to establishing Mongolia as an independent, sovereign republic and guaranteeing a number of rights and freedoms, the new constitution restructured the legislative branch of government, creating a unicameral legislature, the State Great Hural (SGH).

The 1992 constitution provided that the president would be elected by popular vote rather than by the legislature as before. In June 1993, incumbent Punsalmaagiyn Ochirbat won the first popular presidential election running as the candidate of the democratic opposition. In May 2009, Tsakhiagiin Elbegdorj defeated Nambaryn Enkhbayar in the first instance in Mongolia of an incumbent losing a presidential election. This was also the first election as president of a Democratic Party candidate.

As the supreme government organ, the SGH is empowered to enact and amend laws, determine domestic and foreign policy, ratify international agreements, and declare a state of emergency. The SGH meets semiannually for 3-4 month sessions. SGH members elect a chairman and vice chairman who serve 4-year terms. SGH members are popularly elected by district to 4-year terms. The SGH sits for the full 4 years until a subsequent parliamentary election and cannot be dissolved.

The president is the head of state, commander in chief of the armed forces, and head of the National Security Council. He is popularly elected by a national majority for a 4-year term and limited to two terms. The constitution empowers the president to propose a prime minister, call for the government's dissolution in consultation with the SGH chairman, initiate legislation, veto all or parts of legislation (the SGH can override the veto with a two-thirds majority), and issue decrees, which become effective with the prime minister's signature. In the absence, incapacity, or resignation of the president, the SGH chairman exercises presidential power until inauguration of a newly elected president. The president may also declare a state of emergency if the SGH is in recess and cannot be summoned in a timely manner; the SGH may then, upon reconvening, revoke such a declaration of emergency within 7 days of its issuance.

The government, headed by the prime minister, has a 4-year term. The prime minister is nominated by the president and confirmed by the SGH. Under constitutional changes made in 2001, the president is required to nominate the prime ministerial candidate proposed by a party or coalition with a majority of members of the SGH. The prime minister chooses a cabinet, subject to SGH approval. Dissolution of the government occurs upon the prime minister's resignation, simultaneous resignation of half the cabinet, or after an SGH vote for dissolution.

Local hurals are elected by the 21 aimags (provinces) plus the capital, Ulaanbaatar. On the next lower administrative level, they are elected by provincial subdivisions and urban sub-districts in Ulaanbaatar and all aimags.

Political Parties
Mongolian People's Party
Democratic Party
Motherland-Mongolian Democratic New Socialist Party
New National Party
Civil Will Party
Mongolian People's Party
Mongolian Green Party
Mongolian Traditional United Party
Mongol Liberal Democratic Party
Republican Party
Mongolian Women's National Party
Mongolian Liberal Party
Mongolian Social Democratic Party
Freedom Implementing Party
The Civil Movement Party
The Development Program Party
Motherland Party

Legal System
The 1992 constitution empowered a General Council of Courts (GCC) to select all judges and protect their rights. The Supreme Court is the highest judicial body. Supreme Court justices are nominated by the GCC and confirmed by the president; the SGH must be made aware of the nominations but cannot block them. The Supreme Court is constitutionally empowered to examine all lower court decisions upon appeal and provide official interpretations on all laws except the constitution.

Specialized civil and criminal courts exist at all levels and are subject to Supreme Court supervision. Administrative courts exist at the province and city levels only and are also subject to Supreme Court supervision. Local authorities--district and city governors--ensure that these courts abide by presidential decrees and SGH decisions. At the apex of the judicial system is the Constitutional Court, which consists of nine members, including a chairman, appointed for 6-year terms, whose jurisdiction extends solely over the interpretation of the constitution.

PRINCIPAL GOVERNMENT OFFICIALS

The Mongolian parliament has approved the full list of cabinet ministers in the new coalition government. The number of ministries has increased from 11 to 16 and the number of Cabinet ministers has risen to 19 from 15. The increase may well be a reflection of the need for a coalition government of three party groupings.

Four of the ministers come from the Justice Coalition, one from the Civil Will – Green Party (CWGP) and the balance from the largest party, the Democratic Party (DP).

Following the dismissal of Prime Minister J.Erdenebat's Cabinet in early September, Deputy Prime Minister U.Khurelsukh was appointed the 30th Prime Minister of Mongolia on October 4.

Prime Minister U.Khurelsukh did not alter the structure of the previous Cabinet, and proposed new candidates instead, who have been backed by the Mongolian People's Party-ruled Parliament.

Prior to the Parliament meeting, President Kh.Battulga expressed disapproval towards the appointment of Ch.Khurelbaatar as Minister of Finance, but consented the other fourteen candidates. On the other hand, Parliamentary Standing Committees approved all candidates. As such, the new Cabinet now has the full authority to administer the executive branch. The new Cabinet is fully composed of Parliament members.

Parliament members brought up a number of issues and questions to the candidates during the plenary meeting, which was televised live and extended on both Wednesday and Thursday. Following are highlight statements of the new Ministers upon appointment:

Deputy Prime Minister – Enkhtuvshin Ulziisaikhan (voted up by 84.1 percent)

"The corresponding organizations are investigating the alleged MNT 60 billion audio tape controversy. The results of the investigation should be presented to the Parliament. I think that the details should publicized if public positions were really traded," the Minister said.

Head of Cabinet Secretariat – Zandanshatar Gombojav (voted up by 88.1 percent)

"I agree that the productivity of state-owned companies should be increased. I will work on reduction of unnecessary expenditure, and focus on professionalism in public service. Public service should essentially be professional and stable. We can't shake up the public service in the name of new blood," the Minister said.

Minister of Environment and Tourism – Tserenbat Namsrai (voted up by 88.2 percent)

"Air pollution has become a trouble for everyone. I aim to reduce air pollution with the help of three means – building apartments, using natural gas and providing heat. Last winter, a measure to offer night-time electricity discount was taken, benefitting 114 thousand residents, and it will continue this winter as well. We need time to see the results of our actions," the Minister said.

Minister of Defense - Enkhbold Nyamaa (voted up by 84.1 percent)

"Military service is compulsory for those aspiring to be civil servants. I believe that there is a need to extend the length of military service to two years. When it comes to defense sector, 60-70 percent is dependent upon foreign relations. I will ensure Mongolia's continued engagement and contribution to international peacekeeping operations," the Minister said.

Minister of Foreign Affairs – Tsogtbaatar Damdin (voted up by 98.3 percent)

"There are countries with a Ministry of Foreign Affairs and Trade, which is a suitable alternative for small nations. We've been receiving foreign aid and assistance with the help of diplomatic tools. There are opportunities for diplomatic missions abroad to attract investment. I will focus on the Economic Corridor Program, and coordinate with the other Ministries," the Minister said.

Minister of Finance – Khurelbaatar Chimed (voted up by 89.9 percent)

"In order to relieve the budget, I will work efficiently within the existing laws and regulations, promote investment, shorten unnecessary expenditure of the Government and intercept illegal activities," pledged the Minister.

Minister of Labor and Social Protection – Chinzorig Sodnom (voted up by 89.7 percent)

"Teachers and doctors have been warning about a strike, therefore, I am planning to hold a trilateral meeting. I believe that there's a necessity to increase the salary of public servants. But we can't increase wage in compliance with the Extended Fund Facility program. Therefore, I will focus on increasing the real income," the Minister said.

Minister of Justice and Home Affairs – Nyamdorj Tsend (voted up by 89.9 percent)

"I will do everything in my power to declassify S.Zorig's murder case which has been unsolved for 25 years. Justice Minister is responsible for making sure that the Cabinet makes no illegal decision, and I will do my best. I will also assist the Prime Minister in ensuring that no politically incorrect decision is adopted," he said.

Minister of Construction and Urban Development – Badelkhan Khavdislam (voted up by 87.5 percent)

"I think that Tuv aimag should be an administrative center and Ulaanbaatar the industrial-commercial center. About 92 thousand people live in apartment thanks to the Housing Mortgage Loan. I will work on broadening the scope of Housing Mortgage Loan," he said.

Minister of Education, Culture, Science and Sport – Tsogzolmaa Tsedenbal (voted up by 90.8 percent)

"My priority is the three-shift issue in schools. About 10 thousand students are studying in three-shifts in 27 schools in the capital city," she said.

Minister of Road and Transport Development – Bat-Erdene Jadamba (voted up by 88.1 percent)

"At present, there are four provincial capitals that aren't connected to Ulaanbaatar by paved road and I will work on its completion. Connecting soum centers with the provincial capitals is a next issue. I will also focus on roads that will increase circulation of mining products," he said.

Minister of Mining and Heavy Industry – Sumiyabazar Dolgorsuren (voted up by 89.6 percent)

"I will regulate illegal miners and activities of government organizations. I will develop responsible mining," he said.

Minister of Food, Agriculture and Light Industry – Batzorig Batjargal (voted up by 88.1

percent)

“I will focus on ensuring winter preparedness fully. Moreover, my priority is meat export to Mongolia’s two neighbors,” he said.

Minister of Energy – Davaasuren Tserenpil (voted up by 89.4 percent)

“I will promote renewable energy. Eg River Hydro Power Plant project will contribute to the establishment of independent energy source in Mongolia, and the project should move forward,” he said.

Minister of Health – Sarangerel Davaajantsan (voted up by 90.8 percent)

“Mongolia imports 1,800 types of drugs from 45 countries and domestic production makes up only 20 percent of the demand. I will work on increasing this rate to 50 percent. My priority is the wage issue of doctors,” she said.

Mongolia maintains an embassy in the United States at 2833 M Street, NW, Washington, DC, 20007; tel. (202) 333-7117, fax (202) 298-9227, website - **www.mongolianembassy.us/english**.

ECONOMY

Currency	1 tögrög (MNT) = 100 möngö
Fiscal year	Calendar year
Trade organizations	WTO, IMF, World Bank, ADB, SCO (Observer)
Statistics	
GDP	$36.07 billion (PPP, 2015 est.)
GDP rank	136th (nominal) / 118th (PPP)
GDP growth	8.0% (2014), 2.3% (2015), 0.1% (2016e), 2.0% (2017f)[1]
GDP per capita	$12,100 (2015 est., PPP)
GDP by sector	agriculture: 16.6%, industry: 33.1%, services: 50.3% (2011 est.)
Inflation (CPI)	5.9% (2015 est.)
Population below poverty line	21.6% (2014 est.)
Gini coefficient	36.5 (2008)
Labor force by occupation	agriculture: 28.6%, industry: 21%, services: 50.4%
Unemployment	8.3%
Main industries	construction and construction materials, mining (coal, copper, molybdenum, fluorspar, tin, tungsten, and gold), oil, food and beverages, processing of animal products, cashmere wool and natural fiber manufacturing
Ease-of-doing-business rank	64th (2017)[2]
External	
Exports	$5.272 billion (2015 est.)
Export goods	copper, apparel, livestock, animal products, cashmere, wool, hides, fluorspar, other nonferrous metals, coal, crude oil

Main export partners	China 84% Switzerland 9% (2015)[3]
Imports	$3.923 billion (2015 est.)
Import goods	machinery and equipment, fuel, cars, food products, industrial consumer goods, chemicals, building materials, cigarettes & tobacco, soap & detergent
Main import partners	China 39.9% Russia 28.4% Japan 6.4% South Korea 6.2% (2015)[4]
Public finances	
Public debt	$1.9 billion
Revenues	$2.994 billion (2015 est.)
Expenses	$3.354 billion (2015 est.)
Economic aid	$185.94 million (2008)
Credit rating	Standard & Poor's: BB- (Domestic) BB- (Foreign) BB (T&C Assessment) Outlook: Stable Moody's: B1 Outlook: Stable Fitch: B+ Outlook: Stable

Economic activity in Mongolia has traditionally been based on agriculture and livestock. Mongolia also has extensive mineral deposits: copper, coal, molybdenum, tin, tungsten, and gold account for a large part of industrial production. Soviet assistance, at its height one-third of Gross domestic product (GDP), disappeared almost overnight in 1990–91, at the time of the Collapse of the Soviet Union. Mongolia was driven into deep recession. Reform has been held back by the ex-communist MPRP opposition and by the political instability brought about through four successive governments under the DUC. Economic growth picked up in 1997–99 after stalling in 1996 due to a series of natural disasters and increases in world prices of copper and cashmere. Public revenues and exports collapsed in 1998 and 1999 due to the repercussions of the Asian financial crisis. In August and September 1999, the economy suffered from a temporary Russian ban on exports of oil and oil products. Mongolia joined the World Trade Organization (WTO) in 1997.[7] The international donor community pledged over $300 million per year at the last Consultative Group Meeting, held in Ulaanbaatar in June 1999. Recently, the Mongolian economy has grown at a fast pace due to an increase in mining and Mongolia attained a GDP growth rate of 11.7% in 2013.[8] However, because much of this growth is export-based, Mongolia is suffering from the global slowdown in mining caused by decreased growth in China

Mongolia's reliance on trade with China meant that the worldwide financial crisis hit hard,[12] severely stunting the growth of its economy. With the sharp decrease in metal prices, especially copper (down 65% from July 2008-February 2009),[12] exports of its raw materials withered and by 2009 the stock market MSE Top-20 registered an all-time low since its dramatic spike in mid-2007.[13] Just as the economy started to recover, Mongolia was hit by a Zud over the winter period of 2009-2010, causing many livestock to perish and thus severely affecting cashmere production which accounts for a further 7% of the country's export revenues.[12]

According to the World Bank and International Monetary Fund estimates, real GDP growth reduced from 8% to 2.7% in 2009, and exports shrunk 26% from $2.5Bn to $1.9Bn before a promisingly steady increase up until 2008.[12] Because of this, it was projected that between 20,000 and 40,000 fewer Mongolians (0.7% and 1.4% of the population respectively) will be lifted out of poverty, than would have been the case without the global financial crisis.

In late 2009 and the beginning of 2010, however, the market has begun to recover once again. Having identified and learnt from its previous economic instabilities, legislative reform and a tightened fiscal policy promises to guide the country onwards and upwards. In February 2010, foreign assets were recorded at USD1,569,449 million.[14] New trade agreements are being formed and foreign investors are keeping a close eye on the "Asian Wolf".

Mining is the principal industrial activity in Mongolia, making up 30% of all Mongolian industry.[15] Another important industry is the production of cashmere. Mongolia is the world's second largest producer of cashmere, with the main company, Gobi Cashmere, accounting for 21% of world cashmere production as of 2006.[16]

==The Wolf Economy==϶8ם9 The term was coined by Ganhuyag Chuluun Hutagt and subsequently popularized by Renaissance Capital in their report "Mongolia: "Blue-sky opportunity".[17] They state that Mongolia is set to become the new Asian tiger, or "Mongolian wolf" as they prefer to call it, and predict "unstoppable" economic growth.[18] With the recent developments in the mining industry and foreign interest increasing at an astonishing rate, it is claimed that the 'Wolf Economy' looks ready to pounce. The term's aggressive title mirrors the country's attitude in the capital markets, and with newfound mineral prospects it has the chance to retain its title as one of the world's fastest growing economies

Environment

Based on a tradition going back to the era of Chinggis Khan, the government of Mongolia expresses public commitment to restoring and protecting its natural resources. As a result of rapid urbanization and industrial growth policies under the socialist regime, however, Mongolia's deteriorating environment remains a major concern. The burning of soft coal by individual home or "ger" (yurt in Russian) owners, power plants, and factories in Ulaanbaatar has resulted in severely polluted air. Continued overgrazing, increased crop production, and mining development have increased soil erosion and polluted waters. Protecting what remains has policy priority over reclaiming damaged land, although the government recently created a special restoration fund financed by polluter fees. In addition, the government is making significant efforts to introduce sustainable energy projects in an effort to reduce reliance on aging power plants.

FOREIGN RELATIONS

In the wake of the international socialist economic system's collapse and the disintegration of the former Soviet Union, Mongolians began to pursue an independent and nonaligned foreign policy. Mongolia is landlocked between Russia and China and seeks cordial relations with both nations. At the same time, Mongolia has sought to advance its regional and global relations. Ties with Japan and South Korea are particularly strong. Japan has historically been the largest bilateral aid donor to Mongolia, although the ongoing $285 million U.S.-Mongolia Millennium Challenge Compact will put the United States in the top spot until it sunsets in 2013. Mongolia has also made efforts to steadily boost ties with European countries. China is the largest foreign investor in Mongolia.

As part of its aim to establish a more balanced nonaligned foreign policy, Mongolia has sought to take a more active role in the United Nations and other international organizations, and has pursued a more active role in Asian and northeast Asian affairs. The country is a member of the ASEAN Regional Forum (ARF) and the Pacific Economic Cooperation Council. Mongolia is currently seeking to join the Asia-Pacific Economic Cooperation forum (APEC). It is an observer in the Shanghai Cooperation Organization (SCO), but has stated it does not intend to seek membership. Mongolia will begin its 2-year chairmanship of the Community of Democracies beginning in July 2011. The country also serves on the UN Economic and Social Council (ECOSOC).

Mongolia, which has diplomatic relations with both North and South Korea, has also sought to play a supporting role in the Six-Party talks. In late 2007, it hosted a closed meeting between two Six-Party members, North Korea and Japan. Mongolia has also offered to help organize and to host a northeast Asian regional security mechanism. The country is a founding member of the Asia-Pacific Democracy Partnership (APDP) and hosted the group's planning meeting in Ulaanbaatar on July 1, 2008. In January 2011, Mongolia hosted parliamentary delegates from 19 countries for the Asia Pacific Parliamentary Forum (APPF). Mongolia also hosted a regional workshop of the Comprehensive Nuclear Test Ban Treaty Organization in March 2010 and became the Chair of the Board of Governors of the International Atomic Energy Agency in September 2010.

Mongolian relations with China began to improve in the mid-1980s when consular agreements were reached and cross-border trade contacts expanded. In May 1990, a Mongolian head of state visited China for the first time in 28 years. The cornerstone of the Mongolian-Chinese relationship is a 1994 Treaty of Friendship and Cooperation, which codifies mutual respect for the independence and territorial integrity of both sides. China has objected strongly to visits since 1990 of the Dalai Lama; during the 2002 visit, China briefly disrupted railroad links for "technical" reasons. There are regular high-level visits and expanding trade ties. President Hu Jintao visited Mongolia in 2003 (his first international visit as China's President). President Bagabandi visited China in 2004, President Enkhbayar visited in 2008, and Prime Minister Bayar met Premier Wen Jiabao in Beijing in April 2009. Premier Wen visited Ulaanbaatar in June 2010 to open a new cultural center, announce new educational scholarships for Mongolians, and discuss cooperation on infrastructure projects.

After the disintegration of the former Soviet Union, Mongolia developed relations with the new independent states. Links with Russia and other republics were essential to contribute to stabilization of the Mongolian economy. In 1991, Mongolia and Russia concluded both a Joint Declaration of Cooperation and a bilateral trade agreement. This was followed by a 1993 Treaty of Friendship and Cooperation establishing a new basis of equality in the relationship. Mongolian President Bagabandi visited Moscow in 1999, and Russian President Vladimir Putin visited Mongolia in 2000 in order to sign the 25-point Ulaanbaatar Declaration, reaffirming Mongol-Russian friendship and cooperation on numerous economic and political issues. In December 2003, Mongolia believed it had settled the Soviet-era debt it owed to Russia with a negotiated payment of $250 million. In 2009 the Russian Government stated that hundreds of millions of dollars in debt remained unpaid, but the debt was declared settled in December 2010 when Prime Minister Batbold visited Russia and met with Prime Minister Putin and President Medvedev. During the visit, the leaders announced the establishment of a joint venture in Dornod Province to mine uranium. The Mongolian and Russian Governments continue to jointly own the railroad and the large Erdenet copper mine. Prime Minister Putin visited Ulaanbaatar 2 weeks prior to the Mongolian presidential election in May 2009, and President Medvedev visited Mongolia in August 2009 to commemorate the 70th anniversary of the Battle of Khalkhin Gol (aka Battle of Nomonhan), a combined Soviet-Mongolian victory over Imperial Japan, ultimately leading the Japanese Army to sign a non-aggression pact with the Soviet Union and divert its forces into Southeast Asia. After nearly 2 decades of inactivity, Russia is renewing military ties with the Mongolian armed forces through military education and training exchange programs, as well as joint exercises focused on the repair of Mongolia's Soviet-built equipment. As part of the

December 2010 visit, Russia announced it would increase the number of training slots available to Mongolian military officers.

U.S.-MONGOLIAN RELATIONS

The U.S. Government recognized Mongolia in January 1987 and established its first embassy in Ulaanbaatar in June 1988. It formally opened in September 1988. The first U.S. ambassador to Mongolia, Richard L. Williams, was not a resident there. Joseph E. Lake, the first resident ambassador, arrived in July 1990. Secretary of State James A. Baker, III visited Mongolia in August 1990, and again in July 1991. Mongolia accredited its first ambassador to the United States in March 1989. Secretary of State Madeline Albright visited Mongolia in May 1998, and Prime Minister Enkhbayar visited Washington in November 2001. Deputy Secretary of State Richard L. Armitage visited Mongolia in January 2004, and President Bagabandi came to Washington for a meeting with President George W. Bush in July 2004. President Bush, Mrs. Bush, and Secretary of State Condoleezza Rice visited Mongolia in November 2005. Defense Secretary Donald Rumsfeld visited in October 2005 and Speaker of the House of Representatives Dennis Hastert visited Mongolia in August 2005. Agriculture Secretary Mike Johanns led a presidential delegation in July 2006 in conjunction with Mongolia's celebration of its 800th anniversary. President Enkhbayar visited the White House in October 2007 and the two Presidents signed the Millennium Challenge Compact for Mongolia (see below). House Minority Leader John Boehner visited Mongolia in August 2009.

The United States has sought to assist Mongolia's movement toward democracy and market-oriented reform and to expand relations with Mongolia primarily in the cultural and economic fields. In 1989 and 1990, a cultural accord, Peace Corps accord, consular convention, and Overseas Private Investment Corporation (OPIC) agreement were signed. A trade agreement was signed in January 1991 and a bilateral investment treaty in 1994. Mongolia was granted permanent normal trade relations (NTR) status and generalized system of preferences (GSP) eligibility in June 1999. In July 2004, the U.S. signed a Trade and Investment Framework Agreement with Mongolia to promote economic reform and more foreign investment. In July 2007, six members of the U.S. House of Representatives visited Mongolia to inaugurate an exchange program between lawmakers of the two countries. The return visit came in August 2007, with five members of the Mongolian parliament traveling to the U.S. Similar exchanges of lawmakers and staff members have continued. The House Democracy Partnership (HDP), under which members of the U.S. Congress and staff directly assist their parliamentary counterparts in newly democratic countries, is an increasingly prominent means of engagement. In total, 25 Mongolian members of parliament have visited Washington and Macedonia on this program. Several congressional delegations have also traveled to Ulaanbaatar, including that led by House Minority Leader John Boehner in August 2009. Six staffers from the Mongolian parliament also visited Washington during this time. Members of parliament involved have risen in prominence and spearheaded reforms.

The U.S. Agency for International Development (**USAID**) in Mongolia provides targeted bilateral development assistance in two strategic program areas: economic growth and good governance. These activities are conducted with an eye toward assisting Mongolia in managing the expected windfall and the accompanying challenges of its burgeoning mining sector. Between 1991 and 2011, USAID grant assistance to Mongolia totaled $214 million. The FY 2010 economic growth program budget of $6.4 million targets the legal and regulatory environment in the energy, trade, and business sectors to develop a business-enabling environment, strengthen Mongolia's banks and financial markets, facilitate trade, and encourage private sector-led growth. The program also emphasizes building a national consensus among stakeholders on the future of the mining sector. A $1.5 million clean energy earmark added in FY 2010 targets reduction of greenhouse gas emissions in Mongolia. USAID good governance programming continues to focus on anti-corruption activities that include assistance to the independent agency monitoring corruption, building citizen awareness of corruption issues, and improving judicial processes of commercial adjudication. Governance programming in FY 2010 was $1 million.

In August 2009, the United States approved a total of $13 million of FY 2009 supplemental funds to Mongolia to mitigate the negative effects of the global financial crisis. USAID signed a $10 million cash transfer for budget support to the Government of Mongolia, which helped the government meet its deficit reduction targets and ensured essential social safety net transfers to those hardest hit by the economic crisis. Supplemental funds provided $2 million in technical assistance through the Treasury Department's Office of Technical Assistance (OTA) directly to Mongolia's Central Bank to address essential banking and financial sector reforms. Development Credit Authority ($1 million) guarantees are used to mobilize and leverage financing to maintain and generate employment across targeted sectors by promoting lower collateral requirements and longer-term loans.

The second $2 million tranche of FY 2009 global financial crisis supplemental funding was authorized in May 2010. Two-thirds of the funds were granted to social safety net projects to promote the social and economic inclusion of marginal groups to mitigate the effects of the financial crisis and the 2010 dzud (severe weather). The remaining funds were provided to the OTA to continue technical assistance to the country's financial sector.

In addition to regular bilateral and supplemental funding, USAID central funds aim to foster an inclusive environment for local persons with disabilities, to improve responsiveness and inclusiveness of local and national governments through national consensus building, to conserve biodiversity and secure livelihoods of the rural poor, and to promote economic development through cooperative approaches.

In most years since 1993, the United States Department of Agriculture (USDA) has provided food aid to Mongolia under the Food for Progress and 416(b) programs. The monetized proceeds of the food aid ($5 million in 2008) are used to support programs bolstering entrepreneurship, herder livelihood diversification, and better veterinary services. The U.S. Embassy supports a new request from the Government of Mongolia for USDA's Food for Progress assistance.

The United States has also supported defense reform and an increased capacity by Mongolia's armed forces to participate in international peacekeeping operations. Beginning in 2003, Mongolia contributed troops to coalition operations in Iraq and Afghanistan, gaining experience that later enabled it to deploy armed peacekeepers to both UN and NATO peacekeeping missions. While early Afghanistan deployments centered on the provision of artillery mobile training teams, current deployments are far more extensive. Mongolia now has some 200 soldiers in Afghanistan in support of both Operation Enduring Freedom (OEF) and the International Security Assistance Force (ISAF), including fixed-site security missions at Camp Eggers and in support of Germany's ISAF contingent in Feyzabad, as well as 25 artillery trainers and six helicopter trainers. At the recent NATO conference in Lisbon, the President of Mongolia stated his intent to double Mongolia's contributions in Afghanistan to 400.

In addition to deployments in support of coalition operations in Afghanistan and Iraq, Mongolia has deployed over 3,000 of its personnel on UN peacekeeping missions in Chad, Congo, Ethiopia and Eritrea, Georgia, Kosovo, Sierra Leone, Sudan, and Western Sahara. Late 2010 brought Mongolia's first-ever deployment of a UN Level II hospital to Darfur.

The **Peace Corps** has approximately 130 volunteers in Mongolia. At the request of the Government of Mongolia, they are engaged primarily in English teaching and teacher training activities. Other program areas include public health, small-business development, and youth development. In 2005 and 2006 Mongolian Government officials, including then-President Enkhbayar and then-Prime Minister Elbegdorj, requested significant increases in the number of volunteers ("PCVs") serving in country. On August 20, 2010, the largest group of PCVs to serve in Mongolia, numbering 72, took the oath of service. This is the 21st PCV group to serve in Mongolia. PCVs are placed in 20 of the 21 aimags in Mongolia.

Mongolia was one of the first countries eligible for the new Millennium Challenge Account initiative that began in 2004, administered by the Millennium Challenge Corporation (**MCC**). MCC's program focuses on providing grant support to countries that perform above the median in their income peer group on key indicators in three broad policy categories: ruling justly, investing in people, and encouraging economic freedom. MCC-eligible countries propose projects that will significantly reduce poverty in their countries through stimulating economic growth. On October 22, 2007, at a White House signing ceremony, President Bush and President Enkhbayar signed a Millennium Challenge Compact for Mongolia that called for $285 million to be spent on four projects over a 5-year period beginning in September 2008. The Compact supports efforts to broaden and deepen economic development in Mongolia. The original focus of the Compact was on four key areas: rail modernization, property rights, vocational education, and health. In April 2009, the Government of Mongolia requested the termination of the rail modernization project, citing circumstances beyond its control due to the lack of cooperation of the 50% Russian owners of the Mongolian railway. The government proposed areas for reallocation of the rail project funds, and additional funding for the other three projects as well as a new road/bridge construction project and an energy and environment project were approved by the MCC board in late 2009 and finalized in a formal Amendment to the Compact in January 2010, which the Mongolian parliament ratified in February 2010. Implementing MCC projects in Mongolia is enabling key institutions and infrastructure to better support the country's burgeoning urbanized, market-based economy and help Mongolians to increase their incomes by becoming healthier and better trained, by using their land assets more productively, and by increasing their capacity to trade with the world.

Principal U.S. Embassy Official

Chargé d'Affaires a.i. Manuel P. Micaller

The U.S. Embassy is located in Micro District 11, Big Ring Road, Ulaanbaatar; tel. [976] (1) 329-095 and 329-606, fax 320-776. Consular and commercial information are available at the embassy's web site: **http://mongolia.usembassy.gov**.

Investment Climate Statements are available at **http://www.state.gov/e/eb/ifd/**, and Country Commercial Guides can be found at **http://www.export.gov/mrktresearch/index.asp**.

TRAVEL AND BUSINESS INFORMATION

Travel Alerts, Travel Warnings, Trip Registration
The U.S. Department of State's Consular Information Program advises Americans traveling and residing abroad through Country Specific Information, Travel Alerts, and Travel Warnings. **Country Specific Information** exists for all countries and includes information on entry and exit requirements, currency regulations, health conditions, safety and security, crime, political disturbances, and the addresses of the U.S. embassies and consulates abroad. **Travel Alerts** are issued to disseminate information quickly about terrorist threats and other relatively short-term conditions overseas that pose significant risks to the security of American travelers. **Travel Warnings** are issued when the State Department recommends that Americans avoid travel to a certain country because the situation is dangerous or unstable.

For the latest security information, Americans living and traveling abroad should regularly monitor the Department's Bureau of Consular Affairs Internet web site at http://travel.state.gov, where current Worldwide Caution, Travel Alerts, and Travel Warnings can be found. The travel.state.gov website also includes information about passports, tips for planning a safe trip abroad and more. More travel-related information also is available at http://www.usa.gov/Citizen/Topics/Travel/International.shtml.

The Department's Smart Traveler app for U.S. travelers going abroad provides easy access to the frequently updated official country information, travel alerts, travel warnings, maps, U.S. embassy locations, and more that appear on the travel.state.gov site. Travelers can also set up e-tineraries to keep track of arrival and departure dates and make notes about upcoming trips. The app is compatible with iPhone, iPod touch, and iPad (requires iOS 4.0 or later).

The Department of State encourages all U.S. citizens traveling or residing abroad to register via the State Department's travel registration website or at the nearest U.S. embassy or consulate abroad (a link to the registration page is also available through the Smart Traveler app). Registration will make your presence and whereabouts known in case it is necessary to contact you in an emergency and will enable you to receive up-to-date information on security conditions.

Emergency information concerning Americans traveling abroad may be obtained by calling 1-888-407-4747 toll free in the U.S. and Canada or the regular toll line 1-202-501-4444 for callers outside the U.S. and Canada.

Passports
The National Passport Information Center (NPIC) is the U.S. Department of State's single, centralized public contact center for U.S. passport information. Telephone: 1-877-4-USA-PPT (1-877-487-2778); TDD/TTY: 1-888-874-7793. Passport information is available 24 hours, 7 days a week. You may speak with a representative Monday-Friday, 8 a.m. to 10 p.m., Eastern Time, excluding federal holidays.

EU- MONGOLIA RELATIONS

GENERAL FRAMEWORK

Prior to the political reforms of 1990, relations between the EU and Mongolia were extremely limited. Since then, however, these relations have developed fairly rapidly and positively. In January 1991, Mongolia entered into the GSP arrangement. The EU delegate in Beijing was accredited in Mongolia in May 1991, whilst the Mongolian ambassador to the EU presented his credentials in November 1992.

The Trade and Co-operation Agreement was signed on 16.06.1992 and entered into force in March 1993. It is concluded for a period of five years and shall be tacitly renewed. The Agreement includes a commitment to protect human rights. In their trade relations, the two Parties shall accord each other the most-favored-nation treatment. The Agreement doesn't provide the implementation of a trade preferential regime. The adoption of appropriate measures in order to facilitate and to increase the trade is provided. The third meeting of the Joint Committee took place on 25 and 26 April 1996 in Ulaanbatar. The fourth one was held in Brussels on 30 September 1997. The fifth one took place on 19 December 2004 in Ulaanbatar.

Textile agreement: The European Community and Mongolia have concluded an Agreement on trade in Textile Products which has expired on 31.12.97. The textile trade between the EC and Mongolia is now fully liberalized.

TRADE

After China, Switzerland Russia, Korea and Japan, the EU is the sixths biggest trading partner of Mongolia. In 1998 13.4 % of imported goods came from EU-countries, 9.5 % of Mongolia's export went to the EU. The turnover of EU-Mongolia trade amounted to € 115 million in the year 2004. The major EU import commodity from Mongolia is cashmere wool and products (namely imported by Italy and the UK). The major export items from the EU are machinery, agricultural products and chemicals, coming mainly from France and Germany. Statistics on the development of bilateral trade see below.

EC ASSISTANCE

In 1992-1993 Mongolia received nearly ECU 8.0 million in technical assistance under the PUD/ALA Program.

Mongolia became eligible for TACIS support in 1994 when a Aid-Co-ordinating Unit was established in Ulaanbatar.

The 1996-2001 TACIS allocation was 26,5 M €.

The budget of the 1998-1999 Action Program amounted to 11 M €. It covered projects in the field of structural and institutional reform (2,8 M €), support to enterprises and financial development (3,1 M €), infrastructure development (1,6 M €) and Small project programs (3,0 M €) (Reserve: 0,5 M €).

The 2004-2001 Action Program (6,0 M €) was adopted by the Commission at the end of 2004 and is under implementation. It was prepared within the framework of the new Indicative Program (IP) for 2004-2003. Two key priority areas of co-operation had been defined in the new regulation (Council Regulation 99/2004 of 29 December 1999): Development of the Rural Economy (2,9 M €) and Support to the Private Sector and Assistance for Economic Development (1,0 M €). Additionally 1,7 M € have been allocated for Small projects programs.

Since 1994 Mongolia has also actively participated in the TACIS Small Project Program (Tempus, Lien, Democracy, City Twinning, Productivity Initiative Program, ESSN, Statistics, and Customs).

In 2004 1,875 M € have been provided in the framework of ECHO, above all for food aid. In the year 2001 1,03 M € have already been provided to fight against the consequences of the last harsh winter ("Dzud").

FUTURE RELATIONS

The EU-Mongolia relationship has been consolidated over the last few years and will increase in the future given the enlargement of the Union to the East. The new TACIS Regulation, which covers the years 2004-2006, sets out the new priorities for the assistance program and takes into consideration the post-enlargement effects, notably the increase in the trade flow, the need for expanded transport networks, new investment opportunities, demands for increased co-operation on environmental protection, cross border co-operation and co-operation in the field of Justice and Home Affairs. These new priorities take into account the changed economical and political environment in the NIS and Mongolia, and the necessity for a greater concentration in cross-sectoral areas of co-operation. The TACIS assistance will target the Political, Economic, Social, Environmental aspects and the Rural economy.

JAPAN MONGOLIA RELATIONS

BASIC DATA

Number of Residents:
Number of Japanese nationals residing in Mongolia: 229 (Nov. 1999)
Number of Mongolian nationals residing in Japan: 349 (Oct. 1999)

BILATERAL RELATIONS

(1) Diplomatic relations between Japan and Mongolia were established in 1972. However, owing to the international situation prevailing at that time, characterized by East-West antagonism as a result of the Cold War, the environment was not particularly conducive to the vigorous development of the relationship between Japan and Mongolia.

(2) Nevertheless, the moves towards democratization and the transformation to a free-market economic system in Mongolia opened up a new phase in the development of relations by Japan and Mongolia on the previously-established foundation. A visit in April 1989 by the then Japanese foreign minister Sousuke Uno, the first foreign minister of a Western industrialized country to pay a visit to Mongolia, was followed in March 1990 by a visit to Japan by the then Prime Minister Sodnom, in August 1991 by a visit to Mongolia by the then Prime Minister Kaifu, the first prime minister of a Western industrialized country to visit to Mongolia, and by visits to Japan in May 1992 and November 1993 by the Mongolian prime minister. These high-level exchanges resulted in the accelerated development of relations between the two countries.

(3) Based on Japan's belief that the success of democratization and of the transformation to a free-market economy in Mongolia would contribute to peace and stability in the East Asian region, from the outset it has given active assistance to newly democratized Mongolia, and since 1991 has continued to be the largest donor of aid.

(4) In February 1997, the 25th anniversary of the establishment of diplomatic relations between the two countries, the then Prime Minister Enkhsaikhan visited Japan, where a joint announcement was made. Then in May 1998, President Bagabandi has paid an official visit to Japan, which was the first one made by a Mongolian President. During the visit, a joint statement was announced. These confirmed the goal of building a comprehensive partnership between the two countries.

(5) High level exchanges at both political and government level were kept at a good pace, which resulted in an official visit made by the Speaker of the Mongolian Parliament, Mr. R. Gonchigdorj in March and a Foreign Ministerial Meeting held in May.
(6) Assistance from Mongolia

(i) Mongolia has been a firm supporter of Japan in the United Nations, other international organizations, international conferences and international committees. In particular Mongolia has maintained a policy of cooperation with Japan in pursuit of the peace and stability of the northeast Asian region. Mongolia has also been a steadfast supporter of Japan's becoming a permanent member of the United Nations Security Council,
(ii) A memory that remains firmly in the minds of many Japanese people is that of the friendship displayed by the Mongolian people at the time of the Great Hanshin-Awagi Earthquake in 1995, when they were quick to provide a special airlift of relief supplies.

HISTORY AND POLITICAL DEVELOPMENTS

MODERN MONGOLIA--the Mongolian People's Republic--comprises only about half of the vast Inner Asian region known throughout history as Mongolia. Furthermore, it is only a fraction of the great Mongol Empire of the thirteenth and fourteenth centuries that stretched from Korea to Hungary and encompassed nearly all of Asia except the Indian subcontinent and parts of Southeast Asia. Because the Mongol Empire was so vast--the largest contiguous land empire in the history of the world--the Mongols were written about in many languages by numerous chroniclers of divergent conquered societies, who provided a wide range of perspectives, myths, and legends. In addition, because many foreign accounts are about the Mongol invasions and were written by the conquered, the Mongols often are described in unfavorable terms, as bloodthirsty barbarians who kept their subjects under a harsh yoke. Mongol sources emphasize the demigod-like military genius of Chinggis Khan, providing a perspective in the opposite extreme. The term Mongol itself is often a misnomer.

Although the leaders and core forces of the conquerors of Eurasia were ethnic Mongols, most of the main army was made up of Uralo-Altaic people, many of them Turkic. Militarily, the Mongols were stopped only by the Mamluks of Egypt and by the Japanese, or by their own volition, as happened in Europe. In their increasingly sophisticated administrative systems, they employed Chinese, Iranians, Russians, and others. Mongolia and its people thus have had a significant and lasting impact on the historical development of major nations, such as China and Russia, and, periodically, they have influenced the entire Eurasian continent.

Until the twentieth century, most of the peoples who inhabited Mongolia were nomads, and even in the 1980s a substantial proportion of the rural population was essentially nomadic. Originally there were many warlike nomadic tribes living in Mongolia, and apparently most of these belonged to one or the other of two racially distinct and linguistically very different groupings. One of these groupings, the Yuezhi, was related linguistically to the ancient nomadic Scythian peoples--who inhabited the steppes north and northeast of the Black Sea and the region east of the Aral Sea--and was therefore Indo-European. The other grouping was the Xiongnu, a nomadic people of uncertain origins.

Although in the course of history other peoples displaced, or became intermingled with, the Yuezhi and the Xiongnu, their activities, conflicts, and internal and external relations established a pattern, with four principal themes, that continued almost unchanged--except for the conquest of Eurasia in the thirteenth and fourteenth centuries--until the eighteenth century. First, among these four themes, there were constant fierce struggles involving neighboring tribes, engaged in frequently shifting alliances that did not always follow ethnic, racial, or linguistic lines. Second, during periods when China was united and strong, trade with Inner Asian peoples was allowed, and nomadic states either became vassals of the Chinese emperor, or they retreated beyond his reach into the northern steppes; conversely, when China appeared weak, raids were made into rich Chinese lands, sometimes resulting in retaliatory expeditions into Mongolia. Third, occasional, transitory consolidation--of all or of large portions of the region under the control of a conqueror or a coalition of similar tribes--took place; such temporary consolidations could result in a life-or- death struggle between major tribal groupings until one or the other was exterminated or was expelled from the region, or until they joined forces. Fourth, on several occasions, raids into northern China were so vast and successful that the victorious nomads settled in the conquered land, established dynasties, and eventually became absorbed--sinicized--by the more numerous Chinese.

Within this pattern, the Xiongnu eventually expelled the Yuezhi, who were driven to the southwest to become the Kushans of Iranian, Afghan, and Indian history. In turn, the Xiongnu themselves later were driven west. Their descendants, or possibly another group, continued this westward migration, establishing the Hun Empire, in Central and Eastern Europe, that reached its zenith under Attila.

The pattern was interrupted abruptly and dramatically late in the twelfth century and throughout the thirteenth century by Chinggis and his descendants. During the consolidation of Mongolia and some of the invasions of northern China, Chinggis created sophisticated military and political organizations, exceeding in skill, efficiency, and vigor the institutions of the most civilized nations of the time. Under him and his immediate successors, the Mongols conquered most of Eurasia.

After a century of Mongol dominance in Eurasia, the traditional patterns reasserted themselves. Mongols living outside Mongolia were absorbed by the conquered populations; Mongolia itself again became a land of incessantly warring nomadic tribes. True to the fourth pattern, a similar people, the Manchus, conquered China in the seventeenth century, and ultimately became sinicized.

Here the pattern ended. The Manchu conquest of China came at a time when the West was beginning to have a significant impact on East Asia. Russian colonial expansionism was sweeping rapidly across Asia--at first passing north of Mongolia but bringing incessant pressure, from the west and the north, against Mongol tribes--and was beginning to establish firm footholds in Mongolian territory by conquest and the establishment of protectorates. At the same time, the dynamic Manchus also applied pressure from the east and the south. This pressure was partly the traditional attempt at control over nomadic threats from Mongolia, but it also was a response to the now clearly apparent threat of Russian expansionism.

From the late seventeenth century to the early twentieth century, Mongolia was a major focus of Russian and Manchu-Chinese rivalry for predominant influence in all of Northeast Asia. In the process, Russia absorbed those portions of historical Mongolia to the west and north of the present Mongolian People's Republic. The heart of Mongolia, which became known as Outer Mongolia (see Glossary), was claimed by the Chinese. The area was distinct from Inner Mongolia, along the southern rim of the Gobi, which China absorbed--those regions to the southwest, south, and east that now are included in the People's Republic of China. Continuing Russian interest in Mongolia was discouraged by the Manchus.

As Chinese power waned in the nineteenth and the early twentieth centuries, however, Russian influence in Mongolia grew. Thus Russia supported Outer Mongolian declarations of independence in the period immediately after the Chinese Revolution of 1911. Russian interest in the area did not diminish, even after the Russian Revolution of 1917, and the Russian civil war spilled over into Mongolia in the period 1919 to 1921. Chinese efforts to take advantage of internal Russian disorders by trying to reestablish their claims over Outer Mongolia were thwarted in part by China's instability and in part by the vigor of the Russian reaction once the Bolshevik Revolution had succeeded. Russian predominance in Outer Mongolia was unquestioned after 1921, and when the Mongolian People's Republic was established in 1924, it was as a communistcontrolled satellite of Moscow.

EARLY DEVELOPMENT, CA. 220 B.C.-A.D. 1206

ORIGINS OF THE MONGOLS

Archaeological evidence places early Stone Age human habitation in the southern Gobi between 100,000 and 200,000 years ago. By the first millennium B.C., bronze-working peoples lived in Mongolia. With the appearance of iron weapons by the third century B.C., the inhabitants of Mongolia had begun to form tribal alliances and to threaten China. The origins of more modern inhabitants are found among the forest hunters and nomadic tribes of Inner Asia. They inhabited a great arc of land extending generally from the Korean Peninsula in the east, across the northern tier of China to the Kazakh Soviet Socialist Republic and to the Pamir Mountains and Lake Balkash in the west (see fig. 1). During most of recorded history, this has been an area of constant ferment from which emerged numerous migrations and invasions to the southeast (into China), to the southwest (into Transoxiana--modern Uzbek Soviet Socialist Republic, Iran, and India), and to the west (across Scythia toward Europe). By the eighth century B.C., the inhabitants of much of this region evidently were nomadic Indo-European speakers, either Scythians or their kin. Also scattered throughout the area were many other tribes that were primarily Mongol in their ethnologic characteristics.

XIONGNU AND YUEZHI

The first significant recorded appearance of nomads came late in the third century B.C., when the Chinese repelled an invasion of the Xiongnu (Hsiung-nu in Wade-Giles romanization) across the Huang He (Yellow River) from the Gobi. The Xiongnu were a nomadic people of uncertain origins. Their language is not known to modern scholars, but the people were probably similar in appearance and characteristics to the later Mongols. A Chinese army, which had adopted Xiongnu military technology--wearing trousers and using mounted archers with stirrups--pursued the Xiongnu across the Gobi in a ruthless punitive expedition. Fortification walls built by various Chinese warring states were connected to make a 2,300-kilometer Great Wall along the northern border, as a barrier to further nomadic inroads.

The Xiongnu temporarily abandoned their interest in China and turned their attention westward to the region of the Altai Mountains and Lake Balkash, inhabited by the Yuezhi (Yüeh-chih in Wade-Giles), an Indo-European-speaking nomadic people who had relocated from China's present-day Gansu Province as a result of their earlier defeat by the Xiongnu. Endemic warfare between these two nomadic peoples reached a climax in the latter part of the third century and the early decades of the second century B.C.; the Xiongnu were triumphant. The Yuezhi then migrated to the southwest where, early in the second century, they began to appear in the Oxus (the modern Amu Darya) Valley, to change the course of history in Bactria, Iran, and eventually India.

Meanwhile, the Xiongnu again raided northern China about 200 B.C., finding that the inadequately defended Great Wall was not a serious obstacle. By the middle of the second century B.C., they controlled all of northern and western China north of the Huang He. This renewed threat led the Chinese to improve their defenses in the north, while building up and improving the army, particularly the cavalry, and while preparing long-range plans for an invasion of Mongolia.

Between 130 and 121 B.C., Chinese armies drove the Xiongnu back across the Great Wall, weakened their hold on Gansu Province as well as on what is now Nei Monggol Autonomous Region (Inner Mongolia--see Glossary), and finally pushed them north of the Gobi into central Mongolia. Following these victories, the Chinese expanded into the areas later known as Manchuria (see Glossary), the Korean Peninsula, and Inner Asia. The Xiongnu, once more turning their attention to the west and the southwest, raided deep into the Oxus Valley between 73 and 44 B.C. The descendants of the Yuezhi and their Chinese rulers, however, formed a common front against the Xiongnu and repelled them.

During the next century, as Chinese strength waned, border warfare between the Chinese and the Xiongnu was almost incessant. Gradually the nomads forced their way back into Gansu and the northern part of what is now China's Xinjiang-Uygur Autonomous Region. In about the middle of the first century A.D., a revitalized Eastern Han Dynasty (A.D. 25-220) slowly recovered these territories, driving the Xiongnu back into the Altai Mountains and the steppes north of the Gobi. During the late first century A.D., having reestablished the administrative control over southern

China and northern Vietnam that had been lost briefly at beginning of this same century, the Eastern Han made a concerted effort to reassert dominance over Inner Asia. A Chinese army crossed the Pamir Mountains, conquered territories as far west as the Caspian Sea, defeated the Yuezhi Kushan Empire, and even sent an emissary in search of the eastern provinces of Rome.

DONGHU, TOBA, AND RURUAN

Although the Xiongnu finally had been driven back into their homeland by the Chinese in A.D. 48, within ten years the Xianbei (or Hsien-pei in Wade-Giles) had moved (apparently from the north or northwest) into the region vacated by the Xiongnu. The Xianbei were the northern branch of the Donghu (or Tung Hu, the Eastern Hu), a proto-Tunguz group mentioned in Chinese histories as existing as early as the fourth century B.C. The language of the Donghu, like that of the Xiongnu, is unknown to modern scholars. The Donghu were among the first peoples conquered by the Xiongnu. Once the Xiongnu state weakened, however, the Donghu rebelled. By the first century, two major subdivisions of the Donghu had developed: the Xianbei in the north and the Wuhuan in the south. The Xianbei, who by the second century A.D. were attacking Chinese farms south of the Great Wall, established an empire, which, although short-lived, gave rise to numerous tribal states along the Chinese frontier. Among these states was that of the Toba (T'o-pa in Wade-Giles), a subgroup of the Xianbei, in modern China's Shanxi Province. The Wuhuan also were prominent in the second century, but they disappeared thereafter; possibly they were absorbed in the Xianbei western expansion. The Xianbei and the Wuhuan used mounted archers in warfare, and they had only temporary war leaders instead of hereditary chiefs. Agriculture, rather than full-scale nomadism, was the basis of their economy. In the sixth century A.D., the Wuhuan were driven out of Inner Asia into the Russian steppe.

Chinese control of parts of Inner Asia did not last beyond the opening years of the second century, and, as the Eastern Han Dynasty ended early in the third century A.D., suzerainty was limited primarily to the Gansu corridor. The Xianbei were able to make forays into a China beset with internal unrest and political disintegration. By 317 all of China north of the Chang Jiang (Yangtze River) had been overrun by nomadic peoples: the Xianbei from the north; some remnants of the Xiongnu from the northwest; and the Chiang people of Gansu and Tibet (present-day China's Xizang Autonomous Region) from the west and the southwest. Chaos prevailed as these groups warred with each other and repulsed the vain efforts of the fragmented Chinese kingdoms south of the Chang Jiang to reconquer the region.

By the end of the fourth century, the region between the Chang Jiang and the Gobi, including much of modern Xinjiang, was dominated by the Toba. Emerging as the partially sinicized state of Dai between A.D. 338 and 376 in the Shanxi area, the Toba established control over the region as the Northern Wei Dynasty (A.D. 386-533). Northern Wei armies drove back the Ruruan (referred to as Ruanruan or Juan-Juan by Chinese chroniclers), a newly arising nomadic Mongol people in the steppes north of the Altai Mountains, and reconstructed the Great Wall. During the fourth century also, the Huns left the steppes north of the Aral Sea to invade Europe. By the middle of the fifth century, Northern Wei had penetrated into the Tarim Basin in Inner Asia, as had the Chinese in the second century. As the empire grew, however, Toba tribal customs were supplanted by those of the Chinese, an evolution not accepted by all Toba.

The Ruruan, only temporarily repelled by Northern Wei, had driven the Xiongnu toward the Ural Mountains and the Caspian Sea and were making raids into China. In the late fifth century, the Ruruan established a powerful nomadic empire spreading generally north of Northern Wei. It was probably the Ruruan who first used the title khan (see Glossary).

RISE OF THE TÜRK

Northern Wei was disintegrating rapidly because of revolts of semi-tribal Toba military forces that were opposed to being sinicized, when disaster struck the flourishing Ruruan Empire. The Türk, a vassal people, known as Tujue to Chinese chroniclers, revolted against their Ruruan rulers. The uprising began in the Altai Mountains, where many of the Türk were serfs working the iron mines. Thus, from the outset of their revolt, they had the advantage of controlling what had been one of the major bases of Ruruan power. Between 546 and 553, the Türks overthrew the Ruruan and established themselves as the most powerful force in North Asia and Inner Asia. This was the beginning of a pattern of conquest that was to have a significant effect upon Eurasian history for more than 1,000 years. The Türk were the first people to use this later wide-spread name. They are also the earliest Inner Asian people whose language is known, because they left behind Orkhon inscriptions in a runic-like script, which was deciphered in 1896.

It was not long before the tribes in the region north of the Gobi--the Eastern Türk--were following invasion routes into China used in previous centuries by Xiongnu, Xianbei, Toba, and Ruruan. Like their predecessors who had inhabited the mountains and the steppes, the attention of the Türk quickly was attracted by the wealth of China. At first these new raiders encountered little resistance, but toward the end of the sixth century, as China slowly began to recover from centuries of disunity, border defenses stiffened. The original Türk state split into eastern and western parts, with some of the Eastern Türk acknowledging Chinese overlordship.

For a brief period at the beginning of the seventh century, a new consolidation of the Türk, under the Western Türk ruler Tardu, again threatened China. In 601 Tardu's army besieged Chang'an (modern Xi'an), then the capital of China. Tardu was turned back, however, and, upon his death two years later, the Türk state again fragmented. The Eastern Türk nonetheless continued their depredations, occasionally threatening Chang'an.

INFLUENCE OF TANG CHINA

From 629 to 648, a reunited China--under the Tang Dynasty (A.D. 618-906)--destroyed the power of the Eastern Türk north of the Gobi; established suzerainty over the Kitan, a semi-nomadic Mongol people who lived in areas that became the modern Chinese provinces of Heilongjiang and Jilin; and formed an alliance with the Uighurs (see Glossary), who inhabited the region between the Altai Mountains and Lake Balkash. Between 641 and 648, the Tang conquered the Western Türk, reestablishing Chinese sovereignty over Xinjiang and exacting tribute from west of the Pamir Mountains. The Türk empire finally ended in 744.

For more than a century, the Tang retained control of central and eastern Mongolia and parts of Inner Asia. During this century, the Tang expanded Chinese control into the Oxus Valley. At the same time, their allies and nominal vassals, the Uighurs, conquered much of western and northern Mongolia until, by the middle of the eighth century, the Uighur seminomadic empire extended from Lake Balkash to Lake Baykal.

It was at about this time that the Arab-led tide of Islam reached Inner Asia. After a bitter struggle, the Chinese were ejected from the Oxus Valley, but with Uighur assistance they defeated Muslim efforts to penetrate into Xinjiang. The earliest Mongol links with Tibetan Buddhism, or Lamaism (see Glossary), also may have been established in this period (see Religion , ch. 2). During this time, the Kitan of western Manchuria took advantage of the situation to throw off Chinese control, and they began to raid northern China.

Despite these crippling losses, the Tang recovered and, with considerable Uighur assistance, held their frontiers. Tang dependence upon their northern allies was apparently a source of embarrassment to the Chinese, who surreptitiously encouraged the Kirghiz and the Karluks to attack the Uighurs, driving them south into the Tarim Basin. As a result of the Kirghiz action, the Uighur empire collapsed in 846. Some of the Uighurs emigrated to Chinese Turkestan (the

Turpan region), where they established a flourishing kingdom that freely submitted to Chinggis Khan several centuries later (see Early Wars in China , this ch.). Ironically, this weakening of the Uighurs undoubtedly hastened the decline and fall of the Tang Dynasty over the next fifty years.

INFLUENCE OF TANG CHINA

From 629 to 648, a reunited China--under the Tang Dynasty (A.D. 618-906)--destroyed the power of the Eastern Türk north of the Gobi; established suzerainty over the Kitan, a semi-nomadic Mongol people who lived in areas that became the modern Chinese provinces of Heilongjiang and Jilin; and formed an alliance with the Uighurs (see Glossary), who inhabited the region between the Altai Mountains and Lake Balkash. Between 641 and 648, the Tang conquered the Western Türk, reestablishing Chinese sovereignty over Xinjiang and exacting tribute from west of the Pamir Mountains. The Türk empire finally ended in 744.

For more than a century, the Tang retained control of central and eastern Mongolia and parts of Inner Asia. During this century, the Tang expanded Chinese control into the Oxus Valley. At the same time, their allies and nominal vassals, the Uighurs, conquered much of western and northern Mongolia until, by the middle of the eighth century, the Uighur seminomadic empire extended from Lake Balkash to Lake Baykal.

It was at about this time that the Arab-led tide of Islam reached Inner Asia. After a bitter struggle, the Chinese were ejected from the Oxus Valley, but with Uighur assistance they defeated Muslim efforts to penetrate into Xinjiang. The earliest Mongol links with Tibetan Buddhism, or Lamaism (see Glossary), also may have been established in this period (see Religion , ch. 2). During this time, the Kitan of western Manchuria took advantage of the situation to throw off Chinese control, and they began to raid northern China.

Despite these crippling losses, the Tang recovered and, with considerable Uighur assistance, held their frontiers. Tang dependence upon their northern allies was apparently a source of embarrassment to the Chinese, who surreptitiously encouraged the Kirghiz and the Karluks to attack the Uighurs, driving them south into the Tarim Basin. As a result of the Kirghiz action, the Uighur empire collapsed in 846. Some of the Uighurs emigrated to Chinese Turkestan (the Turpan region), where they established a flourishing kingdom that freely submitted to Chinggis Khan several centuries later (see Early Wars in China , this ch.). Ironically, this weakening of the Uighurs undoubtedly hastened the decline and fall of the Tang Dynasty over the next fifty years.

KITAN AND JURCHEN

Free of Uighur restraint, the Kitan expanded in all directions in the latter half of the ninth century and the early years of the tenth century. By 925 the Kitan ruled eastern Mongolia, most of Manchuria, and much of China north of the Huang He. In the recurrent process of sinicization, by the middle of the tenth century Kitan chieftains had established themselves as emperors of northern China; their rule was known as the Liao Dynasty (916-1125).

The period of the eleventh and twelfth centuries was one of consolidation, preceding the most momentous era in Mongol history, the era of Chinggis Khan. During those centuries, the vast region of deserts, mountains, and grazing land was inhabited by people resembling each other in racial, cultural, and linguistic characteristics; ethnologically they were essentially Mongol. The similarites among the Mongols, Türk, Tangut, and Tatars (see Glossary) who inhabited this region causes considerable ethnic and historical confusion. Generally, the Mongols and the closely related Tatars inhabited the northern and the eastern areas; the Türk (who already had begun to spread over western Asia and southeastern Europe) were in the west and the southwest; the Tangut, who were more closely related to the Tibetans than were the other nomads and who were not a Turkic people, were in eastern Xinjiang, Gansu, and western Inner Mongolia (see fig.

2). The Liao state was homogeneous, and the Kitan had begun to lose their nomadic characteristics. The Kitan built cities and exerted dominion over their agricultural subjects as a means of consolidating their empire. To the west and the northwest of Liao were many other Mongol tribes, linked together in various tenuous alliances and groupings, but with little national cohesiveness. In Gansu and eastern Xinjiang, the Tangut--who had taken advantage of the Tang decline--had formed a state, Western Xia or Xixia (1038-1227), nominally under Chinese suzerainty. Xinjiang was dominated by the Uighurs, who were loosely allied with the Chinese.

The people of Mongolia at this time were predominantly spirit worshipers, with shamans providing spiritual and religious guidance to the people and tribal leaders. There had been some infusion of Buddhism, which had spread from Xinjiang, but it did not yet have a strong influence (see The Yuan Dynasty; Return to Nomadic Patterns , this ch.). Nestorian Christianity also had penetrated Inner Asia.

In the eleventh century, the Kitan completed the conquest of China north of the Huang He. Despite close cultural ties between the Kitan and Western Xia that led the latter to become increasingly sinicized, during the remainder of that century and the early years of the twelfth century, the two Mongol groups were frequently at war with each other and with the Song Dynasty (A.D. 960-1279) of China. The Uighurs of the Turpan region often were involved in these wars, usually aiding the Chinese against Western Xia.

A Tungusic people, the Jurchen, ancestors of the Manchu, formed an alliance with the Song and reduced the Kitan Empire to vassal status in a seven-year war (1115-1122; see Caught Between the Russians and the Manchus , this ch.). The Jurchen leader proclaimed himself the founder of a new era, the Jin Dynasty (1115-1234). Scarcely pausing in their conquests, the Jurchen subdued neighboring Koryo (Korea) in 1226 and invaded the territory of their former allies, the Song, to precipitate a series of wars with China that continued through the remainder of the century. Meanwhile, the defeated Kitan Liao ruler had fled with the small remnant of his army to the Tarim Basin, where he allied himself with the Uighurs and established the Karakitai state (known also as the Western Liao Dynasty, 1124-1234), which soon controlled both sides of the Pamir Mountains. The Jurchen turned their attention to the Mongols who, in 1139 and in 1147, warded them off.

THE ERA OF CHINGGIS KHAN, 1206-27

RISE OF CHINGGIS KHAN

After the migration of the Jurchen, the Borjigin Mongols had emerged in central Mongolia as the leading clan of a loose federation. The principal Borjigin Mongol leader, Kabul Khan, began a series of raids into Jin in 1135. In 1162 (some historians say 1167), Temujin, the first son of Mongol chieftain Yesugei, and grandson of Kabul, was born. Yesugei, who was chief of the Kiyat subclan of the Borjigin Mongols, was killed by neighboring Tatars in 1175, when Temujin was only twelve years old. The Kiyat rejected the boy as their leader and chose one of his kin instead. Temujin and his immediate family were abandoned and apparently left to die in a semidesert, mountainous region.

Temujin did not die, however. In a dramatic struggle described in *The Secret History of the Mongols*, Temujin, by the age of twenty, had become the leader of the Kiyat subclan and by 1196, the unquestioned chief of the Borjigin Mongols. Sixteen years of nearly constant warfare followed as Temujin consolidated his power north of the Gobi. Much of his early success was because of his first alliance, with the neighboring Kereit clan, and because of subsidies that he and the Kereit received from the Jin emperor in payment for punitive operations against Tatars and other tribes that threatened the northern frontiers of Jin. Jin by this time had become absorbed into the Chinese cultural system and was politically weak and increasingly subject to harassment by Western Xia, the Chinese, and finally the Mongols. Later Temujin broke with the Kereit, and, in a series of major campaigns, he defeated all the Mongol and Tatar tribes in the region from the Altai Mountains to Manchuria. In time Temujin emerged as the strongest chieftain among a number of contending leaders in a confederation of clan lineages. His principal opponents in this struggle had been the Naiman Mongols, and he selected Karakorum (west-southwest of modern Ulaanbaatar, near modern Har Horin), their capital, as the seat of his new empire.

In 1206 Temujin's leadership of all Mongols and other peoples they had conquered between the Altai Mountains and the Da Hinggan (Greater Khingan) Range was acknowledged formally by a *kuriltai* (council--see Glossary) of chieftains as their khan. Temujin took the honorific *chinggis*, meaning supreme or great (also romanized as *genghis* or *jenghiz*), creating the title Chinggis Khan, in an effort to signify the unprecedented scope of his power. In latter hagiography, Chinggis was said even to have had divine ancestry. The contributions of Chinggis to Mongol organizational development had lasting impact. He took personal control of the old clan lineages, ending the tradition of noninterference by the khan. He unified the Mongol tribes through a logistical nexus involving food supplies, sheep and horse herds, intelligence and security, and transportation. A census system was developed to organize the decimal-based political jurisdictions and to recruit soldiers more easily. As the great khan, Chinggis was able to consolidate his organization and to institutionalize his leadership over a Eurasian empire. Critical ingredients were his new and unprecedented military system and politico-military organization. His exceptionally flexible mounted army and the cadre of Chinese and Muslim siege-warfare experts who facilitated his conquest of cities comprised one of the most formidable instruments of warfare that the world had ever seen (see Historical Traditions , ch. 5).

At the time of his first *kuriltai* at Karakorum, Chinggis already was engaged in a dispute with Western Xia, the first of his wars of conquest. In 1205 the Mongol military organization, based on the *tumen* (see Glossary), had defeated the much larger Tangut forces easily. Despite problems in conquering the well-fortified Western Xia cities, the results were the same in the campaigns of 1207 and 1209. When peace was concluded in 1209, the Western Xia emperor, with substantially reduced dominion, acknowledged Chinggis as overlord.

THE ERA OF CHINGGIS KHAN, 1206-27

RISE OF CHINGGIS KHAN

After the migration of the Jurchen, the Borjigin Mongols had emerged in central Mongolia as the leading clan of a loose federation. The principal Borjigin Mongol leader, Kabul Khan, began a series of raids into Jin in 1135. In 1162 (some historians say 1167), Temujin, the first son of Mongol chieftain Yesugei, and grandson of Kabul, was born. Yesugei, who was chief of the Kiyat subclan of the Borjigin Mongols, was killed by neighboring Tatars in 1175, when Temujin was only twelve years old. The Kiyat rejected the boy as their leader and chose one of his kin instead. Temujin and his immediate family were abandoned and apparently left to die in a semidesert, mountainous region.

Temujin did not die, however. In a dramatic struggle described in *The Secret History of the Mongols*, Temujin, by the age of twenty, had become the leader of the Kiyat subclan and by 1196, the unquestioned chief of the Borjigin Mongols. Sixteen years of nearly constant warfare followed as Temujin consolidated his power north of the Gobi. Much of his early success was because of his first alliance, with the neighboring Kereit clan, and because of subsidies that he and the Kereit received from the Jin emperor in payment for punitive operations against Tatars and other tribes that threatened the northern frontiers of Jin. Jin by this time had become absorbed into the Chinese cultural system and was politically weak and increasingly subject to harassment by Western Xia, the Chinese, and finally the Mongols. Later Temujin broke with the

Kereit, and, in a series of major campaigns, he defeated all the Mongol and Tatar tribes in the region from the Altai Mountains to Manchuria. In time Temujin emerged as the strongest chieftain among a number of contending leaders in a confederation of clan lineages. His principal opponents in this struggle had been the Naiman Mongols, and he selected Karakorum (west-southwest of modern Ulaanbaatar, near modern Har Horin), their capital, as the seat of his new empire.

In 1206 Temujin's leadership of all Mongols and other peoples they had conquered between the Altai Mountains and the Da Hinggan (Greater Khingan) Range was acknowledged formally by a *kuriltai* (council--see Glossary) of chieftains as their khan. Temujin took the honorific *chinggis*, meaning supreme or great (also romanized as *genghis* or *jenghiz*), creating the title Chinggis Khan, in an effort to signify the unprecedented scope of his power. In latter hagiography, Chinggis was said even to have had divine ancestry. The contributions of Chinggis to Mongol organizational development had lasting impact. He took personal control of the old clan lineages, ending the tradition of noninterference by the khan. He unified the Mongol tribes through a logistical nexus involving food supplies, sheep and horse herds, intelligence and security, and transportation. A census system was developed to organize the decimal-based political jurisdictions and to recruit soldiers more easily. As the great khan, Chinggis was able to consolidate his organization and to institutionalize his leadership over a Eurasian empire. Critical ingredients were his new and unprecedented military system and politico-military organization. His exceptionally flexible mounted army and the cadre of Chinese and Muslim siege-warfare experts who facilitated his conquest of cities comprised one of the most formidable instruments of warfare that the world had ever seen (see Historical Traditions , ch. 5).

At the time of his first *kuriltai* at Karakorum, Chinggis already was engaged in a dispute with Western Xia, the first of his wars of conquest. In 1205 the Mongol military organization, based on the *tumen* (see Glossary), had defeated the much larger Tangut forces easily. Despite problems in conquering the well-fortified Western Xia cities, the results were the same in the campaigns of 1207 and 1209. When peace was concluded in 1209, the Western Xia emperor, with substantially reduced dominion, acknowledged Chinggis as overlord.

EARLY WARS IN CHINA

A major goal of Chinggis was the conquest of Jin, both to avenge earlier defeats and to gain the riches of northern China. He declared war in 1211, and at first the pattern of operations against Jin was the same as it had been against Western Xia. The Mongols were victorious in the field, but they were frustrated in their efforts to take major cities. In his typically logical and determined fashion, Chinggis and his highly developed staff studied the problems of the assault of fortifications. With the help of Chinese engineers, they gradually developed the techniques that eventually would make them the most accomplished and most successful besiegers in the history of warfare.

As a result of a number of overwhelming victories in the field and a few successes in the capture of fortifications deep within China, Chinggis had conquered and had consolidated Jin territory as far south as the Great Wall by 1213. He then advanced with three armies into the heart of Jin territory, between the Great Wall and the Huang He. He defeated the Jin forces, devastated northern China, captured numerous cities, and in 1215 besieged, captured, and sacked the Jin capital of Yanjing (later known as Beijing). The Jin emperor did not surrender, however, but removed his capital to Kaifeng. There his successors finally were defeated, but not until 1234. Meanwhile, Kuchlug, the deposed khan of the Naiman Mongols, had fled west and had conquered the state of Karakitai, the western allies that had decided to side with Chinggis.

By this time, the Mongol army was exhausted by ten years of continuous campaigning against Western Xia and Jin. Therefore, Chinggis sent only two *tumen* under a brilliant young general,

Jebe, against Kuchlug. An internal revolt was incited by Mongol agents; then Jebe overran the country. Kuchlug's forces were defeated west of Kashgar; he was captured and executed, and Karakitai was annexed. By 1218 the Mongol state extended as far west as Lake Balkash and adjoined Khwarizm, a Muslim state that reached to the Caspian Sea in the west and to the Persian Gulf and the Arabian Sea in the south.

CONQUEST OF KHWARIZM AND RECONNAISSANCE INTO EUROPE

In 1218 the governor of an eastern province of Khwarizm mistreated several Mongol emissaries. Chinggis retaliated with a force of more than 200,000 troops, and Khwarizm was eradicated by 1220. A detachment of about 25,000 Mongol cavalry, as part of the Khwarizmian campaign, had crossed the Caucasus Mountains, had skirted the Caspian Sea, and had briefly invaded Europe.

After defeating the Georgians and the Cumans of the Caucasus, the small Mongol expedition advanced in 1222 into the steppes of the Kuban. Combining rapid movement with guile, the Mongols again defeated the Cumans, captured Astrakhan, then crossed the Don River into Russia. Penetrating the Crimea, they stormed the Genoese fortress of Sudak on the southeastern coast, then turned north into what later became known as the Ukraine.

The Mongol leaders now thought they had accomplished their mission. Before returning to Mongolia, however, they decided to rest their troops and to gain more information about the lands to the north and the west. They camped near the mouth of the Dnieper River, and their spies soon were scattered throughout eastern and central Europe.

Meanwhile, a mixed Russian-Cuman army of 80,000 under the leadership of Mstislav, prince of Kiev, marched against the Mongol encampment. Jebe and Subetei, another great Mongol general, sought peace; however, when their envoys were murdered, they attacked and routed Mstislav's force on the banks of the Halha River. Historian Charles Halperin estimated that by this time the "destructive power of the Mongol war machine eclipsed anything the Russians had seen before," and the Kievan Russians found themeselves faced no longer with a renewal of the sporadic raids of the past but with the threat of subjugation and foreign domination. In compliance with a courier message from Chinggis, the expedition then marched eastward. As the Mongols were marching north of the Caspian Sea, Jebe died of illness. In 1224 Subetei led the expedition back, after a trek of more than 6,400 kilometers, to a rendezvous with the main Mongol armies, that were returning from their victories over the Khwarizm.

THE LAST CAMPAIGN OF CHINGGIS KHAN

The vassal emperor of Western Xia had refused to take part in the war against the Khwarizm, and Chinggis had vowed punishment. While he was in Iran, Western Xia and Jin had formed an alliance against the Mongols. After rest and a reorganization of his armies, Chinggis prepared for war against his foes.

By this time, advancing years had led Chinggis to prepare for the future and to assure an orderly succession among his descendants. He selected his son Ogedei as his successor and established the method of selection of subsequent khans, specifying that they should come from his direct descendants. Meanwhile, he studied intelligence reports from Western Xia and Jin and readied a force of 180,000 troops for a new campaign.

Late in 1226, when the rivers were frozen, the Mongols struck southward with their customary speed and vigor. The Tangut, well acquainted with Mongol methods, were ready, and the two armies met by the banks of the frozen Huang He. Despite a Western Xia army of more than 300,000 troops, the Mongols virtually annihilated the Tangut host.

Pursuing energetically, the Mongols killed the Western Xia emperor in a mountain fortress. His son took refuge in the great walled city of Ningxia, which the Mongols had failed to conquer in earlier wars. Leaving one-third of his army to take Ningxia, Chinggis sent Ogedei eastward, across the great bend of the Huang He, to drive the Jin forces from their last footholds north of the river. With the remainder of his troops, he marched southeast, evidently to eastern Sichuan Province, where the Western Xia, the Jin, and the Song empires met, to prevent Song reinforcements from reaching Ningxia. Here he accepted the surrender of the new Western Xia emperor but rejected peace overtures from Jin.

A premonition of death caused Chinggis to head back to Mongolia, but he died en route. On his deathbed in 1227, he outlined to his youngest son, Tului, the plans that later would be used by his successors to complete the destruction of the Jin empire.

SUCCESSORS OF CHINGGIS, 1228-59

OGEDEI AND CONTINUING CONQUESTS

In compliance with the will of the dead khan, a *kuriltai* at Karakorum in 1228 selected Ogedei as khan. The *kuriltai* also decided to launch a campaign against the Bulghars, Turks in the region of Kazan on the middle Volga River, and to complete the conquest of the outlying Western Xia territories. By 1229 Batu Khan, grandson of Chinggis, had defeated most of the Bulghar outposts, and in 1231 Ogedei sent an expedition to conquer the Korean Peninsula.

That same year, Ogedei decided to destroy Jin. He formed an alliance with the Song, then sent Tului southward with a large army into Jin territory. In 1232 in the middle of the campaign, Tului died, and Subetei took command. He continued on to besiege Kaifeng, the Jin capital. Despite the defenders' skillful use of explosives, the city fell to the Mongols after a year's siege. Subetei then completed the conquest of the Jin empire, driving many of the Jurchen back into their original homeland, but absorbing others into the Mongol army for the further conquest of China. Ogedei refused to divide the conquered region with the Song, which in 1234 attempted to seize part of the former Jin empire. This was the signal for another war, which lasted fortyfive years.

Ogedei committed the Mongols, whose total population could not have exceeded 1 million, to an offensive war against the most populous nation on earth, while other Mongol armies were invading Iran, Anatolia, Syria, and the steppes of western Siberia and Russia. By this time, ethnic Mongols were a minority of the Mongol armies. The remainder were Turks, Tatars, Tangut, Cumans, Bulghars, and other Inner Asian peoples. Nonetheless, the confidence with which the Mongol armies embarked on these farflung wars was almost as remarkable as the invariable success of their operations.

In compliance with the wishes of Chinggis, as expressed presumably in his legal code, the *yasaq* (see Glossary), his vast empire had been apportioned among his sons (only three survived; the eldest, Jochi, had died in 1227), and his sons' descendants, subject to the overall authority of the khan at Karakorum, which was rebuilt in 1235 by Ogedi. Jochi's son, Batu, ruled the region to the north and the west of Lake Balkash. Chagadai, the second son of Chinggis was given the southwestern region that includes modern Afghanistan, Turkestan (now in the Soviet Union), and central Siberia. He and his successors were known as the khans of the Chagadai Mongols. By implication, this realm extended indefinitely to the southwest, as Batu's did to the northwest. Ogedei and his progeny were awarded China and the other lands of East Asia. Tului, the youngest of the four principal heirs, was to have central Mongolia, the homeland, in accordance with Mongol custom. He and his descendants, however, were to share Mongolia's precious fighting manpower with the other three khanates.

The *kuriltai* of 1235 authorized at least two more major offensive operations: one against Tibet, the other in Eastern Europe. The Tibetan expedition was led by Godan, son of Ogedei, and the conquest was completed in 1239.

REIGN OF KUYUK

It was not until the summer of 1246 that a *kuriltai* assembled at Karakorum to select a successor to Ogedei. This was mainly because of political maneuvering by Batu and other royal princes who had hopes of being elected. While deliberately stalling in Bulghar in 1241, Batu founded Sarai (near modern Leninsk, Russian Soviet Federated Socialist Republic) on the lower Volga River, as the capital of his Khanate of Kipchak, best known to history as the Golden Horde (see Glossary; The Golden Horde , this ch.).

Between 1242 and 1246, Ogedei's widow, Teregene, held power as regent in preparation for the selection of her son, Kuyuk, as the new khan. Present during the *kuriltai* was the Franciscan friar, John of Plano Carpini, a papal envoy sent to ascertain the intentions of the Mongols. He recognized that the Mongols planned the conquest of Europe, and he belatedly urged Europe's monarchs to adopt Mongol strategy and tactics to oppose the coming onslaught.

Kuyuk apparently was torn between completing the conquest of China and continuing the conquest of Europe. The latter project was complicated, however, by Kuyuk's continuing rivalry with Batu. Just as civil war seemed imminent in 1249, Kuyuk died.

MENGKE AND THE WAR IN CHINA

Except for the descendants of Ogedei and Chagadai, most of the royal princes thought that Batu should be elected khan. By this time, however, Batu had decided that he preferred the steppes of the Volga to the steppes of Mongolia. He declined the offer and nominated Mengke, the eldest son of Tului (who had died in 1233), unquestionably one of the most gifted descendants of Chinggis. Mengke's nomination was confirmed by a *kuriltai* in 1251. He executed several of Ogedei's sons who had opposed his election and quickly restored to Mongol rule the vigor that had been lacking since the death of Chinggis.

Taking seriously the legacy of world conquest, Mengke decided to place primary emphasis on completing the conquest of Asia, particularly China; Europe was to be dealt with later. Because the Song had had the benefit of a lull of nearly ten years in which to recover and to reorganize, conquering Asia had become more difficult than it would have been earlier. Mengke himself took command, but he also placed great responsibility on his younger brother, Khubilai. Another brother, Hulegu, was sent to Iran to renew the expansion of Mongol control in Southwest Asia. Mengke encouraged Batu to raid Central Europe, but did not send him additional resources. Thus, although Batu's armies raided deep into Poland, Lithuania, and Estonia, and again overran Serbia and Bulgaria, these campaigns were not so important as the ones being undertaken in Southeast Asia and Southwest Asia.

Mengke also made some major administrative changes in the khanates established by the will of Chinggis. He disinherited the surviving sons of Ogedei, arranging that he and Khubilai would inherit the lands of East Asia. He also placed a limit on the domains of the successors of Chagadai; these were to end along the Oxus River and the Hindu Kush, instead of extending indefinitely to the southwest. Southwest Asia was to be the inheritance of Mengke's brother, Hulegu, the first of the Ilkhans ("subservient khans") or Mongol rulers of Iran (see The Ilkhans , this ch.).

Mengke prosecuted the war in China with intensity and skill. His principal assistant was Khubilai, who was appointed viceroy in China. In 1252 and 1253, Khubilai conquered Nanchao (modern

Yunnan). Tonkin (as northern Vietnam was known) then was invaded and pacified. The conquest ended with the fall of Hanoi in 1257.

Song resistance in southern China was based upon determined defense of its well-fortified, well-provisioned cities. The Chinese empire began to crumble, however, under the impact of a series of brilliant campaigns, personally directed by Mengke between 1257 and 1259. His sudden death from dysentery in August 1259, however, caused another lull in the war with China and put a stop to advances in West Asia.

KHUBILAI KHAN AND THE YUAN DYNASTY, 1261-1368

A NEW KHAN

The overwhelming choice of the *kuriltai* as Mengke's successor was his equally brilliant brother, Khubilai. Khubilai's selection was opposed violently, however, by his younger brother, Arik-Buka. This opposition precipitated a civil war won by Khubilai in 1261. For the next few years, the new khan devoted his attention to administrative reforms of his vast empire (see fig. 3). A major development was Khubilai's establishment in 1260 of a winter capital at what is now Beijing but was then called Dadu ("great capital," also called Khanbalik--Marco Polo's Cambaluc) which shifted the political center of the Mongol empire south into China and increased Chinese influence. Khubilai maintained a summer residence north of the Great Wall at Shangdu (the Xanadu of Coleridge).

In 1268 Khubilai was able to turn his full attention to the war in China. A series of campaigns, distinguished by the skill of Bayan (grandson of Subetei), culminated in 1276 in the capture of Hangzhou, the Song capital. It took three more years to subdue the outlying provinces. The last action of the war--a naval battle in Guangzhou Bay, in which the remnants of the Song fleet were destroyed by a Mongol fleet made up of defectors from the Song navy--took place in 1279.

Khubilai did not share Mengke's fierce desire to conquer the world. He had warred against China with determination, but apparently he realized that there was a limit to the Mongol capabilities for consolidating and for controlling conquered territory. It is likely that he recognized that this limit was being approached because of an event that occurred during the interregnum between Mengke's death and his own accession.

Hulegu, who had seized Baghdad and defeated the Abbasid Caliphate in 1258 and conquered Mesopotamia and Syria, had returned to Mongolia upon receiving news of Mengke's death. While he was gone, his forces were defeated by a larger, Mamluk, army at the Battle of Ain Jalut in Palestine in 1260. This was the first significant Mongol defeat in seventy years. The Mamluks had been led by a Turk named Baibars, a former Mongol warrior who used Mongol tactics.

Neither Khubilai nor Hulegu made a serious effort to avenge the defeat of Ain Jalut. Both devoted their attention primarily to consolidating their conquests, to suppressing dissidence, and to reestablishing law and order. Like their uncle, Batu, and his Golden Horde successors, they limited their offensive moves to occasional raids or to attacks with limited objectives in unconquered neighboring regions. After the failure of two invasion attempts against Japan in 1274 and 1281, Khubilai also gave up his goal of expansion to the east. In January 1293, Khubilai invaded Java and defeated the local ruler, only to be driven off the island by a Javanese ally who turned against him.

After the Song Dynasty had been destroyed, in 1279 Khubilai declared himself emperor of a united China with its capital at Dadu, and he established the Yuan ("first," "beginning") Dynasty

(1279-1368). Khubilai, who took the Chinese-style reign title Zhiyuan ("the greatest of the Yuan"), proved himself to be one of the most able rulers of imperial China.

THE YUAN DYNASTY

A rich cultural diversity evolved in China during the Yuan Dynasty, as it had in other periods of foreign dynastic rule. Major achievements included the development of drama and the novel and the increased use of the written vernacular. The Yuan was involved in a fair amount of cultural exchange because of its extensive West Asian and European contacts. The introduction of foreign musical instruments enriched the Chinese performing arts. The conversion to Islam of growing numbers of people in northwestern and southwestern China dates from this period. Nestorian Christianity and Roman Catholicism also enjoyed a period of toleration. Lamaism flourished, although native Daoism endured Mongol persecutions. Chinese governmental practices and examinations were reinstated by the Mongols in the hope of maintaining order within society. Advances were realized in the fields of travel literature, cartography, geography, and scientific education. Certain key Chinese innovations--such as printing techniques, porcelain playing cards, and medical literature--were introduced in Europe, while European skills, such as the production of thin glass and cloisonné, became popular in China.

The Mongols undertook extensive public works. Land and water communications were reorganized and improved. To provide against possible famines, new granaries were ordered to be built throughout the empire. Dadu was rebuilt with new palace grounds that included artificial lakes, hills, and parks, and the capital became the terminus of the Grand Canal, which was completely renovated. These commercially oriented improvements encouraged overland as well as maritime commerce throughout Asia and facilitated the first direct Chinese contacts with Europe. Chinese and Mongol travelers to the West were able to provide assistance in such areas as hydraulic engineering, and they brought back to China new scientific discoveries, agricultural crops, methods of food preparation, and architectural innovations.

Early records of travel by Westerners to East Asia date from this time. Much that the Western world of the thirteenth and fourteenth centuries knew about the Mongols and Asia was the result of the famous missions of a Venetian trading family. The first mission was by two brothers, Niccolò and Maffeo Polo, from 1260 to 1268. Another started in 1271, when they were joined by Niccolò's son, Marco. Marco Polo, who remained in Asia until 1295, was trusted by Khubilai Khan and undertook a number of diplomatic missions and administrative assignments for him throughout the empire. The account of his travels, *Il milione* (or, The Million, known in English as the *Travels of Marco Polo*), appeared about the year 1299 and astounded the people of Europe, who knew little of the highly developed culture of East Asia. The works of John of Plano Carpini and William of Rubruck also provided early descriptions of the Mongols to the West.

The Mongols sought, but failed, to govern China through its traditional institutions. At the outset, they discriminated against the Chinese socially and politically, monopolized the most important central and regional government posts, and developed an unprecedented and complex six-tier local-government administration. Mongols also preferred employing non-Chinese from other parts of the Mongol domain--Inner Asia, the Middle East, and even Europe--in those positions for which no Mongol could be found. Chinese, in turn, were more often employed in non-Chinese regions of the empire.

In time, Khubilai's successors became sinicized, and they then lost all influence on other Mongol lands across Asia. Gradually, they lost influence in China as well. The reigns of the later Yuan emperors were short and were marked by intrigues and rivalries. Uninterested in administration, they were separated from both their Mongolian army and their Chinese subjects. China was torn by dissension and unrest; bandits ranged the country without interference from the weakening Yuan armies.

The last of the nine successors of Khubilai was expelled from Dadu in 1368 by Zhu Yuanzhang, the founder of the Ming Dynasty (1368-1644), and died in Karakorum in 1370. Although Zhu, who adopted Mongol military methods, drove the Mongols out of China, he did not destroy their power. A later Chinese army invaded Mongolia in 1380. In 1388 a decisive victory was won; about 70,000 Mongols were taken prisoner, and Karakorum was annihilated.

THE ILKHANS

The Mongol defeat at Ain Jalut in 1260 led directly to the first important war between grandsons of Chinggis. The Mamluk leader, Baibars, made an alliance with Berke Khan, Batu's brother and successor. Berke had converted to Islam, and he thus was sympathetic to the Mamluk for religious reasons, as well as because he was jealous of his nephew, Hulegu. When Hulegu sent an army to Syria to punish Baibars, he was attacked suddenly by Berke. Hulegu had to turn his army back to the Caucasus to meet this threat, and he made repeated attempts to ally himself with the kings of France and England and with the Pope in order to crush the Mamluks in Palestine. Berke withdrew, however, when Khubilai sent 30,000 troops to aid the Ilkhans.

This chain of events marked the end of the Mongol expansion in Southwest Asia. Although Hulegu's successors did not exhibit the austere martial qualities of their forebears, they did bring a partial and brief economic revival to Iran. An increase in commerce and the expansion of trade routes brought a measure of cross culturization between Iran and China. The Mongol rulers devoted themselves to a more genteel life and let their provinces be governed by Turkish viziers. Finally these viziers seized control, and the Ilkhan khanate ended with the death of Abu Said in 1335.

THE GOLDEN HORDE

The Golden Horde of Batu had more time and more room for expansion of its territories than any other Mongol khanate. The Mongols maintained sovereignty over eastern Russia from 1240 to 1480, and they controlled the upper Volga area, the territories of the former Volga Bulghar state, Siberia, the northern Caucasus, Bulgaria (for a time), the Crimea, and Khwarizm. By applying the principle of indirect rule, the Golden Horde Mongols were able to preserve the Mongol ruling class and the local dynasties for more than 200 years. The influence that the Golden Horde Mongols came to have over medieval Russia and other areas was immense and lasting. They played a role in unifying the future Russian state, provided new political institutions, influenced imperial visions, and, through indirect rule, facilitated the appearance of a Muscovite autocracy.

The Golden Horde capital at Sarai became a prosperous center of commerce. Here, as in China, Mongol rule meant free trade, the exchange of goods between the East and the West, and also broad religious toleration.

In the mid-thirteenth century, the Golden Horde was administratively and militarily an integral part of the Mongol empire with its capital at Karakorum. By the early fourteenth century, however, this allegiance had become largely symbolic and ceremonial. Although certain Mongol administrative forms--such as census and postal systems--were maintained, other customs were not. The Golden Horde embraced Islam as its state religion and, with it, adopted new and more complex administrative forms to replace those of the old regime that had been devised for conquest. Even though most Mongols remained steppe nomads, new cities were founded, and a permanent urbanized bureaucracy and social structure took shape at Sarai. The Golden Horde allied itself with the Mamluks and negotiated with the Byzantines to combat the Ilkhans in a struggle to control Azerbaijan. Rather than isolating Russia, the Mongol presence and extensive diplomatic system brought envoys to Sarai from central and southern Europe, the Pope, Southwest Asia, Egypt, Iran, Inner Asia, China, and Mongolia.

The Mongols' vast contacts opened Russia to new influences, both Eastern and Western. The reason the Mongols did not occupy Russia itself, but left its administration to local princes, was not inability to administer a society that was both urban and agrarian, or Russian resistance. Rather, some historians believe that Russia had little to offer the Mongols in terms of produce or trade routes, and even tax revenues were insignificant compared with the wealth of the southern realms under their control. The inability of cavalry to operate in forests and swamps--a factor that limited the northward advance of the Mongols and largely determined the northern frontier of their empire--was undoubtedly a distinct disincentive as well.

In time the Golden Horde Mongols and the Mongol Tatars, although still nomads, lost their original identities and--as happened to Mongols in China and Iran--became largely synonymous with the local Turkic peoples, the Kipchak. Arabic and Tatar replaced Mongol as the official language of the Golden Horde, and increasing political fragmentation occurred. The power of the Golden Horde khans slowly declined, particularly as a powerful new state rose in central Russia.

THE MONGOL DECLINE

Contributing to the eventual Mongol decline in Eurasia was a bitter war with Timur, also known as Timur Lenk (or Timur the Lame, from which Tamerlane is derived). He was a man of aristocratic Transoxianian birth who falsely claimed descent from Chinggis. Timur reunited Turkestan and the lands of the Ilkhans; in 1391 he invaded the Eurasian steppes and defeated the Golden Horde. He ravaged the Caucasus and southern Russia in 1395. Timur's empire disintegrated, however, soon after his death in 1405.

The effects of Timur's victory, as well as those of devastating drought and plague, were both economic and political. The Golden Horde's central base had been destroyed, and trade routes were moved south of the Caspian Sea. Political struggles led to the split of the Golden Horde into three separate khanates: Astrakhan, Kazan, and the Crimea. Astrakhan--the Golden Horde itself--was destroyed in 1502 by an alliance of Crimean Tatars and Muscovites. The last reigning descendant of Chinggis, Shahin Girai, khan of the Crimea, was deposed by the Russians in 1783.

The Mongols' influence and their intermarriage with the Russian aristocracy had a lasting effect on Russia. Despite the destruction caused by their invasion, the Mongols made valuable contributions to administrative practices. Through their presence, which in some ways checked the influence of European Renaissance ideas in Russia, they helped reemphasize traditional ways. This Mongol--or Tatar as it became known--heritage has much to do with Russia's distinctiveness from the other nations of Europe.

There were a number of reasons for the relatively rapid decline of the Mongols as an influential power. One important factor was their failure to acculturate their subjects to Mongol social traditions. Another was the fundamental contradiction of a feudal, essentially nomadic, society's attempting to perpetuate a stable, centrally administered empire. The sheer size of the empire was reason enough for the Mongol collapse. It was too large for one person to administer, as Chinggis had realized, yet adequate coordination was impossible among the ruling elements after the split into khanates. Possibly the most important single reason was the disproportionately small number of Mongol conquerors compared with the masses of subject peoples.

The change in Mongol cultural patterns that did occur inevitably exacerbated natural divisions in the empire. As different areas adopted different foreign religions, Mongol cohesiveness dissolved. The nomadic Mongols had been able to conquer the Eurasian land mass through a combination of organizational ability, military skill, and fierce warlike prowess, but they fell prey to alien cultures, to the disparity between their way of life and the needs of empire, and to the size of their domain, which proved too large to hold together. The Mongols declined when their sheer momentum could no longer sustain them.

MONGOLIA IN TRANSITION, 1368-1911

RETURN TO NOMADIC PATTERNS

The end of the Yuan was the second turning point in Mongol history. The retreat of more than 60,000 Mongols into the Mongolian heartland brought radical changes to the quasifeudalistic system. In the early fifteenth century, the Mongols split into two groups, the Oirad in the Altai region and the eastern group that later came to be known as the Khalkha (see Glossary) in the area north of the Gobi. A lengthy civil war (1400-54) precipitated still more changes in the old social and political institutions. By the middle of the fifteenth century, the Oirad had emerged as the predominant force, and, under the leadership of Esen Khan, they united much of Mongolia and then continued their war against China. Esen was so successful against China that, in 1449, he defeated and captured the Ming emperor. After Esen was killed in battle four years later, however, the brief resurgence of Mongolia came to an abrupt halt, and the tribes returned to their traditional disunity.

After nearly two more decades of Oirad-Khalkha conflict, another Oirad chieftain, Dayan Khan, assumed central leadership in 1466 and reunited most of Mongolia. By the end of the fifteenth century, he had restored peace and had established a new confederation comprising a vast region of North-central Asia, between the Ural Mountains and Lake Baykal. He then extended his control eastward to include the remainder of Khalkha Mongolia. The Oirad were surrounded by the Turkic descendants of the Chagadai Mongols who occupied the lowlands to the east and west, in the three independent khanates of Yarkand (modern Xinjiang south of the Tian Shan Mountains), Ferghana, and Khwarizm. Early in the sixteenth century, these three khanates were overwhelmed, however, by the Uzbeks (see Glossary), who earlier had broken loose from Mongol authority. The Uzbeks consolidated their control over Bukhara (Bokhara), Samarkand, Khwarizm, and Herat. During Dayan Khan's rule, quasi-feudalistic administration was reestablished, and tribes became more settled, with more specified grazing areas. What little government existed was exercised by noble descendants of Chinggis (including Dayan), but it met with great resistance.

After the death of Dayan in 1543, the Oirad and the Khalkha disintegrated once more into insignificant and quarrelsome tribal groupings. The Torgut subclan of the Oirad was now perhaps the most vital of the Mongol peoples. The Torgut raided frequently across the Urals into the Volga Valley, which had been conquered by the new Muscovite empire. Farther east the Khalkha roamed the region north and south of the Gobi; the Ordos Mongols and the Chahar Mongols became loosely grouped in a confederation holding most of Southern Mongolia. The boundaries of territories ruled by the Uzbeks remained relatively stable.

Throughout this period of discord among the Mongols, they nonetheless shared a continuing hostility to the Ming. The struggle was maintained principally by the Khalkha. Although the title had become almost meaningless, the line of the khans had continued in the Chahar tribe, the leader of which became the rallying point for the conflict against China.

The war with China was renewed with considerable energy after Altan Khan (1507-83) of the Tumed clan united the Khalkha. Although he was not so prominent in history as his predecessor, Dayan, or his successor, Galdan Khan (1632-97), Altan was probably the greatest of the Mongol princes in the centuries following the collapse of the Yuan. By 1552 he had defeated the Oirad and had reunited most of Mongolia. It soon became obvious to Altan that there was nothing to be gained by continuing the war with the Ming; the empire of Chinggis never could be restored. Accordingly, he concluded a treaty with the Ming emperor in 1571, ending a struggle that had lasted more than three centuries.

In the remaining eleven years of his life, Altan aggressively pushed Mongol power to the south and the southwest, and he raided Tibet extensively. Altan, in turn, was coopted by a Buddhist revival in Tibet, and he became a fervent convert. In 1586 the first lamaist monastery was established in Mongolia, and Buddhism--specifically, Lamaism--became the state religion.

CAUGHT BETWEEN THE RUSSIANS AND THE MANCHUS

By the early seventeenth century, the power of the khan was greatly weakened, and the pattern of decentralized rule reemerged. Small tribes within each *tumen* became petty realms ruled over by individual princes. Division of inheritances further weakened the overall power structure, and *tumen* subdivisions (battalions, referred to in later Mongol history as banners--see Glossary--or *koshuus* in Mongol) were widely dispersed and therefore fragmented. At the same time that Mongol rule was disintegrating, tsarist Russia in the west and the Manchus in the east were expanding steadily. The Mongol and the Turkic peoples, traditionally conquerors, could now be conquered themselves not because their warlike proclivities had decreased, but because the art of war had progressed beyond the capacity of essentially nomadic peoples. Their economic resources would not permit the production or the purchase of muskets and cannon, against which their cavalry could not stand.

A new process of conquest began when most of what is now northeastern China was consolidated by the Manchus. Essentially nomadic in origin, the Manchus were descended from the Jurchen, who earlier had established the Jin Empire. Early in the seventeenth century, under their leader Nurhaci, the Manchus began to press into southern Mongolia.

The westward movement of the Manchu soon involved them in a struggle with the last of the great khans, Ligdan Khan of the Chahar Mongols. Ligdan had been attempting to reestablish Chahar predominance among the Khalkha, particularly among those tribes inhabiting the region south of the Gobi. These efforts alarmed his neighbors, who called upon Nurhaci for assistance. For several years, it appeared that the Manchu conqueror had met his match because Ligdan possessed some of the military prowess of his ancestors. Although he could not prevent the Manchus from gaining control of the territory of the neighboring Ordos Mongols, Ligdan beat back Manchu efforts to move farther west. After his death in 1634, however, Mongol resistance to the Manchus collapsed in southern Mongolia. This is the period of the Mongolian national hero, Tsogto Taji, who is said to have been the only northern Mongol aristocrat to have led his subjects against the Manchus in defense of the southern Mongols.

Meanwhile, many of the Torgut, the westernmost of the Oirad Mongols, began to migrate westward in approximately 1620. Possibly the movement was a reaction to the growing dominance of the Dzungar Mongols, an Oirad subclan and neighbors of the Torgut to the south. In any event, the Torgut fought their way through Kirghiz and Kazakh territory, to cross the Embe River. Becoming better known as the Kalmyk tribe, they subsequently settled in the Trans-Volga steppe and raided Russian settlements on both sides of the river. Finally submitting to Russia in 1646, they maintained autonomy under their own khan. They became an excellent source of light cavalry for the Russians, who later used them in campaigns against the Crimean Tatars and in Inner Asia.

The Mongol interest in Tibet that had been aroused in Altan's campaigns seems to have been transmitted to the Dzungar. They inhabited a region east of Lake Balkash that extended eastward into northern Xinjiang. They carried out a number of campaigns into Tibet, and by 1636 they had established a virtual protectorate over the region. Because of the generally high quality of their leadership at this time, the Dzungar dominated Mongolia for much of the seventeenth century.

Farther east, the religious revival begun by Altan had continued unabated, and it was perhaps the greatest single influence on Mongol life and culture during the seventeenth and succeeding centuries. In 1635 the khan of the Tushetu tribe proclaimed that his son was the reincarnation of an ancient and respected scholar, who had achieved such a state of virtue that he had become known as a buddha. Thus the young Tushetu prince was named the Jebtsundamba Khutuktu or Living Buddha, becoming the highest ecclesiastical figure in Mongolia. This was the beginning of a line of theocratic leaders that was to continue unbroken for nearly three centuries. The successors of the first Jebtsundamba Khutuktu were also believed to be reincarnations, and all were found among the Tushetu.

By the middle of the seventeenth century, Russian exploration and annexation had become very worrisome to the Mongols and the Turks to the southwest. In response to this pressure, in 1672 Ayuka Khan of the Torgut Mongols raided through western Siberia, across the Urals and the Volga, and into Russia. He then made peace with the Russians on terms that enabled him to continue to control his lands in relative tranquility for the remainder of the century.

Later in the seventeenth century, a new effort toward Mongol unity was attempted by Galdan Khan of the Dzungar. He conquered most of Kashgar, Yarkand, and Khotan (Hotan) from the Kirghiz, and he expanded into Kazakh territory. In about 1682, intending to conquer the Khalkha, he turned eastward. In 1688 the hardpressed Khalkha appealed to the Manchus for aid. The Manchus were more than pleased to respond, and a Chinese-Manchu army marched to help. A development that further integrated the Mongols into the Manchu apparatus was the Manchus' adoption of the Mongol banner system, which combined administrative and military functions.

By this time, the Manchus had conquered all of China and had established the Qing Dynasty (1644-1911) with its capital in Beijing. They had become concerned over the steady Russian expansion eastward that, up to this time, had remained far to the north. The Russians had carefully avoided the still-formidable Torgut, who inhabited the region that now comprises central Siberia. In this way, the Russians had reached the Amur Valley and the Pacific Ocean by mid-century. In the period between 1641 and 1652, the Russians gradually conquered the Buryat Mongols, thereby gaining control of the region around Lake Baykal. The Manchus observed with considerable apprehension Russia's growing pressure on the Turkic peoples and the Mongols of Inner Asia. As early as 1653, there were clashes between Manchus and Russians in the Amur Valley. In 1660 the Manchus ejected the Russians from the Amur region, only to see them reappear when the Manchus became occupied with internal troubles in southern China.

In 1683 a second Manchu military expedition began systematic operations to eject the Russians, and in 1685 it seized the Russian stronghold at Albazin. But later that year, when the Manchus withdrew, the Russians reconstructed the fortifications. The Manchus began to prepare for a more extensive war. It was at this time that the Khalkha appealed to the Manchus for aid. The Manchus promptly responded, seeing an opportunity to gain control of Mongolia as a base for possible war with Russia.

This move was probably understood by the Russians. They were conducting a campaign in Europe, and they decided that the dispute with China must be settled peacefully. This led to the Sino-Russian Treaty of Nerchinsk in 1689, in which the Russians agreed to abandon Albazin and the area north of the Amur River. The terms of that treaty were supplemented in 1727 by the Treaty of Kyakhta, which further delineated the Sino-Russian border.

THE END OF INDEPENDENCE

Meanwhile, the Manchus had sent a large army into northern Mongolia to confront Galdan in an effort to preempt any attempts at establishing a new Mongol empire. The employment of artillery had a decisive effect, and the Dzungar were routed. In May 1691, Qing emperor Kangxi called a *kuriltai* of principal Khalkha chiefs at Dolonnur. Those present acknowledged Manchu overlordship in return for protection against the Dzungar. It had become apparent by this time that, although there were strong ties between the Qing court and local Mongol rulers, the relations among individual Mongol leaders were weak. The head of each banner was a vassal of the Qing emperor and was beholden to the Chinese treasury for a pension. Mongols not only pledged personal loyalty to the emperor, but they also became inseparable from their banner and could not serve in any capacity in another banner. Membership was hereditary; class structure was rigid; and the whole feudal-like system helped the Manchus isolate and control the Mongols. The banners, in effect, became petty fiefdoms.

By this time, the Jebtsundamba Khutuktu had fled to escape Galdan's renewed advances. After five years of continued raiding by the Dzungar into central Mongolia, Kangxi led 80,000 troops into Mongolia and in 1696 crushed Galdan near Jao Modo (south of present-day Ulaanbaatar). Galdan retreated, and he died the next year. This ended the influence of the Dzunger in most of Mongolia, although they retained control of the western regions and of parts of Xinjiang and Tibet.

Despite the defeat at Jao Modo, twenty years later the Dzungar again were embroiled in war with the Qing. In 1718 Galdan's nephew and heir, Tsewang Rabdan, invaded Tibet to settle a prolonged dispute over the successor to the Dalai Lama. His troops seized Lhasa, imprisoned the Dalai Lama, and ambushed a Manchu relief force. Kangxi retaliated in 1720; two Chinese armies defeated the Dzungar and drove them from Tibet. This was the first war in which Mongol forces made extensive use of musketry; they were not very effective, however, against the larger, better-armed and better-equipped Qing forces. After the death of the Dalai Lama, a new Dalai Lama was installed by Kangxi, and a Manchu garrison was left in Lhasa. Meanwhile, another Chinese army invaded Dzungar territory to capture Ürümqi and Turpan. Additional Chinese punitive expeditions eventually defeated the Dzungar in 1732 and virtually ended Mongolian independence for nearly two centuries.

The Russian and the Chinese empires continued their expansions into Inner Asia during the eighteenth century. They found it expedient to delimit the borders between the respective areas of ancient Mongolia that they had conquered in the seventeenth century. This was done by the Treaty of Kyakhta in 1727, which established the border between the portions of Mongolia controlled by China and those controlled by Russia.

In the period 1755 to 1757, serious revolts against Chinese rule broke out among the Dzungar in Xinjiang. These were suppressed promptly, and Chinese control over western Mongolia and Oirad territory was strengthened. In 1771 the Chinese government persuaded part of the Kalmyk tribe to return from Russia to repopulate the devastated region.

During the 1750s, as a result of Manchu administrative policies, the first distinction was made between northern and southern Mongolia. The southern provinces--Suiyuan, Chahar (or Qahar), and Jehol (or Rehol), known as Inner Mongolia--were virtually absorbed into China. The remainder of the region--the northern provinces, which became known as Outer Mongolia--was considered an "outside subordinate" by the Manchus, and it was largely ignored. After another 100 years, however, China again became alarmed by Russia's expansionist policy and colonial development in the regions north and west of Outer Mongolia. Increased Chinese activity in Outer Mongolia resulted in some economic and social improvements, but it also revealed to the Mongolians the possibilities of playing off the two great empires against each other. Chinese merchants and moneylenders had become ubiquitous, and the extent of Mongol debt had become enormous, by the early nineteenth century. The debt situation, combined with growing resentment over Chinese encroachment, gave impetus to Mongol nationalism by the beginning of the twentieth century.

During the period of Chinese dominance, Mongolia not only experienced a century of peace, but it became an increasingly theocratic society. Buddhism relatively early had absorbed shamanism, and the result was a unique local religion (see Religion , ch. 2). By the mid-nineteenth century, however, turmoil in China, caused by internal rebellion and by pressures from the West, resulted in a breakdown of the increasingly expensive administrative apparatus in Outer Mongolia. Mounting debts and higher taxes, which led to a growing impoverishment of Outer Mongolia, gradually rekindled traditional Mongol dissatisfaction with the Manchu overlord. Rioting, Mongol troop mutinies, and other anti-Chinese incidents occurred with increasing regularity in the late nineteenth and the early twentieth centuries. Outside help was sought from Russia in 1900, when a mission--which failed--was sent to St. Petersburg. Thereafter, reform-minded Chinese leaders abolished many old social and political proscriptions, and, despite Mongol resentment of the idea and of continued Chinese repression, preparations were being made for constitutional government when revolution broke out in China.

MODERN MONGOLIA

PERIOD OF AUTONOMY, 1911-21

With the end of the Qing Dynasty and the establishment of the Republic of China in 1911, revolutionary ferment also emerged in Mongolia. As early as July 1911, participants in an anti-Chinese meeting in Yihe Huree (see Glossary) had petitioned the Russian government--which long had sought the independence of Outer Mongolia--for help against China. On December 1, 1911, Outer Mongolia in effect proclaimed its independence on the basis that its allegiance had been to the Manchus, not to China. On December 28, the eighth Jebtsundamba Khutuktu became Bogdo Khan (holy ruler) of an autonomous theocratic government; a 20,000-troop army was created; and Russian officers appeared in Yihe Huree (renamed Niyslel--capital--Huree, or Urga) to equip, to organize, and to train the army. The new Chinese government refused to recognize Mongolian independence, but it was too preoccupied with internal discord to enforce its sovereignty.

Meanwhile, Russia was moving rapidly to take advantage of the situation. On November 3 and December 19, 1912, respectively, Mongolian-Russian and Mongolian-Tibetan agreements were signed in Niyslel Huree. The latter agreement granted mutual recognition of independence; the former only affirmed Mongolia's autonomy from China. The Russian agreement and a protocol to it created a tsarist protectorate over Outer Mongolia. The Japanese, too, sought, unsuccessfully, to influence the independence movement in 1911 and 1912 with contributions of arms and money. Following the mobilization of a Mongol army to liberate Inner Mongolia, several other agreements affecting Mongolia were reached. In November 5, 1913, agreement, Russia recognized Chinese suzerainty over Mongolia, and China recognized Outer Mongolia's right to selfrule and to the control of its own commerce and industry. China also agreed not to send troops into Mongolia. On May 25, 1915, a second, tripartite agreement (among China, Mongolia, and Russia), the Treaty of Kyakhta, formalized Mongolian autonomy. Russia's involvement in World War I, however, reduced the attention that the tsar's government could pay to Mongolia. This neglect, which occurred at the same time as new monarchical machinations in China, rekindled Japanese interest in, and aid to, anti-Chinese forces in Mongolia and neighboring Manchuria.

After revolution broke out in Russia in November 1917, Japan moved to aid anti-Bolshevik forces in Mongolia, and a Japanesefostered pan-Mongol movement was established under the influence of the Buryat Mongols. A pan-Mongolia conference was held in February and March 1919 in

Chita, Siberia. The participants decided to establish a Mongol state, comprising Outer Mongolia, Inner Mongolia, and Buryatia (present-day Buryatskaya Autonomous Soviet Socialist Republic) and to send letters to the Versailles Peace Conference that ended World War I. Despite formation of a small provisional government--in which Outer Mongolia refused to participate--and promises of Japanese aid, the movement failed in the face of renewed Chinese efforts to regain control over all of Mongolia. In October 1919, a Chinese warlord army, emboldened by the demise of the tsarist regime, occupied Niyslel Huree and received an acknowledgment of Chinese sovereignty from the Bogdo Khan government. The Mongol army was disarmed and disbanded.

Soon, however, the effects of the upheaval in Russia began to reach Mongolia. In October 1920, Russian White Guard troops under Baron Roman Nicolaus von Ungern-Sternberg invaded from Siberia. In February 1921, after a fierce battle, Von Ungern-Sternberg drove the Chinese out of Niyslel Huree and occupied the city. At first the White Guards were hailed as liberators by Mongolian monarchists, but in the next several months Von UngernSternberg 's reign of terror and destruction aroused popular opposition.

The threatening actions of Chinese, Japanese, and White Russian forces greatly stimulated Mongolian nationalism during this time. Two secret revolutionary circles emerged in Niyslel Huree in 1919, the military-oriented Dzuun (East) Huree Group, under Damdiny Sukhe Bator and Horloogiyn Dandzan, and the civilian-oriented Consul's Group, headed by Horloyn Choybalsan and Dogsomyn Bodoo. The Communist International (see Glossary), also called the Comintern, which was headquartered in Moscow, advised the two groups to merge in order to present a united front to the Chinese and the White Russian occupation forces. The merger was accomplished at a conference in Irkutsk in March 1920, with the formation of the Mongolian People's Party under the leadership of Sukhe Bator. The Jebtsundamba Khutuktu gave his encouragement and support to the revolutionary leaders, and in his name they appealed to Moscow for more assistance.

The Japanese were pressing ahead with efforts to take advantage of the chaos caused by the Russian civil war. A large Japanese force, nominally part of an anti-Bolshevik Allied Expeditionary Force intervening in eastern Siberia, had taken over much of the Trans-Siberian Railway between Vladivostok and Lake Baykal. Japanese funds were provided to von Ungern-Sternberg and other White Russian elements, in order to prevent the Soviet government from establishing control in eastern Siberia and from obtaining too much influence in Mongolia. The Japanese efforts were thwarted to a large degree, however, by the neutralist attitude of United States elements of the Allied Expeditionary Force, and Soviet forces gradually established control over Siberia.

The improved Soviet position in Siberia enabled Moscow to respond to the appeals of the Mongolian nationalists. Earlier, in the 1918 to 1919 period, Moscow had renounced all agreements regarding Mongolia that had been reached with Japan and China. The First Party Congress of the newly formed Mongolian People's Party, was held at Kyakhta (in Siberia, near the Mongolian border) on March 1 to 3, 1921. On March 13, the new party Central Committee formed the Mongolian People's Provisional Government, and, after Sukhe Bator's Mongolian Partisan Army (established in February 1921) captured the Mongolian city of Khiagt (across the border from Kyakhta), a new capital was established. A MongolianSoviet military force also had been formed, and by early July it had driven von Ungern-Sternberg's forces out of Niyslel Huree and had occupied the city. On July 11--the date recognized as Mongolia's national day--the Bogdo Khan government was replaced by a new People's Government of Mongolia, a limited monarchy nominally headed by the Jebtsundamba Khutuktu under the title of khan. Bodoo was named premier and foreign minister; Sukhe Bator continued as commander in chief and became minister of war, with Choybalsan as his deputy. The government was bolstered by Soviet troops, who virtually occupied the country

REVOLUTIONARY TRANSFORMATION, 1921-24

Fighting against the White Russians culminated in the capture of von Ungern-Sternberg in August 1921; the rest of his forces were defeated by January 1922. On September 14, 1921, the independence of Mongolia was proclaimed, and on October 26 a legislative assembly, the National Provisional Little Hural, opened. The formalization of Mongolian-Soviet relations then was accelerated. On November 5, 1921, a bilateral Agreement on Mutual Recognition and Friendly Relations was signed in Moscow. It recognized the People's Government of Mongolia, and it facilitated the exchange of diplomatic representatives. Furthermore, it provided for the self-determination of Tannu Tuva (see Glossary), a region in northwestern Mongolia that had been a Russian protectorate between 1914 and 1917.

At this juncture, discord emerged among the Mongolian factions. When supporters of the Bogdo Khan regime expressed displeasure with the limits placed on the monarchy, the Mongolian People's Party levied further restrictions on it, while giving more power to the party-controlled government. At the same time, some members of the new regime were concerned about Mongolia's close relationship with the Soviet Union. Even Premier Bodoo sought to distance himself from Soviet influence. In August 1922, however, he and forty others were arrested and charged with "counterrevolutionary activities" and with wanting to restore an unlimited monarchy. Bodoo and fourteen others were executed. When the Second Party Congress of the Mongolian People's Party was held in July 1923, Mongolian-Soviet solidarity was reiterated amid calls, for the first time, in favor of purging "oppressor class elements" from the party.

At this critical stage, several key leadership changes occurred that caused momentous political developments. On February 22, 1923, thirty-year-old revolutionary hero Sukhe Bator died of illness (although Choybalsan later claimed he had been poisoned), leaving the way clear for Choybalsan's eventual accession. Next, the Jebtsundamba Khutuktu died on May 20, 1924, and the People's Government, which had resolved to form a republic, forbade the traditional search for the reincarnation of the defunct ruler. This move eliminated the theocratic symbol of Mongolia. At the same time, a new Soviet treaty with China on May 31, 1924 (which provided for the withdrawal of Soviet troops from Mongolia), set the stage for the final step in the nominal independence of Mongolia.

The Third Party Congress of the Mongolian People's Party met in Niyslel Huree from August 4 to 24, 1924, but it quickly became embroiled in a debate led by party chairman Dandzan, who, like Bodoo, hoped to reduce Soviet influence. The congress culminated in the arrest and execution of the "capitalist" Dandzan. Among the achievements of the congress was purging the party of "useless elements" and renaming it the Mongolian People's Revolutionary Party. On November 25, 1924, with the adoption of a Soviet-style state constitution by the First National Great Hural, the new national assembly, the Mongolian People's Republic was formally established. The National Little Hural, the standing body when the National Great Hural was not in session, was elected; it, in turn, elected a cabinet with Balingiyn Tserendorj as premier and Choybalsan as commander in chief of the army. At the same time, Niyslel Huree was renamed Ulaanbaatar (literally, Red Hero).

CONSOLIDATION OF THE MONGOLIAN PEOPLE'S REPUBLIC, 1925- 28

Soviet troops ostensibly were withdrawn in March 1925 (although some historians have debated whether all actually departed). Despite the treaty--between the Soviet Union and China--that acknowledged Outer Mongolia as an autonomous, but integral, part of China, the Soviet Union explicitly recognized Mongolia's independence of China in internal affairs and its ability to pursue an independent foreign policy. While continuing its cautious relationship with Beijing, Moscow made it clear that it would permit no Chinese encroachment on Mongolia. Mongolia's general foreign policy line was based on strong ties with the Soviet Union, "the reliable pillar of [Mongolia's] independence and prosperity" according to the party line.

Under Moscow's guidance, the leftist leaders of Mongolia began to strengthen their still-weak position. The Mongolian communists, with Comintern help, gradually undermined the rightist elements in the Mongolian People's Revolutionary Party and attacked the power of the two great institutions that had dominated Mongolia for centuries: first the nobles; then, the abbots (whose monastic followers comprised at least one-third of the adult males). In this period of cautious consolidation, the party abolished the aristocracy's feudal privileges, a reform which had the initial effect of influencing wealthy nobles to embark on capitalist ventures, such as investing in the new cooperatives. Gradually, however, the revolutionaries built a state-guided economy supported by Mongolian cooperatives and by Soviet trade.

Moscow's economic hold on Mongolia tightened as exports to the Soviet Union rose rapidly from about 14 percent of Mongolia's total production (chiefly livestock and animal products), in 1923 to 1924, to 85 percent, in 1928 to 1929. By 1929 Mongolia's imports lagged far behind its exports. Aside from the provision of technical and political advisers, Soviet trade policy did not yet provide for economic development aid to newer socialist countries as had been envisioned by Lenin in 1920.

Other areas of the economy showed more progress. The Mongolian National Bank, established in 1924 as a joint Mongolian-Soviet company, issued the tugrik, the new national currency, as part of monetary reform. The cooperative movement, directed by the Mongolian Building Cooperative, began to show impressive results. A standardized tax system was instituted, and other administrative reforms slowly took hold. The army, equipped and trained by the Soviets, was steadily growing and improving. The government refrained from a direct attack on the venerated religious establishment, but some higher-level monks were imprisoned and executed.

Although the Mongolian communists had not yet overthrown the conservatives in the government and the economic sectors during this period, they had gained progressively in strength as evidenced by the changes they had made in society. Slowly, the young Soviet-taught Mongols were taking over the political, the military, and the economic apparatus. Many nobles retained their wealth, however, and the number of monastics actually increased between 1925 and 1928. Nearly 90 percent of all trade was controlled by Chinese firms in Mongolia. The Fourth Party Congress (September 1925), the Fifth Party Congress (September 1926), and the Sixth Party Congress (September 1927) had witnessed policy struggles between leftist and rightist elements that presaged the victory of the left.

PURGES OF THE OPPOSITION, 1928-32

A decisive clash between leftists and rightists occurred at the Seventh Party Congress from late October to December 10, 1928. After forty-eight days of debate, party chairman TserenOchiryn Dambadorj was exiled to Moscow, and other rightist members were expelled as the left seized control of the party and the government. With their power now secure at the top and with party opinion united on major policy goals, the leftists accelerated their programs.

Strong Soviet backing was assured by Josef Stalin, who in the meantime had triumphed over his political foes in Moscow. In addition, after 1927 Soviet caution toward China no longer was necessary; Stalin was no longer constrained by his relationship with Chiang Kai-shek's Guomindang (Kuomintang in Wade-Giles romanization), or Chinese Nationalist Party, which had broken with the Chinese Communist Party and had consolidated its rule over eastern China from Nanjing. Both domestic and international changes had freed Mongolian leftists for radical changes.

Policies confirming the party line of developing the country along noncapitalist lines were ratified by the Fifth National Great Hural in December 1928. As conservative officials were eliminated from the government, Choybalsan was chosen as head of the National Little Hural. The leftist leaders called for the immediate confiscation of feudal property, the development of a five-year plan, the collectivization of stockbreeders, the ouster of Chinese traders, and the implementation of the Soviet trade monopoly. These extreme measures followed standard Soviet economic policy. In less-sophisticated Mongolia, however, the economic situation seemed to defy such planning. The basically nomadic society was largely illiterate, and there was no industrial proletariat; the aristocracy and the religious establishment held a large share of the country's wealth; popular obedience to traditional authorities continued to be widespread; the party lacked grass-roots support; and the government had little organization or experience. Nevertheless, the party was receptive to Moscow's directives; and the Mongolian revolutionaries made mistakes similar to those of the Soviets through an excess of zeal, intolerance, and inexperience.

The first harsh repression of opposition came in 1929. Under the direction of Choybalsan, more than 600 feudal estates (herds and fixed property) were confiscated and were given to members of the laity and to monks who left their monasteries. In 1931 and 1932, the property of more than 800 religious and secular leaders was seized, and more than 700 heads of households were killed or imprisoned. The antireligious campaign was three-pronged: ordinary monks were forced to leave the monasteries and enter the army or the economy; monks of middle status were put in prison camps; and those of highest rank were killed. Collectivization followed expropriation, and by 1931 more than one-third of the stock-raising households had been forcibly communized.

The brutal collectivization of herdsmen was rapid, and it caused bloody uprisings. Although the Eighth Party Congress from February to April 1930 had recognized that the country was unprepared for total socialization, the party reaction to opposition was to reenforce its measures nevertheless. The massive shift from private property to collectivization and communization was accelerated. The party then attacked the entire monastic class, the nobility, the nomads, and the nationalists, while purging its own ranks. The government imposed high and indiscriminate taxes, confiscated private property, banned private industry, forced craft workers to join mutual aid cooperatives, and nationalized foreign and domestic trade and transportation.

Extremism produced near-disaster. The power of the monks and the feudal nobles finally was broken, Chinese traders and other foreign capitalists were ousted, and still greater dependence on Soviet aid was required (see The Suppression of Buddhism , ch. 2). The mechanical imposition of communes on an unprepared nomadic sheep-herding and cattle-herding society, however, resulted in the slaughter of 7 million animals in three years by angry and frightened herders. Mongolia's economy, which rested entirely on animal husbandry, was severely affected. The failure of communes, the hasty destruction of private trade, and inadequate Soviet supplies contributed to spreading famine. By 1931 to 1932, thousands were suffering severe food shortages, which, together with the people's reaction to terror, had brought the nation to the verge of civil war. Finally the government was forced to call in troops and tanks; with Soviet assistance, it suppressed the spreading anticommunist rebellion in western Mongolia.

In May 1932, a month after anticommunist uprisings in western Mongolia, the Comintern and the Communist Party of the Soviet Union directed the Mongolian party to end its extremism. The next month, the party Central Committee rejected its prior policy as "leftist deviation" and expelled several top leaders as "leftwing adventurers." Choybalsan announced that "the overall development of our country has not yet entered the stage of socialism, and also it is wrong to copy Soviet experience in every single thing." The entire socioeconomic pattern was swiftly changed. The collective farm experiment was dropped, worker cooperatives were abandoned, the cattle tax was reduced, and herders and peasants again were allowed to hold private property. Foreign trade, still channeled exclusively to the Soviet Union, continued to be controlled by the state, however. Under continuing Soviet protection and domination, Mongolia now settled down to a period of gradual social change.

An underlying reason for Moscow's reversal of the course of Mongolian socialism had been the growing Japanese threat. The September 18, 1931, Mukden incident had opened the way for Japan to establish Manchukuo (Japanese-controlled Manchuria). Mongolians were not alone in the fear that Japan might try to establish a Japanese-controlled Mongolian monarchy, Mengkukuo.

ECONOMIC GRADUALISM AND NATIONAL DEFENSE, 1932-45

THE NEW TURN POLICY, 1932-40

The new policy of socioeconomic gradualism--the New Turn Policy--continued until the mid-1940s, when Mongolian socialism entered its modern stage of collectivization and economic growth. The Ninth Party Congress in September and October 1934 pronounced the New Turn a success, but it became obvious that this gradualism actually had been determined by the basic Soviet need to maintain Mongolia as a stable buffer state against either Japanese or Chinese expansion. At the beginning of this period, the Soviets did not want to enlarge Mongolia's small-scale industries because this might provide a further incentive for Japanese invasion. Instead, Mongolia's raw materials were used to strengthen the Soviet Union, while Soviet Red Army units and a large cavalry-oriented Mongolian People's Revolutionary Army were deployed to defend Mongolia against attack.

On November 27, 1934, a Mongolian-Soviet "gentlemen's agreement" was reached that provided for mutual assistance in the face of Japanese advances in Manchuria and Inner Mongolia. In January 1935, Soviet troops reentered Mongolia as Japanese forces began to probe the Mongolian-Manchurian border. On March 12, 1936, the 1934 agreement was upgraded when the ten-year Mongolian-Soviet Treaty of Friendship--which included a mutual defense protocol--was signed. The pact did not mention Chinese sovereignty over Mongolia, and Moscow ignored Chinese protests.

In addition to concluding defense treaties with the Soviet Union, Mongolia concentrated on building its army with Soviet guidance and military aid. In 1936 military expenditures were doubled, and by 1938 more than half of Mongolia's budget was for defense. The government built paved roads, extended railroads, and established military air bases and communication lines, all with Soviet aid. Military equipment and training also were supplied by the Soviet Union. It is estimated that during World War II the Mongolian Army numbered between 80,000 and 100,000 troops, a huge percentage of the total population of 900,000.

Security concerns and a more conservative economic approach prevented major advances in stock raising and other internal development during this period. A few small Mongolian-Soviet enterprises were initiated to support the war economy. The abandonment of agricultural communes and the return to private enterprise signaled a trend toward gradualism. Voluntary producers' cooperatives were encouraged, but they remained small until the 1950s (see Peacetime Development, 1946-52 , this ch.). Only a few state farms were started. Apart from some veterinary and credit assistance, the government made few efforts to support the nomads, and by 1941 herds had reached the highest recorded growth in Mongolian history. Consumer cooperatives continued to expand, and the state controlled the rest of internal trade.

The policy of gradualism was particularly ineffective in education. In 1941 an estimated 90 percent of the people were illiterate. In 1942 the country's first university--Choybalsan University, later renamed Mongolian State University--was established in Ulaanbaatar, but the spread of general education had to await the late 1940s and the 1950s. The first large-scale literacy program did not begin until 1947 (see Education , ch. 2).

Despite the government's official policy of not overtly persecuting religious beliefs, its antireligious campaign continued slowly but relentlessly. Emphasis was placed on ideological and economic persuasion, which curtailed monastic growth and induced monks of lower rank to return to secular life. Government representatives were attached to monasteries to monitor their activities, construction of new monasteries was forbidden by law, the enrollment of minors was disallowed, and monks became eligible for military service. Many monasteries were destroyed; others were converted to secular use. Methods of suppression became especially bloody in the second half of the 1930s. In 1935 abbots and monks of higher rank were tried publicly; in 1937 and 1938, about 2,000 of them were executed. Thousands of others were arrested and jailed. The financially shattered monasteries gradually were closed in the period 1938 to 1939.

The campaign against the Buddhists was largely successful. Within two decades, the resident monastic population was reduced from about 15,000 to approximately 200 monks. A handful of small monasteries and one large institution were all that were left physically of what had been, at the century's start, the best organized and most intellectual force in Mongolian life.

There also were renewed purges in the inner party ranks in 1937 to 1939. Minor rebellions continued to plague the government, and uncooperative political leaders increasingly were accused of aiding the opposition or the Japanese. One after the other, many top party and government officials fell from power and were executed or were imprisoned. By 1939 Choybalsan had emerged as the premier, the minister of war, and the undisputed leader of Mongolia. It later was acknowledged, in 1956 and in 1962, that Choybalsan had "committed serious errors" and had established a "personality cult" during this period

In March and April 1940, the Tenth Party Congress met. Although it confirmed Yumjaagiyn Tsedenbal as general secretary, Choybalsan continued to be the predominant force in the party. The ensuing Eighth National Great Hural adopted a new state constitution, which, however, made no basic alterations in the 1924 constitution. Although it emphasized the new Mongolian authority structure, the bypassing of capitalism, and the necessity of overall state planning, the 1940 constitution did not change the policy of gradualism. Private ownership, especially of livestock, was allowed until the turn to total communization began in late 1947.

NATIONAL DEFENSE, 1940-45

As political and religious purges finally drew to a close, the international situation worsened. Fighting had broken out, in May 1939, with Japanese forces based in Manchukuo. That summer a Japanese army invaded eastern Mongolia. Soviet General Georgi Zhukov commanded the Soviet-Mongolian army that met this invasion. Between May and September 1939, there was large-scale ground and aerial fighting along the Khalkhyn Gol, a river in northeastern Mongolia. The Mongolian troops and their Soviet allies severely defeated the Japanese, who may have sustained as many as 80,000 casualties compared with 11,130 on the MongolianSoviet side. Hostilities ended on September 16, 1939. The Soviet Union and Japan signed a truce, and a commission was set up to define the Mongolian-Manchurian border. Although Japan did not invade again, it did mass large military forces along the Mongolian and the Soviet borders in the course of the war, while continuing its southward drive into China.

The Soviet position in Mongolia was now fully consolidated. Throughout World War II, Choybalsan followed Moscow's directives, and Mongolia supported the Soviet Union with livestock, raw materials, money, food, and military clothing. The Mongolian army was maintained intact throughout the war; it served as an important buffer force in the Soviet Far East defense system, but it did not actually join the Red Army. Moreover, the Soviets, on the occasion of the

April 13, 1941, Soviet-Japanese Neutrality Pact, obtained a commitment from Japan to respect Mongolia's territorial integrity.

Modernizing the army and keeping it at peak mobilization was a heavy drain on the nation's undeveloped economy and small population. Even so, the party leaders pressed on with what limited social progress they could manage in a wartime situation. As more teachers became trained, literacy began to accelerate, and government efforts to assist the herdsmen in sheltering, feeding, and caring for their livestock continued. Stock raising bore the major war burden, however, and with large Soviet requisitions to fill, herd totals fell sharply during the war.

Mongolia's wartime neutrality ended in the closing days of World War II. On August 10, 1945, two days after the Soviet Union had declared war on Japan, Mongolia also declared war on Japan. The Mongolian army, some 80,000 strong, joined Soviet troops in invading Inner Mongolia and Manchuria. On August 14, 1945, in the Sino-Soviet Treaty of Friendship and Alliance, China agreed to recognize the independence of Mongolia within its "existing boundary," provided that a plebiscite confirmed the Mongolian people's desire for independence. Mongolia obliged, and in an October 20 referendum, 100 percent of the electorate voted for independence from China. On January 5, 1946, China recognized Mongolian independence and, on February 14, agreed to exchange diplomatic representatives. None, however, were exchanged. The ensuing Chinese civil war and the victory of the Chinese communists over the Guomindang government in 1949 led instead to Ulaanbaatar's recognition of the new People's Republic of China.

PEACETIME DEVELOPMENT, 1946-52

On February 27, 1946, Mongolia and the Soviet Union signed the ten-year renewable Treaty of Friendship and Mutual Assistance and the first Agreement on Economic and Cultural Cooperation. With the war over and Chinese and Japanese threat eliminated from Mongolia, the way for renewed assertion of Soviet influence in Mongolia was clear. Mongolia was a strong defense buffer, a trading partner, and a dependable ally in international conferences for the Soviet Union. A further indication of close ties was Mongolia's adoption in February 1946 of the Cyrillic alphabet for use in schools and military units (see Ethnic and Linguistic Groups , ch. 2).

Secure in its relations with Moscow, Ulaanbaatar expanded its other international ties. Diplomatic relations were established with the Democratic People's Republic of Korea (North Korea) and the new communist governments in Eastern Europe. Mongolian participation in communist-sponsored conferences and international organizations increased; Mongolia applied for membership in the United Nations, but representatives from Ulaanbaatar were not seated until 1961 (see Socialist Construction under Tsedenbal, 1952-84 , this ch.). Mongolia was among the first countries to recognize the new People's Republic of China in October 1949.

In its shift to postwar development, the party and the government reduced defense expenditures and shifted personnel from military to civilian enterprises. Rationing was curtailed, and prices for some manufactured items and foodstuffs were reduced. Attention was given to redeveloping the livestock and the agrarian sectors at the same time that modern mining, industrial, transportation, and communications sectors were being established. Initiatives also were taken in raising education and health levels and in improving the general well-being of the people. The First Five-Year Plan (1948-52), presented at the Eleventh Party Congress in December 1947, was important in carrying out postwar construction (see Socialist Framework of the Economy , ch. 3). The first session of the national hural held since 1940, was convened in February 1949 as the Ninth National Great Hural.

SOCIALIST CONSTRUCTION UNDER TSEDENBAL, 1952-84

Choybalsan died on January 26, 1952, and a major era in modern Mongolian history came to an end. He was succeeded as government leader by Tsedenbal who continued to be party general secretary as well.

Economic developments and extensive purges of party and government personnel marked the transition. In March 1953, a party Central Committee plenum was convened to review the results of the First Plan, and in November 1954, the Twelfth Party Congress belatedly approved guidelines for the Second Five-Year Plan (1953-57). A continuing major economic target included in the plan was the development of the livestock sector, and a 72 percent increase in grain production over 1952 levels was envisioned. Special attention also was paid to expanding electrification and international economic cooperation. Also at the Twelfth Congress, Dashiyn Damba was elected general secretary, replacing Tsedenbal as party leader.

In 1956 the party Central Committee condemned the "personality cult" of Choybalsan, specifically pointing out the excesses of the 1937 to 1939 period. Claiming success for the Second Plan, the Thirteenth Party Congress, March 17 to 22, 1958, adopted a special Three-Year Plan (1958-60), aimed at raising Mongolia from a livestock economy to an agricultural-industrial economy, all with Soviet aid. New emphasis was placed on stepping up industrial capacities--particularly in the coal mining, electric power, and construction sectors--and on increasing output of petroleum industry products, minerals, and nonferrous ores (see Industry , ch. 3). Damba was reelected at the Thirteenth Congress, only to be dismissed for ideological reasons and replaced by Tsedenbal several months later. On July 6, 1960, the government adopted the national Constitution that continued to be in force in 1989 (see Constitutional Framework , ch. 4). In January 1962, Choybalsan's "personality cult" again was attacked by the party Central Committee.

Foreign inputs and expansion of international contacts were important to Mongolia's development plans in the 1950s. A result of the close alliance of China and the Soviet Union during this period was Sino-Soviet cooperation in developing Mongolia. In 1952 a ten-year Sino-Mongolian Agreement on Economic and Cultural Cooperation marked an important step in developing relations between the two long-estranged nations. China helped build railroad lines, gave ruble aid and loans for construction projects, and even sent large contingents of laborers in the mid-1950s. Ulaanbaatar also subscribed to the anticolonial stance of the 1955 Bandung Conference and adopted the Five Principles of Peaceful Coexistence (see Glossary; see also Foreign Policy , ch. 4). Relations were developed with countries beyond the communist bloc--for example, India, Burma, Cambodia, nations in Africa and the Middle East, and, later, Cuba.

Soviet troops were withdrawn in 1956, increasing Mongolia's control over its own internal affairs. There were residual fears of a renewed Chinese ascendancy, however, despite Mongolia's signing of the Treaty of Friendship and Mutual Assistance with China on May 31, 1960, and the improved state of bilateral affairs. Memories of Chinese claims to "lost territories"--a theme, in Chinese foreign policy toward Mongolia, raised by Sun Yat-sen in 1912; reiterated by Chiang Kai-shek in the 1920s and by Mao Zedong in the 1930s; and, although rebuffed, raised at the 1945 Yalta Conference, when Chiang asserted China's claim to suzerainty based on the 1924 treaty with the Soviet Union--were strong in Mongolian consciousness.

Soon after the July 1961 Fourteenth Party Congress, Mongolia had garnered enough support from communist countries and from the Third World to be admitted to the United Nations in October 1961. The following June, Mongolia joined the Soviet-sponsored Council for Mutual Economic Assistance (Comecon--see Glossary).

Mongolian-Soviet ties continued to be close during the 1960s; additional aid was granted to Mongolia, and repayment deadlines were extended. In October 1965, a new three-year Agreement on Economic and Cultural Cooperation was signed. A twenty-year Treaty of

Friendship, Cooperation, and Mutual Assistance, which replaced the 1946 treaty, was the culmination of a state visit to Ulaanbaatar by the Soviet leader, Leonid Brezhnev, in January 1966. Soon after the signing of the friendship treaty, which included a defense clause, there was a buildup in Mongolia of Soviet troops and military infrastructure (including bases, roads, airfields, sheltered fighter aircraft sites, radar detection networks, communication lines, and missile sites). Mongolia, more than ever, had become a front line of Soviet defense against China. As part of its alliance with the Soviet Union, Mongolia signed the Nuclear Test Ban Treaty in 1963.

As relations with Moscow grew still closer, there was a corresponding coolness in those with Beijing. Although a difficult bilateral question was resolved with China in December 1962, when a border demarcation agreement was reached, by 1966 serious Mongolian-Chinese differences had surfaced. Chinese aid was stopped; trade decreased to low levels; relations cooled. The Chinese were angry over Ulaanbaatar's siding with Moscow in the Sino-Soviet rift; Mongolia, observing the excesses of China's Cultural Revolution, was concerned anew over China's designs on its sovereignty.

After the Fifteenth Party Congress had approved new economic plans in June 1966, Mongolia continued to try to transform its nomadic economy into ranch-style livestock herding and to expand its industrial sector. The economy, however, continued to have severe problems. For example, poor weather plagued the country; in 1967, blizzards caused a US$37 million loss in livestock alone. Severe winters were followed by drought and by plummeting harvests and exports. Planned increases in agricultural and industrial production did not materialize, and the lack of raw materials continued to hamper even light industry. Some of the blame was placed on the pullout of Chinese economic and technical assistance and the end of trade with China in consumer goods. It was admitted, however, that the economy envisioned in the Fourth Five-Year Plan (1966-70) had "not developed as rapidly as those of fraternal socialist states," and, indeed, achievements fell notably short of goals.

Large infusions of Soviet and Comecon aid eventually had salutary effects in the early 1970s. High-level state visits were exchanged in the 1969 to 1971 period, with the result that Moscow agreed to underwrite the Fifth Five-Year Plan (1971-75). Soviet economic difficulties in the early 1970s, however, had repercussions for Mongolia. The Soviet Union started insisting that trade quotas be honored, a move that caused economic disruption just as Mongolia was recovering from the economic distress of the late 1960s. Nevertheless, some economic progress was achieved between 1971 and 1974, a period during which gross industrial production rose by nearly 45 percent. Severe winters continued to hurt the anticipated growth of livestock herds. By the mid-1970s, direct business and other cooperative links had been established between corresponding Mongolian and Soviet ministries, departments, research institutes, and industries, and cooperative ties also had been established between neighboring Mongolian *aymags* (see Glossary) and Soviet *oblasts*.

More than 100,000 Soviet troops were garrisoned in Mongolia in the early 1970s. Ulaanbaatar's anti-Chinese criticism intensified during this period, ostensibly because of increased numbers of Chinese military exercises along the frontier and alleged anti-Mongolian subversive activities. Mongolia received assurances that Soviet troops would remain; Brezhnev himself, when in Ulaanbaatar, said that Beijing's demand for withdrawal of Soviet troops from Mongolia, as a precondition for the normalization of Sino-Soviet relations, was "absolutely unacceptable."

After a decade of steady growth in party membership, a dramatic change occurred in the composition of those attending the Sixteenth Party Congress in July 1971. Although membership on the Political Bureau, the Central Committee, and the Secretariat remained stable, 82 percent of the delegates were new. As the decade continued, changes at the top began to emerge. In June 1974, Tsedenbal, while retaining his position as general secretary of the Mongolian

People's Revolutionary Party, resigned as chairman of the Council of Ministers--the premiership--to become chairman of the People's Great Hural, the de facto president of Mongolia. The former rector of the Mongolian State University, Jambyn Batmonh, in a move presaging the succession a decade later, was appointed premier; he also was elevated to the party Political Bureau. After these changes, the party leadership was more stable. The closeness of Mongolian-Soviet relations was manifested by meetings in October 1976 in Moscow among Tsedenbal, Batmonh, and three other party Political Bureau members and the Soviet Communist Party general secretary Leonid Brezhnev; the president, Nikolai Podgorny; and the premier, Alexei Kosygin. While the talks were described as "fraternal," they also were characterized as "frank," probably because of increased Mongolian demands for economic aid. Soviet aid was forthcoming for the Sixth Five-Year Plan (1976-80), primarily in support of agriculture, mining, fuel, power, food, and light industries. Mongolian relations with Beijing--following Moscow's lead--were less hostile in the years after the 1976 death of Mao, but fears of China's "predatory aspirations" still lingered in Ulaanbaatar. In 1980 Chinese nationals were expelled from Mongolia on charges ranging from gambling and drug use to public disorder and espionage.

Severe weather in the winter of 1976 to 1977 caused some of the worst damage to animal husbandry in a decade. Heavy snowfalls, severe frosts, disease, starvation, and mismanagement combined to create a perilous economic situation. Recovery was slow, and livestock targets were overestimated continually throughout the rest of the 1970s. Developments in other economic sectors, such as mining and irrigated farming, saw some improvement during the period, however.

The 1980s began with some improvements in the economy, but also with a number of top party and state leadership changes, culminating in the end of Tsedenbal's rule. While Tsedenbal was in Moscow in August 1984, special sessions of the party and the People's Great Hural were held to announce his retirement. Batmonh replaced the reportedly ailing party head, amid tributes to Tsedenbal's forty-four-year career as an "outstanding leader" and "very close friend." In December 1984, Batmonh also was elevated to the chairmanship of the Presidium of the People's Great Hural, and Vice Premier Dumaagiyn Sodnom became premier as Mongolia embarked on historic reforms

STRATEGIC INFORMATION ON MONGOLIA

LANDFORMS

Mongolia is a land-locked country which covers an area of 1,564,118 square kilometers in North East Asia. It has a 3485 km border with Russia in the north and a 4670 km border with the People's Republic of China in the east, south and west. The total area of Mongolia is larger than the combined areas of Great Britain, France, Germany and Italy. It is one of the largest land-locked countries and the world's seventh largest country. It is situated between 42-50°N latitude and 88-120°E longitude.

MOUNTAINS, RIVERS & LAKES

The Mongolian environment has a large variety of features. The northern part of the country is covered by forest mountain ranges and the southern part by desert, desert steppe, and steppe areas with low mountains. The western part is dominated by high snow-capped mountains and glaciers and the eastern part by vast plains and wild heaths. About 81% of the country is higher than 1000 meters above sea level and the average elevation is 1580 meters. The highest mountain is Tavan Bogd in Bayan Ulgii Aimag at 4374 meters and the lowest point is Khukh Nuur in the east at 560 meters.

Highest Peaks	Height / m
Khuiten	4374
Tsambagarav	4195
Otgontenger	4021
Okhbogd	3957
Gurvansaikhan	2825
Asralthairkhan	2800
Bogd Khan	2256

Mongolia has comparatively high levels of surface and ground water resources. The rivers of Mongolia belong to the inland drainage basins of the Arctic Ocean, the Pacific Ocean and Central Asia. The water network is of a greater density in the north of the country. The longest river is the Orkhon at 1124 kilometers in length. There are some 3000 rivers in total with a combined length of 67,000 kilometers. There are also over 3000 big and small lakes, 6,900 springs, 190 glaciers and 250 mineral water springs.

Longest Rivers	Length / m
Orkhon	1124
Selenge	1024
Kherlen	1090
Zavkhan	808
Tuul	704
Khovd	593
Eruu	323
Onon	298
Kharaa	291

Largest Lakes	Area / km^2

Uvs	3350
Khovsgol	2760
Khar Us	1852
Khyargas	1407
Buir	615
Khar	575

LANDSCAPE

Mongolia can be divided into six zones; desert, mountain, mountain taiga, mountain forest steppe, arid steppe and taiga.

The mountain belt of the Mongol Altai, Khangai and Khentii mountainous regions, with their perpetual snow, glaciers, traces and signs of ancient ice covers, has been well preserved due to a constantly cold climate and strong winds. The area is inhabited by some endangered animals (such as the Argali sheep, Ibex, Snow Leopard, Rock Ptarmigan and Altai Snowcock) and plants (such as the Dwarf Siberian Pine and White Gentiana).

The mountain taiga belt comprises about 5% of the Mongolian territory in the Khentii and Khovsgol mountain regions in the northernmost part of the country and experiences a relatively cold and humid climate. Due to a brief warm period, the growing season is not long enough for many plant species. Forests in this belt are dominated by the Siberian Pine and the Siberian Larch and are inhabited by such animal species registered in the Mongolian Red Book as the Musk deer, Elk, Lynx and Eurasian Otter.

The mountain forest steppe belt extends through the Mongolian Altai, Khangai, Khovsgol massifs and borders on the Mongolian taiga belt which is in the southernmost fringe of the Great Eastern Siberian Taiga. One specific feature of the Mountain Forest Steppe is that the back of the slopes of the mountains facing the north, northeast and northwest are covered with different species of forest and woody plants whereas their front slopes facing the east, south and southwest are densely covered by the steppe plants almost up to the sharp ridges of the mountains, giving an impression of sharp habitat boundaries of the mountain forest and steppe species. The Mountain Forest Steppe belt encompasses 25% of Mongolia's territory and is inhabited by such globally endangered animal species as the Manul, Black Grouse and plants threatened by extinction such as the Mongolian Pheasant's Eye.

The Arid Steppe Zone with and area of approximately 20% of the country's territory comprises the entire Eastern and Central Mongolian vast flat plain extending as a tapering zone thousands of kilometers westwards to the northwestern fringe of the Khangai mountain range called Khankhokhii. The Mongolian steppe is part of the great plain which starts from the Don river in Hungary and includes the Pustza, sweeping the east up to the Manchurian steppe in East Asia. The vegetation of the Mongolian steppe is dominated by *Xerophya*, *Caragana* and many forms of feather grass. Mongolian gazelles can be seen roaming and grazing in herds.

The Desert Steppe Zone includes the Depression of Great Lakes, the Valley of Lakes and the Middle and Eastern Gobi lowlands. This area belongs to the semi-arid zone which has an annual precipitation of 100-220 millimeters, loose soil and fewer species of animals and plants compared to the zones, northwards. The Desert Steppe is a habitat for such animal species as the Wild Ass, Saiga Antelope, Black-tailed Gazelle and Houbara Bustard.

The Desert Zone is located in the southern and southwestern parts of Mongolia and has a severe climate with annual precipitation of less than 100 millimeters and high diurnal temperature fluctuation. The Desert Zone is an area of extremely unique physical formations of changing contrasts like hills, hillocks, rolling heaths, and sand dunes. It contains deposits of ancient flora, fauna and mineral resources, and provides a habitat for threatened animal species such as the Wild Camel, Gobi Bear and Mongolian Agama.

CLIMATE

The main characteristics of the climate of Mongolia are sunny days, long and cold winters, low precipitation and large annual, seasonal, monthly and diurnal fluctuations in air temperature. The average mean temperature recorded in January is -34 degrees centigrade in the plateau and depressions, but extreme temperatures have been recorded between -50 and -56 degrees centigrade. In the northern mountains the average mean temperature in the warmest warmth is between +35 and +41 degrees centigrade, depending on the area. The total annual precipitation in mountainous regions averages to about 400 millimeters, in the steppe from 150-200 millimeters and in the desert-steppe less than 100 mm. About 75-85 percent of the precipitation falls during the three summer months. The spring season is often very windy and dust storms are common in the desert regions.

Mongolia is high, cold, and dry. It has an extreme continental climate with long, cold winters and short summers, during which most precipitation falls. The country averages 257 cloudless days a year, and it is usually at the center of a region of high atmospheric pressure. Precipitation is highest in the north, which averages 20 to 35 centimeters per year, and lowest in the south, which receives 10 to 20 centimeters (see fig. 5). The extreme south is the Gobi, some regions of which receive no precipitation at all in most years. The name Gobi is a Mongol meaning desert, depression, salt marsh, or steppe, but which usually refers to a category of arid rangeland with insufficient vegetation to support marmots but with enough to support camels. Mongols distinguish *gobi* from desert proper, although the distinction is not always apparent to outsiders unfamiliar with the Mongolian landscape. *Gobi* rangelands are fragile and are easily destroyed by overgrazing, which results in expansion of the true desert, a stony waste where not even Bactrian camels can survive.

Average temperatures over most of the country are below freezing from November through March and are about freezing in April and October. January and February averages of -20° C are common, with winter nights of -40° C occurring most years. Summer extremes reach as high as 38° C in the southern Gobi region and 33° C in Ulaanbaatar. More than half the country is covered by permafrost, which makes construction, road building, and mining difficult. All rivers and freshwater lakes freeze over in the winter, and smaller streams commonly freeze to the bottom. Ulaanbaatar lies at 1,351 meters above sea level in the valley of the Tuul Gol, a river. Located in the relatively well-watered north, it receives an annual average of 31 centimeters of precipitation, almost all of which falls in July and in August. Ulaanbaatar has an average annual temperature of -2.9°C and a frost-free period extending on the average from mid-June to late August

Mongolia's weather is characterized by extreme variability and short-term unpredictability in the summer, and the multiyear averages conceal wide variations in precipitation, dates of frosts, and occurrences of blizzards and spring dust storms. Such weather poses severe challenges to human and livestock survival. Official statistics list less than 1 percent of the country as arable, 8 to 10 percent as forest, and the rest as pasture or desert. Grain, mostly wheat, is grown in the valleys of the Selenge river system in the north, but yields fluctuate widely and unpredictably as a result of the amount and the timing of rain and the dates of killing frosts. Although winters are generally cold and clear, there are occasional blizzards that do not deposit much snow but cover the grasses with enough snow and ice to make grazing impossible, killing off tens of thousands of sheep or cattle. Such losses of livestock, which are an inevitable and, in a sense, normal consequence of the climate, have made it difficult for planned increases in livestock numbers to be achieved

CLIMATIC STATISTICS

Aimag	Annual Precipitation / mm	Average January Temperature / °C	Average July Temperature / °C
Arkhangai	350.5	-14.9	14.3
Bayan Ulgii	115.5	-17.2	16.3
Bayankhongor	199.4	-18.3	16.2
Bulgan	344.2	-20.5	16.0
Gobi Altai	204.1	-18.0	13.7
Dornogov	116.7	-17.8	22.8
Dornod	247.7	-20.5	19.9
Dundgov	156.0	-17.5	18.7
Zavkhan	217.7	-22.6	15.0
Ovorkhangai	245.2	-14.7	15.3
Omnogov	127.1	-14.9	21.1
Sukhbaatar	201.8	-21.5	19.9
Selenge	289.7	-23.2	19.1
Tog	272.5	-20.4	15.6
Uvs	138.4	-32.3	19.0
Khovd	127.4	-24.4	18.5
Khovsgol	236.9	-22.6	16.2
Khentii	259.4	-23.4	18.7
Ulaanbaatar	258.5	-21.8	16.9
Orkhon	363.8	-16.8	15.5
Govisumber	196.5	-20.5	18.6

PROTECTED AREAS

Mongolia has preserved its virgin nature over vast areas due to the late onset of industrialization and low population density. The Mongolian's traditionally careful attitude to the environment has also been beneficial. The latter is proven among other things by the fact that the mountain range, at the foot of which lies Ulaanbaatar, was proclaimed a protected area over 200 years ago.

Climate change and human activities are leading to the degradation of fragile ecosystems in nature, which ultimately also impact socio-economy. Protected areas play a key role in in the restoration of the environment by maintaining ecosystems, mitigating the loss of biological diversity and creating conditions to naturally increase biological diversity.

Mongolia takes environmental protection seriously and in 1992 at the Rio Earth Summit, pledged to designate up to 30% of Mongolia's surface area as protected areas. The Bogd Khan Strictly Protected Area on the outskirts of Ulaanbaatar is one of the world's first protected areas, being designated in 1778. The Law on Special Protected Areas was passed in 1994 and puts all the protected areas into one of four categories.

- Strictly Protected Areas
- National Parks
- Nature Reserves
- Natural and Historic Monuments

Currently, Mongolia has 48 protected areas which cover 20.5 million hectares or 13.1% of the land surface. There are 12 Strictly Protected Areas, 14 National Parks, 16 Nature Reserves and 6 Monuments. The policy is to cover more areas which are potentially susceptible to human activities and climate change, which have a key role in maintaining ecosystems of different natural zones, as well as, belts and areas which serve as habitats for rare and endangered species. For example, 12.7% of protected areas belongs to the high mountain and mountain taiga zone, 11.7% to the forest steppe zone, 9.6% to the steppe zone, 27% to the desert steppe zone and 39% belongs to the desert zone. Desertification is a growing problem in the latter zone due to the use of saxaul trees and overgrazing.

FLORA

There can be said to be three distinct types of ecosystem related to flora - grassland and shrubs (52% of land surface), forests (15%) and desert vegetation (32%). Crop cultivation and human settlements make up less than 1% of Mongolia's territory. Although there is so much grassland here, used for grazing, overgrazing is a problem in some areas.

Forests - The natural regeneration of Mongolian forests is slow and the forests are often damaged by fires and insects due to the harsh climate. 8.1% of Mongolia's territory is covered by forest totaling 140 species of trees, shrubs and woody plants. Trees are used as a source of fuel, whether it is the larch, pine or birch in the north or the saxaul in the Gobi Desert. Timber is cut in the north of the country for building.

Vascular and Lower Plants - There are 2823 species of vascular plants, 445 species of moss, 930 species of lichen, 900 species of fungi and 1236 species of algae. 845 species of plants are used in Mongolian medicine, 1000 species for fodder, 173 for food and 64 for industry. There are now 128 species of plant listed as endangered and threatened in the 1997 Mongolian Red Book. These include 75 medicinal species, 11 for food and 16 used in industry.

FAUNA

Anyone traveling in Mongolia may find it difficult to distinguish between wild and domesticated animals as both roam freely on the open steppe, for example, Wild Ass are seen among domesticated horses. Although Mongolia doesn't have the large game such as lion, elephant and rhino that attracts visitors to African parks, it does have many very rare and endangered species such as the snow leopard, Argali and Ibex.

Mammals - There are 133 mammals in Mongolia, many of which are endemic to Central Asia and Mongolia, including the Mongolian Vole, Mongolian Gerbil, Gobi Jerboa, Kozlov's Pygmy Jerboa, Mongolian Jerboa and the Mongolian Hamster. The white-tailed gazelle, Saiga Antelope, Przewalski horse, Beaver and Siberian Ibex have been re-introduced to the areas where they have become rare.

Birds - Mongolia has a rich composition of bird species due to the migratory routes from the Pacific and Indian Oceans to the Mediterranean Sea and to the Arctic Ocean and Northern Tundra. A combination of Holarctic, Palearctic and Central Asian species have representatives in the Mongolian bird species assemblage. There are a recorded 434 species of bird, more than 330 of them, migratory. Half of the bird species here are insectivorous, about 25% herbivorous and 10% feed mostly on water plants and animals.

GEOLOGY

Mongolia is rich in many types of mineral resources. Over 6000 deposits of 80 different minerals have been discovered and over 160 deposits are now being exploited. In addition, deposits of construction material such as granite and marble are also being worked.

With assistance from foreign countries, Mongolia is now mining gold, copper, molybdenum, uranium, coal and fluorspar and is a major exporter of these metals and minerals. Silver, tungsten, tin and precious stones mines are small scale operations.

The terrain is one of mountains and rolling plateaus, with a high degree of relief (see fig. 4). Overall, the land slopes from the high Altai Mountains of the west and the north to plains and depressions in the east and the south. Hutyen Orgil (sometimes called Nayramadlin Orgil--Mount Friendship) in extreme western Mongolia, where the Mongolian, the Soviet, and the Chinese borders meet, is the highest point (4,374 meters). The lowest is 560 meters, an otherwise undistinguished spot in the eastern Mongolian plain. The country has an average elevation of 1,580 meters. The landscape includes one of Asia's largest freshwater lakes (Hovsgol Nuur), many salt lakes, marshes, sand dunes, rolling grasslands, alpine forests, and permanent montane glaciers. Northern and western Mongolia are seismically active zones, with frequent earthquakes and many hot springs and extinct volcanoes.

Mongolia has three major mountain ranges. The highest is the Altai Mountains, which stretch across the western and the southwestern regions of the country on a northwest-to-southeast axis. The Hangayn Nuruu, mountains also trending northwest to southeast, occupy much of central and north-central Mongolia. These are older, lower, and more eroded mountains, with many forests and alpine pastures. The Hentiyn Nuruu, mountains near the Soviet border to the northeast of Ulaanbaatar, are lower still. Much of eastern Mongolia is occupied by a plain, and the lowest area is a southwest-to-northeast trending depression that reaches from the Gobi region in the south to the eastern frontier. The rivers drain in three directions: north to the Arctic Ocean, east to the Pacific, or south to the deserts and the depressions of Inner Asia. Rivers are most extensively developed in the north, and the country's major river system is that of the Selenge-Moron, which drains into Lake Baykal. Some minor tributaries of Siberia's Yenisey River also rise in the mountains of northwestern Mongolia. Rivers in northeastern Mongolia drain into the Pacific through the Argun and Amur (Heilong Jiang) rivers, while the few streams of southern and southwestern Mongolia do not reach the sea but run into salt lakes or deserts.

ENVIRONMENTAL CONCERNS

After many years of uncritical fostering of industrial and urban growth, Mongolia's authorities became aware in the late 1980s of the environmental costs of such policies. Belated Soviet concern over the pollution of Lake Baykal encouraged Mongolian actions to preserve their counterpart Hovsgol Nuur, which is linked to Lake Baykal through the Selenge Moron. A wool-scouring plant that had been discharging wastes into Hovsgol Nuur was closed; truck traffic on the winter ice was banned; and the shipping of oil in barges on the lake was stopped. Deforestation in the Hangayn Nuruu, had reduced the flow of northern Mongolia's rivers, which were polluted by runoff from the fertilized and pesticide-treated grain fields along their banks, by industrial wastes, and by untreated sewage from growing settlements.

Ulaanbaatar--located in a valley--with factories and 500,000 inhabitants who depend on soft coal, had severe air pollution, especially when the air was still and cold in winter. Deforestation, overgrazing of pastures, and efforts to increase grain and hay production by plowing up more virgin land had resulted in increased soil erosion, both from wind and from heavy downpours of the severe thunderstorms that bring much of Mongolia's rain. In the south, the desert area of the Gobi was expanding, threatening the fragile *gobi* pasturelands. The government responded by founding the Ministry of Environmental Protection in 1987 and by giving increased publicity to environmental issues.

POLITICAL SYSTEM AND GOVERNMENT

MONGOLIA GOVERNMENT

BASIC INFORMATION

MONGOLIA'S FLAG

The National Flag of Mongolia is red with a vertical blue stripe down the middle. On the left hand red stripe of the flag is a yellow Soyombo (see below). The colours are symbolic. Red is the colour of fire symbolizing progress and prosperity while the blue represents the colour of the sky, meaning peace and eternity.

THE SOYOMBO

The Soyombo is an old ideogram symbolising the Mongol's freedom and independence. As long ago as the 17th Century, it was depicted on the banners of warriors fighting against the Manchurian invaders and later, on the battle standards of the guerillas of the 1921 People's Revolution.

Each element of the symbol has its own meaning. The three tongued flame crowning the emblem symbolise the nation's past, present and future prosperity: from time immemorial fire has meant the continuation of the family and the clan. Depicted underneath the flame are the sun and the crescent, both old Mongolian totems. "We are the people whose father is the new moon and whose mother is the golden sun", say the old legends.

The flame together with the sun and the crescent symbolise the prosperity and progress of the Mongolian nation. The spear or arrow tip turned downwards is supposed to signify victory over the enemy. The two triangles in the upper and lower part of the ideogram tell about the people's determination to uphold their freedom and independence. The rectangle is the symbol of uprightness, honesty and nobility and the two smaller rectangles symbolise honesty of government and rulers. In the centre of the Soyombo is the old symbol signifying the unity of pairs of natural elements; fire and water, earth and sky and man and woman. According to other interpretations, this also denotes two fish swimming in concentric circles. The Mongolians see fish as a symbol of vigilance since fish never close their eyes. Fish also symbolise wisdom and reason.

The two vertical lines at the sides of the emblem mean friendship and staunchness. An old Mongolian saying goes, "Two friends are stronger than stone walls." In the Soyombo, these two lines are understood to be an appeal, "May the whole nation be bound together by ties of friendship turning it into an indestructible stone fortress."

ADMINISTRATIVE STRUCTURE

Power is shared between the President, the Parliament (State Great Khural), the Prime Minister's ten-member cabinet and the Supreme Court. The President and Parliamentary Members are elected directly by the people at two different elections. The Prime Minister is nominated from the party with the largest number of seats in Parliament.

Only the Parliament has legislative power. It determines the basis of domestic and foreign policy, approves and makes changes in laws, determines and announces presidential and parliamentary elections, elects members of the judiciary and the Supreme Court, appoints and dismisses government members, defines the state financial credit, monetary and tax policies and sets base guidelines for the socioeconomic development of the country. It approves and dissolves the territorial and administrative units and regulates the system and the organisational structure of these units. It has Spring and Autumn sessions and consists of 76 full time members elected for four years.

The territories of Mongolia are administratively divided into 21 regions - 18 Aimags and 3 cities. Each Aimag is generally divided into Sums that are further divided into smaller units called bags. The capital city has districts and sub districts.

Aimag & City	Area, (100 km^2)	No. of Sums /Districts	Population in 1998 (x1000)	Name of Capital	Aimag Centre Population (x1000)	Distance from Ulaanbaatar (km)
Arkhangai	55.3	19	103.7	Tsetserleg	18.1	453
Bayan Ulgii	45.7	14	96.2	Ulgii	21.0	1636
Bayankhongor	116	20	91.6	Bayankhongor	23.3	630
Bulgan	48.7	16	66.1	Bulgan	15.6	318
Gobi Altai	141.4	18	74.9	Altai	18.5	1001
Dornogov	109.5	14	49.9	Sainshand	17.7	463
Dornod	123.6	14	84.3	Choibalsan	38.6	655
Dundgov	74.7	16	54.4	Mandalgov	10.9	260
Zavkhan	82.5	24	105.0	Uliastai	24.3	984
Ovorkhangai	62.9	19	116.9	Arvaikheer	20.7	430
Omnogov	165.4	15	46.2	Dalanzadgad	12.6	553

Sukhbaatar	82.3	13	59.7	Baruun Urt	14.7	560
Selenge	41.2	17	107.0	Sukhbaatar	22.3	311
Tov	74	27	113.7	Zuunmod	15.3	43
Uvs	69.6	20	100.5	Ulaangom	26.5	1336
Khovd	76.1	17	93.0	Khovd	27.4	1425
Khovsgol	100.6	23	123.6	Moron	25.6	671
Khentii	80.3	19	77.7	Ondorkhan	16.0	331
Ulaanbaatar	4.7	9	668.8			
Darkhan	3.28	4	94.2	Darkhan	71.4	219
Orkon	0.84	2	72.5	Erdenet	63.5	371
Gobisumber	5.54	3	13.1	Choir	8.7	240

GOVERNMENT STRUCTURE

Mongolia existed for decades as a buffer state between the Soviet Union and China, but amid the collapse of Communism and the Soviet Union's disintegration in 1991, Mongolia too underwent rapid change. In 1990, after months of pro-democracy demonstrations, a new Communist party constitution set the goal of building 'democratic humane socialism' based on a multi-party democracy. Elections in July 1990 brought a coalition government, and the move towards privatisation of the economy.

In January 1992, a new constitution was adopted that renounced socialism, changed the country's name to the State of Mongolia, and made Mongolia a republic with parliamentary government and a directly elected president. Mongolia has remained neutral in international affairs.

In 1996, the Democratic Union Coalition came to power. The Government's Programme of Action was approved by the State Great Khural in November 1996. The programme emphasised the need for consolidation of democratic gains and rapid short and medium-term economic measures to address economical revival. The central government is headed by the President and supported by the Prime Minister and 11 other ministries.

The Head of State is the President, who is elected for four years. President Natsagyn Bagabandi was elected in 1997.

The government is headed by the Prime Minister who is appointed by the State Great Khural for four years. Prime Minister Nambar Enkhbayar was appointed in July 2000.

Prime minister

- Open Government
- Central Intelligence Agency
- State Property Committee
- State Professional Inspection Agency
- Mongolian Radio and Television

- MONTSAME news Agency
- Land relations, Geodesy and Cartography Authority

Cabinet Secretariat of Government of Mongolia
- Press Office of Government of Mongolia
- State Protocol Office
- Management Academy
- Department of Services for Public Organization

Ministry of Finance and Economics
- General Taxation
- General Customs Office

Ministry of Justice and Internal Affairs
- General Police Department
- General Authority for Border Protection
- State Center for Civil Registration and Information
- General Authority for Implementing Court Decisions
- National Archives
- Fire - Fighting Agency
- Intellectual Property Agency

Ministry of Foreign Affairs
- Department of Services for Diplomatic Corps

Ministry of Environment
- National Agency of Meteorology, Hydrology and Environment Monitoring
- Nature, Forest and Water Resources Agency

Ministry of Education, Culture and Science

Ministry of Defense
- General Headquarters of Armed Forces
- Civil Defense Authority

Ministry of Infrastructure
- Civil Aviation Authority
- Coal and Energy Authority
- Road Authority
- Construction, Urban Development, Public Utility Agency
- Tourism Board
- Transportation Agency
- Railway Authority
- Postal and Telecommunications Authority

Ministry of Social Welfare and Labour
- General Authority for social Insurance
- Employment Authority
- State Agency of Social Welfare
- National Authority for Children

Ministry of Industry and Commerce
- Center for Standardization and Measurement
- Foreign Trade and Foreign Investment Agency
- Mineral Resources Authority
- Petroleum Authority

- Petroleum Authority

Ministry of Food and Agriculture

- State Veterinary Agency
- State Reserves Fund

Ministry of Health

- Medical Services Authority

PRESIDENT OF MONGOLIA

The **President of Mongolia** (Mongolian: Монгол Улсын Ерөнхийлөгч, *Mongol Ulsyn Yerönkhiilögch*) is the head of state of Mongolia. The Constitution of Mongolia implements a parliamentary system, so while much of the President's role is ceremonial, he or she does wield significant political power.

5th President of Mongolia	
Incumbent	
Assumed office 10 July 2017	
Prime Minister	Jargaltulgyn Erdenebat Ukhnaagiin Khürelsükh
Preceded by	Tsakhiagiin Elbegdorj
Personal details	
Born	3 March 1963 (age 55) Ulaanbaatar, Mongolia
Political party	Democratic Party

Battulga Khaltmaa born 3 March 1963) is a Mongolian politician who has served as the President of Mongolia since 10 July 2017. He served as Member of the State Great Khural from 2004 to 2016 and Minister of Roads, Transportation, Construction and Urban Development from 2008 to 2012. He was the Democratic Party's candidate in the 2017 presidential election, and was elected President with 50.6% in the run-off, the first ever run-off election in modern Mongolian history.

In 2004, Battulga became a Member of Parliament for the first time from Bayankhongor province. He was re-elected to parliament in 2008 and 2012.

Battulga believes that every Mongolian citizen should benefit from its mineral wealth according to article 6.1 of the Constitution of Mongolia, under which mineral resources are to be developed in consideration of ensuring the nation's economic security and the development of all forms of property and social development of the population. Due to landlocked geography of Mongolia, Battulga views that a unified railway network would enhance the global competitiveness of its national mining industry by creating multiple access points through which the country can target multiple inland and seaborne markets. Furthermore, Battulga believes, given the cyclical nature of commodity markets, industrial clusters designed to do value-add processing of mineral products should be established to create skilled jobs, introduce downstream industrial technologies and diversify the economy, enhancing local purchasing power that would create economic multiplier effect in housing, services and other economic sectors. Battulga thinks that agriculture has a prominent place in diversifying the economy as Mongolia is rich in livestock, about 60 million, with largest consumers of agricultural products as its neighbors. He believes cashmere and leather products could be successfully marketed internationally because of the scarcity factor.

Recognizing these principles, Battulga sponsored the State Policy of Railway Transportation of Mongolia ("Railway Policy") with the Parliament approving it with 84% votes in 24 June 2010 to construct 5,600 km railway base infrastructure in three phases that calls for providing access to multiple seaports in China and Russia, creating three transportation corridors between China, Russia and Europe, as well as establishing and industrial cluster in Sainshand.

Battulga acknowledges that limited human resources and financial capability of Mongolia requires multilateral international participation in the development of the economy, rather than making bilateral arrangement with its neighbors. Battulga strongly opposes control of mineral resources by a few politically connected businessmen reaping of great profits and increase income gap between the rich and the poor, potentially creating political and social instability in the country. For example, as the Minister responsible for development of infrastructure and industrial projects, Battulga encouraged participation of international companies in the development of business cases, feasibility and necessary detailed engineering studies, resulting in selection of Bechtel Enterprises, BNP Paribas, Deutsche Bank, Guggenheim, Fluor, McKinsey & Company, Nippon Koei, Pillsbury Winthrop Pittman Shaw LLP, Samsung, Sidley Austin LLP, Taylor Wessing. As a result, many international companies have expressed their interest to invest, provide technologies and construction services, such as Air Liquide (France), Baotou Steel (China), Dandong Port (China), Overseas Infrastructure Alliance (India), OAO Russian Railways (Russia), Rao UES (Russia), Sembcorp (Singapore), Sinohydro (China), Steel Authority of India Limited (India), among many others.[4][5][6]

On 3 November 2012, the Government of Mongolia announced that it resolved to build 1,800 km railway infrastructure integrating Phase 1 and 2 of the Railway Policy. Stakeholders such as Hong Kong listed Mongolian Mining Corporation greeted such government policy in its press release stating that the policy is particularly beneficial for Mongolian coal exporters.

Battulga was instrumental in background coordination for preparation work and ultimate signing of a Memorandum of Cooperation between Governments of Mongolia and Japan during official visit of Prime Minister Shinzo Abe in 22 October 2015. This memorandum expresses intention of Japan to invest in the construction of railway infrastructure from Tavan Tolgoi coal mine to

Sainshand railway line connecting it to the Trans-Mongolian Railway Network and providing access to Chinese and Russian seaports. Furthermore, plans have been made for Chinese, Russian and Japanese investments in financing the railway in exchange of coking coal sourcing from Mongolia. Investment blueprint and roadmap was agreed with the Japanese government, Japan Bank for International Cooperation and Japanese major trading companies.

Battulga believes foreign direct investment on balanced terms is an important catalyzer for Mongolia's economic development and job creation. His policies has been aimed at enhancing fair, transparent and reciprocal trade.

Battulga criticizes Mongolian economy's heavy dependence on a single trade partner, thus faces fierce opposition and attacks from shareholders and stakeholders of coal miners.

ELECTION

The President is elected by the citizens of Mongolia. Political parties with representation in the State Great Khural nominate candidates. The President can be re-elected only one time. The President can be removed from office if two-thirds of the Khural find him guilty of abusing his powers or violating his oath. Before inauguration, however, the President-elect has to renounce the membership of any political party.

POWERS OF THE PRESIDENT

- Nominating a candidate for the office of Prime Minister, who is then approved or rejected by the State Great Khural (parliament). This is largely a ceremonial responsibility, as the Khural will most likely reject any nominee who is not its own choice — in effect, the Prime Minister is appointed by the Khural.
- Vetoing the Khural's legislation (can be overridden with a two-thirds majority)
- Approving judicial appointments
- Appointing the Chief Judge of the Supreme Court of Mongolia
- Chairing the national security council
- Acting as commander in chief of the armed forces.
- Nominates the Prosecutor General, the official in charge of implementing the laws, who is then approved or rejected by the Khural.

There is debate about who should be considered the first President of Mongolia. The title does not actually date back to before Mongolia's democratisation, but the office itself is seen as extending through Mongolia's period of communist rule. Sometimes, the Bogd Khan (seen as the reincarnations of senior lama) are seen as Mongolia's first "presidents", but more commonly, the title is given to the secular leaders who followed them. Balingiin Tserendorj, who was acting head of state in 1924, is sometimes seen as the first president, but it was not until Navaandorjiin Jadambaa was appointed Chairman of the State Great Khural in November that there was an official leader. Only a day later, the leadership role was reorganised as the Chairman of the Presidium of the State Little Khural (the Little Khural being the executive committee of the Great Khural). Later, the Little Khural was abolished, and its powers were returned to the Great Khural — as such, the title of the president became Chairman of the Presidium of the State Great Khural. This was shortly afterwards changed to Chairman of the Presidium of the People's Great Khural, following a change in nomenclature. Finally, in 1990, the title President of Mongolia was adopted.

ADVISORS TO THE PRESIDENT OF MONGOLIA

LEGAL POLICY AND MINERAL RESOURCE POLICY ADVISOR MR. TSAGAAN PUNTSAG

FOREIGN POLICY ADVISOR MR. PUREVSUREN LUNDEG

NATIONAL SECURITY POLICY ADVISOR MRS. BATCHIMEG MIGEDDORJ

HUMAN RIGHTS AND PUBLIC PARTICIPATION POLICY ADVISOR MRS. SOSORMAA CHULUUNBAATAR

ECONOMIC POLICY ADVISOR MR. DASHDORJ LUVSANDASH

PUBLIC RELATIONS AND PUBLIC POLICY ADVISOR MR. GANBAATAR AMGALANBAATAR

URBAN AND RURAL DEVELOPMENT POLICY ADVISOR MR. ERKHEMBAYAR LOMBO

HEALTH, EDUCATION, SCIENCE AND TECHNOLOGY POLICY AND RELIGION ISSUES ADVISOR MR. BOLD RAVDANSAMBUU

ECOLOGY AND ENVIRONMENTAL POLICY ADVISOR MR. ZORIGT ERDENECHULUUN

POLICY AND ACTION PROGRAM OF THE PRESIDENT OF MONGOLIA

FOR 2009-2013

The President of Mongolia, within the term of his full powers, shall pursue policies and undertake actions to ensure that at all levels of state, policies are centered on citizens, and that Mongolia evolves as a competitive country aspiring nature friendly development.

Confident that the Mongolian people do have the wisdom and knowledge, zeal and will, capacities and resources necessary to support the development of Mongolia and Mongolia's statehood, the President of Mongolia introduces his Policy and Action Program, aimed to effectively implement his election platform, and reflective of the ideas, comments and proposals received from the public.

#	Presidential Election Platform Goals and Proposals from Public	Form of implementation of the Platform within the President's full power term
One. Ensuring National Security and People's Solidarity		
1.1	Fundamental rights and benefits of the Mongolian people shall be upheld ceaselessly	1. Independence, sovereignty, territorial integrity and people's solidarity shall be undyingly safeguarded. 2. Within the full powers of the President, measures shall be undertaken necessary to ensure state and public security. 3. Projects shall be initiated to enhance information security. 4. With the view to improve legal relationship between the state and religion institutions, the Law on State and Religion Institutions Relationship shall be amended

		and submitted to the Parliament.
1.2	Democracy, freedom and independence shall be relentlessly safeguarded.	1.2.1 Support will be rendered to law making, law enforcement and judiciary institutions in the discharge of their legal mandate. 1.2.2. National security system of Mongolia shall be strengthened, the National Security Concepts will be renewed, and the consistency and coordination between and among the core national security institutions shall be bolstered. 1.2.3. Conditions will be created to ensure that Mongolia, while commanding small and capable professional armed forces, effectively ensures her territorial security and the security of her people, and is an active participant in international cooperation, including the United National Peace Keeping Operations.
1.3	The security of a Mongolian shall mean the security of Mongolia.	1.3.1. The security of a citizen of Mongolia shall be seen in association with the security of Mongolia. Within these premises, special attention shall be accorded to creating a safe and secure environment for citizens to live in, as well as to ensuring food and ecological security. Every phenomenon which does and may potentially cause negative effects on human health and security shall be examined, and policies and actions will be taken to eliminate such effects. 1.3.2. A study shall be undertaken to examine the factors negatively affecting the gene pool of Mongolians and necessary policies and measures shall be undertaken. 1.3.3. Step-by-step measures shall be undertaken to support the officers and workers and their families, of the Joint Staff of Mongolian Armed Forces, Mongolian Border Protection Organization, National Emergency Management Agency, General Intelligence Agency, General Police Department, Court Decisions Enforcement Agency and Internal Troops.
Two. Consolidating a Human-Centered Society Upholding Human Rights and Freedom		
2.1	The President shall listen to the voices and concerns of his people.	2.1.1. A Citizen Hall, aiming at receiving public comments for the laws and public acts to be initiated by the President, shall be established, and conditions will be set to establish aimag, cities', soum and local Halls by the model of the Citizen Hall so as to ensure civic participation in decision-making. 2.1.2. State policies and actions shall be open and transparent, and a reform policy shall be run to secure citizens' right to information. The system to deliver to the public information and facts, not subject to state confidentiality, shall be improved.
2.2	A Mongolian citizen shall enjoy his/her rights honestly, and so shall his/her duties be performed	2.2.1. Projects and programs on human rights and civil education and legal assistance shall be widely developed.

	Creativity, pro-activeness and civic culture shall be exercised in conducting a comprehensive legal and political reform in harmony with the values of democracy and freedom.	
2.3	The President shall work to enable the Mongolian citizens to fully enjoy both political and economic rights and freedoms. Help and support will be rendered to everyone to be healthy and aspire education. Help will be offered in pursuing the profession in need. The State shall be made to work for its citizens. People will be freed from pressures and burdens of bureaucrats.	2.3.1. The immunity of titles and honor, private property and homes of citizens shall be guaranteed by law. Compelled self-defense, compelled defense of livestock and other private properties shall be released from criminal obligation. A Law on Property Rights shall be initiated. 2.3.2. Opportunities will be created to enable citizens to get their share of wealth, to become the real owners of wealth and to express their views and positions. Rights will be ensured to enable the citizens support their lives with their share of wealth, generate and dispose their own assets created with their share of wealth. 2.3.3. Public service benefits shall be secured and real estate soft loans to public servants shall be supported. 2.3.4. Incidences of violation of human rights by public servants shall be drastically reduced; furthermore, any practice of infringing upon human rights in public service shall be eliminated. A law will be initiated to intensify the work of the National Human Rights Commission and expand its powers. 2.3.5. Mongolia's policy on death penalty shall be made consistent with the provisions of International Human Rights Treaties, to which Mongolia is a party.
Three. Strengthening Judiciary, Establishing Justice and Eliminating Corruption and Bureaucracy		
3.1	Establishing justice shall be the first and foremost priority of the President. The legal and judiciary system free of prejudice and discrimination to the people shall be supported.	3.1.1 The laws governing the judiciary shall be made consistent with the Constitution of Mongolia and the spirits and ideals of international treaties and conventions on human rights and freedoms, to which Mongolia is a party. 3.1.2 The legal and regulatory environment will be enhanced to ensure that the judicial institutions are enabled to perform their duties to be the guarantor of justice in each and every part of Mongolia. High ethical codes shall be instituted for officers of judicial institutions, and procedures for strict adherence to the code shall be developed and enforced.
3.2	Any law shall, first of all, be dedicated to protecting a citizen, meeting people's demand and heightening responsibility.	3.2.1. The issue of establishing a legal environment to protect a victim and a witness shall be given keen attention. 3.2.2. A legal environment will be created to secure the independence of court proceedings as well as the judges from economic, political and administrative pressures and influences, and to secure official and private independence of judges.

3.3	An environment will be created whereby cases and dispute are resolved in a manner free of any distress and complications for the people. A parochial mentality of treating a citizen like an offender or felon, and themselves - the source of law shall be obliterated.	3.3.1. Legal norms for securing public order, conducting investigations and interrogations shall be discerned, and a law will be initiated to replace the old system whereby a guilt is imposed - to an internationally established norm whereby a guilt is proven. 3.3.2 A Law will be initiated to tighten the legal obligations charged for the crime of abusing official position.
3.4	Corruption will be combated persistently. A system will be put in place whereby economic damages caused by corruption are recovered. Officials will be made to obey laws. The incidences whereby billionaires are born from the state/government shall be exterminated.	3.4.1 An accountability system for corruption, whereby damages caused by corruption to the society, and especially economic damages are paid off, shall be legally instituted. 3.4.2 A law will be initiated on procedures to be followed in case the private interests and benefits of a public servant contradict with his/her official duties. Conflict of interests shall be regulated by law. 3.4.3. A National Integrity Study will be conducted, and its findings publicized on a regular basis.
Four. Strengthening Mongolia's Foreign Relations, and Actively Cooperating With the International Community on Finding Common Solutions to Global Challenges		
4.1	The President shall bridge Mongolia to the world. Mongolia will become relevant to the development and prosperity of the humankind. The President shall work to make Mongolia relevant for the development and prosperity of the humankind, an active, unique and proud participant in the cause of the international community.	4.1.1. The President shall support Mongolia's efforts to develop balanced foreign economic relations and Mongolia's pursuit of active participation in regional economic integration. 4.1.2. Within the framework of her multi-pillar foreign policy, Mongolia will develop active cooperation with two neighbors, third neighbors and other countries with traditional relations. 4.1.3. The President shall develop and implement initiatives to enable Mongolia to most meaningfully participate in international and regional policy-making in a multitude of areas, including in education, technology, finance, agriculture, infrastructure and trade in certain commodities. 4.1.4. Efforts will be made to enhance Mongolia's exposure to the world, expand the rows of Mongolia supporters abroad, and increase Mongolia's contributions to the promotion of democratic values and ideals internationally. 4.1.5. The President shall work to ensure Mongolia's active engagement in political, economic, cultural and humanitarian affairs in North East Asia and Central Asia. 4.1.6. Initiatives will be made to address the challenges caused by global warming, and especially by climate change and desertification in North East Asia, and regional cooperation toward this direction will be supported. 4.1.7. Rights and benefits of Mongolian citizens residing abroad shall be protected, and their efforts to actively contribute to Mongolia's development shall be

		supported. Mongolia will be actively advertised and promoted internationally.
Five. Ensuring Nature-Friendly Sustainable Economic Development Policy Supportive of Rural Development Efforts		
5.1	The President shall support all efforts to make Mongolia a country which best preserved its pristine nature and natural heritages, a country which best protects and rehabilitates its nature and a country with best policies on nature and ecology.	5.1.1. Ecological education of children, youth and general public at large shall be enhanced. 5.1.2. Optimal management of surface and deep water resources shall be introduced, and major projects to establish water reservoirs shall be supported. 5.1.3. Keen attention will be accorded to protecting and reproducing rare animals and animals threatened by extinction. International experiences of and possibilities for establishing ecological police shall be studied and explored.
5.2	Passing pristine nature onto future generations shall become a traditional, fundamental value of the Mongol state and of each and every Mongolian.	5.2.1. A policy will be pursued to prohibit any business operations and activities in mining, agriculture and other sectors of the economy, which although economically profitable, cause negative effects on human health and safe livelihood and on natural environment. 5.2.2. Legal obligations and punishment for damages and criminal offences on nature, wildlife, flora and fauna shall be tightened, and pertinent laws enforced.
5.3	Projects and programs friendly to nature and useful for people's livelihood will be supported.	5.3.1. Green or clean development projects and programs aiming at reducing carbon dioxide and other toxic emissions will be supported. 5.3.2. A nationwide movement of reforestation shall be initiated, and efforts to establish a National Forest Fund shall be supported. 5.3.3. Legal environment for taxation and other incentives encouraging production and use of renewable energy, friendly to nature and human living environment will be created. 5.3.4. Efforts to develop traditional livestock breeding in a nature-friendly manner shall be supported. Veterinary services shall be made consistent with international standards. Farming combined with intensified livestock-breeding shall be encouraged. 5.3.5. Attention shall be accorded to increasing the real income of herders by expanding the exports of animal-originated raw materials, especially meat and meat products.
5.4	All and any policies and actions to restrain desertification in rural areas and reduce air pollution in cities shall be broadly supported.	5.4.1. National and international projects and programs will be supported to restrain and stop desertification in rural areas. 5.4.2. Investments, projects and programs aiming at reducing air pollution in Ulaanbaatar city shall be accorded special attention. 5.4.3. Legal regulation for effective utilization, possession, management, protection and rehabilitation of pasture lands, shall be improved.

5.5	"Made in Mongolia" initiative shall be supported, markets for domestically produced goods and services shall be expanded.	5.5.1. Production and services to expand domestic industries, substitute imports and diversify the range of export commodities shall be supported. 5.5.2. Attention shall be accorded to creating the optimal structure and organization for developing domestic and international tourism. 5.5.3. Initiatives and ideas to diversify the Mongolian brand products and services shall be supported. 5.5.4. In line with supporting the healthy environment for economic competition, a legal environment will be created to prohibit carteling to inflate prices and impose them on customers, and/or any attempts to seek any preferential rights 5.5.5. Efforts to intensify banking, financial, and capital markets development including mortgage sub-sector will be supported.
5.6	The President will support rural development. Transfer of political, economic and financial powers to local governments shall be supported. Citizens' rights to use, dispose and monitor the use of local wealth shall be secured.	5.6.1. Projects and programs to establish Business Incubators to help translating into reality constructive business ideas, initiatives and proposals by rural citizens and communities, shall be supported. 5.6.2. Efforts to improve the system and mechanisms to protect the intellectual properties of the Mongolian citizens will be firmly supported
5.7	The President shall initiate decentralization of state functions out to rural communities – citizens, private sector and local governments, and shall persistently support policies to reduce and alleviate bureaucratic pressures and costs.	5.7.1. The President shall initiate an action to consolidate and improve laws regulating state central and local budget relations. 5.7.2. Opportunities will be created to enable local governments generate their tax revenues, plan for development and finance this development with generated incomes 5.7.3. Investments in rural areas will be supported. Soums and villages will be supported in their efforts to mobilize their advantages for their development. 5.7.4. Regardless of place of residence, a citizen of Mongolia will be enabled to equally participate in social relations and receive the necessary services without discrimination, barriers and impediments.
Six. Supporting Families and Protecting Rights and Benefits of Social Groups		
6.1	Efforts to promote family development and wellbeing will be supported	6.1.1. 1 A social atmosphere intolerant to any forms of domestic violence shall be created. 6.1.2. Protection of children's and women's violated rights shall be a priority. 6.1.3. The role of women in the family, community and the society shall be strengthened through all means. 6.1.4. The conditions for eligibility for the Order of an Honored Mother title shall be softened and the Order premium increased. 6.1.5. Humane policies and equal and equitable social relations for citizens with development challenges shall be enforced.
6.2	Policies to care for the elderly	6.2.1. A comprehensive range of policies shall be

	encourage the youth and secure their future shall be pursued.	pursued to increase the pensions and benefits to pensioners, and to create the most enabling environment for the youth to pursue their intellectual and physical development.
6.3	Concerted attention shall be paid to education reform. Enhancing the competitiveness of a Mongolian citizen shall be deemed as the basis of Mongolia's competitiveness.	6.3.1. The President shall support the youth to acquire their desired profession. As tuition is one of the key issues under education reforms, initiatives will be made to create a clear legal and financial mechanism. 6.3.2. Support will be rendered to conforming to international standards and implementing the state unified examination to establish the quality of training at all levels of education system. 6.3.3. Science-Production-Training bond shall be enhanced. 6.3.4. Any initiative, proposal, program and action to enhance Mongolia's scientific Research and Development potentials and capacities shall be welcome and supported.
6.4.	Health, education, sports, culture and arts shall be supported through fiscal policies	6.4.1. Without cutting the current fiscal expenditures on health, education, sports, culture and arts, efforts will be made to adopt national program-based government financing, seeking to enhance efficiency and performance. 6.4.2. Health sector reform shall be implemented in consistency with fiscal expenditure reform and health insurance system improvement. 6.4.3. Special attention shall be paid to supporting sportsmen and athletes' material supply, and to duly rewarding the success and achievements of athletes, coaches and trainers, and to supporting public sports and physical training at large. 6.4.4. Efforts and initiatives to establish sports and fitness centers for youth, and to develop public sports, competitions and games to help the population relieve stress and help enjoy healthy leisure and pastime, shall be supported.

The President of Mongolia shall motivate and encourage the progressive thinking and innovative ideas of his people, and shall spare no effort to create more opportunities for development and prosperity of Mongolia.
The Policy and Action Program of the President of Mongolia is open for further enrichment and expansion, subject to the needs and realities, with initiatives, proposals and ideas of Mongolian scholars, scientists and the public.

GOVERNMENT AND POLITICS

THE MONGOLIAN PEOPLE'S REPUBLIC was undergoing a major transition in the development of its government and political institutions in the late 1980s. Beginning in 1984, the country had embarked on a program to restructure its political and economic system in ways that engaged the entire population and made it responsible and accountable for the country's modernization. Much of the inspiration for this program came from the Soviet Union's examples of *glasnost* (see Glossary) and *perestroika* (see Glossary).

Nevertheless, in developing its policies, Mongolia's senior leadership displayed a realistic awareness not only of the severe challenges, but also of the opportunities, afforded by Mongolia's unique political, social, economic, and geophysical conditions. There were efforts by mid-1989 to revive key elements of the Mongolian cultural heritage. This effort apparently was inspired by the recognized need to instill vitality in a polity long stifled by the wholesale imposition of Soviet models. Openings to the West, including the 1987 establishment of diplomatic relations with the United States, increased Mongolia's options within the international diplomatic community and provided additional developmental models. Finally, by mid-1989, the gradual normalizing of Sino-Soviet relations had helped significantly to reduce the tensions inherent in Mongolia's strategic location, enveloped between these giant countries, which facilitated a resurgence of Mongolian national identity and allowed a small measure of Mongolian political independence.

CHARTER OF THE PRESIDENTIAL OFFICE

1. General provision

1. The Presidential Office of Mongolia /hereinafter refer to as the Office/ is the state institution that is responsible to assist the President of Mongolia /hereinafter refer to as the President/ on exercising the power and implementing his manifesto.
1.2. The Office shall conduct its activities according to the Constitution, the Presidential Law, other legal acts as well as orders and decrees of the President of Mongolia.
1.3. The Office shall direct its activities to ensuring the exercise of power and implementing the manifesto and objectives of the President in accordance to coherent relationship with related state institutions.
1.4. The President shall appoint the Head of the Office.
1.5. The Head of the Office shall be responsible for the activities of the Office in front of the President.
1.6. The Office shall have a consultative council. A form of the council activity shall be meeting. The council shall comprise of Head of the Office, Advisors to the President, Deputy Head of the Office and heads of Departments.
1.7. An advisor shall be accountable to the President of Mongolia though, as a civil servant, supervised by the Office according to the Presidential Law.
1.8. The Office shall be responsible for providing working group, responsible for assisting the President to conduct activities, as well as non-staff advisors, their correspondence and other relevant services.
1.9. The Office shall use seal, stamp and letterhead according to the fixed standard.
1.10. The Office shall plan its activities annually and quarterly. The President shall approve annual work plan and the Head of the Office shall approve quarterly working plan.

2. Obligation and responsibilities of the Presidential Office

2.1. The Office shall have the following responsibilities:
2.1.1. Make comments and develop proposals by processing foreign and domestic information related to exercising the power of the President, and provide the President with relevant information.
2.1.2. Advertise internally and externally orders, decrees, reports, messages, vetoes, proposals, directions and other documents of the President through press and media.
2.1.3. Set up information database collecting domestic and foreign press and information materials on the President's activities.
2.1.4. Inform the President regularly on on-time fulfillment and resolution of issues, which are discussed during the presidential meeting with citizens, state institutions and NGOs, proposals, concerns and requests of the citizens addressed to the President through studying, analyzing and monitoring activities.

2.1.5. Study and process proposals of related organizations on granting State and military awards and titles and make them resolved.
2.1.6. Set up information database and release legal reference related to the exercise of power by the President.
2.1.7. Receive, study, and make comments mercy requests and make them resolved.
2.1.8. Assist the President on executing the policy of state civil servants.
2.1.9. Keep a record of official correspondence of the President and the Office and ensure a proper decision fulfillment, exercise control on implementation, take necessary measures and report on implementation to related officials.
2.1.10. Organize official visits, State protocol and other activities of the President, exercise control on provide for guarding and service, take additional measures if necessary.
2.1.11. Formulate annual budget of the Office, provide for adequate spending, exercise control on its implementation and make quarterly report to responsible officials on budget spending.
2.1.12. Create archive, PC information database and network of the President and provide for its confidentiality.
2.2. The Office shall have the following rights:
2.2.1. Develop proposals on exercising power of the President and introduce to the President.
2.2.2. Claim statistic indices, information, research, introduction and comments necessary for the President's activities from related organizations and their authorities.
2.2.3. Work out proposal, recommendation and jurisdiction on activities of central and subordinate state administrative institutions based on the presidential direction or suggestion.
2.2.4. Involve relevant professionals in conducting researches and developing issues within the scope of power.
2.2.5. Demand related organizations on providing necessary working condition, equipment, materials, and technical facilities.
2.2.6. Spend adopted budget sparingly, provide for certain amount of saved budget can be spent on resolving social issues of employees.
2.2.7. Cooperate with the Parliament, the Government, state institutions, NGOs, other related organizations and relevant officials on other issues in order to assist the President to exercise the power.

3. Structure of the Presidential Office

3.1. The Office shall comprise of Internal Affairs and Monitoring Department, Department of Advisors Task force, Press and Information Department and Correspondence Department. Some other departments may be added or even disbanded as subject to official necessity.

4. Staff of the Presidential Office

4.1. The Presidential Office shall comprise of Head and Deputy of the Presidential Office, Advisors to the President, Heads of Departments, senior staff-members, staff-members and state service officials.

5. Obligation and duties of the Office employees

5.1. Head of the Presidential Office:
5.1.1. Is a political assignee who leads the state institution, which is responsible for assisting the President to exercise the power.
5.1.2. Shall coordinate Advisors' activities coherently
5.1.3. Shall submit proposals to the President on issues related to exercising the presidential power.
5.1.4. Shall approve a quarterly working plan of the Office, and report to the President on annual and quarterly performance.

5.1.5. Shall monitor the President and the Office annual budget implementation.
5.1.6. Shall identify an agenda of management council Meeting of the Office, arrange and head the meeting.
5.1.7. Shall coordinate an activity of the Presidential developing orders, decrees and reports drafting, check drafts of speeches, messages and other documents.
5.1.8. Shall assist the President on implementing the civil servants policy within the scope of the presidential power.
5.1.9. Shall organize official visits, State protocol and other activities of the President, provide for adequate guarding and make additional measures according to the law, if necessary.
5.1.10. Jointly with the advisors, shall study and process proposals of related organizations on granting state and military awards and titles and make them resolved.
5.1.11. Shall provide for resolving claims, concerns, complaints and requests of citizens and organizations.
5.1.12. Shall provide for the presidential orders and decrees implementation.
5.1.13. Shall issue decree in compliance with the laws of Mongolia, the presidential orders and decisions and ensure its proper implementation.
5.1.14. Shall cooperate with the Parliament, the Government, the Supreme Court, General Commission of the Court, State Prosecutor General's Office, the Constitutional Court, Ministries, agencies and local subordinate administrative authorities directly in implementing above mentioned activities.
5.1.15. In case of the Head's absence, any of the Advisors shall be acting whereas, the Deputy Head of the Office shall be responsible for other activities.
5.1.16. The Head of the Office shall be provided with salaries and working conditions an equivalent of that of ministers.

5.2. An advisor to the President:

5.2.1. The President shall have political, economic, legal, military and foreign policy advisors. The President may have advisors on other matters.
5.2.2. Shall advise the President on related matters in developing a proposal on Government structure, composition and changes to it.
5.2.3. Shall assist the President on exercising the power and executing the manifesto by providing with true and practical advise on initiating law and resolution drafts, submitting proposals concerning external and internal issues to the Parliament, vetoing on laws and giving directions to the Government on issues under his consideration.
5.2.4. Shall be fully responsible for implementing issues, reflected in the election manifesto by incorporating them in the annual and quarterly plan of the Presidential Office.
5.2.5. Shall develop drafts of orders, decrees, vetoes, speeches, messages, reports, proposals, directions and other documents of the President and monitor them in accordance to their policy directions.
5.2.6. Shall suggest and give comments to the President on resolving claims, complaints and requests of citizens in accordance to own policy directions and responsibilities.
5.2.7. Shall be provided with salaries and working condition an equivalent of that of vice-ministers.

5.3. Deputy Head of the Presidential Office:
5.3.1. Shall coordinate internal activities of the Office, provide with adequate management the Departments and have internal rules followed.
5.3.2. Shall develop draft of annual budget of the President and the Office by incorporating into it a financing need of sub-structures including working group and non-staff council and organize its implementation.
5.3.3. The Head of the Office shall determine other obligations and responsibilities of the Deputy

PRIME MINISTER

Ukhnaagiin Khürelsükh is a Mongolian politician currently serving as Prime Minister of Mongolia since October, 2017. He was elected to the Parliament of Mongolia three times – in 2000, 2004 and 2012, served in the Cabinet of Mongolia as Minister for Emergency Situation from 2004 to 2006, Minister for Professional Inspection from 2006 to 2008, and in 2014–2015 and 2016–2017 as Deputy Prime Minister of Mongolia. Also he was the Secretary-General of Mongolian People's Party from 2008 to 2012.

Prime Minister and his Power

The Prime Minister of Mongolia is the head of the Government, the highest executive body of the State.

- The Prime Minister leads the Government under the Constitution, and is responsible to the Parliament for the implementation of state laws.
- It is the prerogative right of the country's President to propose to the State Ih Hural (Parliament) the candidature for the appointment to the post of Prime Minister in consultation with the majority faction or parties in Parliament if none of them has majority of seats, as well as to propose to the State Ih Hural the dissolution of the Government.
- The Government comprises the Prime Minister and his/her Cabinet members. The Prime Minister, in consultation with the President, submits his/her proposals on the structure and composition of the Government and on the changes in these to the Parliament. The latter considers the nominees proposed by the Prime Minister one by one, and takes decision on their appointment.
- The State Ih Hural is entitled to take decisions regarding the Government resignation or formation of a new one, resignation of its member or revealing him/her from the duty, assignment of a new Cabinet member, and a vote of confidence to the Government in accordance with the Constitution and other relevant laws.
- The term of the mandate of the Government is four years and its term of office starts from the day of the appointment of the Prime Minister by the Parliament and terminates upon the appointment of a new Prime Minister.
- The Prime Minister may tender his/her resignation to the National Parliament before the expiry of his/her term of office if he/she considers that the Government is unable to exercise its powers.
- The Government steps down en masse upon the resignation of the Prime Minister or if half of the members of the Government resign at the same time.
- The Parliament considers the matter and makes a final decision within 15 days after taking the initiative to dissolve the Government or receiving the President's proposal or the Prime Minister's statement on resignation.

- The Parliament considers and takes decision on the dissolution of the Government if not less than one fourth of lawmakers formally propose the dissolution of the Government.
- The Government is entitled to the right of a legislative initiative in the same manner as the President and the members of the State Ih Hural.
- If the Government submits a draft resolution requesting a vote of confidence, the National Parliament makes a final decision within 15 days after receiving the draft resolution.

GOVERNMENT OF MONGOLIA

The Government of the country is the highest executive body of the State under the Constitution of Mongolia.

In discharging its duty of directing economic, social, and cultural development of the country in observance of State laws, the Government exercises the following powers:

- to organize and ensure nation-wide implementation of the Constitution and other laws;
- to work out a comprehensive policy on science and technology, guidelines for economic and social development, the State budget, credit and fiscal plans, to submit these to the Parliament, and to execute decisions taken thereon;
- to elaborate and implement comprehensive measures on sectoral, intersectoral, as well as regional development;
- to undertake measures on the protection of the environment and on the rational use and restoration of natural resources;
- to provide efficient leadership of central state administrative bodies and to direct the activities of local administrations;
- to strengthen the country's defense capabilities and to ensure national security;
- to take measures for the protection of human rights and freedoms, enforcement of public order, and prevention of crime;
- to realize the State foreign policy;
- to conclude and implement international treaties with the consent of and subsequent ratification by the Parliament as well as to conclude and abrogate intergovernmental treaties.
- the specific powers, structure, and procedure of the Government are determined by law.

Ministries and other government offices are constituted in accordance with the law.
The Government is to make decisions based on the opinion of the majority of the Cabinet members, however, giving a due consideration to the arguments of those with a different position on the matter, and it bears a collective responsibility to the Parliament for the implementation of its decisions. The Government is to conduct its policy in combination of both regional and sectoral principles.
Under the administrative division of the territory, Mongolia is divided into aimags (provinces) and the capital city; the aimag consists of soums (counties), and the latter of bags. The capital city is divided into districts consisting of horoos (quarters).
Chief administrators of bags, horoos, soums, and districts are nominated by the relevant local Hurals (Assemblies), and are appointed by the Governors of the provinces and the capital city for the term of four years. Nominees to the office of the province and the capital city Governors are proposed by the aimag and capital city assemblies to be appointed by the Prime Minister for the tenure of four years.

CABINET SECRETARY

Cabinet Secretariat of Government of Mongolia,
Government House, Ulaanbaatar - 12, Mongolia
tel: 976 - 11 - 322408
fax: 976 - 11 - 310011

FUNCTIONAL STRUCTURE OF THE CABINET SECRETARIAT

The internal functional structure of the Cabinet Secretariat

As a result of the State Great Khural /Parliament/ Election of 2000, the functional structure of the Government has been changed. The status of the Cabinet Secretariat has become higher and its scope of activities has become broader. The Chief of the Cabinet Secretariat is a Cabinet Member. Under the Government Resolution of September 13, 2000 and the Cabinet Secretariat has 6 departments and 80 employees.

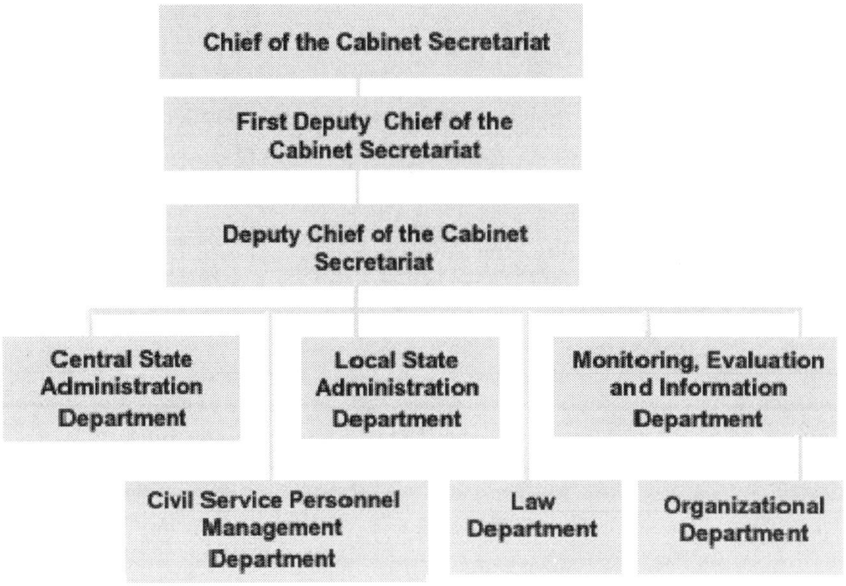

External Functional Structure of the Cabinet Secretariat

According to its general functional structure as well as under the legislation, State Protocol Office, Government Press Office and the Prime Minister's Office are included in the structure of the Cabinet Secretariat. Furthermore, within the scope of the Cabinet Secretariat functions, Academy of Management, State Services & Management Agency are included in the external functional structure of the Cabinet Secretariat. In addition, the Cabinet Secretariat provides support and advice to the Prime Minister and the Cabinet on issues related to the workings of the Government agencies such as the Central Intelligence Agency, the State Property Committee, the Mongolian Radio and Television, the News Agency "MONTSAME."

Informal structure of the Cabinet Secretariat

In the Informal structure of the Cabinet Secretariat, included are the following:

- “Economic policy support project”
- “Public Administration Reform project”
- “Local Government and Decentralization project,”
- “Water Policy project”
- “Social Policy project”
- “Strengthening of Democracy”
- “Good Governance for the Human Security Program”
- Representatives of the International Monetary Fund

and some National committees and commission led by the Prime Minister:

- National Regulatory Committee for preventing and fighting against AIDS
- National Poverty Alleviation Committee
- Sustainable Development Commission

The aforementioned programmes and projects conduct their activities independently within the scope of the Cabinet Secretariat functions. For instance, the project “Good Governance for Human Security” has 4 components and led by the Prime Minister. The component “Sound Governance” of the said project is directed by the Chief of the Cabinet Secretariat.

LOCAL STATE ADMINISTRATION DEPARTMENT

Local state administration department (the head of department is B. Shatar) has 7 posts and it is structured to serve local administrative organizations and Citizen's Representative Offices with professional and methodological assistance and supports on their administration and management.

№	Names of staff	Function	E-mail address
1	B.Shatar	Deputy chief	Shatar_b@prime.pmis.gov.mn
2	B.Sharbandi	Government senior officer	Sharbandi_b@prime.pmis.gov.mn
3	M.Sandag-Ochir	Government officer	Sandag_ochir@prime.pmis.gov.mn
4	L.Erhembayar	Government officer	Erkhembayar@prime.pmis.gov.mn
5	D.Ulziibat	Government officer	Ulziibat@prime.pmis.gov.mn
6	D.Odmaa	Analyst	Odmaa_d@prime.pmis.gov.mn
7	Z.Tuul	Analyst	Tuul_z@prime.pmis.gov.mn
8	Ts.Sharav	Analyst	Sharav_ts@prime.pmis.gov.mn

CENTRAL STATE ADMINISTRATION DEPARTMENT

The Central state administraion department (the head is L. Khangai) have 16 posts and it coordinates activities of ministries and agencies and serves the Government with whole range of supports and advice in implementing Government action plan and setting sectoral policy, regulation and management.

№	Names of staff	Function	E-mail address
1	L.Khangai	First deputy chief	Khangai@prime.pmis.gov.mn

2	Ts.Bazar	Government senior officer	Bazar_ts@prime.pmis.gov.mn
3	D.Guunee	Government senior officer	Guunee_d@prime.pmis.gov.mn
4	E.Sumiya	Government senior officer	Sumiya@prime.pmis.gov.mn
5	N.Buyandelger	Government senior officer	Buyanaa@pmis.gov.mn
6	D.Delgertsogt	Government senior officer	Delgertsogt_d@prime.pmis.gov.mn
7	N.Bayaraa	Government senior officer	N_bayaraa@prime.pmis.gov.mn
8	D.Ganchimeg	Government senior officer	Ganchimeg_d@prime.pmis.gov.mn
9	N.Ulziikhutag	Government officer	Ulziikhutag_n@prime.pmis.gov.mn
10	J.Rentsen-Amgalan	Government officer	Ramgalan_j@prime.pmis.gov.mn
11	J. Uranchimeg	Government officer	Uranchimeg@prime.pmis.gov.mn
12	M.Erdene-Ochir	Analyst	Erdeneochir_m@prime.pmis.gov.mn
13	G.Batbayar	Analyst	Batbayar@prime.pmis.gov.mn

MONITORING, EVALUATION AND INFORMATION DEPARTMENT

Monitoring, Evaluation and Information division (Head is L.Ishdorj) has 8 staffs. The division's key function is to ensure timely and quality provision of information to the Prime Minister, its Cabinet, Minister for Cabinet Secretariat and other related stakeholders through regular monitoring and evaluation of Central Governments and Local Administration performances and the implementation processes of Government policy objectives and resolutions, decision, programs and projects. Its final outcome is strengthening the Public Administration accountability and reporting, and transparency of the Decision Making Processes.

№	Names of staff	Function	E-mail address
1	L. Ishdorj	Head of department	Ichdorj@prime.pmis.gov.mn
2	N.Orgodol	Government senior officer	Orgodol_n@prime.pmis.gov.mn
3	L.Tulga	Government senior officer	Tulga_l@prime.pmis.gov.mn
4	G.Yumjab	Government officer	Yumjav_g@prime.pmis.gov.mn
5	Sh.Chingerel	Government officer	Chingerel_sh@prime.pmis.gov.mn
7	L.Tsegmid	Analyst	Tsegmid_l@prime.pmis.gov.mn
8	D.Solongo	Analyst	Solongo_d@prime.pmis.gov.mn

CIVIL SERVICE PERSONNEL MANAGEMENT DEPARTMENT

Civil Servant Personnel Department (Head: Ts.Samballkhundev, Ph.D.) has 8 personnel. The department is in charge of managing and regulating all matters related to civil servants management and providing the Public Service Committee with basic and essential assistance and services.

№	Names of staff	Function	E-mail address

1	Ts.Samballhundev	Head of department	Samballhundev@prime.pmis.gov.mn
2	G.Dagva	Government senior officer	Dagva_g@prime.pmis.gov.mn
3	D.Yadamsuren	Government officer	Yadamsuren@prime.pmis.gov.mn
4	B.Jugder	Government officer	Jugder_b@prime.pmis.gov.mn
5	B.Erdenebileg	Government officer	Erdenebileg_b@prime.pmis.gov.mn
6	T.Bumtsend	Analyst	Bumtsend_t@prime.pmis.gov.mn
7	D.Baatarsaihan	Analyst	Baatarsaihan_d@prime.pmis.gov.mn

LAW DEPARTMENT

Law Department /Head Sh. Solongo/ has 6 personnel. Its functions are lawmaking; provision of professional and methodological services and support to ensure that Government resolutions are in accord with existing laws and regulations; provision of all kinds of assistance and advise to the the Government to administer policy formulation and coordination in legal sector.

№	Names of staff	Function	E-mail address
1	Sh.Solongo	Head of department	Solongo_sh@prime.pmis.gov.mn
2	N.Batbold	Analyst	N_batbold@prime.pmis.gov.mn
3	Sh.Radnaased	Analyst	Radnaased@prime.pmis.gov.mn
4	J.Otgontsetseg	Analyst	Otgontsetseg_j@prime.pmis.gov.mn
5	J.Batmagnai	Analyst	Jmagnai@prime.pmis.gov.mn
6	E. Samdan	Analyst	Samdan@prime.pmis.gov.mn

ORGANIZATIONAL DEPARTMENT

The organizational department (the head of department is Sh.Buuveebaatar) has 34 posts and it is structured to provide official services such as protocol recording, archive keeping, secret service, letter responding, postal service, faxing and copying, government information server and urgent information service under its main functions including organizing Government decision making, drafting, documentation and information activities; common service policy setting and planning; and maintaining internal service quality of Cabinet Secretariat as well as consistent operation of Government information network. For instance, the government information computer server has information network in which connected 22 central government organizations, 6 aimags and one soum. Also it has connected the Cabinet meeting room in 2000, allowing central and local public administration organizations instant access and information exchange during the Cabinet meeting.

№	Names of staff	Function	E-mail address
1	Sh.Buuveebaatar	Head of dcpartment	Buuveebaatar_sh@prime.pmis.gov.mn
2	G.Chingel	Government senior officer	Chingel_g@prime.pmis.gov.mn
3	N.Dan-Aajav	Government senior officer	Danaajav_n@prime.pmis.gov.mn
4	Ts.Tsendjav	Government officer	Tsendjav_ts@prime.pmis.gov.mn

5	Boldkhuyag	Officer	Boldkhuyag@prime.pmis.gov.mn
6	G.Tsedendagva	Officer	Tsedendagva@prime.pmis.gov.mn
7	Ya.Yandag	Government senior officer	Yandag_ya@prime.pmis.gov.mn
8	Ts.Tsendeehuu	Analyst	Tsendeehuu_ts@prime.pmis.gov.mn
9	N.Oyun	Analyst	Oyun_n@prime.pmis.gov.mn
10	H.Bilguun	Analyst	Bilguun_h@prime.pmis.gov.mn
11	D.Bayaraa	Analyst	Bayaraa_d@prime.pmis.gov.mn
12	N.Enkhtuya	Operator	Enkhtuya_n@prime.pmis.gov.mn
13	D.Bat-Erdene	Government officer	Baterdene@prime.pmis.gov.mn
14	B.Byambadorj	Analyst	Byambadorj_b@prime.pmis.gov.mn
15	D.Altansukh	Analyst	Altansukh@pmis.gov.mn
16	Ch.Enkhzaya	Analyst	Enkhzaya@pmis.gov.mn
17	J.Tamir	Analyst	Tamir@pmis.gov.mn
18	T.Oyun	Analyst	Oyun_t@prime.pmis.gov.mn
19	B.Tuya	Analyst	Tuya_b@prime.pmis.gov.mn
20	Ch.Uran	Analyst	Uran_ch@prime.pmis.gov.mn
21	E.Onorzul	Analyst	Onorzul@prime.pmis.gov.mn
22	B.Enkhtuya	Officer	Enkhtuya_b@prime.pmis.gov.mn
23	Z.Batbayar	Government officer	Batbayar_z@prime.pmis.gov.mn
24	D.Byambajav	Analyst	Byambajav_d@prime.pmis.gov.mn
25	P. Gantumur	Analyst	Gantumur@prime.pmis.gov.mn
26	S.Tseveenpurev	Analyst	Tseveenpurev@prime.pmis.gov.mn
27	Ch.Purevdorj	Analyst	Purevdorj@prime.pmis.gov.mn
28	H. Batchuluun	Analyst	Batchuluun@prime.pmis.gov.mn
29	S.Gandanbaavar	Officer	Gandanbaavar@prime.pmis.gov.mn
30	A.Altantulkhuur	Officer	Altantulkhuur@prime.pmis.gov.mn
31	G. Bol-Erdene	Officer	Bolderdene@prime.pmis.gov.mn
32	D.Dendev	Officer	-
33	M.Khishigjargal	Senior operator	Khishigjargal_m@prime.pmis.gov.mn
34	Sh.Dorjsambuu	Operator	Dorjsambuu_sh@prime.pmis.gov.mn

POLITICAL SITUATION

Politics of Mongolia takes place in a framework of a semi-presidential representative democratic republic, and of a multi-party system.[1][2][3] Executive power is exercised by the President and the Government. Legislative power is vested in both the government and parliament. The Judiciary is independent of the executive and the legislature. The Economist Intelligence Unit has rated Mongolia as "flawed democracy" in 2016

After seven decades of communist rule in Mongolia the nation's first free multiparty elections took place in July 1990. The new parliamentary body, the Great Hural (Ikh Hural), elected P. Ochirbat as President and D. Byambasuren as Prime Minister, both belonging to the formerly communist Mongolian People's Revolutionary Party (MPRP).

Since 1990 Mongolia has made important progress in consolidating its democratic institutions. Early in 1992, a new Mongolian Constitution was adopted enshrining human rights and the ownership of land and a state structure based on separation of power between legislative and judicial branches. The People's Republic was renamed as Mongolia, and a new single chamber 76-seat national assembly, the Great Hural, was established. In 1992, during the first parliamentary elections under the new constitution, the MPRP won 71 of the 76 places in the Ikh Hural, though it received only 60% of the popular vote ("first past the post"-system).

On 6 June 1993 incumbent President P. Ochirbat, who had left the MPRP to join the Mongolian National Democratic Party, was re-elected with 58 percent of the votes in the country's first direct presidential elections. 38 percent of the electorate voted for the candidate of the MPRP, L. Tudev.

The second parliamentary elections in June 1996, resulted in a overwhelming victory for the Democratic Union Coalition (DUC), consisting of the two principal opposition parties (National Democratic Party and the Social Democratic Party) and several minor ones. The DUC won 50 of the 76 seats in the Ikh Hural with a turnout of 87 % of the votes. MPRP won just 25 seats, the remaining seat went to the Conservative Party. Mr. M. Enksaikhan, Head of the DUC, was elected the new Prime Minister. The transition from MPRP to Democratic Union proved to be peaceful and smooth, an important step toward democracy. The new Government adopted a radical reform agenda, which was pursued with vigor up to April 1998 date of its demise.

On 19 May 1997 Mr. N. Bagabandi, candidate of the MPRP won the second presidential elections. He was supported by 60.8 % of the electorate on a platform of slowing down political and economic reforms. Incumbent President P. Ochirbat of the Democratic Union trailed with 30 percent. Turnout was 85 percent of the 1.1 million eligible voters. (Next presidential elections: 20 May 2001).

In the years 1998/99 the country's government was dismissed three times: After the removal from office of M. Enksaikhan in April 1998, a new government was set up in May 1998, headed by PM Ts. Elbegdorj. The latter was released on 28 July 1998. After a political turbulent summer, the Parliament elected J. Narantsatsralt as the new PM on 9 December 1998. He and his cabinet were replaced on 22 July 1999 by the government of PM R. Amarjargal.

Thc third parliamentary elections on 2 July 2000 were assessed as free and fair by the international community. They resulted in a victory of the MPRP, which landed 72 out of the 76 seats, though it received only 50.3 % of the vote. The new Prime Minister Nambaryn Enkhbayar has officially stated that the new government will not introduce a major change in path towards transition process. The landslide victory of the MPRP ended two years of political instability and economic drift.

FOREIGN POLICY

The main objective of Mongolian foreign policy is to keep a good balance between the two big neighbors Russia and China. Mongolia is looking to develop and deepen relations with other partners such as the EU, the US or Japan. For the moment 140 countries have diplomatic relations with Mongolia.

ECONOMIC SITUATION

Mongolia began its transition from a centrally planned economy to a market oriented economy in 1990. The disintegration of the USSR, and of the socialist trading system, threw the Mongolian economy into difficulties. Like other transitional economies which lost large external subsidies from the Soviet Union (in the Mongolian case about US $ 900 million a year), Mongolia experienced a sharp depression and increased poverty in the first part of the 1990s. Between 1990 and 1992 GDP declined by 20 %. According to the Living Standards Measurement Survey (LSMS) of the World Bank in 1998, 35.6 percent of the population lived below the weighted national average poverty line of US $ 17 per month.

Decisions of economic reform: During the 1990s, Mongolia made considerable progress in laying the institutional and policy foundations for a private, market-based economy, including price and trade liberalization, launching large-scale privatization (retail sector and herding industry), curtailing budget transfers and lending to state enterprises, and setting-up a commercial banking system. During 1995-99, Mongolia also drastically curtailed inflationary financing of the public sector and pursued tight monetary policies. In 1991 Mongolia became a member of international financial institutions like the World Bank and the IMF. Mongolia joined the WTO on 29 January 1997.

Structure of the economy: In 1999, agriculture, almost exclusively livestock production, accounted for about 35 % of GDP; commerce, 29 %; services, 18 %; mining, 10 %; and industry, 7.5 %. Mining, mainly copper and gold, generated more than 80 % of the economy's export earnings. Industry includes wool and cashmere processing, leather goods production, food processing, construction, and, in recent years, garments. 40 % of Mongolian labor force is employed in livestock production (32 million heads of livestock in 1998). In 1999 70 % of the GDP was generated by the private sector (compared with 10 % in 1990). In 1999 the country's trade balance deficit amounted to US $ 112.9 million.

Growth: After 1994 the economic downturn could be stopped and macro-economic stability could be reached. In 1994 GDP increased by 2.3 % and by 6.3 % in 1995. In 1996, economic growth slowed down to 2.6 % essentially because of the drop of international copper prices by 33 % and of cashmere prices by 10 % which adversely affected export earnings. Since then the growth rate stayed comparatively stable between 3.5 and 4 %. In 1999 GDP reached an amount of US $ 920 million, US $ 350 per capita. Despite the recovery of the economy between 1996 and 1999, per capita income stagnated over the course of that period. In 1999/2000 and 2000/2001 Mongolia had to suffer from extremely harsh winters. Each so called "Dzud" killed about ten percent of the country's livestock. This affected seriously husbandry production, which is the major sector of the country's economy. In the face of the suffering of the country's agriculture, growth rate of GDP amounted only to 1 percent in the year 2000.

Inflation: The average annual rate of inflation has been reduced from 425% in 1992 to 44.6 % in 1996, 20.5 % in 1997, 8 % in 1998. In 1999 it accelerated to a level of 10 % mainly due to huge external price shocks. In 2000 the rate could be kept at a single digit level.

Challenges: The main challenges the new Government has to facing are to progressively reduce poverty and improve living standards for all Mongolians. The government is facing the objective to reduce the budget deficit which amounted in 2000 to more than 10 % of GDP. The new Government's budget for 2001 intends to keep the fiscal deficit to 7 %. Regional development and the diversification of the countries exports are further aims in the future. In order to guarantee a higher level of economic growth, international financial institutions pledge for further economic reforms, in particular for the privatization of major industries such as banking, cashmere processing, and copper mining. In August 2000, the new Government, headed by Prime Minister N. Enkbayar, adopted its 2000-04 Action Program, a Poverty Reduction Strategy Paper (IPRSP) is under preparation in collaboration with the international financial institutions (IFIs). It aims at a decrease of unemployment and an increase of living standards of people through macroeconomic stabilization and economic growth.

International Assistance: The IMF, the World Bank and the Asian Development Bank (ADB) have worked with the government of Mongolia to accomplish many of the key reforms taken to date and to establish detailed policy agendas, including transportation and energy. With the support of the IMF and the World Bank Mongolia has been able to mobilize the international community of donors through various big donor conferences. The seventh assistance group meeting took place in Ulaanbatar in June 1999. A large number of external donor organizations are committed to assisting the process of economic transition in Mongolia. For the period 1991-1998 total commitments of assistance (grant and loan) of the international donor community amounted to USD 2.08 billion. A new consultative group meeting will be organized in May 2001.

GENERAL DATA

Geography: Mongolia is a landlocked country, located between the Russian Federation in the North and the PR China in the South. It expands on a territory of 1.565 Mio km². The country is increasingly urbanized – 63% of the population lives in cities, 600.000 inhabitants live in Ulaanbatar ("The Red Hero"), the country's capital since 1924. The other major urban centers are Darhan (90.000 inhabitants) and Erdenet (65.000 inhabitants)

Population: 2,4 million (2000). Mongolia has a population density of only 1.7 people per km² - one of the lowest in the world. **Ethnic groups**: 86% Kalkh Mongols, 7% of Turkic origin, mostly Kazakhs, living in the far west of the country. The rest belong to a wide variety of ethnic groups, including the Buryat, Dariganga, Bayad, Zakchin and Uriankhai. More than 6 million Mongols live outside Mongolia, most of them in Russia and in Chinese Inner Mongolia.

Religions: Tibetan Buddhist, Muslim (Kazakhs).

Official language: Mongolian.

Political system: Mongolia is a parliamentary republic.

Legislature: One-cameral Parliament, the Ikh Hural, with 76 seats, elected for four years.

Head of the State: President elected for four years.

Government: Prime Minster appointed by Ikh Hural for four years.

Judicial system: Mongolian judicial system consists of a Constitutional Court, a Supreme Court, *aimag* (provinces) and capital city courts, and *somon* and district courts.

Incumbent government: HoS President Natsagyn Bagabandi (Mongolian People's Revolutionary Party) elected for a four-years-term on 26 June 1997 (next presidential elections: 20 May 2001). Prime Minister: Nambariin Enkhbayar (MPRP), elected 26 July 2000, Foreign Minister: L. Erdenechuluun.

ADMINISTRATIVE STRUCTURE

Power is shared between the President, the Parliament (State Great Khural), the Prime Minister's ten-member cabinet and the Supreme Court. The President and Parliamentary Members are elected directly by the people at two different elections. The Prime Minister is nominated from the party with the largest number of seats in Parliament.

Only the Parliament has legislative power. It determines the basis of domestic and foreign policy, approves and makes changes in laws, determines and announces presidential and parliamentary elections, elects members of the judiciary and the Supreme Court, appoints and dismisses government members, defines the state financial credit, monetary and tax policies and sets base guidelines for the socioeconomic development of the country. It approves and dissolves the territorial and administrative units and regulates the system and the organisational structure of these units. It has Spring and Autumn sessions and consists of 76 full time members elected for four years.

The territories of Mongolia are administratively divided into 21 regions - 18 Aimags and 3 cities. Each Aimag is generally divided into Sums that are further divided into smaller units called bags. The capital city has districts and sub districts.

Aimag & City	Area, (100 km^2)	No. of Sums /Districts	Population in (x1000)	Name of Capital	Aimag Centre Population (x1000)	Distance from Ulaanbaatar (km)
Arkhangai	55.3	19	103.7	Tsetserleg	18.1	453
Bayan Ulgii	45.7	14	96.2	Ulgii	21.0	1636
Bayankhongor	116	20	91.6	Bayankhongor	23.3	630
Bulgan	48.7	16	66.1	Bulgan	15.6	318
Gobi Altai	141.4	18	74.9	Altai	18.5	1001
Dornogov	109.5	14	49.9	Sainshand	17.7	463
Dornod	123.6	14	84.3	Choibalsan	38.6	655
Dundgov	74.7	16	54.4	Mandalgov	10.9	260
Zavkhan	82.5	24	105.0	Uliastai	24.3	984
Ovorkhangai	62.9	19	116.9	Arvaikheer	20.7	430
Omnogov	165.4	15	46.2	Dalanzadgad	12.6	553
Sukhbaatar	82.3	13	59.7	Baruun Urt	14.7	560

Selenge	41.2	17	107.0	Sukhbaatar	22.3	311
Tov	74	27	113.7	Zuunmod	15.3	43
Uvs	69.6	20	100.5	Ulaangom	26.5	1336
Khovd	76.1	17	93.0	Khovd	27.4	1425
Khovsgol	100.6	23	123.6	Moron	25.6	671
Khentii	80.3	19	77.7	Ondorkhan	16.0	331
Ulaanbaatar	4.7	9	668.8			
Darkhan	3.28	4	94.2	Darkhan	71.4	219
Orkon	0.84	2	72.5	Erdenet	63.5	371
Gobisumber	5.54	3	13.1	Choir	8.7	240

MONGOLIAN ARMY AND DEFENCE POLICY

MILITARY OF MONGOLIA

STRATEGIC INFORMATION

	Leadership
Commander in Chief	Nambaryn Enkhbayar
Minister for Defense	Luvsanvandangiin Bold
Chief of General Staff	Tsevegsurengiin Togoo
Military age	18
Conscription	yes
Available for military service	736,182 males, age 15–49 (2005 est.), 734,679 females, age 15–49 (2005 est.)
Fit for military service	570,435 males, age 15–49 (2005 est.), 607,918 females, age 15–49 (2005 est.)
Reaching military age annually	34,674 males (2005 est.), 34,251 females (2005 est.)
	Expenditures
Budget	$23.1 million (FY02)
Percent of GDP	2.2%

The **military of Mongolia** has three branches: general purpose forces, border defense forces and internal security forces. This is a peace-time structure. In case of war or war-like situations, the structure could be changed and reorganized.

POLICY

Due to its geopolitical positions and economical powers, Mongolia has a unique military policy. Being between two of the world's largest nations, Mongolian armed forces have a limited capability to protect its independence against foreign invasions; the country's national security therefore depends strongly on diplomacy. The country's military ideal is to create and maintain a small but efficient and professional armed forces.

MONGOLIAN ARMED FORCES IN PEACEKEEPING MISSIONS

Mongolian armed forces are performing peacekeeping missions in Sierra Leone, Iraq, Ethiopia, Eritrea, and Afghanistan, and with the United Nations Mission in Liberia. Mongolian forces in Afghanistan mostly assist NATO/ISAF personnel in training on the former Warsaw Pact weapons that comprise the bulk of the military equipment available to the Afghan National Army. In 2005/2006, Mongolian troops also served as part of the Belgian KFOR contingent in Kosovo.

CAPABILITY

Ground forces possess over 600 tanks, 450 mobile artillery pieces, 100 mobile anti-air defence vehicles and other military vehicles and equipment. Most of them are old Soviet Union models designed between the late 50's to early 70's.

LIGHT EQUIPMENT

- AK-74
- AK-47
- NSV (machine gun)
- SVD (rifle)

TANKS

- T-62 - 250
- T-55 – 350

INFANTRY FIGHTING VEHICLES

- BMP-1 – 310 in 2003, 400 in 1996, originally 420 were delivered.

ARMORED PERSONNEL CARRIERS

- BTR-40 - ?
- BTR-152 - ?
- BTR-60 – 300
- BRDM-1 - ?
- BRDM-2 – ?

MONGOLIAN PEOPLE'S AIR FORCE

The small **Mongolian People's Air Force** is the national air force, administered by the Army.

Aircraft	Origin	Type	Versions	In service	Notes
Antonov An-24 Coke	Soviet Union	tactical transport	An-24	4	
Antonov An-26 Curl	Soviet Union	tactical transport	An-26	3	
Antonov An-2 Colt	Soviet Union	biplane transport	An-2	10	
Harbin Y-12	People's Republic of China	light transport	Y-12	4	
Mikoyan-Gurevich MiG-21 Fishbed	Soviet Union	fighter	MiG-21PFM/UM	8/2	grounded
Mil Mi-24 Hind	Soviet Union	attack helicopter	Mi-24V	4	
Mil Mi-8 Hip	Soviet Union	attack helicopter	Mi-8	20	Anti-tank
Mil Mi-8 Hip	Soviet Union	transport helicopter	Mi-8	12	Transport only

MINISTRY OF DEFENCE

Ulan Bator
Mongolia
Tel: +976 1 358477
Fax: +976 1 358477

Military branches:	Mongolian Armed Forces (includes General Purpose Forces, Air and Air Defense Forces, Civil Defense Troops); note - Border Troops are under Ministry of Justice and Home Affairs in peacetime
Military manpower - military age:	18 years of age
Military manpower - availability:	males age 15-49: 748,779 (2001 est.)
Military manpower - fit for military service:	males age 15-49: 486,491 (2001 est.)
Military manpower - reaching military age annually:	males: 30,230 (2001 est.)
Military expenditures - dollar figure:	$25.5 million (FY01)

THE BASIS OF THE STATE MILITARY POLICY OF MONGOLIA

I. GENERAL PROVISIONS

The basis of the state military policy of Mongolia is the fundamental legal document defining the defense policy, a constituent of the national security.

The state military policy is the official view of the state defining the attitude of the state *inter alia* armed aggression, averting the threats of wars and armed conflicts, safeguarding the country from external armed intervention, organizational development of military, and on conducting armed struggle, and it shall be based on the self-defense principles of the Constitution of Mongolia.

The political base of the military structure of Mongolia is the civilian control on the armed forces.

The self-defense principles of Mongolia shall be based on the integrated defense system relying on territorial defense.

The basis of the state military policy shall form the foundation of the laws and legislation, international treaties and agreements of Mongolia with respect to defense activities.

The implementation of the state military policy of Mongolia shall be regulated through laws and legislation, and the National Security Council of Mongolia shall oversee how the state military policy is being reflected in these laws and legislation.

The State Ikh Khural, in keeping with the proposal of the President of Mongolia, taking due account of the changes in the international and regional military, political, economic, scientific, technological and military affairs, shall make adjustments to the basis of the state military policy of Mongolia.

II. THE BASIC DIRECTIONS OF THE STATE POLICY ON AVERTING THE THREAT OF ARMED AGGRESSION

Although mutual understanding, trust and partnership are becoming a predominating trend in international relations, the threats of wars and armed conflicts have not fully dissipated and a collective security system is non-existent in the world, and in the Asia-Pacific region including. Proceeding from this premise, the danger and threats of local wars and border armed skirmishes continue to persist.

Mongolia shall conform its peace-loving policy of creating a favorable external environment of ensuring its national security and averting the threat of all kinds of wars and armed conflicts with the following universally-recognized international legal principles:

- Mongolia shall not consider the use or the threat to use military force as the solution to disputed issues and shall not recognize any kind of violence and aggression;
- Under no circumstances will it resort to the first use of military force against another country, it shall not pose any military danger or threat, and it shall not take part in any war or armed conflict unless it itself becomes a target of armed aggression from outside;
- It shall honor, in keeping with the UN Charter, its commitment to provide, mediate and conciliate support and good-offices in the activities of the United Nations Organization;
- It shall not join any military alliance or bloc unless the independence, sovereignty and territorial integrity of Mongolia comes under military threat or danger, or if such a danger and threat become imminent;
- It shall strictly pursue the policy of barring entry into, stationing of and passing through its territory foreign military force in the event of the absence of such a Mongolian law.

Any country which threatens the use of military force or unleashes an armed aggression against the independence, sovereignty and territorial inviolability of Mongolia or all allies of such an armed invasion shall be considered enemies. Mongolia shall wage its own armed struggle for self-defense against foreign armed aggression.

Mongolia shall regard the following instances as cases of armed aggression against the country:

- Intrusion into or invasion of the territory of Mongolia by military force by any country;
- Armed attack on Mongolia or its military installations from outside its borders;
- Armed forces of a foreign country, while stationed in or passing through the country's territory, violates the Law of Mongolia inter alia such a provision;
- Any country, which is leasing the territory of Mongolia temporarily or on a long-term basis in keeping with the laws and legislation of the country, uses that territory for the purpose of armed aggression against a third country;
- Any country which intentionally infiltrates specially trained mercenaries into Mongolia for subsequently carrying out terrorist, subversive and other illegal operations on the territory of Mongolia;
- Any party involved in a domestic armed conflict in any country violates or intrudes into the borders of Mongolia.

Mongolia, while implementing its self-defense objectives, relying on the concepts of its national security and foreign policies, shall make political and diplomatic means its precedence.

The supreme objectives of the state of Mongolia are to officially conduct multi-lateral security-related talks and negotiations on the international level and in the Asia-Pacific region; take an active part in preventing all kinds of wars and armed aggressions, and consolidating bilateral and multi-lateral military confidence; maintain many partners; and, consistently conduct a foreign policy designed at guaranteeing its security through political means while upholding its vital national interests.

Mongolia shall make its territory a nuclear-weapons-free zone and shall strengthen its through multilateral guarantees, and it shall take an active part in the policies and activities designed at prohibiting nuclear-weapons tests and upholding the nuclear non-proliferation regime.

Mongolia shall actively support international effort at banning the development, production, stockpiling and employing of mass destruction weapons and their subsequent destruction, and shall cooperate with other countries and international organizations in this respect.

Mongolia shall promote all-round friendly relations and cooperation with the nations of the world and with the neighboring powers, in particular, and it shall prevent the rise to any cause or reason for any external military threat by way of refraining from or preventing the danger of being drawn into any activity that could have a detrimental effect on the establishment of military confidence and on the vital national interests as well.

Mongolia shall establish and promote military ties with the United Nations, international military organizations and with other countries.

Mongolia shall set up and reinforce an integrated defense system and build up its military capacity.

Mongolia shall undertake the following actions in the event armed aggression from another country becomes obvious:

- Conduct talks and negotiations with the country or subject preparing to mount an armed aggression, and conduct an energetic political and diplomatic effort designed at averting the threat of the armed aggression and protecting itself by way of appealing to seeking the support of the United Nations and other related international organizations, as well as, influential nations;
- Conclude, without delay, defense-related treaties and agreements with the United Nations, international military alliances and influential countries supporting Mongolia, establish relations of military alliance with them, deploy their armed force on the country's territory in conformity with the laws and legislation, and seek military hardware assistance;
- Carry out actions, strictly in keeping with the laws and legislation, designed at declaring a state of war in the country or at repulsing the armed aggression.

The policy of preventing mass disturbance and disorder within the country spearheaded against the foundations of state and social structures, established in compliance with the Constitution of Mongolia, and against national unity and harmony.

III. THE DIRECTIONS OF PREPARING THE POPULATION, THE ECONOMY AND THE TERRITORY FOR DEFENDING MONGOLIA

The state shall implement the following schemes with the objective of ensuring the nation's preparedness in safeguarding the independence, sovereignty, territorial integrity and the inviolability of the state borders of Mongolia from external armed aggression:

- The effort of government agencies at all levels and non-government organizations shall be coordinated and directed towards inculcating in all the citizens and the young people the ideals of patriotism, and promoting military-civilian relationship;
- The health, educational, psychological and physical training of the population shall be improved and public order and discipline shall be tightened;
- A policy incorporating social and economic incentives shall be developed and implemented designed at enhancing the interest and striving of the citizens to serve in the army;
- The military and strategic training of senior officials of the central and local state and administrative institutions and agencies shall be upgraded by way of involving them in drills and training;
- An integrated system of top defense management shall be set up and strengthened;
- An integrated system of protecting the civilians from the dangers of destructive means, natural and other mass calamities, and industrial accidents, and eliminating their consequences;
- While determining the basic guidelines of economic and social development, defense interests should also be given due consideration;
- Set up a buffer stock of essential commodities and materials that could be invariably required by the defense and the population in times of both peace and war;
- Ensure that the central and local state and administrative institutions and agencies, industrial and business enterprises, cultural and scientific institutions are prepared in well advance to switch from peace-time to a war status;
- Business entities and enterprises, irrespective of their form of ownership, must be prepared to transfer, supply and manufacture the necessary machinery, equipment and materials for use by the defense;
- A set of measures shall be implemented permanently to equip the territory of Mongolia for the purpose of self-defense.

IV. THE DIRECTIONS OF TRAINING THE ARMED FORCES

Mongolia shall have a compact, capable and a professionally-oriented armed forces tailored to the peace-time defense needs and the economic potentials of Mongolia.

The armed forces shall have military equipment and materiel suited to the self-defense policy.

The personnel of the armed forces shall be replenished by a mixed method bringing it closer to the standard of a professional army.

The structure and branches of armed forces and the appropriate correlation of them shall be established by law with due consideration for the military and political situation, and the defense needs and requirements.

The illegal establishing of military organizations on the territory of Mongolia shall be prohibited.

The function and the principles, structure and leadership of the armed forces as well as the rules and procedures for services in the armed forces shall be established by law.

The armed forces shall, while checking and repudiating external armed aggression and up until decisive actions are taken to ensure pressure and influence are imposed on the aggressors on the part of the United Nations and other related international organizations, as well as influential states, work to create the necessary conditions for the leadership of the country to conduct an active political and diplomatic effort.

The armed forces shall fulfill the following functions in time of peace:

- It shall be prepared to safeguard the national independence, sovereignty and territorial integrity from external armed aggression;
- It shall protect the state borders and monitor the inviolability of the country's airspace;
- It shall guard important state projects;
- It shall render assistance in protecting the population and other material assets from the dangers of destructive means, natural and other mass calamities, and industrial accidents;
- It shall set up a mobilization reserve and train the population in military matters;
- It shall render support and assistance in humanitarian acts;
- It shall carry out functions within the UN Peace-keeping forces and other functions as stipulated in the law;

The armed forces shall, in times of peace, ensure the preparations necessary for carrying out its duty of checking and repudiating potential armed aggression.

Should Mongolia become a target of external armed aggression, the country shall wage a struggle to check and repulse the aggression by uniting and mobilizing all the available means of force and by relying on the support and involvement of the civilians. In this regard, Mongolia reserves the right to seek the support and assistance of other countries and international organizations in conformity with the UN Charter.

The armed forces shall be readied in the following manner in order to repulse any potential armed aggression:

- Streamline the structure and organizational set-up of the armed forces, increase the number of professionally-oriented army units and formations and enhance their capability;
- Set up a mobilization system with united management and planning tailored to the specific features of the country's market-oriented relations and the roles and duties of the army;
- Streamline the system of training military personnel, and upgrade the knowledge and skill of senior and professional military personnel;
- Introduce scientific and technological achievements in the defense sector, set up a reliable information network, and promote the development of military science and traditional art of warfare;
- Study and analyze the changes and progress in the global and regional military and political policies, and the status of military, the lessons of the local wars, conflicts and border protection, and, streamline the rules and regulations of replenishing the military personnel and the form of doing military service.

MONGOLIA'S INTERNAL AND EXTERNAL SITUATION AFTER 1990

It is more than common to start virtually any article or book on Mongolia with a reference to Mongolia being the *huge, landlocked country between China and Russia*. As much as this is commonplace it is unarguably true and contributes a lot to the socio-political pecularities of this country with such a huge area and a rather small population.

When *glasnost'* came to transform the former Soviet Union, its waves spilled over to Mongolia, too. In the early 1990s, Mongolia underwent what became known internationally as *peaceful revolution*, and since then, with a new constitution passed in 1992, several democratic elections and a landslide victory of a democratic party coalition in 1996 the very foundations of Mongolia's society and national identity have been exposed to continuous transformation. Mongolia's national economy virtually collapsed after the breakdown of the COMECON, and after several years of negative growth Mongolia is now recovering and developing a privatized national economy. Democratic reform and economical transformation on the interior side force Mongolia's defense system to restructure and to scale down significantly; the end of the Cold War, the collapse of the Soviet Union as a Bloc and China's new international position prompt a wholly new international situation which, though being far from the so-called New World Order of the early 1990s, profoundly determines the basis of Mongolia's international relations and security doctrine.

National security of a country with a small population cannot depend on military power; Mongolia's vital security interests should rather be seen

> within a framework of political and diplomatic actions compatible with the patterns of human development and values, equitable relations and confidence among nations

as it is stated in the introduction to the White Paper (p. 6).

The White Paper was introduced at an international press conference (Feb. 23rd, 1998) by the Minister of Defense, D. Dorligjaw. One of the first questions raised by members of the national press was the concern that such a White Paper unprecedented as it is could seriously hamper Mongolia's national security by betraying military and diplomatic secrets. D. Dorligjaw answers this question in his foreword to the White Paper:

> With the rapid advance of democratic reforms in Mongolia and the associated profound changes in its political and economic systems and social consciousness, the notions of war and peace, military and army are becoming enriched with new substance and content. All this draws the keen interest of our people which also has become an important justification for the publication of the White Paper. As the country increasingly embraces democracy, the people of Mongolia have received greater freedom to express their views and opinions on all issues related to the activities of the state, including its defense policy. All citizens of Mongolia, military personnel and reservists icluded, are entitled to concrete information on our defense policy and armed forces.
>
> It is our firm conviction that the people of Mongolia and the world community will understand and respect the fact that the defense policy being pursued by us is forthright, with a vision that is compatible with the universal trend of human

development, and is of a firm adherence to the principles of mutual trust and confidence.

SECURITY ISSUES AND THE NATIONAL DEFENSE CONCEPT

The national security concept of Mongolia changed dramatically after the end of the Cold War and the complete withdrawal of Soviet troops in 1992 from Mongolia's territory. While Mongolia used to serve as a buffer state between China and Russia during the Cold War, the Mongolians participated in the defense system of the Warsaw Pact States acting as the Eastern frontier, effectively shielding the former Soviet Union from direct contact with her estranged former comrade, the People's Republic of China. China was regarded *the* enemy, a threat not only to the USSR but also to Mongolia. It was the mission of the Mongolian army to build up armaments and the number of military personnel to a level sufficient to carry out joint operations with the Soviet armed forces (p. 5) in order to minimize the military threat from the south.

With the diminishing rôle of ideology and military power as a primary means of defining global and regional relations and the end of the Cold War one of the major blocs disappeared from the map and a major reason for a military build-up at the crossroads of the political, economic and cultural interests of the regional countries and super powers, and at the junction of influence of the major world religions (p. 4) ceased to exist. The former concept is now replaced by a strict neutral stance.

In peacetime, Mongolia no longer permits the stationing of foreign troops in her territory and has written this new position into the new Constitution promulgated in 1992.

Due the dramatical changes of the external security environment Mongolia is now developing new approaches for her external relations and her national security. The first, most important factor is a balanced relationship with the two neighbours Russia and China which is ideally complemented by ``relying on a third force" as this key orientation in the country's foreign policy is called.

This is on one hand made possible through the cessation of military confrontation between both neighbours as well as their refraining from striving for military influence in Mongolia. On the other hand, Mongolia is not only bound to seek influential partners in the Asia-Pacific region but is also determined to develope a strategy serving both the country as well as fostering regional security and stability.

Mongolia considers, however, the potential of internal instability in China and China's contradictions in dealing with some other countries as a cause of concern. Though political and territorial claims of China against Mongolia were settled long ago and China is now rapidly developing as an influential power in Asia due to her open door policy and economic growth, Mongolia does not see that there is no garantuee that the future development of internal social, political and ethnic controversies will not lead to a situation similar to that in the former Soviet Union. (p. 21/22) Mongolia signed treaties on friendly relations and cooperation with the Russian Federation in January 1993 and with China in April 1994.

Both countries respect Mongolia's non-aligned, non-nuclear policy, and Mongolia hopes that the relations between Russia and China may further improve as it seen as eventually possible that a trilateral framework between Russia, China and Mongolia can be built.

MONGOLIA'S MILITARY DOCTRINE AND LEGISLATION

Only in 1992 Mongolia started building an integrated system of legal regulations covering all aspects of security, armed forces and defense issues. Under the former socialist system, these questions were handled in the form of decrees issued by the Politburo of the MPRP and the Council of Ministers. This structure now being defunct, legal provisions had to be designed to fill the vacuum. The first and most significant step was to cover all basic aspects of national security and defense in appropriate articles in the Constitution promulgated in February 1992, the Law on the Defense of Mongolia was adopted in 1993, and in 1994 the State Great Xural adopted a document called ``Fundamentals of the Military Doctrine of Mongolia". The Doctrine puts forward the principles of conformity with universally recognized principles of international law, and in particular Mongolia discards the use of force or the threat to use force as a means of settling disputes. Furthermore it will not participate in wars and conflicts unless it falls victim to foreign aggression. Mongolia shall fulfill her UN Charter obligations and support UN activities

> by dispatching observers and/or by offering its good offices, mediation and conciliatory services; (p. 44)

Mongolia will not be part of any Military alliance unless the independence and sovereignty of Mongolia is directly threatened, and will strictly adhere to the policy of not allowing foreign troops to enter, be stationed in or pass through the national territory in the absence of relevant Mongolian legislation. Formal agreements on military-to-military cooperation have been signed with the United States of America and at least 15 other regional and international partners including Japan, Kazakstan, India, France and Germany.

The White Paper offers detailed information on the structure of the defense system, Mongolia's framework of international cooperation, its defense budget and its personnel, and reveals an outline of the armed forces and their mission, structure and organization. It offers additional information on civilian activities of the armed forces (Construction Corps), and shows trends and pending issues like linking defense expenditures to a fixed percentage of the GNP (following Japan's example).

MONGOLIA DEFENCE UNIVERSITY

Defence University of Mongolia
Mongolia, Ulaanbaatar-22. BKHIS.
Tel/Fax: 976 - 11 - 458673
Email: dum@dum.edu.mn

The Damdiny Sukhbaatar Defense University, one of the first professional educational institutions in Mongolia, was founded in 1921. It provides professional military and academic educational programs in all degrees.

Rich with glorious battle experience and historical traditions, the University, since its founding, has been a part of the Mongolian educational system and the sole source for preparing military personnel for the Armed Forces of Mongolia. It has produced thousands of distinguished officers and specialists, who served the country loyally and honorably. The University and its graduates have significantly contributed to the defense of the nation from foreign aggression as well as the development of the country's economy. A clear illustration of this are the five Heroes of Mongolia, one Hero of Labor and many other meritorious persons and scientists, renowned statesmen and military leaders who count among the graduates. Therefore, for its commitment and contribution the University has been awarded the highest state awards, namely, the Order of Sukhbaatar and Red Banner Order for Merits in Combat.

In accordance with the new organizational structure done within the framework of the policy that is to bring the defense educational, training, and research establishments under one administration and organization, the Defense University is structurally comprised of the following:

- The Defense Management Academy,
- The Defense Research Institute,
- The Academic Education Institute,
- The General Purpose Military College,
- The Military Orchestra College,
- The NCO Training Center and
- Sixteen academic and military branch departments as well as administrative, logistic, finance and other sections.

At the University's disposal are 100 classrooms and laboratories, a central library and libraries at each respective college and institute, a gymnasium, a soccer field, obstacle courses, behind-the-wheel driving area, a center for cultural activities, and a field training center, all dedicated to provide high standards of education and training and support recreational and social activities.

The University integrates both military and civilian faculty. Of the entire faculty, military command and staff college graduates constitute 29.0 percent, military academy graduates 44.0 percent, and civilian university or college graduates 27 percent. 30.0 percent of the total amount of researchers have graduated from military command and staff colleges, 40.0 percent from military academies, and 30.0 percent from civilian universities and colleges. About 30 percent of the faculty members and researchers hold a Doctor of Science or Philosophy and the rest hold master degrees. Forty percent of them are professors and associate professors. Of the entire faculty, researchers and staff, 50 percent are uniformed personnel and the rest are civilians.

Many faculty and staff members have been recognized and rewarded for their distinguished service. The University has three Distinguished Workers of Science, nineteen Distinguished Workers of Education, nine Distinguished Workers of Culture, one Distinguished Worker of Health Care, and four Distinguished amateur singers, dancers, and musicians.

The Defense University is fulfilling its goals and objectives to provide the Armed Forces with capable, well-educated, and knowledgeable personnel. It runs Ph.D. programs in military law, military history, and military and technical sciences, and master's degrees, bachelor's degrees and diploma educational programs in 14 military and 11 civilian specialties.

- **The Defense Management Academy** gives students graduate military education, specialized in combined arms and services strategy, tactics, and military leadership and confers a Master of Military Science degree upon the completion of a thesis.
- **The Defense Research Institute** conducts a diversity of researchand scientific works tailored to meet specific needs of the Science and Technical Council of the Ministry of Defense and other defense agencies as well as the Defense University. It is currently working on more than 20 research projects.

- **The Academic Education Institute** runs a four-year bachelor degree program in 10 specialized areas and a two-year master degree program in law, state administration, economics and a variety of engineering degrees.
- **The General Purpose Military College** confers a Bachelor degree in 10 civilian specialties, such as public administration management, economics, and a variety of engineering degrees, and a Diploma of Completion in 10 military specialties, thus producing officers with both civilian and military specialties.
- **The Military Orchestra College** confers a Bachelor of Arts degree to students specialized as conductors of orchestras and as officers of units' orchestral services and gives a Diploma of Completion to professional musicians.
- **The NCO Training Center** prepares professional noncommissioned officers in 30 different specialties.

Since 1998, the Defense University's international relations have greatly expanded. It has direct and productive relations with eight foreign defense and military universities, colleges, and schools. About 40 instructors, researchers, and cadets from the University are studying or undergoing training in the Russian Federation, the People's Republic of China, the United States of America, the Federal Republic of Germany, Republic of Korea, Great Britain, Japan and Turkey.

In order to improve the content, structure, organization, design and implementation of the curricula and courses and to enhance the model and environment of learning and instruction, all to be consistent and relevant to meet the new requirements in preparing the defense personnel, the Defense University has developed, and since the academic year 1999-2000, is implementing "Development Program of the Defense

University through the Year 2005," including a "Business Plan," new curricula and others. As a result, the content and technology of the academic and military training programs have been modified and renewed, thus bringing up the University's standard to those of domestic as well as foreign defense and military universities and colleges and creating the legal base to develop it as a complex of academic and military training and research.

On behalf of the Defence University of Mongolia, one of the foremost professional educational institutions of the country with its rich historical traditions and great combat experiences, I would like to express my appreciation for your participation and wish you a lot of success in your jobs, happiness in your life and all the best.

It is certain that globalization, because of the dynamic change in economics and technology, has touched the whole world. It is clear, then, that aspiration to value the common interests of mankind will be major factors in the growth of the world in the beginning of the XXI century. Higher education in the XXI century will continue to be a primary factor in determining human rights, democracy and prosperity. Peacemaking efforts will also continue to determine a nation's well-being as has been the trend embracing the world.

Social changes taking place since 1990 have forced the reform of the old education system in accordance with the new circumstances and arising needs. These tendencies have encompassed the preparation of the cadres for the defence of the nation which include the Defence University of Mongolia. Accordingly, we have been changing the content and technology of training and scientific research and are converting from the former tendency to prepare only military specialists. Training is being changed and organized in order to prepare patriotic, physically strong and morally sound elite personnel with higher academic education as well military branch specialization that could meet the needs and requirements of the armed forces and public services. As a result, Defence University graduates could serve not only in the Armed Forces but also in public or business professions after serving a certain amount of time in the military. Thus, The University assume its proper place in a democratic, free enterprise-economy society and respect for basics of human rights.

Our University is always open to those who are well trained and motivated and accepts individuals determined to serve their country, government and its people with honour as officer-citizens and public servants

The Defense University's mission is to prepare state servants and commissioned and non-commissioned officers who highly respect and value the national vital interests and historical and cultural heritage; have a high sense of patriotism; have Leadership skills; are morally and physically sound and courageous; are loyal and honest to the state and military service; are highly educated in civilian and military affairs and professionally competent; and to conduct defense research and scientific works of high quality.

TRAINING CURRICULA ARE AS FOLLOWS:

- **The Defense Management Academy** gives students graduate military education, specialized in combined arms and services strategy, tactics, and military leadership and confers a Master of Military Science degree upon the completion of a thesis.
- **The Defense Research Institute** conducts a diversity of researchand scientific works tailored to meet specific needs of the Science and Technical Council of the Ministry of Defense and other defense agencies as well as the Defense University. It is currently working on more than 20 research projects.
- **The Academic Education Institute** runs a four-year bachelor degree program in 10 specialized areas and a two-year master degree program in law, state administration, economics and a variety of engineering degrees.
- **The General Purpose Military College** confers a Bachelor degree in 10 civilian specialties, such as public administration management, economics, and a variety of engineering degrees, and a Diploma of Completion in 10 military specialties, thus producing officers with both civilian and military specialties.
- **The Military Orchestra College** confers a Bachelor of Arts degree to students specialized as conductors of orchestras and as officers of units' orchestral services and gives a Diploma of Completion to professional musicians.
- **The NCO Training Center** prepares professional noncommissioned officers in 30 different specialties.

ARMY HISTORY

THE ARMY AND THE EMPIRE[1]

Never before and never since has the world witnessed anything like the avalanche of conquests that followed Jenghiz Khan's election as supreme ruler of the Mongol nation. There has never been anyone to equal him. Someone said he was like a desert storm that tore up cities in its path. The Mongol assault was the last and greatest of all predatory incursions of nomadism on the civilized world, both East and West. From the thirteenth century to the fifteenth century nomadism from Central Asia dominated the known world. Some authorities have called these three centuries the Age of the Mongols.

[1] By Catriona Macpherson

From the beginning of history there has been conflict between nomad and civilized or sedentary people. It could be called a clash between the "haves" and the "have-nots". Civilization bred complacency, an open invitation to predatory men. Again and again the aggressive nomad brought fresh blood and leadership to a static, civilized people. The Chinese civilization was a prime example of people ripe for invasion.

The conquests of Jenghiz Khan and his immediate successors surprised the civilized world and no doubt the Mongol khans themselves, with the probable exception of Jenghiz. From relative obscurity in the twelfth century, he welded the Mongols into an awesome military machine which was feared and hated by most of the known world.

In the Year of the Tiger, 1206, all the clans of the steppes, the people who lived in felt tents, met at a Great Kuriltai at the source of the Onon River. Under the nine-tailed white banner, the clansmen swore allegiance to the 39 year old Jenghiz Khan and proclaimed him Emperor of the Steppes. Under his strong leadership, for the first time, the Mongols achieved national unity. To strengthen his position, he sent armies to intimidate any tribes around his borders who did not submit to his authority.

His was a new power, based on tribal unity, centered on one person who had already shown his ability to conquer and provide security and stability. His election to supreme ruler of all the people who would henceforth be known as Mongols, should have caused the rest of the world to sit up and take notice. For the first time the united tribes had a common name, Mongol, which soon attracted many other warriors who sought adventure and wealth. It was under Jenghiz Khan's leadership that the Mongols began their conquest of countries with a more advanced civilization than their own. The Mongol people and their ruler had the same objective and now they did not stop with booty but began to build a huge, powerful state which ultimately was to reach from the Pacific Ocean to Hungary and from Russia to northern India. It was the largest contiguous land empire in the history of man. Not even Alexander the Great, the Romans, or Napoleon conquered and ruled such a large empire.

To conquer territory and mold it into an empire, required a well-trained, well-equipped army, which took time, skill and patience to build. Jenghiz Khan laid the foundations for his army before he was elected Khan, as one by one he conquered the tribes of the steppes and incorporated them into his army, the best of the thirteenth century world. Twentieth century soldiers would recognize in their own military experience the tactics and training principles, the structure of command, and the organization of the Mongol army. Armies of today still use the military tactic of softening up the enemy by artillery fire, pioneered by the Mongols, the difference being, the Mongols used arrows, and stones and other missiles fired from siege engines, instead of heavy artillery cannon.

His old night and day guards were increased to 1,000 men each. Later they were strengthened to 10,000 and became the Imperial Guard, keshik, which was under the control of the commander-in- chief. 1,000 of these were the emperor's personal guard, and only fought when Jenghiz Khan went to war. During times of peace, they acted as part of the court guard: supervising the palace staff, tents, ox and camel herds, had charge of the palace wagons, the Yak's tail banners, lances, kettledrums, dishes and drinking bowls. They also handled the storage and issue of quivers, bows, armor and all other weapons. They saw to the horses, loading and unloading the palace tents, and the issuing of raw silk. They assisted Shigikutuku who carried out the law.

The Mongols now formed one united army, organized on a decimal system, which was not new, as armies before Jenghiz Khan's time had been so organized. It was a simple but effective system. A troop of 10, called an arban, was the smallest unit. A squadron of 100, made up of 10 arbans, was called a jagun. A regiment of 1,000, made up of 10 jaguns, was called a minghan. A division of 10,000, made up of 10 minghans, was called a tumen. Generally there would be two to three tumens in a Mongol army. All able-bodied men between 14 and 60 years of age were liable for military service.

The army was divided into three parts. The Jun-gar was the Army of the Left Wing or East, the Baran-gar was the Army of the Right Wing or West, and the Khol was the Army of the Center.

The decimal system facilitated giving orders. No officer had to give orders to more than 10 men and everyone was responsible only to the officer above him. Order and discipline could be effectively maintained. Not only in organization but in discipline the Mongol Army was superior to other armies of its time and for some time to come.

On a campaign 200 men were sent two days' ride ahead to act as scouts, 200 more to the rear, and 200 on each flank so that the army could not be attacked by surprise. They carried no baggage with them on long campaigns. Each man carried two leather flasks to hold milk and a pignate, a small earthen pot for cooking meat. If they killed an animal and had no pot, they took out the stomach, emptied it, filled it with water, and cooked it over a fire. When it was done, they ate flesh, pot and all. Shelter from rain was provided by a small, felt tent. They could ride ten days without food or fire, living on blood from their horses. They slit open a vein, drank the blood and then carefully bound up the wound for horses were too important to sacrifice . Sometimes they carried dried blood with them, which they dissolved in water before drinking. They carried dried milk in a leather flask, to which they added water, before drinking. While they rode ,the milk dissolved in the water and provided them with a nourishing drink. In addition to dried milk, they carried qumiz, millet and dried meat. The dried milk (iron rations) and the small tents (one-man `dog-tents') were centuries ahead of their time.

The Mongols' chief weapons were speed and surprise. No army equaled theirs in mobility, horsemanship or archery. Training provided discipline and organization, factors which for some time to come, made their army invincible. Early on Jenghiz Khan found that sound military decisions could only be made when he was well- informed. He employed a network of spies, to obtain information from travellers, merchants, dissidents, scouts, and anyone else who might have an iota of useful information. He learned about mountain passes, river fords, roads, fortified places, towns, cities and military forces they might encounter on a campaign. His battle plans would be drawn up based on this information. At a kuriltai plans for a campaign would be discussed, how many men and horses would be needed, (at least two to three for each man), what supplies and livestock on the hoof would be necessary and what would be a suitable season to campaign. The Russian campaign was timed so the Mongols would be crossing frozen rivers and moving through Russia on terrain similar to their homeland. When everything had been discussed down to the minutest detail, and preparations completed, the commander would review the army to see if it was up to strength. A general inspection would be made of the horses and equipment, and orders given for the troops to march. Mongols usually entered a country in widely spaced columns but in the face of a large enemy they were able to unite with unbelievable speed. They used a system of messengers, out of which grew the imperial postal service, yam, which could transmit information over vast distances in an incredibly short time. It operated somewhat like the Pony Express of the American West.

Unquestioned obedience to his commander, ability to endure unspeakable hardships, unbelievable mastery of the bow, excellent horsemanship, with horses obedient to their riders, made the Mongol warrior superior to his enemy. The horse archer could ride in, fire a deadly volley of arrows, turn and disappear, and reappear just as suddenly, to harrass and demoralize the enemy until he finally gave up. Only after the enemy and his horses were worn down by charges did the Mongols fight at close quarters.

The Mongols were the first armies in military history to use "fire power", arrows and siege engines to precede an assault. Each warrior carried a file for sharpening arrowheads, a small axe, a lasso, rope for pulling siege engines, needle and thread, and an awl. Some troopers carried lances with hooks on the end, used to drag a man from his saddle. The Mongol horsemen carried a composite bow, their favorite, and a long bow. The long bow was used when they were fighting at long range and the composite bow was used in a charge and in fighting from the saddle at close quarters. The composite bow had a pull of 166 pounds and was deadly accurate at a range of 200 to 300 yards. The horse archers carried three quivers each containing different types of arrows for different ranges and uses. One type could penetrate armor, another was used against unprotected troops, and still a third type was used for arrow grenades and flaming naptha. In addition to mounted archers, the army had both light and heavy cavalry. The light cavalry carried bows and javelins, and the heavy cavalry carried lances with hooks on the ends, and sometimes maces.

They both carried sabers for hand to hand fighting. Shields were generally used when on guard duty. Eventually their light artillery used various missile-throwing machines, mangonels, catapults, ballista and trebuchets. Smaller siege engines could be taken apart, packed on animals or in carts and go anywhere. Their fire was accurate and rapid. In 1220 when Jenghiz Khan invaded the west, he took with him a corps of Chinese artillerymen and machines they called ho pao, or fire projectors. In the fall of 1225 he fielded the greatest war machine the world had ever seen. His armies gained experience in campaigns from the Yellow Sea to the Crimea, and they possessed every siege engine known to man at that time. It looked as if the army was invincible.

For protection the Mongols wore armor, of leather or iron, with a raw silk coat under their armor for additional protection. An arrow, when it hit its target, would carry the unpierced silk into the flesh and the arrow could be removed by pulling gently at the coat; the Mongols did not abandon their wounded. Their lamellar armor consisted of four pieces of overlapping plates. These were lacquered to provide protection against humidity. The helmet was of iron or steel and the drop or neck protection was leather. Some Mongols made horse armor in five sections; one on each side from head to tail, fastened to the saddle and behind the saddle on its back and also on the neck, a third section stretched over the hindquarters and was tied to the side parts, with a hole through which the tail emerged, a fourth piece covered the breast and a fifth piece, an iron plate for the forehead, was fastened on each side of the neck.

The tulughma, a typical Mongol battle formation, was made up of five ranks spaced at wide intervals. The heavy cavalry in the two front ranks wore complete armor, carried swords, lances, and maces; and their horses were armored. The three rear ranks were light cavalry, wore no armor and carried bows and javelins. When the battle began part of the light cavalry swept around the ends to harry the enemy as he advanced. As the enemy drew near, the rest of the light cavalry moved forward through the spaces in the front lines and overwhelmed the enemy with arrows and javelins. When the enemy ranks were thrown into disorder, the rear ranks retired back through the intervals and the front lines charged in for the kill.

Mongol battle movements were controlled by signals with the black and white flags of the squadrons during the daylight and by lanterns at night. Thus the troops could be deployed speedily in comparative silence further demoralizing the enemy. At the start of a charge the Mongols were accompanied by the naccara, war drums carried on camel's backs. Once the drums pierced the silence, the Mongols rushed forward, screaming ferociously.

Other tactics included a feigned retreat to lure the enemy into a prepared ambush. There they would pour down on the enemy and annihilate them. When they met a superior force they often sent out riders to stir up the dust behind their horses by using branches tied to their horse's tails. The enemy would think large reinforcements were coming up and would retreat.

The Mongols had no equal in field warfare. At first they had no experience in siege warfare, and did not know how to effectively break into a walled city, nor did they know what to do with the city once they did break in. Realizing their lack of training in siege warfare, they used captured foreign siege experts and soon the Mongols were attacking cities, with newly acquired catapults, mangonels, ladders and burning oil; and battalions of Chinese engineers and artillerymen. It is true that atrocities were committed under the leadership of Jenghiz Khan, but in the Mongol milieu of his time, they knew no other way of warfare; only the nomad's way. Much of the barbarity of the Mongols came from ignorance; they perceived the settled areas useful only for raids to capture slaves, women and booty. Because they had had no experience with conquered cities, they killed the inhabitants and burned the cities. When they realized they could use cities to consolidate and expand their power, and be a source of future wealth, they were spared. Because they lacked the time and knowledge, the Mongols employed many foreigners to help with the administration of their captured cities.

Many historians believed that Mongol victories were due to an overwhelming superiority of numbers. Further research disproves this excuse of medieval historians and shows that often the Mongols were outnumbered. Their superior fire power and military tactics led their opponents to believe the Mongols outnumbered them. The basis of Mongol power was their undeniable prowess on the battlefield. In addition they wasted nothing, adopted anything useful: Greek and Persian physicians, naptha incendiary missiles, western-style weight-and-counterpoise siege catapults (trebuchet, ballista, and Mangonel). The Emperor was supreme commander, but once a battle plan was decided upon, the generals carried out the operations without interference from the Emperor. Command of the armies was held by the royal princes in name only. The actual control went to the experienced generals, the most famous of whom were Jebe Noyan and Subodai Bahadur in the Western campaigns and Mukhali in China. Promotions were by merit, not seniority, and both Jebe and Subodai were made generals before they were twenty five. Through the years students of military tactics have studied the campaign strategies of Subodai; among the most well-known were Napoleon, Gustavus Adolphus, Rommel and Patton.

Discipline was harsh, but Mongol warriors were treated fairly, and by and large were better off than the soldiers of most armies up until recent times. They received no pay but were given a fair share of the booty. Officers usually came from the Mongol aristocracy and a class of freemen, darkhat. The Mongols were convinced they were invincible and had been sent by The Everlasting Blue Sky to conquer the world, and this could not help but have a positive effect on their fighting.

They believed the Sulde or guardian spirit of the Altan Uruk, Golden Family resided in the great white standard that led the Army to near world conquest. Many Mongols, to this day, preserve and revere the White Banner of the Sulde believing it is the same one that led the armies of Jenghiz Khan to victory. They believe that the soul of the emperor entered the banner and he became the guardian of his clan. There is a Messianic belief among large numbers of Mongols that he will rise again and lead them to new power and glory.

Jenghiz Khan died in 1227 at the height of his power. He was master of the largest empire ever created in the lifetime of one person. Under the khanships of Ogodai, Guyuk, Mongke, and Qublai, the rest of the Mongol Empire was forged. It reached from the Pacific Ocean to Hungary and from Russia to northern India, being not only conquered but governed by the Mongols. Other territories, such as Mien and Novgorod, paid them tribute.

Jenghiz Khan had not only created a huge, well-organized empire, but had also built an experienced, victorious army, the command of which he entrusted to his brilliant generals. He had laid the ground-work for an administrative structure and had given them a rigid code of laws. However, he could not have risen to a position of such power and glory without the aid of his trusted companions, andas, who had worked just as hard as he had to build up his empire. He was not surrounded by flattering, servile followers but devoted, reliable men who could carry out any assignment he gave them. His greatest gifts to his sons were the Mongol Army and this body of loyal, talented servants, whom he counted upon to maintain the integrity of the empire. According to his will, Ogodai, Jagadai and Tolui divided up the main horde, his personal army. The system of mobilizing, training and maneuvering continued as before. The veteran generals were there to carry on the extension of the empire.

Jenghiz, a man of iron will, foresight, political and military genius, held the empire together during his lifetime. At one point in his earlier years he voiced a fear that his descendants would dress in fine silks, eat rich food, drink sweet wines and surround themselves with luxury, forgetting their nomad roots. He always kept a square of gray felt under his throne as a reminder of his nomad heritage. Just prior to his death, however, it was evident that he planned for his descendants and the Mongol aristocracy to continue to follow the nomad ways, which he believed to be superior to the lifestyle of sedentary people. The nomads had an independent, less complicated way of life compared to sedentary people. Jenghiz saw sedentary people as forever being slaves either to material possessions, conquerors or both. He believed nomads were destined to rule over sedentary people.

Late in 1226, word came to Jenghiz Khan that his oldest son, Jochi, planned to revolt and was assembling an army for that purpose. Details are scanty as to an open revolt but it was known that Jochi wanted his own kingdom. He had been openly critical of his father's and brothers' policy during the Khwarezm campaign. After the war he retired to his appanaged territory in what is now part of Russia and thereafter made many excuses not to go to Karakorum when summoned by his father. He died in February of 1227 just six months before the Conqueror, but his successors were to follow his policy and remain aloof from the Khan. Looking back it would seem that this was the first sign of dissension from within. In anticipation of his death, he divided up his empire.

To the sons of his deceased eldest son, Jochi, he gave the still-to- be-conquered western Eurasian steppe, the land to the north and west to the Altai, as far as Mongol arms could conquer. To his second son, Jagadai, went the old Khwareizmian Empire and the land east of it to the Altai Mountains. Ogodai, his third son, was made ruler of China and to his youngest son, Tolui, went the Mongolian homeland, a nomad custom. Each had his own territory and armies, each was to cooperate with and obey the new emperor, who would be the first to assume the title of Khaghan (Great Khan) to further expand the empire's frontiers.

Jenghiz chose his third son, Ogodai, as his successor. According to custom, Jenghiz was elected as Khan of the Mongols because he was the strongest chief. Ogodai wasn't selected because he was the strongest, but because he was generous and forgiving, had enough willpower not to get involved in irresponsible actions and he could act severly when it was necessary. Because of their nature, neither Jagadai nor Tolui could obey each other, if one were chosen khan; but both could give their allegiance to Ogodai. Jenghiz Khan's decision to choose one of his sons as his successor led the aristocracy and the princes to believe that future khans should be chosen from the line of Ogodai. This departure from custom was to cause trouble within the Empire.

The Conqueror believed that if enough Mongols were educated, they could eliminate the employment of foreigners in civil administration, although while he needed them, he never hesitated to use them. He regarded the kind of education that was needed to keep the empire together as compatible with a nomadic life. He thought that an educated pastoral society could be organized like his army but that proved impossible.

Jenghiz Khan's empire survived for some thirty or so years after his death, but by 1260 the vigor of conquest had passed its zenith and their story became one of division and decay, as they began to abandon the policies and ideas of the Conqueror. Ogodai was a decent enough ruler but he was no Jenghiz. The events that followed chipped away at the central authority and cohesiveness of the empire, weakening it, causing it to fall apart from within.

The absence of an orderly system of succession led to conflicts and inevitably to the destruction of the empire. When Ogodai died, his widow, Toregene, served the empire as regent for five years before his son Guyuk was elected Great Khan. During these five years, political scheming and intrigue tore away at the inner strength of the empire; a strength which had grown out of unity. Batu, leader of the line of Jochi, refused to attend Guyuk's enthronement ceremonies. There was `bad blood' between them, stemming from a petty argument over who should take the first drink, a point of honor among the Mongols, at a feast held to celebrate the army's victories in the Russian campaign. During Guyuk's brief reign, the authority of the central government fell to a new low, in part because of the khan's addiction to alcohol and in part because of Batu's lack of support. Dynastic troubles continued to plague the Mongol empire. Each of the following successions brought its own schemes and intrigues further dissipating the strength of the empire. After the death of Guyuk, Batu wasn't about to allow a descendant of Ogodai to mount the throne. He condescended to allow Guyuk's widow, Oghul Gaimish, to act as regent. With the support of Tolui's widow, Sorghaghtani, he convened a kuriltai south of Lake Balkash in 1250; and Mongke, Tolui's oldest son, was proclaimed khaghan. The lines of Jagadai and Ogodai refused to attend, saying it wasn't official unless the kuriltai was held in the capital, Karakorum. Eventually Mongke bowed to tradition and a second coronation was held in Mongolia in 1251. An election which was stamped by intrigue, was followed by a ruthless purge of his opponents. He was a strong leader but the process of disruption of the Mongol Empire had already begun. Under Mongke's khanship, Batu and the Golden Horde became independent of the rest of the empire.

Mongke, like Ogodai before him, did not set forth a clear line of succession and in 1260 civil war broke out between Qublai and Arygh Boke, son of Tolui,each seeing himself Mongke's successor. Arygh Boke led the conservative Mongols who wanted the old way of life, taking wealth from the empire without mingling with the conquered people or getting involved in their government. Qublai knew an empire won on horseback could not be governed on horseback, something Jenghiz Khan had come to realize many years before. He intended to establish a permanent, sophisticated government in China.

Qublai succeeded in establishing himself as Great Khan, but not without a price. Mongol fighting Mongol continued to undermine the unity of the empire.

Alliances between appanages of the Mongol empire caused further fragmentation. Hulagu, Ilkhan of Persia, Mesopotamia and Syria, joined forces with Qublai while he was pressing his claim to the throne of the empire. Arygh Boke, at the same time, reached an agreement with Berke, Khan of the Golden Horde, the Mongol kingdom in south Russia. After Qublai moved the capital from Karakorum to Peking, the empire of the Ilkhan severed ties with Peking, followed by the smaller Mongol groups in Turkestan. When Qublai died, the supremacy of the Great Khan died too. Civil war broke out between Arygh Boke and Hulagu in 1260. Berke ordered his troops who had been fighting in the service of Hulagu to leave his service and go to Egypt. For the first time a Mongol agreement with a foreign power took precedence over an agreement with another Mongol kingdom. Still later there was friction between the Golden Horde and Persia. The Ilkhan Ghazan refused to restore the Caucasus to the Golden Horde. Political intrigue and conspiracy continued to weaken the empire, resulting in the loss of many of their external possessions, among them

Georgia and Lesser Armenia. Persia was ravaged and plundered by the Golden Horde, decimated by the Black Plague, torn apart by ruthless internecine wars, and by 1359, the Mongol Empire in Persia ceased to exist.

The boundary between the Jagadai Khanate and the kingdom of Ogodai had never been defined by Jenghiz when he was dividing his empire among his sons. Over the years this led to occasional clashes. Prince Alghu of the House of Jagadai took possession of Khorazm and Otrar, which belonged to the Golden Horde; civil war followed. Qaidu Khan, Ogodai's grandson, allied himself with Berke of the Golden Horde against the Il-khan of Persia. Fragmentation continued; the Jagadai state was divided into two parts and the Golden Horde broke away from the Mongol Empire.

The power of the Golden Horde declined as fighting with Persia continued; the bone of contention still being the Caucasus. Parts of the Golden Horde were drifting away, namely Bulgaria and Byzantium. Discord between various Russian princes forced the Mongols to pay more attention to what was happening within their kingdom. As in Persia, due to increasing Turkish influence, the Yassa was gradually replaced with the Muslim canon law, the shari'a. In 1354 the Ottoman Turks captured the Dardanelles, cutting off trade between the Horde and Egypt. The status of the Golden Horde was finally reduced to a state of Eastern Europe. Internal upheaval, plots and assassinations followed in quick succession and the state disintegrated just as Persia had done a few years earlier.

Religion played an important part in the breakup of the empire. Jenghiz had always practiced an extraordinary religious tolerance. For a number of years his successors appeared to sway this way and that. In 1295, the Ilkhan Empire restored Islam as the official state religion. With religion no longer a barrier between Turk and Mongol, they blended into a new nation, with Turkish becoming the common language. The Mongol language disappeared, the Empire of the Il-khans was completely dominated by Turkish influence; and a true Mongol state no longer existed in Persia. At the beginning of the 14th century, the Jagadai Khanate and the Golden Horde restored Islam as the state religion.

The fusion of Turk and Mongol produced a mixed race, and led to the replacement of the Mongol language with an eastern form of the Turkish language. Qublai installed Buddhism as the state religion, alienating the Chinese Confucian gentry, a loss which played a major role in the decline of Mongol power in China. Palace intrigues, plots and plans against the Mongol aristocracy produced its share of disruption to the empire. Inflation, stemming from the use of paper money, and exorbitant taxes levied on the peasants, to support the Mongol aristocracy, sparked a Chinese nationalist movement which brought about the rapid collapse of the Yuan Dynasty. The last khaghan of the Mongol Empire fled Peking in 1368, just ahead of the Chinese rebel armies, and he took refuge in Mongolia.

The Mongols adapted themselves to the sedentary societies they ruled. Eventually this affected their mobility which led to the decline of their military supremacy. While conservative Mongol opposition to Qublai produced splits in the political structure, the process of cultural assimilation was more dangerous. The Mongols in China had become Sinicized, and after 1260, Chinese histories refer to Qublai as a Chinese monarch, founder of the Yuan Dynasty (1280-1368). The Mongols of the Golden Horde came under Russian influence and the Ilkhanate in Persia fell under the cultural influence of Islam and Iran. The only pure Mongols remaining, Conservatives, were those in the homeland, Mongolia. In addition to political disunity, cultural differences played a part in the separation of the eastern parts of the empire from the western parts.

In the Pamirs, Eastern and Western Turkestan and to the north, the Mongols fell back to the tribal conditions of pre-Jenghiz time. The Mongols of the Golden Horde reverted to a similar nomad life. In China, the Mongols who were left behind when the last Mongol emperor returned to Mongolia, found work with the new regime, the Ming Dynasty. In the homeland, the Mongols slipped back into the old system of intertribal warfare; fighting over grazing lands. Six hundred years after the birth of Jenghiz Khan, the last of his decendants handed over his territories; in Hindustan the British conquered the Moghuls (a corruption of Mongol), and the Mongols in the east yielded to Chinese armies. The Tatar khans of the Crimea became subjects of Catherine the Great and at the same time, the Kalmuk Horde left the Volga region and by a long and terrible march eastward, returned to their homeland.

The final refuge of Jenghiz Khan's decendants was the land between Lake Baikul and the Aral Sea. Here in the steppe of mid- Asia, they wandered from summer to winter pasture, living in their felt tents, following their herds, true nomads once more. Did they talk around the fire at night? Did they know that through these same valleys the fierce Mongol warriors, who followed the yak-tail standard of Jenghiz Khan, surged forth to terrify the world? And so the Mongol Empire passed, fragmenting into nomad tribes from which it had come. The brief and terrible parade of the Mongol horse archers, conquerors of half the world, passed by leaving almost no traces of their conquests. Karakorum, their capital, is buried in the desert sand and even the site of the grave of their mightly leader is unknown.

THE NATIONAL SECURITY SYSTEM: IMPORTAN T DEVELOPMENTS

The people of Mongolia were subject to the control of a variety of political, economic, and social organizations inside and outside the government. The entire system was guided by the party, which directed the overall policies of the government agencies; other political groups, such as the youth and labor organizations; and the network of herding and agricultural cooperatives that extended to include the lowliest *arad* (see Glossary). Through this hierarchy of formal control and the dynamics of its politico-social activities, the central government extended its general, and often extremely particular, direction over the entire population

In the government structure itself, the security system comprised the Ministry of Public Security under which were the central Militia Office and the network of police departments, called militia departments; the State Security Administration; the Fire Prevention Administration; the Border and Internal Troops Administration; and the offices handling correctional organizations. In addition, both governmental and public auxiliary law-enforcement groups helped these agencies to maintain public order and safety

The national police apparatus, commonly called the militia, had a department in each *aymag* and a militia office in each district. The militia was responsible for the registration and supervision of the internal passports that all citizens aged sixteen and older were required to carry, and for enforcement of the passport regulations at the national and local levels. A passport was necessary for internal travel, and persons wishing to travel first had to obtain permission from the militia. After arriving at their destination, they had to register with the militia. The militia collected the passports of those entering military service. The passports of persons under criminal investigation and detention were held by the investigative organ, but those who were sentenced to prison surrendered their passports to the militia. A system of tight control was imposed upon the movements of all citizens. The militia also had been designated as the organ of criminal investigation--giving central direction to police work and combining the functions of criminal investigation and criminal arrest. The procurators supervised the militia's crime-detection work. Militia investigators were expected to have strong political convictions, a knowledge of jurisprudence, extensive working experience, loyalty, and honesty.

Militia organs, together with local assemblies administered compulsory labor sentences of convicted criminals. Militiamen, as well as the executive committees of local governments, had authority to put intoxicated persons into detention houses for twenty-four hours or less and to fine them.

Each militia office had a motor-vehicle inspection bureau, which regulated vehicular traffic, investigated accidents, issued licenses, and could impose fines on operators guilty of minor law infractions. Detectives attached to motor vehicle inspection bureaus also investigated vehicular accidents. Militia members directed motor traffic, and they were stationed along the railroads.

The Ministry of Public Security also was responsible for the Fire Prevention Administration and the State Security Administration. The Fire Prevention Administration supervised all fire-prevention and fire-fighting activities. The State Security Administration was a counterintelligence organization thought to oversee anti-espionage, antisubversion, and anti-sabotage activities.

The Border and Internal Troops Administration was in charge of 15,000 troops responsible for border patrol, for guard duties, and for immigration control. Border defense troops were equipped with fixed-wing aircraft, helicopters, tanks, motor vehicles and motorcycles, radio communications equipment, engineering equipment, and automatic weapons.

THREAT PERCEPTION

In the early 1980s, despite improved Sino-Soviet relations, Mongolia maintained its traditional distrust of Beijing and was unwilling to reduce its own armed forces or the level of Soviet forces stationed in Mongolia. By 1985 Soviet troops in Mongolia still numbered 75,000; they included two tank and three motorized infantry divisions. China insisted that Soviet forces in Mongolia be withdrawn as a condition for improved Sino-Soviet relations. Soviet communist party general secretary Mikhail Gorbachev responded to that demand in a July 1986 Vladivostok speech in which he offered to withdraw Soviet troops from Mongolia. Two weeks later, the Mongolian government gave its support for "the withdrawal of a considerable part of the Soviet troops from Mongolia...to promote the establishment of the overall Asian and Pacific security and serve the cause of strengthening trust and good neighborliness in Asia." Between April and June 1987, the Soviet Union announced the withdrawal of one full-strength motorized rifle division and several separate units, which reduced Soviet forces in Mongolia to approximately 55,000

Mongolia's relations with China also improved during this period; the exchange of government, trade, and friendship delegations culminated in the November 1988 signing of a Mongolian-Chinese border treaty. In December 1988, Mongolia's first deputy minister of foreign affairs, Daramyn Yondon, commenting on a Soviet offer to withdraw the majority of its troops stationed in Mongolia within two years, stated that "if relations with China continue to improve, all Soviet troops will be withdrawn." In February 1989, official Mongolian news sources quoted Mongolian military leaders as calling for a reduction in the size of the Mongolian armed forces. Mongolia's concern over the Chinese threat, although by no means eliminated, was at its lowest level in nearly thirty years.

AUXILIARY SECURITY FORCES

Various governmental and public organizations assisted the regular law-enforcement agencies in keeping order. Public brigades had been organized as auxiliaries to help the militia in crime detection and prevention, in gathering evidence, in observing public gatherings, in finding stolen goods, and in tracking escaped criminals. In addition, there were mass social organizations, including block and district committees, and parents' committees in schools. These citizens' groups were used to help fight such crimes as murder, burglary, theft, and arson. They also could function as deputies or special police, as the occasion demanded. In addition, there were administrative committees, special police courts, committees of public-spirited citizens to deal with juvenile delinquents, and anticrime commissions in the larger cities and towns.

The most important of these bodies were the Crime Fighting and Crime Prevention Councils, which were voluntary and informal party organizations operating without paid staffs at all levels of the party-government structure. These councils were strictly advisory bodies, and they had no authority to replace judicial or law-enforcement agencies in any way. Their function was to discuss in general terms the problems of crime and how best to combat it.

CIVIL-MILITARY RELATIONS

In the Mongol military tradition, all men were warriors, and therefore military training was not confined to the regular army. In the early days of the Mongolian People's Republic, before universal military conscription, party and youth league members received sporadic special military training in the reserve and in physical culture detachments. Women were admitted to this training on a voluntary basis. In 1929 the League for Assisting the Defense Aims of the Mongolian State was established by the party Central Committee; it was based on the Soviet Voluntary Society for Cooperation with the Armed Forces. In 1942 the league was reorganized as the People's Volunteer Self-Defense Detachment and was used in home defense against the Japanese. In 1945, at the end of World War II, it again was reorganized and renamed-- this time the Auxiliary Defense Organization. A 1975 decree of the Political Bureau of the party Central Committee specifically assigned the Auxiliary Defense Organization the task of fostering patriotism and support for the army through sponsorship of annual defense popularization months, Mongolian-Soviet friendship months, and military sports competitions throughout the year. In the late 1980s, the Auxiliary Defense Organization still was responsible for these activities and for providing spare-time schools and courses to train all seventeen-year-old males in basic military skills and specialties of use to the military. "To protect the economy against weapons of mass destruction," all citizens were obliged to participate in civil defense training organized by the Civil Defense Office of the Ministry of Defense. In 1982 there reportedly were 600 civil defense units in Mongolia.

MONGOLIA'S SECURITY POLICY: REGIONAL AND INTERNATIONAL ASPECTS[2]

NEW GEOPOLITICAL ENVIRONMENT

The disintegration of the so-called socialist world and of the Soviet Union itself, the end of the cold war, normalization of sino-soviet and later of sino-russian relations and some other developments in international relations have favorably changed Mongolia's geopolitical environment. These changes have allowed Mongolia to expand its relations, define its own national interests and priorities, and pursue them.

Though international relations are undergoing changes due to new geopolitical realities, including increasing interdependence of states, nevertheless the very nature and basic laws as international relations based on puerperal striving and even struggle of states for power and influence remains almost unchanged. Only the accent is being shifted from predominantly political and military fields to economic, scientific-technological and informational fields, in other words from geopolitics to geoeconomic.

NATIONAL SECURITY CONCEPT

It is under these circumstances that Mongolia had undertaken to review its security and foreign policies, which resulted in the adoption in June 1994 by the State Ih Hural (Parliament) of national security and foreign policy concepts as well of the military doctrine -all of them bound by single notion of national security and national interest, including vital national interests, of way and means of ensuring national security, of security guaranties, etc.

According to the national concept, vital national interests imply the existence of the Mongolian people and their civilization, the country's independence, sovereignty, territorial integrity, inviolability of State frontiers, relative economic independence, sustainable ecological development and national unity.

Mindful of the political realities in Mongolia and in international relations, as well as the trends of evolution of international relations and power politics, Mongolia has defined the following as the primary areas of its concern:

[2] *by J. Enkhsaikhan, Secretary, National Security Council, Mongolia*

-security of the existence of Mongolia,

-security of the social order and state system,

-security of citizens' rights and freedom,

-economic security, scientific and technological security,

-of information,

-security of the Mongolian Civilization (culture and way of life),

-security of the population and its gene pool, and

-ecological security.

EXTERNAL ASPECTS OF SECURITY

The national security of Mongolia is a part of the international security and as such it is directly dependent on the latter. International guarantees of national security consist of political, legal and moral-psychological components. They are secured and strengthened through the combination of unilateral, bilateral and multilateral measures. Military-political security, the concept underlines, can be best ensured through a collective security system by joint efforts or by participation in such a system. Mindful of the misperception in foreign policy, including excessive ideologization, subordination of the national interests to those of others, full and unreserved support of foreign policy of and excessive dependence on one particular state, the national security concept stipulates that in its foreign relations Mongolia shall exercise political realism, accord the priority to the vital national interests, seek to secure many partners in international relations and promote a non-aligned policy so long as it does not threaten the country's national interests.

Any external threat to Mongolia, whether political, military, terrorist, economic, or other, will somehow be directly or indirectly connected with one or both of our two neighbors. By the same token, it could be said that its security is also one way or other connected with two neighbors as well as with their mutual relations. Therefore it is logical that relations with the two neighbors constitute the cornerstone of our security policy and thus are accorded top priority in our foreign relations.

RELATIONS WITH CHINA AND RUSSIA

Having served as a geopolitical buffer and political pawn in the relations between the two neighbors, Mongolia is now trying to pursue a balanced relationship with them, bearing in mind at the same time the need to maintain balance of forces and interests in the region.

However, balanced relationship does not necessarily mean keeping mechanical equidistance from both neighbors or taking identical position on all issues. When defining its own policy towards them, Mongolia would be taking into account their policies in regard to the national interests of Mongolia, above all its vital national interests.

In the past few years, Mongolia has been able to define the basic principles of relations and main fields and forms of cooperation with Russia and China, and reflect them in bilateral treaties of friendly relations and cooperation, signed with them in 1993 and 1994 respectively.

The treaty with Russia, unlike the previous treaty with the Soviet Union, does not contain provisions of collective self-defense or automatic collective action in case of perceived threat. Article 4 of the new Treaty stipulates that the parties shall not participate in any military-political alliance against each other, nor conclude with third countries any treaties and agreements running counter to the interest of sovereignty and independence of the other party. They have also agreed that neither of them would allow the use of their territory by third states for aggressive or other violent acts against the other party, i.e. for undermining the security interest of the other party.

Furthermore, Russia has pledged to respect Mongolia's policy aimed at nonstationing on its territory or transit through it of foreign troops as well as nuclear and other weapons of mass destruction. The treaty with China also stipulates that the Parties shall not allow countries to use their territory against stale sovereignty and security of the other party. Unlike Russia, China has pledged to respect Mongolia's policy of nonstationing on its territory or transit through it of foreign troops as well as nuclear and other weapons of mass destruction in a separate press statement. Nevertheless, these treaties with its two neighbors, together with Russian-Chinese joint declaration of 18 December 1992, whereby the two sides pledged not to use or threaten to use force in any form against each other, including the use of the territory, territorial water and airspace of third countries that border with any one of them, constitute a solid base for ensuring predictability and thus stability and security among the three countries and in the subregion in general.

Despite these treaties, in case of abrupt changes in the balance of forces or interests in the region, one cannot exclude attempts to impose indirectly, through political, economic and other means, control over Mongolia, or future massive inflow of refugees due economic hardships or political considerations in neighboring states. Again, judging from our past experience, one can not rule out spillover into Mongolia of internal disturbances if they occur in the neighboring states.

MONGOLIA NATIONAL SECURITY SYSTEM

The people of Mongolia were subject to the control of a variety of political, economic, and social organizations inside and outside the government. The entire system was guided by the party, which directed the overall policies of the government agencies; other political groups, such as the youth and labor organizations; and the network of herding and agricultural cooperatives that extended to include the lowliest *arad* (see Glossary). Through this hierarchy of formal control and the dynamics of its politico-social activities, the central government extended its general, and often extremely particular, direction over the entire population (seeSociety , ch. 2; Major State Organizations , ch. 4).

In the government structure itself, the security system comprised the Ministry of Public Security under which were the central Militia Office and the network of police departments, called militia departments; the State Security Administration; the Fire Prevention Administration; the Border and Internal Troops Administration; and the offices handling correctional organizations. In addition, both governmental and public auxiliary law-enforcement groups helped these agencies to maintain public order and safety (see Local Administration , ch. 4).

The national police apparatus, commonly called the militia, had a department in each *aymag* and a militia office in each district. The militia was responsible for the registration and supervision of the internal passports that all citizens aged sixteen and older were required to carry, and for enforcement of the passport regulations at the national and local levels. A passport was necessary for internal travel, and persons wishing to travel first had to obtain permission from the militia. After arriving at their destination, they had to register with the militia. The militia collected the passports of those entering military service. The passports of persons under criminal investigation and detention were held by the investigative organ, but those who were sentenced to prison surrendered their passports to the militia. A system of tight control was imposed upon the movements of all citizens. The militia also had been designated as the organ of criminal investigation--giving central direction to police work and combining the functions of criminal investigation and criminal arrest. The procurators supervised the militia's crime-detection work. Militia investigators were expected to have strong political convictions, a knowledge of jurisprudence, extensive working experience, loyalty, and honesty.

Militia organs, together with local assemblies administered compulsory labor sentences of convicted criminals. Militiamen, as well as the executive committees of local governments, had authority to put intoxicated persons into detention houses for twenty-four hours or less and to fine them.

Each militia office had a motor-vehicle inspection bureau, which regulated vehicular traffic, investigated accidents, issued licenses, and could impose fines on operators guilty of minor law infractions. Detectives attached to motor vehicle inspection bureaus also investigated vehicular accidents. Militia members directed motor traffic, and they were stationed along the railroads.

The Ministry of Public Security also was responsible for the Fire Prevention Administration and the State Security Administration. The Fire Prevention Administration supervised all fire-prevention and fire-fighting activities. The State Security Administration was a counterintelligence organization thought to oversee anti-espionage, antisubversion, and anti-sabotage activities.

The Border and Internal Troops Administration was in charge of 15,000 troops responsible for border patrol, for guard duties, and for immigration control. Border defense troops were equipped with fixed-wing aircraft, helicopters, tanks, motor vehicles and motorcycles, radio communications equipment, engineering equipment, and automatic weapons.

NATIONAL SECURITY STRATEGY DEVELOPMENT

EARLY- TO MID-1990S: "SECURITY THROUGH DEMOCRATIZATION"

Mongolia became the world's second socialist country in 1924, and was destined to become the first Asian nation to denounce the old system through a peaceful revolution in 1990. The period of peaceful change between 1990 and 1994 marked a watershed in Mongolia's historical development, and the change has been no less dramatic in nature and in scope for having been achieved without violence and bloodshed.

The new constitution of 1992 instituted a solid legal framework for genuine democratic reforms. Pluralism and a multi-party system became a reality. Free market rules were introduced to govern the economic life of the country. Mongolia joined the International Monetary Fund, the World Bank, the Asian Development Bank, and the World Trade Organization. These developments were a breakthrough in the process of integrating Mongolia into the world economy, and that integration itself was a breakthrough. Having been dominated by China for two centuries and then by Soviet Union for seven decades, Mongolia has learned a single indelible lesson in terms of national sovereignty and security – that the nation should seek balanced, equidistant relations with its two neighbors while seeking wider recognition and global interaction to the utmost possible degree.

However, Mongolia was considered one of the least likely cases to achieve a successful transition to democracy. The scholar M. Steven Fish has noted that often a country's transition to democracy and its success are often assisted by a history of previous liberal governance, its political culture, prior experience with elements of a capitalist free market economy, and even proximity to other democratic states. This helps explain the relative ease with which many East and Central European nations have undergone their transitions. Mongolia had none of these. It is because of these reasons that Fish described Mongolia's successful transition as "democracy without prerequisites."

Now it is widely believed that the initial assurance of national security was closely linked to, and exclusively depended on, the processes of liberalization and democratization. Mongolia had to become an open country to ensure international recognition. In doing so, Mongolia had to equally distance itself from the political domination of the then-still existing Soviet Union and post-Tiananmen China and move closer to the so-called "third neighbors," major democracies like the United States and Japan. This international recognition and, moreover, appreciation of Mongolia's transition to liberal democracy, served as the single most important factor of assuring national security in this otherwise unfavorable historical and geographical environment.

MID- TO LATE-1990S: "SECURITY THROUGH PROACTIVE DIPLOMACY"

Mongolia's foreign policy achievements were direct results of its strategy of assuring maximum national security through democratization. In 1994 the Parliament adopted two principal documents based on the spirit of the 1992 Constitution.

First, the Foreign Policy Concept heralded fundamental changes in the modus operandi of the nation's engagement with the rest of the world as the end of the ideological confrontation of the Cold War opened up opportunities for Mongolia to pursue an independent foreign policy. In securing its interests, Mongolia pursues the following broad objectives:

- maintaining friendly relations with both Russia and China;
- developing friendly relations with developed countries in both the West and the East;
- strengthening the nation's position in Asia and participating in the political and economic integration process in the region;
- seeking cooperation with international institutions such as the United Nations, its affiliated agencies, and international financial institutions;
- developing friendly relations with countries of the former socialist countries, including the newly independent states;
- promoting friendly relations and cooperation in the pursuit of common objectives with developing countries.

In addition, as a plausible counterweight to the dominance of Russia and China, especially in the wake of their strategic partnership and like-mindedness in nearly all issues of concern to global and regional security, first Mongolian scholars and then practitioners coined the term and pursued the "Third Neighbor Policy," developing ever closer political, economic, cultural and security ties to developed democracies, including the United States, Japan, India, and European nations, as well as the international organizations.

The National Security Concept, also legislated in 1994, demonstrates how a comprehensive, human-centered, development-oriented security approach can complement the nation's political will to pursue liberal democracy. Given the aforementioned foreign policy agenda and its ultimate success, the national security perception is based on the liberal institutionalist approach which many developing countries adhere to. It is composed of nine areas of concern including security of the existence of state, security of constitutional order, security of national economy, security of information, security of population and genetic composition, security of the environment, security of Mongolian culture and way of life, security of science and technology and finally, most importantly, security of civil liberties.

Within this context of a proactive foreign policy and liberal institutionalist approach to national security, Mongolia has offered a number of unique initiatives within the Northeast Asian region as active contributions to regional security. Mongolia declared its territory nuclear-free, a status recognized by the five permanent members of the United Nations Security Council, and has proposed to expand the nuclear-free zone beyond its boundaries throughout Northeast Asia. Though sounding utterly unrealistic within the neighborhood of nuclear Russia and China, this proposal can be understood as Ulaanbaatar's call to Pyongyang to curtail its nuclear ambitions, which can destabilize the whole sub-region. As part of its multi-pillar foreign policy, the Mongolian government continues to offer good-will gestures and has a vested interest in maintaining stable relations with the two Korean states. Mongolia declared its interest in the peaceful resolution of the Korean crisis and its willingness to offer its contribution to the mutual understanding among the major actors of the region. In particular, it was declared that although North Korea faces difficulties in communicating to other actors, Mongolia's stable and friendly relations with the two Koreas, Japan, and the United States can serve as an asset in enhancing the mutual understanding and building the confidence. A vivid example of such a policy was Ulaanbaatar's hosting of Japan-North Korea working group discussions within the framework of the Six-Party Talks in August 2007.

Mongolia strives to become a full participant in the process of Asian regional integration. Mongolia is a member of the Association of Southeast Asian Nations (ASEAN) Regional Forum, and is seeking ASEAN Dialogue Partner status and membership in Asia-Pacific Economic Cooperation (APEC) and the East Asian Community.

In sum, the second half of the 1990s was marked by the strategy of proactive diplomacy, a more sophisticated tool of security assurance than merely a political democratization. Having secured stable and harmonious relations with both Russia and China while pursuing greater visibility in the region, this was the period of strengthening the "third neighbor" concept. This stage was built upon democratization, and did not replace it; moreover, this stage has paved the foundation for a third stage – increased international commitments of the Mongolian military – even has some features of the second stage are still in practice.

THE 21ST CENTURY: "SECURITY THROUGH PEACEKEEPING COMMITMENTS"

The beginning of the new century was especially productive with regard to Mongolia's contribution to regional and global security. In 2002 the Parliament of Mongolia adopted legislation on dispatching military and/or law enforcement personnel to international peacekeeping operations. This legislation was reflected in certain unprecedented decisions that can be labeled as "bold" for some and "adventurous" for others. In March 2003, the Mongolian government declared that the country had become a member of the "coalition of the willing," and offered political support for Operation Iraqi Freedom – a position not shared by its two immediate neighbors. Mongolian servicemen were sent to assist in the reconstruction of Iraq, performing their duties within the multinational command. Ten rotations of troops, each consisting of detachments 100 plus-strong, served in Iraq before the mission was declared successfully completed in 2008. In addition to the successful completion of peacekeeping duties by several officers as United Nations military observers in the Democratic Republic of the Congo, Western Sahara, Sudan, and Bangladesh, Mongolian military instructors are involved in the training of Afghan National Army units. In 2005, Mongolian troops successfully completed peace support duties in Kosovo as part of the NATO mission there. Under the aegis of the United Nations, the Mongolian Armed Forces continue to send their premier peacekeeping units to Sierra Leone, and an initial detachment will soon land in the African nation of Chad.

To facilitate increased participation in UN peacekeeping operations, Mongolia has set up a regional peacekeeping training center, and has hosted the annual international peacekeeping exercise "Khaan Quest" at that installation ever since 2005.

Mongolia's participation in the U.S.-led coalitions in both Operation Iraqi Freedom and Operation Enduring Freedom in Afghanistan sometimes triggers criticism that it contradicts to the non-aligned stance of Mongolia's foreign policy that is mandated in the nation's Constitution. Some critics debate whether these steps automatically make Mongolia an ally of the U.S., or any other country in the coalition. The answer is rather negative; by signing-in to the ad hoc coalition of the willing, Mongolia remains a neutral country and stays away from building military alliances with any of the aforementioned countries, and from binding mutual security treaties.

Mongolia has certainly earned a so-called "peace dividend" from the international commitments undertaken by its reforming military. Ulaanbaatar has begun to attract the geo-strategic attention of other capitals, including Washington. In 2005 George W. Bush became the first sitting U.S. president to visit Mongolia and has proclaimed that the United States "is proud to be called the third neighbor of Mongolia" – a clear demonstration that willful actions made slogans a reality.

THE NEW ERA: "SECURITY THROUGH VESTED INTERESTS"

More recently Mongolia has been blessed with an unprecedented opportunity for growth and an anticipated economic boom due to ongoing discoveries of its vast mineral resources and continuing investment bids. But this blessing could become a curse, as real world problems challenge the capacity of the state. Health issues, poverty, crime, underdeveloped domestic legal frameworks and institutions, and widespread perception of corruption all present enormous challenges to the national search for security. In general, Mongolia's human security condition is inherently weak, and this is where the geo-economic dimension enters Mongolia's pursuit of security – the government is now taking into consideration not only gigantic regional powers, but also giants of the transnational corporate world. Until now, Mongolia has quite successfully handled Moscow and Beijing and courted Washington, Tokyo, and Delhi. Now, however, it has to deal with new actors from across the globe, less bound by protocol courtesies of bilateral and multilateral diplomacy.

More stressing is the fact that where huge cash and high expectations meet week laws and poor management, the usual outcome is not prosperity but disaster. From a dream of becoming the "Persian Gulf of Northern Asia," Mongolia still can slide down the path of the Zimbabwean model and its problems may be multiplied by strains of Dutch disease in which exploitation of natural resources leads to a decline in industrial production. It is therefore vital to remember that the nation's perception and pursuit of security was successful up to now only because each of its stages, from geo-political to geo-strategic, were logically consecutive and evolutionary. Just as the proactive diplomacy was built upon the foundations of democratization, Mongolia's peacekeeping commitments evolved from its multi-pillar foreign policy. In the same manner, Mongolia's attraction of multi-billion mineral sector investment should resemble less of a cold-blooded monetary deal and more of a carefully weighed resource diplomacy, following the nation's time-tested pattern of equidistant balancing of diverse actors. This is the real challenge. As a citizen, it is my hope that Mongolia comes out of this challenge as a winner, as it did in the past twenty years.

MONGOLIA NATIONAL SECURITY STRATEGY

Mongolia is strategically located between two of the major powers: Russia and China. That location has influenced her international standing and foreign policy. Thus in the XX century alone Mongolia was able to regain her freedom from two century Manchu rule, pursue a struggle for total independence and international recognition, accept the tripartite (Russo-Chinese-Mongolian) agreement imposed on Mongolia by the two neighbors scaling down her independence to a mere autonomy under Chinese 'suzerainty', brief Chinese occupation, national revolution achieved with the support of the soviets and as a consequence - seven decades of 'sovietization'. Unlike other countries, during the post World War II period, Mongolia was subject to double 'cold wars': East-West (taking the side of the East) and Sino-Soviet (taking the side of the latter).

Since early 1990s Mongolia is pursuing a foreign policy based on its national interests and political realism, aimed at overcoming its isolation, diversifying its political and economic relations by acquiring new friends and partners, ensuring its security primarily by political means. To this end it has adopted a foreign policy concept, the English translation of which is reproduced below.

INTRODUCTION TO MONGOLIA'S NATIONAL SECURITY POLICY

As in other countries, national security considerations play a very important role in the country's foreign and domestic policies. Mongolia's geographical location has always been a major, and in many cases decisive factor in its security policy. Thus until very recently, the main actors and factors that influence Mongolia's external status and destiny have been, besides itself, China and Russia.

Since the end of World War II, Mongolia has been caught up in two 'cold wars': East-West and Sino-Soviet, which left little room for maneuver. Because of its historical experience, until recently Mongolia has been identifying its security interests with those of the so-called socialist community of nations, which boiled down to soviet interests. Mongolia was under Soviet security umbrella. Therefore it was thought at that time that whatever was good for the Soviets by implication was good for Mongolia. Thus logically Mongolia's national interests were subordinate to Soviet interests, meaning in many cases that Mongolia's own interests were undermined.

The disintegration of the so-called socialist world and of the Soviet Union itself, the end of the cold war, normalization of Sino-Soviet and later of Sino-Russian relations and some other developments in international relations were favorably changed Mongolia's geopolitical environment. At the same time Mongolia began to pursue a foreign policy based on its own national interests and political realism.

Thus in 1990 Mongolia started reviewing its foreign and internal policies and priorities and in 1994 the Mongolian parliament has overwhelmingly adopted three very important documents: concepts of national security, of foreign policy and the military doctrine, which enjoy the broad support of all political forces. The national security concept has duly reflected the country's geopolitical situation and role, and for the first time in its history the concept concretely defined Mongolia's vital national interests as well as the ways and means of ensuring them. The five vital national interests are: a) existence of the Mongolian people and their civilization, b) the country's independence, sovereignty, territorial integrity, inviolability of State borders, c) relative economic independence, d) sustainable ecological development and e) national unity. All other interests are subordinate to them.

Today the external environment for ensuring its vital national interests is relatively favorable. The relations with the two powerful neighbors are normal, there are no political problems with any of them. Both have pledged to respect Mongolia's sovereignty and territorial integrity. Moreover, as a result of open foreign policy, Mongolia has many well-wishers, sympathizers and supporters, as seen and felt by the support of donor countries and agencies.

As to national security priorities, there is a number of them. The immediate security concerns today are primarily of economic nature. Bringing down the inflation and reducing the budget deficit, restructuring the banking and financial systems, conducting fair privatization of enterprises, of housing and of land are all important to ensuring accelerated economic development. Externally, ensuring economic security is the cornerstone of the country's independence and sovereignty. It is not an easy task bearing in mind the sheer size of economic might if its neighbors. Bringing down poverty, the crime rate, ensuring the security of citizen's rights and freedoms, ecological security - are also high on the agenda (The Permanent Mission shall carry the extracts of the National Security Concept in its homepage in November). .

THE CASE FOR THE SINGLE-STATE NUCLEAR-WEAPON-FREE ZONE

Recent years have witnessed intensification of the creation of nuclear- weapon-free zones /NWFZs/. In the last three years two new multilateral treaties established such zones: one in South-East Asia and the other comprising the entire African continent. Existing NWFZs in Latin America and the Caribbean as well as in the South Pacific, created respectively by the Tlatelolco and Rarotonga treaties, have been further strengthened both qualitatively and quantitively. Initiatives for new NWFZs in Central Asia, in the Middle East and in other regions are under discussion.

The spread of NWFZs is due to a large measure to the end of the Cold War and ensuing positive developments in international political and security environments. These developments have increased the appeal of NWFZs as important security measures contributing to regional peace and security.

NWFZs are important for large, medium and small states alike. They provide an opportunity, especially for the small states to contribute, in their own way, to non-proliferation of nuclear weapons while strengthening their national security. They, therefore, have a wide practical appeal to the more than 60 countries that are not covered by the existing NWFZ regimes. These countries can make, in due time, their contribution to nuclear non-proliferation by establishing NWFZs, either individually or collectively.

As a rule, the notion of a NWFZ denotes a vast area comprising territories, regions, adjacent waters of several states or even entire continents. This is quite natural, since until recently those were known cases. However, if we take the notion of the "zone" in general, it could be interpreted differently depending on the meaning that one would like to put in or convey. Thus depending on the context, the term "zone" could even mean a region or an area within a state as well. Therefore in respect of NWFZ, even single-states can form such zones, bearing in mind the specifics of the region concerned. In fact a 1976 comprehensive study of the question of NWFZs in all its aspects, undertaken in accordance with General Assembly resolution 3261 F of 9 December 1974, provided for the possibility of single-state zones. Its first principle reads: "obligations relating to the establishment of NWFZs may be assumed not only by groups of States, including entire continents or large geographical regions, but also by smaller group of states and even individual countries". The reference to "individual countries" as a variation of

NWFZs was unanimously recognized in the study. But it was not pursued during the height of the Cold War and block politics.

Although some 20 years have passed since the study had been undertaken, it has lost none of its importance and significance. On the contrary, the post Cold War period is expanding and deepening the understanding of nuclear issues and the maximalist approach of "all or nothing" is giving way to practicality and more flexibility. As the earlier period of the creation of the Tlatelolco regime shows, single-state zones could be precursors of wider group-State (so-called conventional) zones to be joined by other States later on.

Single-state zones, just like the conventional zones, are not only important for non-proliferation of nuclear weapons. They also represents an additional political and legal assurance against external pressures on small States that could entail, if national efforts are not seconded by international support, the deployment of nuclear weapons or parts of their system on territories of such small States.

Some 6 years ago, after the withdrawal of Soviet troops (then already Russian) from its territory, Mongolia declared its territory, which is parger than Central Europe, a NWFZ. It was a bold and innovative approach to the concept of NWFZs and the first case of its kind. By declaring its territory a NWFZ, Mongolia took into due account not only the lessons of the past, but also the importance of and trends for NWFZs. It was trying to ensure its security by political means, to contribute, at the same time and in its own way, to reinforcing stability and enhancing predictability in its sub-region. This policy of Mongolia was welcomed by all the five nuclear-weapon-states, including its two immediate neighbors - Russia and China. It was also welcomed by the entire membership of the Non-Aligned Movement.

Naturally, a single-state NWFZ can be credible only when it has sound legal basis, containing the commitments of the zonal state as well as those of neighboring and nuclear weapon states not to take any measure that would directly or otherwise violate the status of the zone. The single-state zones, in the view of Mongolia, have many common features and elements with the conventional zones. They share, inter alia, the same fundamental objective - total absence of nuclear weapons, consent of the parties concerned, promotion of non-proliferation of nuclear weapons, etc. Nevertheless there can be major differences, for instance, as to the type of monitoring mechanisms and scope of their functions as well as comparative advantages: its geographical scope is apriori well-defined; there is no need for intra-zonal negotiation or coordination; the parties responsible are apparent, etc. An essential requirement, however, seems to be for the zonal state to have the acquiescence, if not support, of not only nuclear weapon powers but also neighboring states and not to have any territorial or border problems with its neighbors.

Taking into account the over-all significance of the above initiative and in order to complement and expand the existing practice of establishing zones by groups of States, Mongolia proposed to the 1997 session of the United Nations Disarmament Commission, the consideration of the concept of a "single-state NWFZ" and adoption of guidelines on the principles and modalities for the creation of such zones and presented a working paper to that effect. In doing so, it proceeded from the assumption that consideration and adoption of such guidelines could be of conceptual importance as well as have practical implications for the 1/3 of the U.N. membership that is not covered by the existing zones. More delegations extended their support during the 1998 session of the U.N. Disarmament Commission, for the consideration of the single-state zone concept. This was reflected the working paper of the Chairman of the Working Group on Nuclear-Weapon-Free Zones as follows: "The international community may consider further initiatives, proposals and issues linked to nuclear-weapon-free zones and should be more actively engaged in the consideration of all aspects of the establishment of a single-State nuclear-weapon-free zone".

NWFZs are not the ultimate security solution. They are, however, an inseparable part of the active quest for international peace and security and represent a valuable practical measure capable of contributing to the gradual reduction and, perhaps even elimination of nuclear weapons. In this the role of single-state zones should not be underestimated.

1.GENERAL PROVISIONS

1. The Constitution of Mongolia expresses the integrated interests of the people, all groups and strata of Mongolian society.

2. The national security, of Mongolia (hereinafter referred to as " national security") represents the status when favourable external and internal conditions are secured to ensure vital national interests of Mongolia. The ideological basis of the policy ensuring national security is national patriotism.

3. The vital national interests of Mongolia consist in the existence of the Mongolian people and their civilization, in the country`s independence, sovereignty territorial integrity, inviolability of State frontiers, relative economic independence, sustainable ecological development and national unity. The vital national interests of Mongolia constitute the object of special care and protection on the part of the State and the people.

4. The ensurance of national security implies State policy aimed at creating all-round guarantees of protecting and strengthening of Mongolia`s vital national interests, actions taken by the State, its agencies and functionaries to that effect as well as measures implemented by its citizens. Those measures shall be of both preventive and creative nature. Mongolia shall strive to develop its international competitiveness in the economic, cultural, scientific and technological and educational fields.

ONE. STRUCTURE OF NATIONAL SECURITY

5. The national security shall consist of the following main components:

1) Security of the existence of Mongolia,
2) Security of the social order and state system,
3) Security of citizens' rights and freedoms,
4) Economic security,
5) Scientific and technological security,
6) Security of information,
7) Security of Mongolian civilization,
8) Security of the population and its gene pool,
9) Ecological security

TWO. FACTORS AFFECTING NATIONAL SECURITY

6. Factors affecting the national security are divided into internal and external by their origins, and into immediate, temporary, long-term and permanent by their duration. The vital national interests of Mongolia are interests of a permanent nature.

7. The factors that may have a negative impact on national security are divided into objective and subjective by their character, and into real and possible by the probability of danger they might cause. The policy of ensuring and strengthening the national security aims at identifying and eliminating any threats at the "probable" stage of its occurrence, as well as at reducing or preventing objective threats by the timely elimination of subjective ones.

8. External factors affecting national security:

The national security of Mongolia constitutes a part of the international security and as such is directly dependent on the latter. In terms of political spatial security, it is divided into global, regional and subregional.

9. Internal factors affecting national security:

In terms of internal spatial dimension, national security shall be of national, regional, aimag, the capital, soum levels.

THREE. WAY AND MEANS OF ENSURING NATIONAL SECURITY, SECURITY GUARANTEES

10. National security is ensured by social, political, organizational. economic, diplomatic, military, intelligence and legal means, unilaterally or through the development of international cooperation.

11. The main means of ensuring national security consists of taking measures designed to forecast and forestall the trends and the development of events on the basis of reliable information and thorough its evaluation and assessment.

12. The main guarantors of national security are the people of Mongolia and the Mongolian State.

13. International guarantees of national security consist of political, legal and moral-psychological components. They are secured and strengthened through the combination of unilateral, bilateral and multilateral measures. Military-political security can be ensured through a collective security system by joint efforts or participation in such a system.

FOUR. SYSTEM OF ENSURING NATIONAL SECURITY

14. The duties to ensure national security are incumbent on the State Great Hural, the President of Mongolia, the National Security Council headed by the President, the Government, the central and local law enforcement and State administrative agencies.

15. The legislative, executive, judicial and local self-governing bodies are obligated to implement, within their competence, the tenets of this Concept, strengthened by the Constitution, legislation and other relevant legal acts.

16. Political and public organizations, as well as citizens shall strictly observe the legislation on ensuring national security and the present Concept, and shall actively participate in the realization thereof.

17. The National Security Council is charged with thc coordination of the strategies and tactics of the implementation of the present Concept with due regard to existing circumstances. It shall monitor the state of safeguarding national security, and annually inform the State Great Hural thereon.

18. The organizations concerned shall provide for funds needed to implement this Concept in their budgets. In cases of special measures, expenses shall be covered by the State budget.

FIVE. INFORMATION DATABASE OF NATIONAL SECURITY

19. Every kind of information necessary to coordinate and implement the State policy of ensuring national security shall be obtained from relevant authorities, citizens, and from foreign sources. The information database shall be set up under the National Security Council.

II. SECURITY OF THE EXISTENCE OF MONGOLIA

20. The security of the existence of Mongolia means the ensurance of its independence, sovereignty, territorial integrity, and inviolability of state frontiers of Mongolia.

21. External factors which may adversely affect the security of the existence of Mongolia:

1. Armed aggression or threat of armed aggression against Mongolia from any State or force;

2. Policies designed to forcibly abolish the State independence of Mongolia or to disrupt the national unity of the people;

3. Impeding or pressuring the sovereign relations of Mongolia with other States developed on the basis of international law;

4. Organization of terrorist and subversive activities, espionage against Mongolia and its people, as well as the abetting and conspiring in such acts;

5. Imposition by any State of its own interests and policies on Mongolia or attempts to resolve disputes by force;

6. Imposition of political, military, economic and ideological control over Mongolia;

7. Emergence of global, regional and subregional crises and conflicts which they may affect Mongolia,
or may draw it into war.

8. Destabilization of the Mongolian economy, attempts at or organizing coup d`etat or using Mongolia as a bridgehead for policies and activities directed against other States;

9. Changing of state frontiers, illegal border crossing and border violations;

10. Disputes and conflicts between the neighbouring States, and being affected by their internal contradictions and crises;

11. Massive inflows of migrants from a neighbouring State;

12. Occurrence of natural and ecological calamities, outbreak or spread of acutely infectious human or animal diseases.

22. Internal factors which may adversely affect the national security of Mongolia:

1.Breakdown of statehood, or designs and/or attempts at turning Mongolia into a satellite State;

2. Political, economic and military acts aimed at disrupting national unity and or/ undermining the independence of Mongolia;

3. Emergence of conditions leading to acute religious, ethnic or local disputes and confrontations;

4. Organization of subversive and/or espionage activities aimed at weakening the potential of Mongolia;

5. Division within the armed forces and other military entities, loss of their defence capability or military-patriotic conscience, or confrontation between the military and civilian population or armed insurgency and conflicts.

23. Ways and means to ensure the security of the existence of Mongolia:

Mongolia shall:

One. 1) Uphold universally accepted principles of contemporary international law in relations with any State and make others observe them as well;

2) Support the activities of the United Nations Organization and other international institutions aimed at strengthening world peace and security, and closely cooperate with them to that end;

3) Establish and protect bilaterally and multilaterally the legal foundations the unilateral or collective protection of the country from aggression in conformity with Article 51 of the UN Charter;

4) Promote the policy of maintaining strategic stability and establishing a reliable system of strengthening the peace and security in Asia and the Pacific, particularly in Northeast Asia and Central Asia;

5) Strictly observe the policy of not allowing the use of the country's territory against other States. Ensure the nuclear-weapons-free status of Mongolia at the international level and make it an important element of strengthening the country's security by political means. Pursue the policy of turning Central Asia into a nuclear-weapon-free zone;

6) Ensure timely and sound reactions to acts capable of affecting or contradicting the vital national interests of Mongolia or damaging its prestige and, if necessary, duly reflect them in the politics and activities of the government;

7) Promote an atmosphere conducive to understanding and supporting Mongolia in other countries, particularly in neighbouring and influential countries through the wide use of the policy of "people's diplomacy", an important channel of foreign relations;

8) Promote legal acts that determine the overall number of foreigners and stateless persons that may reside in Mongolia and regulate their movement within the country, and monitor their compliance. Establish a mechanism of control to prevent illegal residence or stay in Mongolia.

Two. 1) Cooperate with other countries and relevant international organizations in the military field, and in pursuit of the policy of safeguarding itself against possible aggression and seeking collective defence, she shall follow the policy of making use of the armed force of neighbouring or of third States or the United Nations and/ or other integrated international armed forces;

2) Have national armed forces, other troops capable of safeguarding the country's independence, territorial integrity and inviolability of frontiers;

3) Implement defence objectives on the basis of the universal defence system in accordance with its own military doctrine. In case of having to defend against armed encroachment or aggression solely by its own forces, a self-defence war shall be waged through the mobilization of all internal forces and means while also making wide use of external factors;

4) Participate to the greatest extent possible in international efforts and cooperation designed to strengthen trust in the military field and establish a mechanism for ensuring regional security.

III. SECURITY OF SOCIAL ORDER AND STATE SYSTEM

24. Security of the social order and State system means the ensurance of the state and socioeconomic structure, fundamental principles of State activities, as well as human rights and freedoms as provided for in the Constitution of Mongolia.

25. External factors which may adversely affect the security of the social order and state system:

1. Policies aimed at the destruction of the State, and social and economic structure of Mongolia;

2. Sowing discord among nationalities, different social groups and national leadership in order to disrupt the integrity of the state system, or disrupting the national unity of the people or an attenipt to do so;

3. Divulging state secrets including military and technological ones;

4. Espionage activities by foreign intelligence services and their accomplices.

26. Internal factors which may adversely affect the security of the social order and state system:

1. Impair the sovereignty of Mongolia provided for by the Constitution ;

2. Illegal seizure of state power or an attempt to do so;

3. Breach of the equality of forms of property and violation of the right to own property;

4. Breach of principles of non-interference by the state agencies in religious affairs and by religious entities in state affairs;

5. Breach of the principle of separation of State powers of Mongolia;

6. Emergence of different splinter groups due to difference of views, of ethnic origin, religion, place of origin, contradictions within the national leadership on issues of national security;

7. Weakening of the country's defence potential and the ties between the people and the military;

8.Weakening of the respect for law and order in society, slackening of discipline and responsibility that lead to public disorders, weakening State governance, accountability and vigilance, disclosure of state secrets;

9.Aggravation of corrupt practices taking the form of organized crime;

10. Exhaustion of strategic and other national resources, outbreak of famine and natural calamities, spread of plagues leading to a large number human deaths.

27. Ways and means to ensure the security of the social order and state system :

Mongolia shall:

One. 1) Enact legislation in compliance with the spirit, principles and provisions of the Constitution of Mongolia, and ensure strict observance thereof;

2) establish a political mechanism for the coordination of activities of political parties and movements;

3) provide conditions needed for protecting the top national leaders from influences contrary to the national interest, and take preventive and safeguarding measures;

4) make government activities transparent to the public except for cases prohibited by law for national security reasons.

Two. 1) In foreign relations, exercise political realism and consistently principled approach, according top priority to the vital interests and other national considerations, and seek to secure many partners in international relations. Promote a nonaligned policy so long as it does not threaten the country`s vital interests. Whenever Mongolia's interests conflict with those of other countries, a flexible approach shall be sought bearing in mind the vital national interests of Mongolia ;

2) accord top priority to the question of relations with the two neighbouring countries and adhere to the principle of a balanced relationship with them. Maintaining a balanced relationship does not mean keeping equidistance between them or taking identical positions on all issues but this policy does mean strengthening trust and developing all-round goodneighbourly, relations and mutually beneficial cooperation with both of them. In relations with these countries, due account shall be taken of their policies in regard to the national interests of Mongolia, above all its vital interests. A policy of non-involvement and neutrality shall be pursued in relation to the disputes between the two neighbours unless the disputes affect the vital national interests of Mongolia;

3) pursue an open foreign policy. Promote the policy of consultation with influential countries on issues of strengthening world peace and security, of developing international cooperation, of enhancing the country's strategic significance and fostering strategic interests of major powers in Mongolia;

4) in its relations with other developing and landlocked countries, pursue the line of jointly defending and promoting the shared interests on the international arena.

IV. SECURITY OF CITIZENS` RIGHTS AND FREEDOMS

28. The security of the citizens` rights and freedoms means the situation when conditions are ens ured for individuals to fully devote their physical and intellectual potential to their own benefit, to the interests of the country and the people, and for Mongolia to carry out its international obligations with respect to human rights.

29.External factors which may adversely affect the ensuring of the security of the citizens` rights and freedoms :

1.Violations of constitutionally, provided and guaranteed democracy, justice, equality and the citizens` rights and freedoms as a result of provocative actions and pressures by other States ;

2. Breach of the unity among the population and between citizens by making use of ethnic and religious distinctions, as well as differences of opinion ;

3. Restrictions of the rights, freedoms and equal status of Mongolian citizens traveling abroad on business or private trips, or residing there permanently or temporarily ;

4. Entrapping of Mongolian citizens by foreign agencies and services through promises, incitement and brainwashing and using them to the detriment of Mongolia's interests;

5. Emergence of dual citizenship which would result in the loss of guarantees to ensure the citizens' rights on the part of the State.

30. Internal factors which may adversely affect the ensuring of the security of the citizens` rights and freedoms :

I .Grave violations of human rights provided for by the Constitution and other laws of Mongolia, and by international treaties and conventions to which Mongolia is a party ;

2. Lack or loss of real political, economic, social and other guarantees capable of ensuring the citizens' rights and freedoms provided for by the Constitution and other legislative acts of Mongolia;

3. Loss of citizens' sense of patriotism due to hard social and economic conditions.

31. Ways and means to ensure the security of the citizens` rights and freedoms:

Mongolia shall :

1.guarantee the specific rights and freedoms of citizens provided for by the Constitution of Mongolia through the enactment of relevant legislation;

2.besides acceding to multilateral treaties and conventions protecting human rights and freedoms, conclude bilateral treaties and agreements ensuring the interests of this country's citizens;

3.set up a mechanism for providing Mongolian citizens traveling abroad with the needed information on their rights and obligations, on legal means of self-protection, as well as enhance the role and responsibility of the diplomatic missions of Mongolia abroad in the protection of the rights of citizens ;

4.identify and determine the root causes of political repression, rehabilitate the victims of repression and create political and legal guarantees to prevent the recurrence of such tragedies ;

5.support the activities of the non--governmental organizations aimed at protecting human rights and freedoms ;

6.have the option to introduce appropriate restrictions on human rights and freedoms in accordance with the law whenever the population and the gene pool of the nation are endangered due to the outbreak of acutely infections diseases and disparities in the age and sex ratios of the population ;

7.enact legislation prohibiting dual citizenship and conclude international treaties and agreements thereon ;

8.ensure that the citizens of Mongolia and foreign residents are prohibited from violating the rights and freedoms of others or cause damage to others while exercising their own rights and freedoms, as well as to infringe upon the security and the vital national interests of the country.

V. ECONOMIC SECURITY

32. Economic security means building an economic structure which has the potential for effective economic reproduction through the use of internal resources, for meeting the basic needs of the people and strengthening the country`s independence, and in cases of need to sustain the country for a definite period of time.

Economic security represents the cornerstone of the independence and sovereignty of Mongolia.

33. Fxternal factors which may adversely affect the ensuring of economic security :

1. Restricting or impeding the development of foreign trade and economic cooperation ;

2. Turning into a raw materials appendage to other countries ;

3. Plummeting of prices of the country's export items of strategic importance and/or loss of markets for them;

4. Direct dependence on any one country in economic branches of strategic importance.

34. Internal factors which may adversely affect economic security:

1. Failure of the ecological policy leading to the depletion of water and forest resources, reduction of agricultural lands ;

2. Widening of disparity in regional development leading to economic unbalances ;

3. Depletion of the gene pool of Mongolian domestic farm animals and acclimated varieties of grains ;

4. Failure of customs policy leading to penetration of items which may adversely affect the security of Mongolia and its population, to the reduction of sources of budget revenues which may have a negative impact on national production ;

5. Increase of the State's current budget deficit, failure of the State policy to protect the national currency, the togrog ;

6. A sharp rise in inflation resulting in the fall of the togrog's exchange rate, and increase in the number of families with incomes below the minimum level of subsistence ;

7. Growth of the debt to other countries or international organizations and thus increasing the vulnerability to externl pressures and dependence ;

8. Sharp increase in the number of foreigners and stateless persons resident in Mongolia, and mass emigration of nationally trained personnel and skilled workers ;

9. Sharp increase in the share in the overall population of the unemployed, including the number of persons of working age with disabilities.

35. Ways and means to ensure economic security :

Mongolia shall :

One. 1) pursue a uniform government policy in the following fields :

- economic structural changes
- foreign economic relations
- issues related to indebtedness and debt servicing
- budget policy
- monetary policy
- scientific and technological policy
- economic reporting, accounting and information

Two. 1) recognize the following branches as having strategic importance due to their role in ensuring economic security :

a) in the spheres of production :
- food and agriculture
- mining

- light industry
- chemical industry

b) in the sphere of infrastructure :

- energy
- fuel
- telecommunications and information
- roads and transport

2) Encourage foreign investments in the following areas :

- developing strategically important branches
- increasing the production of export items and foodstuffs
- internally processing raw materials, mechanical components and spare parts thus substituting imports

Three. Pursue the following guidelines in the formulation and implementation of the national policy on ensuring economic security :

1. develop economic and social infrastructures;
2. set up economic zones capable of providing conditions for the relatively independent and integrated development of local areas;
3. develop industries producing ecologically clean products and introduce wasteless technologies ;
4. determine, secure and replenish annually reserves of essential food and consumer goods; produce domestically certain types of goods of strategic importance ;
5. maintain the country's hard currency reserves at an amount equalto the total import costs of not less than two months ;
6. protect the gene pool of Mongolian farm animals as well as the acclimated varieties of grains ;
7. when developing trade and economic relations with various countries, safeguard against situations where the country`s economy, especially its branches of strategic importance, may become the object of dominance by one country, or a group countries or where the country may turn into a raw materials appendage. Impart an interest in the developed countries to freely maintain and expand relations with this country ;
8. ensure the right of Mongolia to leave access to the sea on the basis of international legal norms ;
9. with a view to ensuring economic security, expand bilateral and multilateral equitable mutually beneficial trade and economic cooperation with neighbouring countries, and the developed countries of the West and East; secure the country's appropriate place in the regional trade and economic network ;
10. keep the amount of strategically important raw materials and equipment to be imported, as well as the number of experts and workers to be received from any one country at the level not capable of affecting national security;
11. avoid situations where incentives and concessions accorded to foreign investors to protect their economic interests surpass the concessions and economic allowances provided to the national investors and producers; oversee compliance therewith ;
12. when receiving loans from foreign countries and international organizations, care should be taken so that their total does not exceed the country`s capacity to pay back within a specified time period ;
13. settle the issues of repayment of loans before 1990 and their interests in accordance with international practices taking into States as well as causes that led to such debts ;
14. when promoting the policy of increasing the share of' exports in foreign trade, care should be ttaken to market processed and finished goods.

VI. SCIENTIFIC AND TECHNOLOGICAL SECURITY

36. Scientific and technological security means the ensurance of conditions for the use of technologies, information and research for the purpose of the country`s development adapted to its ecological conditions, for enhancing the national scientific potential and intellectual competitiveness.

37. External factors which may adversely affect the ensuring of scientific and technological security are :
1. Technological dependence on a country in an economic branch having strategic importance for the
development of the country ;
2. Backwardness in scientific and technological development.

38. Internal factors which may adversely affect the ensuring of scientific and technological security :
1. Lack of a uniform government policy for scientific and technological development ;
2. Loss of Mongolian traditional time-tested technologies ;

3. Insufficient government protection of specific Mongolian technologies as well as studies of and information on the gene pool of the population, plants and animals, and loss of scientific and technological secrets ;

4. Failure to introduce world advanced technologies due to the absence of favourable economic and legal conditions and guarantees ;
5. Loss of competitiveness of national techniques and technologies due to non-introduction of modern achievements of science and technology, and resultant retardation therein ;
6. Inability to make full use of the national intellectual potential and of trained personnel in the country ; 7. Lack of conditions for the utilization of new and innovative technologies in production.

39. Ways and means to ensure scientific and technological security :

Mongolia shall:

1. define a uniform scientific and technological policy and its priority tasks allocate not less than three percent of the national income to financing scientific activities ;

2. encourage research, secure scientific discoveries and intellectual products, create legal guarantees for introduction of foreign technologies adapted to Mongolian conditions.

3. develop and introduce technologies suitable for Mongolian conditionsfor the exploitation of natural resources, food and agricultural rawmaterials ;

4. set up an integrated national scientific and technological information network and database and place them under Government protection ;

5. encourage fair competition for the introduction of scientific and technological achievements in industry, and the development of industrial technologies. Apply the principle of providing tax allowances and soft loans on priority, basis to private enterprises and institutions which gain achievements in the development of scientific and technological researches and find new

technological solutions of national importance and in using their results in production and practical work ;

6. strengthen the competitiveness of science and technology, its capability to develop through increasing involvement of the private sector in scientitific technological development;

7.create a technological infrastructure and favourable environment, introduce a system of proper assessment of the content, potentiality and status of national technology ;

8. concentrate the intellectual potential of science and technology, and the available funds and resources primarily in the implementation of nationally important research projects ;

9. improve steadily the quality of the educational system, and encourage and develop people's talents ;

10. promote special-purpose training of highly skilled specialists in particularly needed technological fields, create intellectual and materia prerequisites and conditions for national scientists to work and prosper in their own country ;

11. introduce the practice of selecting promising children from the secondary school level for subsequent work in scientific and technological research fields as well as in processing and manufacturing industries, of providing them with facilities and conditions for individualized education and apprenticeship training ;

12. ensure priority development of artificial intellingence management technology and biotechnology. While paying special attention to acquiring the technologies of assembling computers and other electronic equipment, the use of solar and wind energy, as well as to the establishment of an integrated telecommunications network based in modern technology, expand work in the development of research-intensive new materials ;

13. develop national scientific and technological cooperation and secure the country`s place in international and regional integration ;

14. preserve national scientific and technological traditions and methodologies, adapt them to modern conditions.

VII. INFORMATION SECURITY

40. Information security means the situation where conditions are ensured for the Government to assess objectively the country`s actual internal and external situation and make correct decisions, for government organs and the people to have the necessary information for the exercise of their powers and rights provided by the Constitution and for the dissemination abroad of information about Mongolia. Freedom of information constitutes an important means for the development and strengthening of democracy.

41. External ffactors which may adversely affect the ensurance of information security are :

1. Dissemination of false information by outside sources that may sow doubts about Mongolia's independence and territorial integrity in other countries, lead to interference in its internal affairs by any State or sow distrust between ethnic groups in Mongolia, and lead to disputes and

conflicts as well as to internal instability ;

2. Dependence upon one country or a group of countries in the field of information.

42. Internal factors which may adversely affect the ensurance of information security are :

1. Use of the mass media by any force as an instrument to increase tension in the country, settle a personal score or damage others' reputation ;
2. Curtailment of the right to seek, receive and impart information ;

3.Disclosure of state secrets related to ensuring national security and defence as well as public law and order ;

4.Curtailment of the rights of citizens and institutions calumniated in the mass media to protect themselves
through the mass media or courts of justice ;

5.Causing damage to others by supplying incomplete or false information ;

6. Failure to keep abreast of the course of events or of scientific and technological developments as a
result of the breach of information freedom or lack of access to information.

43. Ways and means to ensure information security:

Mongolia shall:

1. have a multi-source information database on external and domestic situations ;

2. safeguard mass media agencies and means against becoming subservient to foreign organizations or citizens ;

3. create the legal basis for the dissemination of true and objective news and information by the mass media ;

4. establish a national structure and legal safeguards for the protection of computerized information ;

5. join international information networks and carry out efficient dissemination of true and objective
information on Mongolia ;

6. have the mass media serve the cause of developing and strengthening democracy and pluralism, and disallow deliberate distortion and abuses of truth and objective reality ;

7. guard against informational intrusion detrimental to Mongolia's independence, culture and way of life customs and traditions ;

8. have the mass media and other information sources create an information environment conducive to national security through the dissemination of authentic information and communications on security matters.

41. External ffactors which may adversely affect the ensurance of information security are :
1. Dissemination of false information by outside sources that may sow doubts about Mongolia's independence and territorial integrity in other countries, lead to interference in its internal affairs by any State or sow distrust between ethnic groups in Mongolia, and lead to disputes and conflicts as well as to internal instability ;

2. Dependence upon one country or a group of countries in the field of information.

42. Internal factors which may adversely affect the ensurance of information security are :

1. Use of the mass media by any force as an instrument to increase tension in the country, settle a reputation ;

2. Curtailment of the right to seek, receive and impart information ;

3.Disclosure of state secrets related to ensuring national security and defence as well as public law and order ;

4.Curtailment of the rights of citizens and institutions calumniated in the mass media to protect themselves through the mass media or courts of justice ;

5.Causing damage to others by supplying incomplete or false information ;

6. Failure to keep abreast of the course of events or of scientific and technological developments as a result of the breach of information freedom or lack of access to information.

43. Ways and means to ensure information security:

Mongolia shall:
1. have a multi-source information database on external and domestic situations ;
2. safeguard mass media agencies and means against becoming subservient to foreign organizations or citizens ;
3. create the legal basis for the dissemination of true and objective news and information by the mass media ;

4. establish a national structure and legal safeguards for the protection of computerized information ;
5. join international information networks and carry out efficient dissemination of true and objective information on Mongolia ;

6. have the mass media serve the cause of developing and strengthening democracy and pluralism, and disallow deliberate distortion and abuses of truth and objective reality ;

7. guard against informational intrusion detrimental to Mongolia's independence, culture and way of life,customs and traditions ;
8. have the mass media and other information sources create an information environment

conducive to national security through the dissemination of authentic information and communications on security matters.

VIII. SECURITY OF MONGOLIAN CULTURE AND WAY OF LIFE

44. The security of Mongolian culture and way of life means the situation where conditions are ensured for the preservation of the national language, history, culture, customs and traditions that constitute the basis for the existence and development of the Mongolian nation and its statehood, and conditions for the eternal existence of the Mongolian people.

45. External factors which may adversely affect the security of Mongolian culture and way of life :

1. Emergence of conditions where the blurring of the distinctive features of Mongolian culture and way of life may lead to its eventual assimilation into others' as a result of political, economic and sociocultural policies of foreign countries and external forces ;

2. Indoctrination of inhumane ideologies such as chauvinism, racism, fascism, and reactionary religious teachings, uncontrolled dissemination of materials inciting violence, murder, and pornography.

46. Internal factors which may adversely affect the ensurance of the security of Mongolian culture and way of life are :

1. Disregard for and belittling of the cultures of other peoples and exaggeration of the values of the historical traditions of Mongolian culture and way of life, which may ultimately lead to the country's self-isolation as a nation ;

2. overestimation and blind imitation of civilizations of other nations or failure to safeguard against the negative side- effects of a market economy and modern science and technology ;

3. Emergence of an intellectual vacuum in society due to the external internal situations, and lapsing of society, into intellectual degradation ;

4. Smuggling of objects of historical and artistic value abroad.

47. Ways and means of ensuring the security of Mongolian civilization:

Mongolia shall:

1. formulate and pursue an active policy for reinforcing and enriching the basic characteristics of the nomadic civilization; preserve all valuable an progressive elements of Mongolian culture and traditions in economy statehood, material and intellectual life, and develop them in a harmonious combination with the values of world civilization ;

2. perfect the Mongolian language in line with the extant trends by mastering both the traditional and
Cyrillic scripts ;

3. create an educational system in accordance with the traditions of the Mongolian Enlightenment and present-day world standards, protect and enhance the national intellectual potential ;
4. create conditions for learning about and perceiving the history, culture and mentality of the people as well as the nature of the homeland, inculcate in every citizen, particularly the younger generation, a strong sense of patriotism and an aspiration to cherish the country's name; make the study, instruction and popularization of Mongolian history, religion and culture the special object of the government`s constant care and support ;

5. pursue a policy of encouraging the search, protection, recovery and restoration of the relics of Mongolian culture, prevent the illegal outflow of historical and cultural treasures ;

6. carefully preserve and rely on the intrinsic ability of the Mongols to live in harmony with Nature, their traditional abiding respect for statehood, knowledge and talent displayed in thought and in deed, and their keen sense of community ;

7. restore and preserve specific types of the traditional economic Mongolian know-how and technology and the heritage of national culture and craftsmanship ; and protect their work and masterpieces ;

8. respect freedom of conscience and religious belief, refrain from interfering in the affairs of the church on the part of the state; make possible for the church to freely conduct its services ; keep under state supervision the number of places of worship, their locations and the actual number of the clergy ;

9. keep inter-confessional relations under particular care of the state and forestall crises and conflicts; keep the activities of any church within the legal customs and traditions;

10. expand relations and ties with Mongols living in other countries, help them maintain and develop Mongolian culture and traditions ; Mongoliabeing the ancestral homeland of the Mongols, while pursuing the policy of encouraging the desire of Mongols living abroad to see Mongolia develop, shall particularly, eschew the injection of any political intent in these relations ;

11. prevent the spread of such man-hating ideologies as racism and fascism, which may undermine the national unity of the Mongolian people, the public morals and spirit; the publication, display and dissemination of productions advocating violence, murder, war and pornography shall be permitted exclusively, within the legal framework under special regulations.

IX. SECURITY OF THE POPULATION AND ITS GENE POOL

48. The security of the population and its gene pool implies a situation where conditions are ensured for the maintenance and protection of the health and gene pool of the Mongolian population and its sustained growth.

49. External factors which may adversely affect the ensurance of the security of the Mongolian population's gene pool :

1. transgression of radioactive substances, chemical pollution, acid rains and epidemics through atmosphere, water and soil ;

2. joining the international decision of labour as a country, engaged in production harmful to the ecology and the population's health ;

3. influx of foodstuffs, chemicals and consumer goods adversely affecting the health of the population and its gene pool due to erroneous foreign trade policy and slackened control over the quality of imported goods.

50. Internal factors which may adversely affect the ensurance of the security of the population and its gene pool :

1. outbreak of acute human and animal diseases ;

2. damage of the gene pool as a result of inbreeding ; an increase in the number of mentally deficient and intellectually retarded persons exceeding the admissible ratio to that of normal people and thus exceeding the world average indicator ;

3. spread of alcoholic addiction affecting the overall health of the population and its gene pool ;

4. imbalance in the age and sex structure of the population ;

5. spread of famine and dystrophy among the population ; shortage of drinking water or its pollution ;

6. breach of sanitary and other established hygienic standards by domestic producers; production and uncontrolled distribution of foodstuffs, consumer goods and other products harmful to the health of the population ;

7. breach of safety rules of handling chemicals resulting in the negative impact on the health and gene pool of the population.

51. Ways and means of ensuring the security of the population and its gene pool :

Mongolia shall :

I. formulate and pursue a comprehensive Government policy, aimed at ensuring the gene pool, health and sustained growth of the Mongolian population ; revive, on public initiative, the tradition of keeping track and being aware of the family genealogy up to 7-9 generations of one's ancestors;

2.make prophylaxis the basis of Government policy and activities in health protection;

3. consider as a priority task the prevention of inbreeding, alcoholism and drug addiction which would negatively affect the Mongol gene pool and comprehensive study of Mongols as human beings and of the Mongolian population ; promote the policy of early diagnosis of and preventive measures against mental diseases and ensurance of psychological security of the population ;

4. establish a monitoring system for safeguarding against radioactive and chemical pollution, bacteriological contamination, as well as diseases and epidemics originated therefrom in the contiguous areas of neighbouring countries ;

5. prohibit the importation into or transit through territory of Mongolia of particularly poisonous chemical and biological substances having direct and residual effect on human genes and the health of the population as well as proscribe economic activities connected with storage or processing of hazardous wastes of foreign countries ;

6. institute regular control over the incidence and frequency cycles of genetic diseases, anomalies and mental deficiencies ;

7. exercise constant control over the accumulation in the environment of chemicals harmful to human genes ;

8. keep food security under special Government care, exercise control over the quality, of foodstuffs to safeguard against the possible presence of toxic substances hazardous to human health and genetic system, set up a national laboratory ;

9.pursue the policy of closely monitoring the social, biological and environmental factors which may adversely affect the health of the population, as well as developing pharmaceutical and biopreparation technologies so as to domestically produce at least fifty percent of the essential drugs needed, and ensure a priority use of domestic raw materials of mineral, plant and animal extraction in pharmaceutics ;

10. attain world average indices of population health, reduction of maternal and infant morbidity, and mortality rates; promote the policy of appropriate management of birth rate in order to achieve a sound solution to certain pressing problems of child and maternal health.

X. ECOLOGICAL SECURITY

52. Ecological security means the situation where conditions are ensured for the prevention of a negative impact on human environment and the economy as a result of ecological and climatic changes, and of irrational rise and insufficient protection of natural resources.

53. External factors which may adversely affect the ensurance of ecological security :

1. Intensification of desertification, changes in the level and distribution of precipitation and increased frequency of droughts and blizzards as a result of global climatic transformations; thinning of the ozone layer ;

2. increase in the levels of radiation, chemical pollution acid rain transgressing the borders by atmospheric
and water currents; outbreak of human and animal epidemics; inroads of rodents and insects harmful to forests, pastures and vegetation ;

3. turning into a supply base of raw materials for production of raw materials for he production of hallucinogens, of psychotropic and other substances harmful to human intellect and health.

54. Internal factors which may adversely affect the ensurance of ecological security :

1. Destabilization of ecological balance, increase of soil erosion and destruction, depletion of the gene pools of plants and animals ;

2. Depletion of the vegetation and forests, drying up of rivers and lakes draining of subterranean waters and parching of pastures ;

3. Exploitation of natural resources in a skimming and wasteful manner ;

4. Accumulation of wasteful techniques and technologies; increase of industries producing hazardous wastes; turning into a dumping ground for toxic wastes of foreign countries.

55. Ways and means to ensure ecological security :

Mongolia shall :

1. make the concern of Government policy, the activity designed to revive the national traditions of caring for and protecting Nature, and to impart them to the entire society ;

2. apply the principles of meeting the basic human needs within the limits of renewable natural resources, and using non-renewable or gradually renewable resources for the country's development as additional factors ;

3. develop the economy with ecological orientation and promote the policy of securing an appropriate position in the world market with its ECOMARK products ;

4. protect certain parts of the country's territory, turning them into national reserves while gradually drawing the rest of the territory into economic circulation in line with policies and mechanisms designed to maintain ecological balance ;

5. avoid turning land into ownerless wastes in the name of free ownership fragmenting it into pieces
for the alleged purpose of giving shares to everyone, and the irreversible exhaustion of pastures ;

6. pursue a course aimed at establishing eco-economic zones to develop complexes comprising suitable combinations of economic infrastructure and natural resources capable ensuring ecological balance, while avoiding further fragmentation of the present administrative and territorial divisions ;

7. in planning and building towns and settlements avoid overcrowding the population which may become the cause of ecological disturbances any given region ;

8. implement the policy designed to restrict the use as fuel of shrubs which are effective in nblocking sand movements and retaining soil moisture, make use of the possibilities of neighbouring States in meeting the country's needs in lumber; goals aimed at carrying out goals the complex of measures aimed at carrying out reforestation, prevention of fires, protecting the sources of springs and rivers as well as crop
fields by green belts ;

9. plant greenery in degrading areas, expand year by year the areasunder vegetation ; species in t world and in Mongolia ; valuable finds of animal and plan extractions native to Mongolia;

10. constantly update the national Red Data Book, promote a systematipolicy for protection of the gene pools of endangered

11. organize the commercial use of valuable herbs, edible and technicalplants through their acclimation and planting; restrict the export for economic reasons of economically

12. make lakes, rivers. water pools and all other water resources of Mongolia the object of special protection by the Government and the people, establish a system of managing and monitoring the rational use of water resources, water preservation, building reservoirs for collecting rain and snow drainage, and exercise control over the quality and reserves of clean water for drinking and industrial usage ;

13. conduct through effective means and methods sustained activities against the testing and emplacement of nuclear weapons in the territory of Mongolia and in areas adjacent to its borders ;

14. apply the principle of restricting economic activities harmful to the environment through legal and economic means;

15. cease production activities which emit gases damaging the ozone layer, and impose restrictions on such products ;

16. establish a system of prevention and combating natural calamities, and other unforeseen disasters ;

17. conduct researches on traditional measures of survival that enable the population to live in arid and desert regions ; and develop the national capacity, and preparedness to survive any possible climatic changes ;

18.while fully incorporating the habitats of unique wildlife and vegetation as well as the intersections of biospheres in Mongolia in the national reserve areas, take measures to secure international status for some of them by including them in the register of world heritage of civilization ;

19. promote the policy of having the territory of Mongolia included in the internationally protected ecological zones ;

20. acquire advanced technology, and know-how concluding or becoming party to international treaties and agreements concerning environmental protection and rehabilitation by realizing ecologicalprojects in cooperation with international organizations and donor countries; set up a system environmental disaster prevention designed to enable the country to survive the least possible damage under any conditions.

XI. OTHER PROVISIONS

56. The State Great Hural shall make appropriate changes and amendments with regard to the basic structure and content of the Concept of National Security of Mongolia on the proposal of the

National Security Council, taking into account the changes and trends in the global, regional and domestic situations and the development of events.

MONGOLIA'S SECURITY POLICY: REGIONAL AND INTERNATIONAL ASPECTS

by J. Enkhsaikhan, Secretary, National Security Council, Mongolia

NEW GEOPOLITICAL ENVIRONMENT

The disintegration of the so-called socialist world and of the Soviet Union itself, the end of the cold war, normalization of sino-soviet and later of sino-russian relations and some other developments in international relations have favorably changed Mongolia's geopolitical environment. These changes have allowed Mongolia to expand its relations, define its own national interests and priorities, and pursue them.
Though international relations are undergoing changes due to new geopolitical realities, including increasing interdependence of states, nevertheless the very nature and basic laws as international relations based on puerperal striving and even struggle of states for power and influence remains almost unchanged. Only the accent is being shifted from predominantly political and military fields to economic, scientific-technological and informational fields, in other words from geopolitics to geoeconomic.

NATIONAL SECURITY CONCEPT

It is under these circumstances that Mongolia had undertaken to review its security and foreign policies, which resulted in the adoption in June 1994 by the State Ih Hural (Parliament) of national security and foreign policy concepts as well of the military doctrine -all of them bound by single notion of national security and national interest, including vital national interests, of way and means of ensuring national security, of security guaranties, etc.

According to the national concept, vital national interests imply the existence of the Mongolian people and their civilization, the country's independence, sovereignty, territorial integrity, inviolability of State frontiers, relative economic independence, sustainable ecological development and national unity.

Mindful of the political realities in Mongolia and in international relations, as well as the trends of evolution of international relations and power politics, Mongolia has defined the following as the primary areas of its concern:
-security of the existence of Mongolia,
-security of the social order and state system,
-security of citizens' rights and freedom,
-economic security, scientific and technological security,
-of information,
-security of the Mongolian Civilization (culture and way of life),
-security of the population and its gene pool, and
-ecological security.

EXTERNAL ASPECTS OF SECURITY

The national security of Mongolia is a part of the international security and as such it is directly dependent on the latter. International guarantees of national security consist of political, legal and moral-psychological components. They are secured and strengthened through the combination of unilateral, bilateral and multilateral measures. Military-political security, the concept underlines, can be best ensured through a collective security system by joint efforts or by participation in such a system. Mindful of the misperception in foreign policy, including excessive ideologization, subordination of the national interests to those of others, full and unreserved support of foreign policy of and excessive dependence on one particular state, the national security concept stipulates that in its foreign relations Mongolia shall exercise political realism, accord the priority to the vital national interests, seek to secure many partners in international relations and promote a non-aligned policy so long as it does not threaten the country's national interests.

Any external threat to Mongolia, whether political, military, terrorist, economic, or other, will somehow be directly or indirectly connected with one or both of our two neighbors. By the same token, it could be said that its security is also one way or other connected with two neighbors as well as with their mutual relations. Therefore it is logical that relations with the two neighbors constitute the cornerstone of our security policy and thus are accorded top priority in our foreign relations.

RELATIONS WITH CHINA AND RUSSIA

Having served as a geopolitical buffer and political pawn in the relations between the two neighbors, Mongolia is now trying to pursue a balanced relationship with them, bearing in mind at the same time the need to maintain balance of forces and interests in the region.

However, balanced relationship does not necessarily mean keeping mechanical equidistance from both neighbors or taking identical position on all issues. When defining its own policy towards them, Mongolia would be taking into account their policies in regard to the national interests of Mongolia, above all its vital national interests.

In the past few years, Mongolia has been able to define the basic principles of relations and main fields and forms of cooperation with Russia and China, and reflect them in bilateral treaties of friendly relations and cooperation, signed with them in 1993 and 1994 respectively.

The treaty with Russia, unlike the previous treaty with the Soviet Union, does not contain provisions of collective self-defense or automatic collective action in case of perceived threat. Article 4 of the new Treaty stipulates that the parties shall not participate in any military-political alliance against each other, nor conclude with third countries any treaties and agreements running counter to the interest of sovereignty and independence of the other party. They have also agreed that neither of them would allow the use of their territory by third states for aggressive or other violent acts against the other party, i.e. for undermining the security interest of the other party.
Furthermore, Russia has pledged to respect Mongolia's policy aimed at nonstationing on its territory or transit through it of foreign troops as well as nuclear and other weapons of mass destruction. The treaty with China also stipulates that the Parties shall not allow countries to use their territory against stale sovereignty and security of the other party. Unlike Russia, China has pledged to respect Mongolia's policy of nonstationing on its territory or transit through it of foreign troops as well as nuclear and other weapons of mass destruction in a separate press statement. Nevertheless, these treaties with its two neighbors, together with Russian-Chinese joint declaration of 18 December 1992, whereby the two sides pledged not to use or threaten to use force in any form against each other, including the use of the territory, territorial water and airspace of third countries that border with any one of them, constitute a solid base for ensuring predictability and thus stability and security among the three countries and in the subregion in general.

Despite these treaties, in case of abrupt changes in the balance of forces or interests in the region, one cannot exclude attempts to impose indirectly, through political, economic and other means, control over Mongolia, or future massive inflow of refugees due economic hardships or political considerations in neighboring states. Again, judging from our past experience, one can not rule out spillover into Mongolia of internal disturbances if they occur in the neighboring states.

GOVERNMENT ACTION PROGRAM ABOUT DEFENCE AND FOREIGN POLICY

1. The defense set-up of Mongolia and military reform policy shall be implemented consistently in accordance with the principles of the State military policy and measures shall be taken to eradicate distortions and problems accumulated in this field in recent years. Within the framework of these aims following actions shall be taken:

Revise and work out Defense and other laws & regulations, incorporate and enforce ways & forms of civic control over activities of Armed forces and other military organizations;

Define priorities and implement an initial stage of upgrading weapons & armament and technical renovation of Armed forces & Border Security Force;

Improve the organization of military, intensify the reforms, and increase the capabilities of military force;

Upgrade qualification of personnel of professional military units through improvement of terms and conditions of voluntary military services on agreement basis;

Revise and improve the training concept of military personnel of Armed forces in conformity with the contemporary needs and goals, conduct training in the areas different from basic responsibilities, such as natural disaster relief, rectification of damages of industrial accidents and humanitarian assistance to civilians;

Conduct training for those of substitute military service in particular cases such as to take measures to avoid natural disaster or to prevent industrial accidents and to fight them.

Ensure preparatory measures and undertake initial steps to participate in UN peace-keeping activities by personnel of Armed forces;

2. Independence and sovereignty of Mongolia shall be protected and conducive environment for peaceful life to its people shall be created. Within the framework of these aims following actions shall be taken:

Evaluate implementation of the State policy on the Border of Mongolia, laws and regulations related to border and of international agreements to which Mongolia acceded and improve their legal regulation. Create an independent set-up of Border Security Forces;

Conduct activities to stop and eliminate cross-border pilferage, intensify preventive measures against violations of State border, especially in Uvs, Zavkhan, Huvsgul, Dornod and Sukhbaatar aimags and ensure the integrity and non-violability of the borders of Mongolia;

Improve step by step the process of renovation of communication, technical supplies and transport of the Border Security Forces;

Improve the system of involvement of citizens, local organizations in regions in the protection of State border;

Undertake measures to further perfecting and renewing the agreements with the Russian Federation and the People's Republic of China on border regime and border ports and cross-points;

Develop incentives for stable and constant work by military officers and warrant officers in regions;

Improve living conditions and social security of military officers and warrant officers, assist them in obtaining civil profession simultaneously. Support the provision of job opportunities for family members of military officers and warrant officers serving at the border;

Actively participate in multilateral activities on strengthening regional security and military confidence building, expand external military relations and cooperation;

Resolve issues of creation of funds for rectification of damages caused by natural disasters and major industrial accidents;

Ensure all aspects of national security such as political, economic, civilizational, ecological etc. and prevent internal and external factors that may adversely affect on national security;

Create conducive environment for peaceful life of citizens and expand mutual cooperation between citizens and police;

Create legal environment which will ensure protection of the rights of Mongolian citizens working abroad and foreign citizens living in Mongolia ;

3. The Government shall thoroughly carry out, in line with the new realities at home and abroad, the principles and priority directions defined in the National Security as well as Foreign Policy Concepts of Mongolia and actively pursue an independent, open and multi-pillared foreign policy in accordance with its national interests and goals of sustainable development. The government shall uphold the continuity and integrity of foreign policy and shall continue to strengthen the independence, sovereignty and international position of Mongolia . Within the framework of this objective, the foreign policy program of the government is defined as follows:

The neighboring countries:

Good neighborly, friendly relations and all-round cooperation with the neighboring countries shall be maintained and promoted on the basis of traditions and confidence.

Good-neighborly, friendly relations, and equal, mutually beneficial cooperation with the Russian Federation shall be developed and expanded in all spheres and directions according to the provisions and spirit of the Treaty on Friendly Relations and Cooperation between Mongolia and the Russian Federation and all outstanding problems shall be solved in an appropriate way.

The good-neighborly, friendly relations and equal, mutually beneficial cooperation with the People's Republic of China shall be developed in a stable manner in accordance with the provisions and spirit of the Treaty on Friendly Relations and Cooperation as well as of the Joint Declaration of 1998 signed between Mongolia and People's Republic of China .

Cross-border pressing issues with neighboring countries shall be settled, the opportunities and potentials of economic cooperation shall be optimized, its efficiency shall be increased, cultural and humanitarian relations shall be promoted.

Relations with the countries of the Asia-Pacific region:

An active foreign policy shall be pursued in the Asia-Pacific region, bilateral relations and cooperation with countries of this region shall be developed and expanded.

Bearing in mind that the relations with the USA are significant in strengthening Mongolia 's democracy and market economy system, the relations and cooperation with this country shall be further developed and enhanced.

The comprehensive partnership relations and cooperation with Japan shall be further strengthened and expanded.

Friendly relations and cooperation with countries of the Asia- Pacific region such as the Republic of Korea and the Republic of India shall be promoted.

Level of political relations with ASEAN member states, as well as with Australia , New Zealand and Canada shall be upgraded and the framework of cooperation with these countries shall be expanded and enhanced.

Cherishing historical and cultural traditions, friendly relations and cooperation with Central Asian countries such as the Republic of Turkey and the Republic of Kazakhstan shall be developed.

While promoting cooperation with Latin American countries within the framework of international organizations, efforts shall be exerted to establish trade and economic relations with influential nations of this region.

Active bilateral dialogues and talks on Asia Pacific and North East Asia regional security issues shall be promoted on regular basis.

Relations with European countries:

Bearing in mind the significance of relations with European countries in achieving the objectives of strengthening democracy and market economy in Mongolia , mutually beneficial cooperation shall be developed with these countries.

Partnership relations with the European Union shall be enhanced, cooperation shall be expanded and developed with its member states, in particular with the FRG, the UK , France and Italy .

Mutually beneficial cooperation shall be developed with other European countries.

Relations with Middle Eastern and African countries:

Within the open foreign policy of Mongolia , relations, especially trade and economic cooperation with countries of Middle East and Africa shall be developed.

Relations with the UN and other international organizations:

The Government shall effectively participate in the activities of the United Nations Organization, its specialized agencies and other international organizations, in an endeavor to fruitfully benefit from the potentials of these organizations for guaranteeing national security, achieving social and economic goals.

The UN GA resolution on International security and the nuclear free status of Mongolia and the National Law on Mongolia 's nuclear weapon-free status shall be implemented, and the nuclear weapon-free status of Mongolia shall be secured at the international level by an appropriate international law.

The Government] shall actively participate in the works of the Nonaligned Movement and the Group of 77, cooperate with them on issues consistent with the common goals of developing countries and of its own national interests, and shall support to advance the North-South dialogue in order to reach an agreement.

Duties assumed under international organizations and international treaties shall be fulfilled.

Prospects of accession to international treaties on issues of human rights, protection of environment, improvement of situation of vulnerable strata of society, transnational issues, including combating organized crimes, terrorism and narcotics shall be explored, and Mongolia shall cooperate with international organizations in this field.

Participation in the Multilateral Processes

Mongolia shall work in a constructive and efficient manner to have its participation in the multilateral processes and dialogues on the issues related to the Asia-Pacific, Northeast and Central Asian security and in the regional economic and political integration processes.

Mongolia shall participate actively in the ASEAN Regional Forum /ARF/ activities and shall engage in the APEC and other multilateral dialogues aimed at developing political and economic cooperation between Asia and Europe .

Promoting External Economic Relations

The Government shall pursue a policy aimed at ensuring the unity of political and economic facets of the Mongolian foreign policy, managing the foreign economic relations in such a manner so that it should help in solving the outstanding social and economic tasks of the country.

While promoting close cooperation with donor countries [The Government] shall create favorable conditions for foreign trade and ensure conducive environment to attracting foreign direct investment. For these purposes the related laws and regulations shall be perfected.

Protection of Mongolian citizens' rights abroad

The Government is committed to facilitate the external travel regime for Mongolian citizens and attaches importance to the creation of an optimal legal environment for their study and work abroad. It shall also bring the consular service quality to the international standard.

Cultural and Humanitarian Relations

In developing humanitarian relations with foreign countries due attention shall be attached to the close cooperation with individuals, NGOs and local administrations and shall encourage their activities.

Shall promote active relations with international educational, cultural, art, sports and information organizations and foundations and accede to relevant treaties, stimulate active engagement of Mongolia in the international humanitarian activities.

Through promotion of Mongolian national culture abroad [The Government] shall expand the ranks of well-wishers and supporters of Mongolia .

Through expanding ties with people of Mongolian origin abroad endeavors shall be made to employ and encourage their potentials.

IMPORTANT OFFICIAL AND ANALYTICAL MATERIALS

GOVERNMENT ACTION PROGRAM ABOUT DEFENSE AND FOREIGN POLICY

1. The defense set-up of Mongolia and military reform policy shall be implemented consistently in accordance with the principles of the State military policy and measures shall be taken to eradicate distortions and problems accumulated in this field in recent years. Within the framework of these aims following actions shall be taken:

Revise and work out Defense and other laws & regulations, incorporate and enforce ways & forms of civic control over activities of Armed forces and other military organizations;

Define priorities and implement an initial stage of upgrading weapons & armament and technical renovation of Armed forces & Border Security Force;

Improve the organization of military, intensify the reforms, and increase the capabilities of military force;

Upgrade qualification of personnel of professional military units through improvement of terms and conditions of voluntary military services on agreement basis;

Revise and improve the training concept of military personnel of Armed forces in conformity with the contemporary needs and goals, conduct training in the areas different from basic responsibilities, such as natural disaster relief, rectification of damages of industrial accidents and humanitarian assistance to civilians;

Conduct training for those of substitute military service in particular cases such as to take measures to avoid natural disaster or to prevent industrial accidents and to fight them.

Ensure preparatory measures and undertake initial steps to participate in UN peace-keeping activities by personnel of Armed forces;

2. Independence and sovereignty of Mongolia shall be protected and conducive environment for peaceful life to its people shall be created. Within the framework of these aims following actions shall be taken:

Evaluate implementation of the State policy on the Border of Mongolia, laws and regulations related to border and of international agreements to which Mongolia acceded and improve their legal regulation. Create an independent set-up of Border Security Forces;

Conduct activities to stop and eliminate cross-border pilferage, intensify preventive measures against violations of State border, especially in Uvs, Zavkhan, Huvsgul, Dornod and Sukhbaatar aimags and ensure the integrity and non-violability of the borders of Mongolia;

Improve step by step the process of renovation of communication, technical supplies and transport of the Border Security Forces;

Improve the system of involvement of citizens, local organizations in regions in the protection of State border;

Undertake measures to further perfecting and renewing the agreements with the Russian Federation and the People's Republic of China on border regime and border ports and cross-points;

Develop incentives for stable and constant work by military officers and warrant officers in regions;

Improve living conditions and social security of military officers and warrant officers, assist them in obtaining civil profession simultaneously. Support the provision of job opportunities for family members of military officers and warrant officers serving at the border;

Actively participate in multilateral activities on strengthening regional security and military confidence building, expand external military relations and cooperation;

Resolve issues of creation of funds for rectification of damages caused by natural disasters and major industrial accidents;

Ensure all aspects of national security such as political, economic, civilizational, ecological etc. and prevent internal and external factors that may adversely affect on national security;

Create conducive environment for peaceful life of citizens and expand mutual cooperation between citizens and police;

Create legal environment which will ensure protection of the rights of Mongolian citizens working abroad and foreign citizens living in Mongolia ;

3. The Government shall thoroughly carry out, in line with the new realities at home and abroad, the principles and priority directions defined in the National Security as well as Foreign Policy Concepts of Mongolia and actively pursue an independent, open and multi-pillared foreign policy in accordance with its national interests and goals of sustainable development. The government shall uphold the continuity and integrity of foreign policy and shall continue to strengthen the independence, sovereignty and international position of Mongolia . Within the framework of this objective, the foreign policy program of the government is defined as follows:

THE NEIGHBORING COUNTRIES:

Good neighborly, friendly relations and all-round cooperation with the neighboring countries shall be maintained and promoted on the basis of traditions and confidence.

Good-neighborly, friendly relations, and equal, mutually beneficial cooperation with the Russian Federation shall be developed and expanded in all spheres and directions according to the provisions and spirit of the Treaty on Friendly Relations and Cooperation between Mongolia and the Russian Federation and all outstanding problems shall be solved in an appropriate way.

The good-neighborly, friendly relations and equal, mutually beneficial cooperation with the People's Republic of China shall be developed in a stable manner in accordance with the provisions and spirit of the Treaty on Friendly Relations and Cooperation as well as of the Joint Declaration of 1998 signed between Mongolia and People's Republic of China .

Cross-border pressing issues with neighboring countries shall be settled, the opportunities and potentials of economic cooperation shall be optimized, its efficiency shall be increased, cultural and humanitarian relations shall be promoted.

RELATIONS WITH THE COUNTRIES OF THE ASIA-PACIFIC REGION:

An active foreign policy shall be pursued in the Asia-Pacific region, bilateral relations and cooperation with countries of this region shall be developed and expanded.

Bearing in mind that the relations with the USA are significant in strengthening Mongolia 's democracy and market economy system, the relations and cooperation with this country shall be further developed and enhanced.

The comprehensive partnership relations and cooperation with Japan shall be further strengthened and expanded.

Friendly relations and cooperation with countries of the Asia- Pacific region such as the Republic of Korea and the Republic of India shall be promoted.

Level of political relations with ASEAN member states, as well as with Australia , New Zealand and Canada shall be upgraded and the framework of cooperation with these countries shall be expanded and enhanced.

Cherishing historical and cultural traditions, friendly relations and cooperation with Central Asian countries such as the Republic of Turkey and the Republic of Kazakhstan shall be developed.

While promoting cooperation with Latin American countries within the framework of international organizations, efforts shall be exerted to establish trade and economic relations with influential nations of this region.

Active bilateral dialogues and talks on Asia Pacific and North East Asia regional security issues shall be promoted on regular basis.

Relations with European countries:

Bearing in mind the significance of relations with European countries in achieving the objectives of strengthening democracy and market economy in Mongolia , mutually beneficial cooperation shall be developed with these countries.

Partnership relations with the European Union shall be enhanced, cooperation shall be expanded and developed with its member states, in particular with the FRG, the UK , France and Italy .

Mutually beneficial cooperation shall be developed with other European countries.

RELATIONS WITH MIDDLE EASTERN AND AFRICAN COUNTRIES:

Within the open foreign policy of Mongolia , relations, especially trade and economic cooperation with countries of Middle East and Africa shall be developed.

Relations with the UN and other international organizations:

The Government shall effectively participate in the activities of the United Nations Organization, its specialized agencies and other international organizations, in an endeavor to fruitfully benefit from the potentials of these organizations for guaranteeing national security, achieving social and economic goals.

The UN GA resolution on International security and the nuclear free status of Mongolia and the National Law on Mongolia 's nuclear weapon-free status shall be implemented, and the nuclear weapon-free status of Mongolia shall be secured at the international level by an appropriate international law.

The Government] shall actively participate in the works of the Nonaligned Movement and the Group of 77, cooperate with them on issues consistent with the common goals of developing countries and of its own national interests, and shall support to advance the North-South dialogue in order to reach an agreement.

Duties assumed under international organizations and international treaties shall be fulfilled.

Prospects of accession to international treaties on issues of human rights, protection of environment, improvement of situation of vulnerable strata of society, transnational issues, including combating organized crimes, terrorism and narcotics shall be explored, and Mongolia shall cooperate with international organizations in this field.

PARTICIPATION IN THE MULTILATERAL PROCESSES

Mongolia shall work in a constructive and efficient manner to have its participation in the multilateral processes and dialogues on the issues related to the Asia-Pacific, Northeast and Central Asian security and in the regional economic and political integration processes.

Mongolia shall participate actively in the ASEAN Regional Forum /ARF/ activities and shall engage in the APEC and other multilateral dialogues aimed at developing political and economic cooperation between Asia and Europe .

PROMOTING EXTERNAL ECONOMIC RELATIONS

The Government shall pursue a policy aimed at ensuring the unity of political and economic facets of the Mongolian foreign policy, managing the foreign economic relations in such a manner so that it should help in solving the outstanding social and economic tasks of the country.

While promoting close cooperation with donor countries [The Government] shall create favorable conditions for foreign trade and ensure conducive environment to attracting foreign direct investment. For these purposes the related laws and regulations shall be perfected.

PROTECTION OF MONGOLIAN CITIZENS' RIGHTS ABROAD

The Government is committed to facilitate the external travel regime for Mongolian citizens and attaches importance to the creation of an optimal legal environment for their study and work abroad. It shall also bring the consular service quality to the international standard.

CULTURAL AND HUMANITARIAN RELATIONS

In developing humanitarian relations with foreign countries due attention shall be attached to the close cooperation with individuals, NGOs and local administrations and shall encourage their activities.

Shall promote active relations with international educational, cultural, art, sports and information organizations and foundations and accede to relevant treaties, stimulate active engagement of Mongolia in the international humanitarian activities.

Through promotion of Mongolian national culture abroad [The Government] shall expand the ranks of well-wishers and supporters of Mongolia .

Through expanding ties with people of Mongolian origin abroad endeavors shall be made to employ and encourage their potentials.

POTENTIAL THREAT OF TERRORISM IN MONGOLIA

An extensive network of international terrorism, has long embraced all regions of the world becomes increasingly global in scope and unpredictability of challenges. Terrorism is linked with problems such as proliferation of weapons of mass destruction, geopolitical rivalries, religious strife, the clash of civilizations, ethnic and cultural differences. According to analysts, the risk inherent dangers of terrorism in particular are not involved in the regional security system to underdeveloped countries, with their own disabilities to ensure their safety. From all this it is clear that more and more difficult to ensure reliable security for our citizens and protect them from attacks of international terrorism.

Since the terrorist activity, we still generally small, let me share my thoughts about the theoretically possible terrorist machinations in Mongolia. In a number of accepted documents, such as "The National Security of Mongolia," a decree on "performing various destructive and destructive action and espionage," "Policy framework of government armed forces," stated the thesis that "the actions of any country, especially in an organized and prepared the armed men for implementation in Mongolia for the purpose of further destructive, disruptive and other unlawful acts on the territory of Mongolia, "will be treated as an armed terrorist act against Mongolia.

In addition, the Armed Forces Act, the law of emergency, the instructions on the use of armed forces in the Charter of the General Staff of the Armed Forces and many other instruments are clearly defined legal framework for the participation of armed forces in the fight with fighter operations. In Mongolia, terrorism can be shown as follows:

1. The attack on prominent politicians, high government officials, diplomats and executives of banking institutions, businesses, seizure of kindergartens, schools or hostage-taking of people with the presentation of certain terms and conditions. 2. The nomination of the political, economic and criminal claims to political parties, international organizations and the mass public, the implementation of major attacks on strategic targets of the country, places of mass gatherings, temporary seizure of objects. 3. Carrying out destructive actions and explosions using the airports, densely populated areas, machinery, equipment and construction projects. 4. Negative environmental habitat and ecological conditions, as well as implementation of constant pressure and violence. 5. With the aim of undermining international relations, an attempt of hijacking, hostage taking of foreign guests and representatives, or the attempt on their lives. A. Consider the external factors of a hypothetical terrorist threat in Mongolia. In our neighboring two countries, Russian Federation and the Republic of China, has long been seen terrorism, which is based on Islamic fundamentalism, terrorism and they are now under intensive development. Superseded

by the anti-terrorism, the terrorists from these countries in search of a safe haven, can move to Mongolia - a country more comfortable for their existence. The external factors contributing to the rise of the terrorist threat in Mongolia, include the following: - the nature of the geopolitical changes in the region - transparency boundaries in the overall process of globalization; - vnegranichnaya relationship nationalists; - boycott extremist ideology of terrorists - the use of the spread of nuclear technology to create a "dirty bomb"; - part of terrorists in illegal immigration, human trafficking, cross-border conflicts; - influence on the masses by means of transportation and use of drug - use of territorial disputes; - illegal trans-border trade, organized crime, - growing difference between rich and poor, deteriorating conditions of life - freedom of information flow, new technology. There are the following possible dangers of terrorism in Mongolia - the ravages of ; - an attempt on the life - of people stealing and taking of hostages; - burglary / theft of cattle near border areas, etc. - the seizure of buildings and objects - an armed attack; - bioterrorism; - cyberterrorism. Types of possible terrorist attacks from the outside: - Explosion or seizure of a foreign embassy in Mongolia, representatives of international organizations, the presentation of political and other requirements. - The assassination attempt on the heads of state and government of foreign countries who came to visit Mongolia. - Trying to thwart rallies, meetings and symposia of international level, carried out in Mongolia . - The attack on the industrial and economic facilities with foreign investment. - Capture of international flights and airport security to attempt flight. - hostage-taking of major political and public figures, representatives of the banking and financial institutions, an attempt on their lives. - The attack on the State Bank , financial and commercial organizations. - Attack of the international railway and border posts and their capture. - Trying to terrorists, members of terrorist groups or their supporters to enter the territory of Mongolia, to temporarily hide it or to create a terrorist base. - Illegal introduction of capital for the financing of terrorist organizations under the pretext of assisting Mongolia, or under the guise of tax transactions or money laundering. - Trying to illegal cross-border implementation or transport of drugs through Mongolia, drugs, firearms and explosives. The negative impact of possible international terrorist attacks include: - The death of foreign nationals, damage to their health. - Risk for Mongolian citizens to be subjected to violence. - psychological distress and disruption of normal life for citizens. - The emergence of the crisis in the stable development of society and the economy of Mongolia. - Violation of the normal functioning of the social and political organizations. - Negative impact on environmental safety. The main danger of terrorist attacks coming from the organization of Inner Mongolia-Shinzan Uygar China, terrorists Muslims in Chechnya (Russian Federation), the Muslim group "Al Qaeda", "Muslim Brotherhood" opposing any U.S. activity. B. Consider the background of possible domestic terrorism threats in Mongolia. Today we can say that in Mongolia there is no direct terrorist threats. This is because: - In Mongolia, had not yet formed terrorist organization. - There is no experience of terrorist training, voluntary suicide. - There is no ground for extremist views of Muslims. - There is currently no nation or nationality, which has set out a direct order to separatism and the declaration of independence. - Not yet formed any movement, political parties or groups who have contact with foreign terrorist organizations. - stopped by inciting ethnic hatred - the prerequisites for terrorist activity. - There is a sharp deterioration in living conditions. Factors contributing to the eventual emergence of terrorism in Mongolia: - Wide public access via the Internet and mass media to information about terrorist activity allows some citizens to use their acquired knowledge as a practical guide to drawing methods and techniques of terrorism. Moreover, the information channels of the Internet and mass media have the opportunity to receive both moral and financial support from international terrorist organizations. - We have no experience of fighting against terrorism, there is no organization to this appointment, did not come out and the anti-terrorism that may impact negatively. - Increase in the number of victims of alcohol makes it easier to distabilizatsii situation in the country by involving drunken crowd to destructive actions - Terrorists could be used vital strategic facilities, airports, capital cities and major provinces, petrol stations, public buildings and public places of destination. - Increase the number of people consciously ready to commit suicide, commit crimes, drug addicts, can recruit volunteers from among the bombers (kamikaze), persons wishing to participate in terrorist acts. What, however, creates advertising and set a good example for the ranks of terrorists. V. The most terror-vulnerable areas and facilities for terrorists choose their targets places crowded and densely populated areas. In Mongolia, for such are the following places: - Public and government buildings in Mongolia. - International organizations and the various offices in Mongolia. - The capital and provincial centers. - International items with non-stop service. - International airports. - Production strategic objects. - Companies and the economy to foreign investment. - Military facilities. - of culture, education and science. - Places of entertainment. - Public transport. - nurseries, kindergartens, schools and hospitals. - Business services (hotels, markets, department stores). - Railways and railway stations. - Embassies of foreign countries. - Monasteries and cultural attractions. G. Opportunities and ways to combat terrorism today, when there is a range of international terrorism worldwide, the most urgent goal is to bring together law enforcement agencies, such as law enforcement, organizations for the fight against organized crime, law enforcement agencies, to develop unified and concerted action to counter terrorism. The many manifestations of terrorism complicates counterterrorism. However, some systematization of knowledge about the threat of terrorist attack can more accurately plan for countermeasures to neutralize the call. The scheme works with terrorist threats is approximately as follows: - you need to pinpoint and foreign citizens, as well as the most important items that may be susceptible to terrorist attacks; - should be pre-estimate potential losses and negative impacts; - to develop a specific plan for rapid response and a point to counter terrorist the act. As terrorism has acquired an international character, and one country is difficult to cope with this threat, you need to counter-terrorism cooperation with other states. Therefore, to participate in anti-terrorism should all states from bringing intelligence and armed forces which will depend on success in the fight against terrorism. It is also important to exchange information in this regard between the two countries, to establish control over the financing of terrorist organizations and their supply of weapons to try once and for all stop terrorism. Conclusion In Mongolia, while relatively calm situation with regard to terrorism, but with the deepening of the market economy and to participate in processes of globalization, Mongolia does not avoid involvement in this issue. I must say that due to the increase of foreign investments in larger companies in our country and with an increase in the interest of the leading countries in the world to our country, we can not deny the fact that Mongolia could be in the area of terrorist activity. From the bitter examples of terrorism in other countries We can draw the following conclusions: 1. Terrorism has become to grow both qualitatively and quantitatively, that is likely to continue in the future. 2. Our neighboring countries began to change in the territory, favorable for the activity of terrorist groups and organizations. 3. Personal characteristics and suicide bombings mechanism increasingly improved. Expanding base of terror and stepped up its display. 4. In order to minimize social disruption shocks should be in the fight against terrorism, greater use of special forces. 5. Terrorists try to capture whole countries and regions and to establish over them the control. Therefore, increasing the scale of threats and changes to an adequate system to counteract new challenges. 6. Terrorists are completely focused on the acquisition of weapons of mass destruction and make it their main objective the capture of large strategic sites. For reliable protection of the country against terrorist attacks, you must first begin preparations for the joint fight against the combined forces and unified plan of action, and therefore should be held the following Activities: - to protect objects of national importance to joint exercises, and develop an overall plan for counter-terrorism operations; - to be held in the armed units trained to fight terrorism - the exchange of information and familiarization with practical experience in combating terrorism through cooperation with international organizations ; - to develop a joint plan of action corresponding to the modern level of defense. In the fight against terrorism should follow a common pattern: the identification of terrorist groups in the early stages of their creation, the prevention of terrorist activity, timely control them, good planning and the elimination of neutralizing their gangs. If we work together we can forge a united front against terrorism, then we will have a wholly owned possibility to prevent large-scale terror and we contribute to the overall victory over terrorism. Epilogue Eugene Vertlib to the article, Major-General Mihlaya Borbaatora "potential terrorist threat in Mongolia," Unfortunately in Mongolia is not all so well, just hypothetically ugrozno. U.S. President George W. Bush will not casually called Mongolia "bastion of democracy" in Asia. On arrival in Ulan Bator, he held talks with Prime Minister Democrat, a typical "orange" leader Edbegdorzhem (Harvard graduate), although, according to Article 32 of the Constitution of Mongolia, a country in the international arena is its president, which is the representative of the People's Revolutionary Party (MPRP) Enkhbayar. The situation after such diplomatic nonsense is extremely acute. After partial dismissal of the government of Mongolia and raise fares on public transport in Ulan Bator, the events occurred, reminiscent of the revolution in Kyrgyzstan. More than 1.5 thousand people stormed the headquarters of the MPRP. The current political climate in Mongolia like "drawn" version of the "orange revolution." The first raid, said K. Goloskokov associated with raising the question of the legitimacy of the election and are judged to have been spent to automatism, not quite reached the goal. Perhaps due to the fact that not a nationalist resource: the architects of this campaign, apparently sought to "get rid of a little blood," and used mainly the rhetoric about democracy and the future of life "in America," ie, worked on the scheme of Yugoslavia (Mongolian experience was taken into account while preparing for the "orange revolution" in Ukraine, where nationalist factor has played a crucial role). As a result of this first swoop revolutionaries share power and responsibility with his adversary, and, eventually, discredit themselves. But the banner of the revolution must carry on, because the victory was so close. Here, it turns out, demanded the "right" bias. So much for social unrest, provoking terrorist livelihoods bacilli. In a society where a lot of unemployed and poor, growing social tensions. In 1990. realized in Mongolia religious pluralism, which changed the face of this Buddhist country. Freedom of religion has led to Mongolia Protestant missionaries and Western culture. In order to counter the threat of destabilization in the country is currently developing "a single national policy" out of the crisis, taking into account and the revival of Buddhism as an ideological foundation for the preservation of national identity, culture and traditions of the Mongols. The ideological confrontation between the factor of cultural and religious orientations contributes to rise of terrorism. And more. As a result of global climate change and the impoverishment of the soil fertile opustynivaetsya Mongolia, its cultivated area is reduced annually - country's food security is deteriorating, as there is no guarantee of supply of wheat from Russia and China, buying her own. to try once and for all stop terrorism. Conclusion In Mongolia, while relatively calm situation with regard to terrorism, but with the deepening of the market economy and participation in the processes of globalization, Mongolia did not avoid involvement in this issue. I must say that due to the increase of foreign investments in larger companies in our country and with an increase in the interest of the leading countries in the world to our country, we can not deny the fact that Mongolia could be in the area of terrorist activity. From the bitter examples of terrorism in other countries We can draw the following conclusions: 1. Terrorism has become to grow both qualitatively and quantitatively, that is likely to continue in the future. 2. Our neighboring countries began to change in the territory, favorable for the activity of terrorist groups and organizations. 3. Personal characteristics and suicide bombings mechanism increasingly improved. Expanding base of terror and stepped up its display. 4. In order to minimize social disruption shocks should be in the fight against terrorism, greater use of special forces. 5. Terrorists try to capture whole countries and regions and to establish over them the control. Therefore, increasing the scale of threats and changes to an adequate system to counteract new challenges. 6. Terrorists are completely focused on the acquisition of weapons of mass destruction and make it their main objective the capture of large strategic sites. For reliable protection of the country against terrorist attacks, you must first begin preparations for the joint fight against the combined forces and unified plan of action, and therefore should be held the following Activities: - to protect objects of national importance to joint exercises, and develop an overall plan for counter-terrorism operations; - to be held in the armed units trained to fight terrorism - the exchange of information and familiarization with practical experience in combating terrorism through cooperation with international organizations ; - to develop a joint plan of action corresponding to the modern level of defense. In the fight against terrorism should follow a common pattern: the identification of terrorist groups in the early stages of their creation, the prevention of terrorist activity, timely control them, good planning and the elimination of neutralizing their gangs. If we work together we can forge a united front against terrorism, then we will have a wholly owned possibility to prevent large-scale terror and we contribute to the overall victory over terrorism. Epilogue Eugene Vertlib to the article, Major-General Mihlaya

Borbaatora "potential terrorist threat in Mongolia," Unfortunately in Mongolia is not all so well, just hypothetically ugrozno. U.S. President George W. Bush will not casually called Mongolia "bastion of democracy" in Asia. On arrival in Ulan Bator, he held talks with Prime Minister Democrat, a typical "orange" leader Edbegdorzhem (Harvard graduate), although, according to Article 32 of the Constitution of Mongolia, a country in the international arena is its president, which is the representative of the People's Revolutionary Party (MPRP) Enkhbayar. The situation after such diplomatic nonsense is extremely acute. After partial dismissal of the government of Mongolia and raise fares on public transport in Ulan Bator, the events occurred, reminiscent of the revolution in Kyrgyzstan. More than 1.5 thousand people stormed the headquarters of the MPRP. The current political climate in Mongolia like "drawn" version of the "orange revolution." The first raid, said K. Goloskokov associated with raising the question of the legitimacy of the election and are judged to have been spent to automatism, not quite reached the goal. Perhaps due to the fact that not a nationalist resource: the architects of this campaign, apparently sought to "get rid of a little blood," and used mainly the rhetoric about democracy and the future of life "in America," ie, worked on the scheme of Yugoslavia (Mongolian experience was taken into account while preparing for the "orange revolution" in Ukraine, where nationalist factor has played a crucial role). As a result of this first swoop revolutionaries share power and responsibility with his opponent and, eventually, discredit themselves. But the banner of the revolution must carry on, because the victory was so close. Here, it turns out, demanded the "right" bias. So much for social unrest, provoking terrorist livelihoods bacilli. In a society where a lot of unemployed and poor, growing social tensions. In 1990. realized in Mongolia religious pluralism, which changed the face of this Buddhist country. Freedom of religion has led to Mongolia Protestant missionaries and Western culture. In order to counter the threat of destabilization in the country is currently developing "a single national policy" out of the crisis, taking into account and the revival of Buddhism as an ideological foundation for the preservation of national identity, culture and traditions of the Mongols. The ideological confrontation between the factor of cultural and religious orientations contributes to rise of terrorism. And more. As a result of global climate change and the impoverishment of the soil fertile opustynivaetsya Mongolia, its cultivated area is reduced annually - country's food security is deteriorating, as there is no guarantee of supply of wheat from Russia and China, buying her own. to try once and for all stop terrorism. Conclusion In Mongolia, while relatively calm situation with regard to terrorism, but with the deepening of the market economy and participation in the processes of globalization, Mongolia did not avoid involvement in this issue. I must say that due to the increase of foreign investments in larger companies in our country and with an increase in the interest of the leading countries in the world to our country, we can not deny the fact that Mongolia could be in the area of terrorist activity. From the bitter examples of terrorism in other countries We can draw the following conclusions: 1. Terrorism has become to grow both qualitatively and quantitatively, that is likely to continue in the future. 2. Our neighboring countries began to change in the territory, favorable for the activity of terrorist groups and organizations. 3. Personal characteristics and suicide bombings mechanism increasingly improved. Expanding base of terror and stepped up its display. 4. In order to minimize social disruption shocks should be in the fight against terrorism, greater use of special forces. 5. Terrorists try to capture whole countries and regions and to establish over them the control. Therefore, increasing the scale of threats and changes to an adequate system to counteract new challenges. 6. Terrorists are completely focused on the acquisition of weapons of mass destruction and make it their main objective the capture of large strategic sites. For reliable protection of the country against terrorist attacks, you must first begin preparations for the joint fight against the combined forces and unified plan of action, and therefore should be held the following Activities: - to protect objects of national importance to joint exercises, and develop an overall plan for counter-terrorism operations; - to be held in the armed units trained to fight terrorism - the exchange of information and familiarization with practical experience in combating terrorism through cooperation with international organizations ; - to develop a joint plan of action corresponding to the modern level of defense. In the fight against terrorism should follow a common pattern: the identification of terrorist groups in the early stages of their creation, the prevention of terrorist activity, timely control them, good planning and the elimination of neutralizing their gangs. If we work together we can forge a united front against terrorism, then we will have a wholly owned possibility to prevent large-scale terror and we contribute to the overall victory over terrorism. Epilogue Eugene Vertlib to the article, Major-General Mihlaya Borbaatora "potential terrorist threat in Mongolia," Unfortunately in Mongolia is not all so well, just hypothetically ugrozno. U.S. President George W. Bush will not casually called Mongolia "bastion of democracy" in Asia. On arrival in Ulan Bator, he held talks with Prime Minister Democrat, a typical "orange" leader Edbegdorzhem (Harvard graduate), although, according to Article 32 of the Constitution of Mongolia, a country in the international arena is its president, which is the representative of the People's Revolutionary Party (MPRP) Enkhbayar. The situation after such diplomatic nonsense is extremely acute. After partial dismissal of the government of Mongolia and raise fares on public transport in Ulan Bator, the events occurred, reminiscent of the revolution in Kyrgyzstan. More than 1.5 thousand people stormed the headquarters of the MPRP. The current political climate in Mongolia like "drawn" version of the "orange revolution." The first raid, said K. Goloskokov associated with raising the question of the legitimacy of the election and are judged to have been spent to automatism, not quite reached the goal. Perhaps due to the fact that not a nationalist resource: the architects of this campaign, apparently sought to "get rid of a little blood," and used mainly the rhetoric about democracy and the future of life "in America," ie, worked on the scheme of Yugoslavia (Mongolian experience was taken into account while preparing for the "orange revolution" in Ukraine, where nationalist factor has played a crucial role). As a result of this first swoop revolutionaries share power and responsibility with his opponent and, eventually, discredit themselves.

But the banner of the revolution must carry on, because the victory was so close. Here, it turns out, demanded the "right" bias. So much for social unrest, provoking terrorist livelihoods bacilli. In a society where a lot of unemployed and poor, growing social tensions. In 1990. realized in Mongolia religious pluralism, which changed the face of this Buddhist country. Freedom of religion has led to Mongolia Protestant missionaries and Western culture. In order to counter the threat of destabilization in the country is currently developing "a single national policy" out of the crisis, taking into account and the revival of Buddhism as an ideological foundation for the preservation of national identity, culture and traditions of the Mongols.

The ideological confrontation between the factor of cultural and religious orientations contributes to rise of terrorism. And more. As a result of global climate change and the impoverishment of the soil fertile opustynivaetsya Mongolia, its cultivated area is reduced annually - country's food security is deteriorating, as there is no guarantee of supply of wheat from Russia and China, buying her own.

ACTION PROGRAM OF THE GOVERNMENT OF MONGOLIA

The Government of Mongolia formed as a result of the third parliamentary elections defines its Action Program for the next four years on the basis of the election program of the MPRP.

The key objectives of the Action Program of the Government of Mongolia are to:

- **Continue and deepen the economic reform and ensure higher economic growth;**
- **Pursue an export-oriented economic policy and sustain higher economic growth;**
- **Respect and preserve education and culture, and promote human factor - the keystone of the development;**
- **Improve the living standard of people by streamlining the distribution of wealth and income, and develop an effective system of social welfare;**

- **Adopt and implement regional development concept and on this basis, narrow the gap between the development and living standard in the rural and urban areas;**
- **Formulate and effectively implement a social and economic development policy, tailored to the specific conditions of Mongolia, and set up highly efficient and accountable Governance.**

ONE. SOCIAL POLICY

The key objectives of the social sector lie in creating an environment for human development, improving the living standard of citizens, ensuring an equal access to social services, and reducing unemployment and poverty.

1. An environment which provides people with equal opportunity and access to education shall be created; the system of basic education and all types of professional training shall be developed in compliance with individual's interest, needs of the society and the market force; and a system that provides with modern education shall be established.

- **Increase investment and capital repair in the education sector;**
- **Expand and construct buildings for crowded schools and maintain the rural school buildings to meet the normal requirements of educational activities;**
- **Support and encourage private Investment in the education sector;**
- **Computerize all secondary schools and install the Internet;**
- **Redesign the education content in order to prepare young generation for the future life and work and to teach them the traditional and as well as modern production technologies; Enforce educational environment standards; and, adopt the quality evaluation system;**
- **Actively seek possibilities for mutual acceptance of educational documents by domestic and foreign schools;**
- **Review regulations on accreditation of professional schools and take measure to improve quality of schooling;**
- **Improve text book writing, publishing and distribution systems;**
- **Expand secondary school attendance and fully subsidize expenses related to the school dormitory;**
- **Provide children of vulnerable group famllies and those families with more than three children attending schools starting 2000-2001 school year with free textbooks and stationary;**
- **Expand scope of pre-school education activities, improve kindergarten attendance and introduce a new method of training children at home school;**

- **Welcome branches of colleges and universities of developed countries in Mongolia and provide them an opportunity to function normally and permanently; Support with tuition to students of such institutions;**

- **Resolve issues of providing grants and awards to talented and academically brilliant students of domestic universities and colleges;**

- **Grant scholarships to domestic universities and college students of poor and herder's family and a student of a family with more than two children attending higher education schools;**

- **Take measures to ensure that domestic university and college students receive the same benefits and allowances in accordance with the international practice, and support students to improve their lives by working during non-class hours;**

- **Effectively conduct informal and distance education, and specialized training; Provide drop-outs with necessary training and reduce substantially illiteracy rate;**

- **Formulate a policy designed at staffing Government institutions and organizations with qualified personnel; Make an request of such personnel according to needs and requirements and ensure that contracted students have a guaranteed job upon graduation;**

- **Increase the number of students in MA and Ph.D. degrees in developed countries; Set up the requirements to learn and use internationally accepted languages as a door to the latest information and new technology;**

- **Renew training and retraining system of teacher and education management staff;**

- **Upgrade and intensify professional training.**

2. The quality of health service and health preventive measures shall be developed to international standards and on this basis the objectives to improve population health and increase the average life expectancy shall be achieved. These objectives include the following:

- **Budget allocations to the basic health care and services shall be increased each year;**

- **Free preventive medical check-ups, diagnosis and laboratory testing at Government–run hospitals shall be introduced by way of revising the types of medical car and services covered by health, insurance and the latter shall be developed independently;**

- **A system of providing basic medical assistance through family doctors shall be introduced;**

- **An immunization fund shall be set up measures designed at gradually decreasing and eventually eliminating infectious diseases using preventive vaccines shall be taken;**

- **Free medical services shall be provided to vulnerable groups, i.e., the elderly, female headed households with many children, adolescents and handicapped people;**

- **Programs on protecting maternal and infant health, and reducing infant and maternal mortality shall be financed and implemented by the Government;**

- **Within the framework of an integrated drug policy the availability of medical drugs shall be improved and quality control shall be tightened. Abnormal practices of patients paying the ambulance fuel cost and drugs used during therapy shall be eliminated;**

- **A national Healthcare Technology Program shall be formulated and implemented**

- **Diagnostic and therapeutic centers shall be set up in economic regions and they shall be furnished with modern medical equipment and staffed with qualified & doctors;**

- **Not less than 40% of ambulance fleet in soums and 60% in aimag centers and the capital city shall be renovated;**

- **Soum hospital development program shall be implemented and soum hospitals shall be provided with designated premises and equipment, the access to and the quality of medical services to rural population shall be improved by way of creating the and create conditions and incentives for doctors and health workers to improve their knowledge and profession, and to work continuously in one place;**

- **Measures shall be taken to protect the health of the population, and in particular by encouraging the extensive utilization of mineral spring care services in rehabilitative therapy;**

- **Private health institutions shall be supported and their coverage by the health insurance fund shall be expanded;**

- **The quality of medical services to the population shall be improved by way of improving the quality of certified health institutions & medical doctors system;**

- **Big sports shall be patronized. Mass physical culture and sports shall be developed extensively to protect population health and promote physical health of shall be patronized young people.**

3. The Government shall work to ensure an intensive development of national culture and arts in conformity with the world cultural achievements and values and the unique features of Oriental culture. Within this context, the Government shall:

- **Improve institutional set up of cultural and art institutions and strengthen their management;**

- **Develop traditional culture and art in combination with classical and modern art; Introduce into practice universal norms and standards of civilized human relations such as the study and advocacy of and respect for national language and culture;**

- **Implement projects on the protection and rehabilitation of monuments in Harhorin and of those pertaining to the period of the Turks in Mongolia;**

- **Patronize classical and children's art and books, Increase financial support to their creators in order for them to take part in international contests and to improve their professionalism;**

- **Re-open soum culture centers and libraries and increase the scope and coverage of cultural, art and information services provided to the rural population;**

- **Build a Children's Book Palace;**

- **Support outstanding artists and sportsmen;**

- **While ensuring the religious freedom of people, the Government shall support the research of traditional religion which is a cultural, intellectual and ethical heritage of the Mongolian people and shall support the revival, inheritance and development of religious culture;**

- **The activities of all educational institutions, and cultural & scientific organizations shall be directed at promoting national spiritual traditions of the Mongolians such as respect for the elderly and complying with humane morality of ancestors.**

4. The Government shall implement a national program on acquiring a relative development edge by way of boosting scientific & technological capabilities, and shall work to increase the evaluation of works by scientists and researchers. Within this framework, the Government shall:

- **Formulate and start implementing a long-term national program on the development of Mongolia's science and technology up to the year 2010;**

- **Establish a self-financing and independent science-education-production complex in line with the Long-term development program priorities;**

- **Increase government orders for priority research on traditional technology, biotechnology, new materials, information technology and new energy sources, support & encourage their application into production;**

- **Increase the number of researchers and scholars to be trained in the country and abroad in priority areas of science and technology;**

- **Establish an integrated scientific and technological information network and database; enrich research libraries fund and improve their usage;**

- **Increase the supply of necessary instruments, equipment, chemical reagents and other materials for research institutions ;**

- **Improve and expand cooperation and coordination among scientific, educational and production organizations; increase the evaluation of intellectual products and streamline related legislation;**

- **Cooperate actively with international organizations and foreign countries in the field of science and technology; and support the establishment of joint laboratories and centers.**

5. The Government shall improve the system of wealth and income distribution, halt the decline in the living standard of the people, narrow income gap among social groups and eliminate absolute poverty. For this purpose, the Government shall:

- **Reduce by twice, as compared to 1999, the number of poor households living under the poverty line through the implementation of a set of social and economic measures to prevent living standard decline and the creation of jobs for able-bodied and working age poor citizens;**

- Starting this year, gradually increase the minimum wage to triple it as compared to the level at the beginning of 2000;
- Increase the salary of civil servants every year starting from 2001 to double it more than the present level;
- Improve the working and living conditions of civil servants and set up a concessional credit fund designed at providing loan to them for construction of private houses;
- Grant special allowances to civil servants, teachers and doctors working in remote and desert areas;
- Streamline the national social welfare system and increase its capacity;
- Improve social insurance relations and take measures to protect children, family members and relatives from risks by bringing them under the insurance system;
- Gradually increase the size of pensions and allowances provided from the Social Security Fund starting from 2001 to twice that of today's level;
- Increase to the minimum pension level the compensatory pension of those who have retired before their retirement age due to administrative arrangements;
- Fully introduce the notional individual pension account;
- Expand social insurance coverage and strengthen the responsibility of timely payment of insurance contributions; improve self financing of the social insurance fund;
- Revise and enforce labor safety and sanitary standards in accordance with the Labor Code;
- Enforce new regulation on payment of benefits from industrial accident and professional illness insurance fund for disabled people during their injury period caused by industrial accident and professional illness, and expenses incurred during care and treatment;
- Cover herders and self employed citizens under social insurance and improve their social welfare;
- Establish and enforce a procedure on granting long-term soft loan to young families for construction of private houses; resolve the issue of privatization of apartments owned by organizations;
- Increase the number and types of benefits and services rendered to senior veterans;
- Improve social care for poor and disabled people, and mothers with many children;
- Support and encourage the creation of new jobs as a part of a set of measures to create better employment opportunities. Promote microcredit;
- Provide opportunities for people not covered by unemployment insurance and for long-term unemployed people with professional training and labor market activities;

- **Pay attention to creating favorable conditions for neglected children to live in their own homes and take measures to provide them with assistance and services;**

- **Improve the quality of training at vocational education and production centers;**

- **Establish a credit fund to promote small and medium size enterprises and small-scale crop, vegetable, fruit, berry, and poultry farming in rural areas;**
- **Create a favorable legal environment for the protection of the rights of Mongolian citizens working abroad and for export and import of labor;**

- **Formulate and implement a policy on population migration in accordance with regional development.**

TWO. ECONOMIC POLICY

Sustainable and high economic growth shall be ensured by reinforcing macro economic stability and intensifying structural reforms based on export-oriented and private sector led economy. Priority shall be given to improving the level of processing mining and animal-origin raw materials and developing export-oriented and tourist industries.

Economic growth shall be accelerated, and shall be increased by 6 percent 2004. In order to achieve these objectives, the following policies shall be implemented:

- **Ensure macroeconomic stability;**
- **Build up sound banking and financial sectors;**
- **Continue the privatization process and improve its efficiency;**
- **Restore domestic industries and promote export;**
- **Intensively develop infrastructure.**

1. Ensure macroeconomic stability:

- **Stabilize the real exchange rate of the national currency and maintain the inflation rate at an adequate level that would stimulate the economy, production and investment;**

- **Reduce budget deficit;**

- **Decrease unemployment by not less than 50%;**

- **Reduce foreign trade deficit;**

- **Take a set of legal and economic measures to eliminate the shadow economy;**

- **Strengthen the independent status of the statistics office and ensure transparency by improving official statistics information system.**

Tax issues:

- **Expand the basis assessment and develop it to support production, improve collection of taxes, and take comprehensive measures aimed at building the capacity of tax authorities;**

- **Tighten control on tax imposition and payment, enhance the management for tax arrears and tighten legal regulations;**

- **Resolve the issue of dual taxation and make the relevant decision available to the public. Reduce tax concession and exemption;**

- **Pursue a differentiated and flexible customs duty and tax policy in order to promote production and investment in the regions; reduce tax burden on business entities by up to 30 percent;**

- **Exempt from corporate income taxes for a definite period of time those investors, that have created jobs other than in alcoholic production and its trade in rural areas;**

- **Take measures to gradually reduce individual income tax imposed on low income people;**

- **Impose an average of 10% import duty;**

- **Grant tax holidays on the importation of machinery and equipment, raw and other materials by business entities exporting their goods and products;**

- **Make public information on registration of customs duty, exemptions, and tax payments.**

Fiscal issues:

- Formulate and implement a policy directed at ensuring a stable growth of budget revenue sources;
- Formulate budget proposals in conformity with medium and long-term macroeconomic policies; improve budget financing process and gradually introduce output-based financing;
- Improve the basis of budget expenditure financing norms and standards;
- Streamline treasury cash management system;
- Establish a price risk-proof mechanism of protecting main strategic commodities as gold, copper and cashmere;
- Clearly determine the sources and utilization of special funds, improve their management and organization, and ensure their transparency;
- Provide local governments greater opportunity to generate local budget independently and take measures to strengthen the duties and responsibilities of local representative authorities.

2. Build up sound banking and financial sectors:

- **Develop a sound banking system by accelerating the structural reform process, privatizing commercial banks, improving their management and by attracting foreign investment;**

- **Tighten legal procedures in order to improve responsibilities of debtors and creditors in repayment of the loans extended by commercial banks;**

- **Restructure the Agricultural Bank into Development Bank, and enhance its competitive edge;**
- **Create the necessary legal environment related to supporting non-banking financial institutions and developing a better system that mobilizes the remaining balance of insurance companies;**
- **Pursue flexible monetary and credit policies to expand production services activities and to encourage and promote domestic industry and investment;**
- **Create a favorable environment for development of securities market, expand its scope and increase information and public awareness campaign;**
- **Improve supervision over participants' activities in the securities market, develop a system on allocation and distribution of dividends to shareholders, and protect their interests;**
- **Broaden insurance coverage and increase the number of different types of insurance. Take measures to increase the accountability of insurance companies and make information about them available to the public;**

3. Continuation of the privatization process and improving its efficiency:

- **Eliminate distortions of the privatization process, strengthen law enforcement and improve accountability;**
- **Improve the management of privatized entities and pay attention to the final results and efficiency improvement;**
- **Privatize business entities on the basis of the most appropriate methods allowed by law and accelerate the privatization process;**
- **Privatize most valuable enterprises with an eye on their economic efficiency and national security concerns;**
- **Restructure the energy sector and gradually market the government shares in state-owned enterprises in the energy and mining sectors;**
- **Create a legal environment for privatization of the social sector, and commence social sector privatization;**
- **Adopt a principle of mobilizing privatization earnings solely for investment purposes.**

1. Revival of domestic industries and promotion of export:

PROMOTING DOMESTIC INDUSTRIES:

- **Implement the "Cashmere" program, increase export of Mongolian cashmere products and improve their competitiveness on the world market;**
- **Establish a reserve fund of strategic raw materials such as cashmere and wheat grain and support domestic producers by giving loans for working capital and raw materials purchase;**

- Improve the quality of processing of animal-origin raw materials, particularly meat, cashmere, sheep and camel wool, skin and hides;

- Implement "Wool", "Skin and Hides" sub-programs and increase the export of scoured wool and processed skin. Encourage export through revision of standards for preparation of sheep and camel wool, yak and horse hair, skin and hides and improvement of quality of raw materials and products;

- Adopt the "Meat" program, and increase the export of meat and meat products;

- Create greater opportunities for export of meat, wool and leather products by acceding into agreements on veterinary and sanitary conditions;

- Implement projects and programs designed at improving business entity management capacity, enhancing business activity and quality of products;

- Support production and service cooperatives through tax and credit policies, and encourage the creation of new jobs;

- Create the legal environment for establishing free economic zones in Altanbulag, Zamiin Uud and Tsagaannuur and start its implementation;

- Develop an appropriate system of procurement, transportation, storage, and processing of agricultural produce according to market forces. Raw material procurement system shall be organized through the creation of a wholesale trade network;

- Increase foreign and domestic investment, and strengthen the country's competitiveness on the world market;

- Reduce administrative red-tape and develop a "one-stop" system in order to facilitate foreign investment;

- Mobilize revenues generated from the sale of foreign aid products for the purpose of expanding production and services, and improve control through greater information transparency;

- Develop the legal environment for protecting consumer rights, prohibiting unfair competition, and combating monopoly.

Increase mining product export:

- Increase export revenues from the mining industry;

- Support Erdenet plant's efficiency improvement through technological renovation and deepening the level of copper concentrate processing;

- Increase the production capacity of cathode copper to produce 10-15 thousand tons of refined copper a year;

- Increase gold production by 1.5 times from the present level;

- **Create conditions for the construction of plants for processing zinc ore deposits in Tomort, gold in Boroo, placer gold deposits in Toson and Bayangol, and start production in the next few years;**

- **Develop a project for the exploitation of coking coal deposit in Tavan Tolgoi and submit it for consideration by foreign investors;**

- **Create conditions for the utilization of gold deposit in Tavt, copper deposit in Tsagaan Suvarga and silver ore deposit in Asgat;**

- **Create an internationally accepted legal environment to protect domestic and foreign investors' rights and set up a tax and financial system in order to attract investment in the geology and mining sectors.**

Intensifying geological surveying and creating mineral reserves:

- **Enhance geological surveying of oil and oil extracting activities;**

- **Gradually increase the scale and scope of geological surveying financed from the central government budget to increase it annually at a constant rate of 2.5 times;**

- **Take a step-by-step measure to create a 1:200,000 scale geological map of Mongolia;**

- **Conduct a general prospecting work in and create a 1:50,000 scale geological map in a field, not less than 50,000 square kilometers, and with possible long-term mineral deposit and close to the border areas ;**

- **Support private investment in geological surveying by way of creating a favorable investment and taxation environment;**

- **Continue the work on developing geological information database meeting international information technological requirement and based on geographical information network.**

STOP THE DECLINE IN THE FARMING INDUSTRY:

- Arrest the decline in the farming industry and create a favorable legal and economic environment to ensure its stable growth;
- **With a view to improving arable land utilization and ownership, increase the size of fee for neglected arable land and exempt companies, organizations and individuals of land fee provided they harvest a stable crop and efficiently utilize fallow and arable land;**

- **Meet the domestic needs in high quality grain-seed by way of supporting seed production business entities and research institutions;**

- **Increase the utilization of irrigated arable land;**

- **Support initiatives and activities to produce fertilizer;**

- **Formulate and implement a constructive credit policy of promoting the crop farming industry;**

- **Support efforts to establish business entities that provide technical services to crop farming companies and individuals;**

- **Intensify the implementation of the "Green Revolution" national program;**
- **Accelerate the implementation of the "White Revolution" national program and improve the supply of dairy products to urban population;**
- **Improve the food production standard and quality control system, and create an environment that ensures food security.**

Developing the tourist industry as a priority sector:

- **Streamline cross-sectoral coordination and management of the implementation of the National Tourism Master Plan;**
- **Develop tourist infrastructures in Ulaanbaatar, Harhorin, Omnogobi and Huvsgul;**
- **Upgrade the quality of tourism services international standard.**

2. Development of regional infrastructure:

- Extensively engage unemployed people in road construction, repair and maintenance work in order to provide them with a regular source of income.

THREE. REGIONAL AND RURAL DEVELOPMENT POLICY

The economy shall be developed according to regions, infrastructure will be set up in the rural areas and a rural-oriented taxation, investment and credit policies shall be implemented which would create favorable conditions for people in the given regions to continue to live and work there. Towards this end, the Government shall:

- **Take a set of measures designed at developing a concept of regional development and its legal coordination, defining the strategy for regional, aimag and rural development and ensuring their relatively uniform progress;**
- **Implement a differentiated tax and customs policy designed at encouraging investment and industrial growth in the rural areas;**
- **Set up a network of wholesale trade of raw materials, goods and food stuffs in each region and take measures to supply the herders and the general rural population with cheap but good quality food and consumer goods;**
- **Regulate by law economic and legal relations of herder households and farmers, support initiatives by herders to improve their livelihood and business through the establishment of co-operatives and farms;**
- **Improve the system of maintaining herds under state protection in conformity with the market forces, direct the government policy towards supporting veterinary services, irrigation of pastureland and the creation of buffer fodder stock;**
- **Introduce a livestock insurance system;**

- Set up a mechanism of protecting livestock from natural disasters and establish a disaster relief network. Establish inter-aimag reserve pastureland in the regions;

- Take measures to recover within the next 2-3 years the damage caused by the zud disaster in 1999-2000. Under community scrutiny and participation, implement measures on restocking herder households whose income level has dropped below the poverty line due to the zud disaster;

- Promote cooperation between herders, farmers, business entities and research institutions, and support initiatives designed at fostering close linkage between production and science;

- Improve the system of protecting livestock health, renew, in conjunction with market forces, legal regulations on animal gene pool, animal health protection and quarantine;

- Improve the quality of work to fight animal diseases: brucellosis, glanders, tuberculosis, leukocyte, anemia in the horses, build up the capacity of veterinary laboratories and support efforts to intensify animal husbandry;

- Improve water supply in not less than 70 per cent of the pastureland in the desert and steppe regions by constructing new wells and repairing the damaged and abandoned ones;

- Resolve the issue of ownership of watering points;

- Improve water supply and public services in aimag centers, take a set of measures on supplying the population with clean and safe water meeting hygienic and health requirements. A stage-by-stage measure shall be taken to soften and purify human-consumption water with a high level of mineralization and hardness;

- Public bath houses will be built in all aimag and soum centers;

- Public services in Ulaanbaatar, Hovd, Ulaangom, Ulgii, Murun and Uliastai will be reintroduced and the rehabilitation of similar services in the central and eight eastern aimags will be implemented;

- Renew diesel generators in more than 80 soums, hook 2 aimag and 40 soum centers to the central power grid;

- Renewable sources of energy will be supplied to large consumers in soum centers;

- Measures will be taken to meet the basic needs of 100,000 herder households with solar and wind generators;

- Measures will be taken to improve and renew the railway rolling stock and railway lines, and implement anti-flood security measures;

- Measures will be taken to enhance the competitiveness of the Mongolian railway in the regional and continental railway network;

- Air space usage on the territory of Mongolia will be improved through the introduction of new navigation and communication technology in the civil aviation sector;

- Support will be given to renovating the fleet of civil aviation;

- The system of inspecting the technical conditions of automobiles shall be renewed and streamlined to meet internationally recognized standards;

- International road communication link will be expanded and developed;

- Reinforced concrete bridges along the major highways in Bulgan's Egiin, Zavkhan's Tes and Buyant, Selenge's Zuunburen rivers will be commissioned, and the construction of reinforced concrete bridges over Khumuult river in Hentii and Sarkhairkhan river in Zavkhan will commence;

- Technical support will be provided to equip all aimag centers with IDD and DDD connections, the automation level of trunk-call telephone lines will be increased to 85%, and the number of telephone subscribers will be raised by 20%;

- Digital technology will be introduced at radio and TV studios, and the entire transmission network, and all aimag centers will have FM radio stations;

- Increase the number of radio and TV channels beamed to rural areas and improve the quality of radio and TV broadcast transmission;

- Improve the quality of basic and introduce new types of postal services. Improve delivery services of subscribed newspapers and posts to baghs;

- Expand the range of mobile communication. Develop information technology and internet as a tool for intensifying economic relations;

- Efforts will be exerted to implement the Mongolian Law on the Use of Sea and Marine Wealth;

- Elaborate and implement a Master Plan of construction and building materials industry;

- Support technological renovation of coalmines and take measures to improve coal supply in the rural areas.

In the western region:

- Measures will be taken to build hydropower stations on Durgun, Ulaangom and Uyench rivers and set up an independent energy system of the western zone;

- The airports in Khovd and Ulgii will be renovated;

- The construction of the Khovd-Ulaangom-Khandgait and Ulgii-Tsagaannuur roads, and the work to link the Gobi Altai-Khovd-Uvs-Bayan Ulgii highway to he Arvaikheer-Bayankhongor highway will be continued. The construction of the Tsetserleg-Tosontsengel-Uliastai road and Bulgan-Yarant road in Khovd will begin;

- Measures will be taken to install VSAT stations in the administrative centers of Bayankhongor, Gobi-Altai, Khovd, Bayan-Ulgii, Uvs and Zavkhan aimags;

- The radio transmission system between Zavkhan and Uvs aimag centers as well as regional radio relay stations will be transferred into digital technology.

In the khangai region:

- The Chargait hydropower station will be built and effort to seek funding for the Egiin hydropower station will be intensified. A thermal power station will be built basing on the Bayanteeg coal deposit and the center of Bayankhongor aimag will be hooked to the central power grid;
- The construction of the Erdenet-Bulgan-Murun road will begin. The Harhorin-Tsetserleg highway will be commissioned;
- Measures will be taken to expand and renovate automatic telephone exchanges and cable lines will be laid to the centers of Arkhangai and Huvsgul aimags.

In the central region:

- The thermal power station in Dalanzadgad will be commissioned;
- The Darkhan-Erdenet and Nalaikh-Maant-Choir paved roads will be commissioned and the construction of the Choir- Sainshand- Zamyn Uud road will begin;
- Measures will be taken to transfer the radio communication systems in the soums of Tuv and Selenge aimags from single to multiple spots;
- Measures will be taken to install VSAT stations in Gobisumber, Dornogobi, Dundgobi and Umnugobi aimag centers.

In the eastern region:

- The expansion and renovation of the Choibalsan thermal power station will be completed to provide reliable sources of energy to the regional consumers;
- The construction of the Erdene soum-Baganuur-Undurkhaan-Choibalsan road will be continued;
- The Choibalsan and Baruun Urt airports will be expanded and renovated;
- A fiber cable network, connecting the centers of Hentii, Sukhbaatar and Dornod aimags will be established and the communication equipment of nearby soums and settlements will be expanded and renovated with digital technology;

In the capital city:

- Consumers will be provided with reliable services through the introduction of new technology in the power, heating and water supply systems of Ulaanbaatar. The Master Plan of developing Ulaanbaatar city will be revised;
- A special fund for the construction of apartment houses will be set up designed at increasing the availability of housing and alongside this a housing complex for 1000 families of civil servants and young people will be built;
- The City Road Fund will be used for the repair and renovation of roads and bridges, and roads in the residential estates will be repaired thoroughly;
- International Direct Dialing exchange will be expanded;

- **The ger districts will be developed under an integrated policy matrix and their water, communication, transport supply and everyday services will be upgraded. Land entitlement rights will be consolidated which will guarantee a normal livelihood.**

FOUR : NATURE AND ENVIRONMENT POLICY

The Government shall aim to rationally utilize and rehabilitate natural resources with due consideration of their capacity to ensure an eco-oriented economic growth; precisely define civil rights and responsibilities related to the utilization and protection of local natural resources and create a mechanism of nature and environment protection by the citizens themselves. Proceeding from this premise, the Government shall:

- **Consecutively implement a long-term environment policy and program designed at promoting sustainable growth with due consideration of regional social and economic development;**

- **Improve legal co-ordination designed at ensuring concerted actions of the ministries, local governments, NGO's and individuals successfully implementing environment policy and policy measures;**

- **Support the introduction of advanced and eco-friendly technology and the development of ecologically clean products;**

- **Determine the eco-economic and deficiency cost and criteria of nature and its main riches, and on this basis, adopt and enforce standards for the utilization, protection and rehabilitation of the natural resources;**

- **Establish anew fees and dues for the utilization of natural resources and pollution of the nature and environment, and on this basis, set up a reliable financial base for the protection and rehabilitation of the nature and environment;**

- **The rational utilization, protection and rehabilitation of the forest resources will be intensified. Actions will be taken to implement the initial goals set forth in the National Forest program;**

- **Put in place a legal monitoring and incentive system for the introduction of eco-friendly technology in mines;**

- **Expand the network of protected areas, improve their management. Implement measures to improve the living standards of communities living in protected parks and areas;**

- **Take measures to multiply rare and endangered species of flora and fauna;**

- **Streamline the system of environment monitoring and make it more efficient. Renew the system of monitoring the environment, meteorology, pollution and radiation levels, and renew its technology;**

- **Bring the system of environment information and statistical database to international standard;**

- **Expand the rights of citizens to land ownership and utilization, and on this basis the relevant legal environment shall be streamlined to ensure that the citizens reap the benefits of the land for a long period of time;**

- Raise interests in employing land for business purposes and improve land utilization in order to ensure that citizens and organizations have a long-term ownership of land;

- The mechanism of long-term land entitlement shall be streamlined to attract foreign investment and ensure a stable operation of foreign invested entities;

- The process of desertification on the territory of Mongolia will be studied within the framework of projects and in collaboration with international organizations, and on this basis, desertification and soil erosion will be prevented;

- Measures will be taken to prevent soil erosion. Actions will be taken to protect cultivated crops from hail, increase the level of precipitation for the purpose of increasing the harvest yield and extinguishing forest and steppe fires in remote inaccessible areas;

- Efforts to combat forest and steppe pests and rodents, check the spread of harmful plants will be intensified by introducing eco-friendly technology, and starting in the year 2000, the acreage of land for destroying *Brandt vole* shall be increased by 1.5 times;

- The question of classification, transportation and disposal of wastes in Ulaanbaatar city and building an eco-friendly recycling plant will be considered in a systematic manner. Preparatory work will be made on classifying, transporting and disposing of wastes and building recycling plants in the larger cities of Darkhan, Erdenet and Choibalsan;

- Consecutive measures will be taken to providing households with efficient stoves in order to reduce pollution level in Ulaanbaatar;

- Bilateral and multilateral cooperation in the sphere of nature and environment protection will be expanded. Measures will be taken to increase support and assistance from foreign countries and international organizations in addressing pressing ecological problems.

FIVE. DEFENSE AND FOREIGN POLICY

1. The defense system and military reform policy of Mongolia will be implemented consistently in accordance with the principles of the state military policy and measures will be taken to eradicate distortions and drawbacks that emerged in the system in recent years. To accomplish the above, the Government shall:

- Revise the defense and other related laws and legislation, and strengthen civil monitoring of activities of the armed forces and other military organizations;

- Define the priorities in upgrading the technical capacity of the armed forces and the frontier troops, and the initial stage of the program will be launched;

- Streamline the structure of military forces, deepen reforms, and build the capacity of the military;

- Upgrade the professionalism of military personnel by way of improving the terms and conditions for contractual military service on a voluntary basis;

- **Revise and improve the content of training and preparedness of the personnel with due consideration of the present objectives and needs, and at the same time, besides their major duties and responsibilities, to render humanitarian assistance to the civilians in eliminating the consequences of natural disasters and industrial accidents;**

- **Train people recruited for alternative military service in such concrete areas as preventing and fighting natural disasters and industrial accidents;**

- **Armed forces personnel shall be trained to serve in UN peacekeeping efforts.**

2. Measures will be taken to protecting and preserving the independence and sovereignty of Mongolia and creating an environment for a peaceful life to its people. Proceeding from this premise, the Government sets forth the following objectives:

3. The implementation of the Mongolian state border policy, laws and legislation on border and international agreements acceded to by the country shall be evaluated and their legal coordination shall be improved. An independent frontier troop system will be created;
4. Actions will be taken to check cross-border robbery and in particular measures to prevent border violations Uvs, Zavkhan, Huvsgul, Dornod and Sukhbaatar aimags will be intensified and the inviolability of the border will be guaranteed;
5. Communication and technical supply as well as transport means of the frontiers troops will be improved stage-by-stage;
6. The system of mass voluntary involvement of local organizations and the local community in the protection of the state border will be further improved;
7. Measures will be taken to streamline and renew treaties and agreements on border regime, border ports and passes concluded with the Russian Federation and the People's Republic of China;
8. Efforts will be made to create an environment whereby officers and company sergeant majors in the border areas will have continued interest in working in those areas they are stationed in;
9. The living conditions and social status of military officers and company sergeant majors will be improved; support will be given to their effort to simultaneously acquire dual civilian profession. Assist the family members of military officers and company sergeant majors serving on the border by helping them find a job;
10. Take active part in multilateral effort to strengthen regional security and military confidence and trust, expand bilateral cooperation and foreign relations of the armed forces;
11. Fully address the question of creating funding resources for fighting major industrial accidents and natural disasters;
12. Prevent and eliminate all internal and external factors that could adversely affect the political, economic, civil and ecological aspects of national security;
13. Create peaceful living conditions for the civilians, and expand cooperation between the civilians and the police;
14. Create a legal environment that protects the rights of Mongolian citizens working overseas and foreign citizens living in Mongolia.

3. The Government is committed to consistently implement all the principles and directions outlined in the concepts of national security and foreign policy of Mongolia in keeping with the new national and global circumstances and will energetically pursue an independent, open and multi-prop foreign policy that is

consistent with the vital national interests and the principles of sustainable development. The Government, upholding the continuity and integrity of its foreign policy, shall consistently conduct activities designed at strengthening Mongolia's independence, sovereignty and its international position. Within this framework, the Government shall undertake the following actions:

In respect to neighboring countries:

Extend good-neighborly relations and all-round cooperation with the neighboring countries on the basis of traditions and trust;

Extend good neighborly relations, equitable and mutually beneficial cooperation with the Russian Federation in all spheres and directions in keeping with the provisions, the letter and spirit of the Treaty of Friendly Relations and Cooperation between Mongolia and the Russian Federation, and shall make consistent efforts to resolve all outstanding issues;

Extend good neighborly relations, equitable and mutually beneficial cooperation with the People's Republic of China in accordance with the ideas and provisions of the Treaty of Friendly Relations and Cooperation between Mongolia and the People's Republic of China and the Joint Statement of 1998;

Promote cultural and humanitarian relations designed at regulating pressing border problems, tapping to the full the opportunities and potentials of economic cooperation, and enhancing its efficiency.

In respect to Asia-Pacific regional countries:

Conduct an active foreign policy in the Asia-Pacific region, and develop bilateral relations and cooperation with the regional countries;

The Government shall work to further extend relations and cooperation with the United States of America, taking into consideration the importance of established relationship with the USA in strengthening democracy, the market system in and foreign ties of Mongolia;

Relations and cooperation of comprehensive partnership established with Japan will be further strengthened and extended;

Friendly relations and cooperation will be developed with the Republic of Korea, Republic of India and other countries of the Asia-Pacific region;

Political relations established with the ASEAN member countries, Australia, New Zealand and Canada shall be extended, and the scale and scope of cooperation with them will be strengthened;

With due respect for traditional historical and cultural links, friendly relations and cooperation will be promoted with the Republic of Turkey, Republic of Kazakhstan and other countries of Central Asia;

Cooperation with Latin American countries will be fostered within the framework of international organizations and the Government will work to establish trade and economic relationship with the major countries of the region;

Exchange of bilateral opinions and holding of talks and negotiations on security in the Asia-Pacific region and South East Asia will be conducted energetically and on a regular basis.

IN RESPECT TO THE COUNTRIES OF EUROPE:

- **Considering the importance of the relations established with European countries in strengthening democracy and free market economy in Mongolia, the Government will promote mutually beneficial cooperation with them;**
- **Partnership relations will be developed with the European Union and cooperation with its member countries, such as Germany, Great Britain, France and Italy will be extended;**
- **Mutually beneficial cooperation will be developed with other European countries.**

IN RESPECT TO THE COUNTRIES OF MIDDLE EAST AND AFRICA:

- **Within the framework of its open foreign policy, the Government will extend relations and in particular, commercial and economic cooperation with the Mid-East and African countries.**

ON RELATIONS WITH THE UN AND OTHER INTERNATIONAL ORGANIZATIONS:

- **Mongolia will take an active part in the activities of the United Nations, its specialized agencies and other international organizations, and will make efforts to apply their influence and capacity in guaranteeing national security and implementing social and economic objectives;**
- **The UN General Assembly Resolution on Mongolia's international security and Non-Nuclear Weapon Status, and the Law of Mongolia on a nuclear-weapons free status will be implemented, and the country's Non-Nuclear Weapon Status will be consolidated legally at the international level;**
- **Mongolia will take an active part in the activities of the Non-Aligned Movement and the Group of 77, and work closely with them on issues that meet the common objectives and interests of developing countries, and will contribute to furthering North-South talks and understanding;**
- **Mongolia will honor its commitments before international organizations and international agreements;**
- **Mongolia will study the possibility of acceding to international agreements on human rights, environmental protection, improving the situation of the society's vulnerable groups, multinational issues such as combating organized crimes, terrorism, and drug trafficking, and will cooperate with international organizations in these directions.**

PARTICIPATION IN MULTILATERAL ACTIVITIES:

- **Mongolia will seek constructive means for an effective participation in multilateral processes, talks and negotiations on Asian-Pacific, North-East Asian and Central Asian security issues as well as regional political and economic integration;**
- **Mongolia will take an energetic part in the ASEAN Regional Forum (ARF) and in the multilateral talks and negotiations of APEC and Asia-Europe designed at promoting political and economic cooperation.**

PROMOTING FOREIGN ECONOMIC RELATIONS:

- **Mongolia will conduct a policy designed at preserving the integrity of Mongolia's foreign and economic policies, and directing foreign economic relations to addressing pressing social and economic objectives;**

- **The Government will work closely with the donor countries and on this basis create a favorable environment for foreign trade and direct foreign investment. Proceeding from this premise, relevant laws and legislation will be improved.**

PROTECTING MONGOLIAN CITIZEN'S RIGHTS IN FOREIGN COUNTRIES:

- **The conditions for overseas travel by Mongolian citizens will be eased, priority will be given to creating the most favorable legal environment for study or work overseas and consular services will be developed to international standards.**

IN THE FIELD OF CULTURAL AND HUMANITARIAN RELATIONSHIP:

- **While developing humanitarian relations with foreign countries, the Government will work closely with individuals, NGO's and local authorities and will give priority to encouraging and supporting their activities;**

- **Mongolia will deal closely with international education, culture, sport and information organizations and funds; acceded to the necessary treaties and agreements; and step up its participation in international humanitarian activities;**

- **Mongolia will work to increase international interest in Mongolia through the promotion of national culture;**

- **The Government will conduct a policy of extending ties and relationship with Mongolians living overseas, utilizing and supporting their capacity.**

SIX. POLICY OF OVERCOMING GOVERNANCE CRISIS AND STRENGTHENING PUBLIC ORDER AND DISCIPLINE

1. The Government shall strive to put in place good governance that would develop and implement state policies efficiently, effectively serve the people, meet their basic needs and establish justice. Proceeding from this premise, the Government shall:

- **Develop an integrated legal system of structural and management set-up of the Government, ministries, agencies, administrations and local units, and create a favorable legal framework for their operation;**

- **Streamline the division of rights and responsibilities, objectives and strategy of the Government and the administrative institutions of all levels in order to eliminate duplication of duties, responsibilities and interruptions in the services provided by the Government to the public;**

- **Extend the reform in the Government administration and civil services, enhance the knowledge and skills of civil servants, and implement in stages projects and programs designed at building up the capacity of the government institutions;**

- **Ensure quality and efficiency of services extended by government institutions to the population in terms of taxation, finance, social insurance, civil registration, health and granting of land tenure license;**

- **Streamline the legal basis of the public sector administration and financing for their subsequent transition to a new constructive and cost-effective structure;**

- **Eliminate duplicity in granting official licenses and permissions, take measures to reduce the number of licenses and permissions granted by way of enforcing related laws and legislation. Illegal distribution of licenses and permissions will be stopped;**

- **Improve the forms and methods of interpreting and educating the public in new laws and legislation, support informal training and expand the involvement of NGO's in this effort. Establish the legal framework of an integrated state information network, take measures to ensure efficient distribution of information through the use of modern technology. Define and enforce standards of information exchange among government agencies;**

- **Improve the registration and monitoring of foreign citizens and set up an information network;**

- **Give citizens greater opportunity to directly monitor the performance of their elected Citizen's Representative Hural and the executive agencies nominated by the Hural;**

- **Support the activities of NGO's, expand their involvement in the development and implementation of government policy and in particular in the social sector;**

- **Integrate the activities of local department, sections and agencies under local governors, and make them directly accountable to the latter;**

- **Expand trilateral partnership and cooperation of the Government, the trade unions and the employer's association, take measures to involve non-governmental organizations in executing some of the government functions and services on a contractual basis;**

- **Develop a special policy for homeless children and adults, and alcohol addicts, and take measures for their integration into the society;**

- **Improve traffic safety and traffic police inspection and patrol activities, and renew their car park;**

- **Create a peaceful and safe environment for citizens by raising the efficiency and increasing the number of patrol police in towns and settlements, and expand cooperation between the citizens and the police.**

2. Improve accountability system of public service, raise and strengthen its reputation and capacity.

Define the needs for the improvement of the qualification and skills of civil servants, introduce new forms of free training, systematically involve them in post-graduate training both inside the country and overseas, and on this basis the professional skill and knowledge of the civil servants will be improved;

Improve the registration of the wealth and income of all political appointees and those working in the key state and government positions, and conclude anti-corruption agreement with them;

Amend the clauses in the Law on Public Service, create an efficient mechanism of protecting the rights of professional civil servants from all kinds of political pressure, concretize job description and terms of reference at all stages, create and introduce a system of accountability and bonus;

Tighten and improve the efficiency of control on budget revenue and expenditure, utilization, preservation and protection of government property and the ethics of civil servants, and introduce new procedures on independent auditing of financial statements and performance of government organizations;

Decisively oppose all forms of pressure by state administrative and service organizations on citizens and consumers, all manifestations of abuse of power, introduce rules that will oblige government organizations to consider and monitor applications from citizens;

DEEPEN LEGAL REFORM AND IMPROVE THE IMPLEMENTATION OF LAWS.

- **Introduce a system of studying, monitoring and evaluating the implementation and efficiency of laws and legislation;**
- **Streamline the enforcement of court decisions;**
- **Draft and submit to the State Ikh Hural for consideration and approval the guidelines on amending laws and legislation by the year of 2004;**
- **Institute a national human rights organization, take measures to fine tune national laws and legislation with international treaties and conventions on Human Rights to which Mongolia is a party;**
- **Ensure the equality of parties involved in legal process;**
- **Create conditions for the safety of state archives and take measures to improve the system of filing and documenting government correspondence;**
- **Intensify the work on bringing to international standards the coordination of intellectual property rights and accord intellectual property rights laws and legislation with that of international treaties and agreements. Improve the legal environment for the protection of national and traditional intellectual property;**
- **Improve the organizational structure, linkages and responsibilities of government institutions, and ensure the transparency of their activities;**

3. Tasks will be set to decisively combat corruption, bribery and crime, and destroy the basis of their appearance.

- **Develop and implement a national anti-corruption Program;**
- **Improve work on uncovering and preventing new forms of serious crimes such as armed robbery, drug and narcotics trafficking and drug abuse, and production and circulation of counterfeit money;**

- **Root out gratuity acceptance for providing the government services like income tax collection, imposition of customs duty, issuing of licenses and permissions;**

- **Reinvestigate obscure criminal cases related to privatization, customs, taxation and banking operations, and inform the public in a transparent manner;**

- **Introduce a system of public monitoring of discipline and ethics of lawyers and improve the mechanism of their resignation, withdrawing their appointment and making them accountable for their actions;**

- **Develop and consecutively implement a strategic program guaranteeing independence of lawyers.**

CONCEPT OF MONGOLIA'S FOREIGN POLICY AND NATIONAL SECURITY

The Cold War which dominated international relations since the end of World War II has come to an end , the mutually opposing bipolar world structure has collapsed and a process of forming a new international order is gaining momentum.

In line with trends of advancing human society, in particular with requirements of economic and technological progress, the nations of the world are drawing closer together, and conditions for enhancing their relationship are taking shape.

The disintegration of the world socialist system and the Soviet Union has dramatically changed the external situation of Mongolia which used to be aligned with them. The major changes taking place in Mongolia's two neighbouring countries have a direct impact on its external environment.

The restructuring and reforming of the country's political, social and economic systems provide it with favorable conditions for conducting a foreign policy based on realism and according priority to its national interests.

Based on these external and internal factors, the concept of Mongolia's foreign policy is defined as follows.

1. GENERAL PROVISIONS

1. Independent and sovereign Mongolia, in terms of its state structure, is a unitary State upholding rights, freedoms and free economy; in political and geographical respects, it is a developing country in Asia, landlocked between two great powers. Mongolia's foreign policy shall be based on its national interests, as defined in its Constitution ; the country`s specific external and internal situation constitutes the basis for determining its foreign policy objectives, principles and priorities.

2. Mongolia`s foreign policy objectives reside in ensuring its independence and sovereignty by following the trends of human society`s advancement, maintaining friendly relations with all countries, strengthening its position in the international community and forming with influential countries in the region and in the world a network of relationships based on the interdependence of political, economic and other interests.

3. Mongolia shall pursue an open and non-aligned policy. While following a policy of creating realistic interest of the developed countries in Mongolia, it will seek to avoid becoming overly

reliant or dependent on any particular country.

4. In formulating Mongolia`s foreign policy and determining its priority directions and objectives, flexible approach shall be applied, paying close attention to the development of international relations and to the regional and world political situations.

5. The priority of Mongolia`s foreign policy shall be safeguarding of its security and vital national interests by political and diplomatic means, and creating a favorable external environment for its economic, scientific and technological development.

6. Considerations of foreign relations shall be in political, economic, scientific, technological, cultural and humanitarian fields of foreign policy.

II. MONGOLIA`S FOREIGN POLICY IN THE POLITICAL FIELD

7. Mongolia's foreign policy in the political field is an important instrument for ensuring and strengthening its security. Thus its results will be measured first and foremost by how the country's security and independence interests are met, and to what extent its international position has been strengthened and its prestige enhanced.

8. In developing its relations with other countries, Mongolia shall be guided by universally recognized principles and norms of international law as defined in the Charter of the United Nations, including mutual respect for each other's sovereignty, territorial integrity and unviolability of frontiers, right to self-determination, non-interference in internal affairs, non-use of force, settlement of disputes by peaceful means, respect for human rights and freedoms, and equal and mutually beneficial cooperation.

9.In its foreign policy Mongolia shall uphold peace, strive to avoid confrontation with other countries and pursue a multi-base policy. While always championing its national interests, it will at the same time respect the legitimate interests of other countries and its partners. Mongolia will not interfere in
the disputes between its two neighboring countries unless the disputes affect Mongolia's national interests. It shall pursue a policy of refraining from joining any military alliance or grouping, allowing the use of its territory or air space against any other country, and the stationing of foreign troops or weapons, including nuclear or any other type of mass destruction weapons in its territory.

10. Mongolia shall seek to guarantee its interests in the international arena through bilateral and multilateral treaties and agreements. Mongolia shall respect and observe international law, and fulfill in good faith its obligations under international treaties.

11. As a member of the world community Mongolia shall strive to make active contribution to the common cause of settling pressing regional and international issues. In doing so, it shall be guided primarily by its national interests, values and fundamental principles.

12. In implementing its foreign policy, Mongolia shall be guided by the following :

a) Maintaining friendly relations with the Russian Federation, People`s Republic of China shall be a priority directions of Mongolia`s foreign policy
activity. It shall not adopt the line of either country but shall maintain in principle a balanced relationship with both of them and shall promote all-round
neighbourly cooperation. In doing so, the traditional relations as well as the specific nature of our economic cooperation will these two countries will be
taken into account.

b) The second direction of Mongolia's foreign policy activity shall be developing friendly relations with highly developed countries of the West and East such as the United States of America, Japan and the Federal Republic of Germany. At the same time it will also pursue a policy aimed at promoting friendly relations with such countries as India, the Republic of Korea, Thailand, Singapore, Turkey, Denmark, the Netherlands, Finland, Austria. Sweden, Switzerland and at creating and bringing to an appropriate level their economic and other interests in Mongolia.

c) The third direction of Mongolia's foreign policy activity shall be strengthening its position in Asia and securing a constructive participation in the political and economic integration process in the region. Within the framework of this objective, greater attention shall be given to Asia and the Pacific region, in particular to North-East and Central Asia. Mongolia shall take an active part in the process of initiating dialogues and negotiations on the issues of strengthening regional security and creating a collective security mechanism. It will strive to become a member of the Asia, Pacific Economic Cooperation forum (APEC). Prerequisites for participating in regional integration shall be created primarily through expanding and promoting bilateral relations with the countries of the region.

d) The fourth direction of Mongolia's foreign policy, activity shall be promoting cooperation with the United Nations Organization and its specialized agencies, and with international financial and economic organizations, including the International Monetary Fund, the World Bank and the Asian Development Bank.

c)The fifth direction of Mongolia's foreign policy activity will be developing friendly relations with countries of the former socialist community, as well as the newly independent states. When developing relations with these countries, a flexible approach will be adopted, reinforcing the positive legacy of our past relations while at the same time taking into account the potential of promoting relations in conformity with the new circumstances. Particular attention will be given to promoting relations with Poland, Hungary and the Czech Republic in Eastern Europe as well as with Kazakhstan, the Ukraine, Belarus, Kyrgizstan and Uzbekistan.

f)The sixth direction of Mongolia`s foreign policy activity shall be developing friendly relations with developing countries and cooperating with them, as much as possible, in the solution of common objectives. Beyond the framework of bilateral relations with these countries, this task will be realised mainly through cooperation within the framework of international organizations and movements, such as the United nations, the Group of 77 and the Non-Aligned Movement.

13. The placement of Mongolia`s plenipotentiary (diplomatic) representatives abroad shall be carried out with due regard to directions of foreign political relations so as to ensure conditions for their implementation.

14. Assignment of highly qualified and competent personnel from the economic, scientific and technological spheres to Mongolia`s diplomatic missions abroad shall be deemed a matter of principle.

III. ECONOMIC FOREIGN POLICY

15. The fundamental objective of Mongolia`s policy concerning foreign economic relations lies in the optimal use of external factors to adequate solutions to long-term and current economic goals in the light of the concept of sustainable development and in eventually securing a proper place for its economy in regional economic integration.

16. In developing economic relations and cooperation with foreign countries, Mongolia, while safeguarding against any adverse impact on it economic security and against becoming dependent on any given country, shall pursue a policy designed to ensure conditions leading to equality, mutual benefit and faithful fulfillment of obligations, freedom political and other pressures, based on the principles and norms of international economic relations.

17. In the implementation of projects connected with establishing economic, customs and trade special zones, joint ventures or enterprises with full foreign investment or with granting concessions, their political and economic consequences shall be thoroughly examined to ensure that they do not adversely affect the country` s economic security and that they will bring economic gains.

18. In selecting partners in the implementation of projects of crucial importance to the national interests, political interests shall have a significant role to play.

19. External debt issues shall be settled without detriment to national economic security, and loans will be accepted on the basis of a thorough assessment of guarantees of their repayment and effective utilization.

20. In developing foreign economic relations. Mongolia shall adhere to the following main guidelines :

a) Foreign economic activities should be focused on enhancing the country's potential, increasing export resources, developing economic infrastructure and producing import substituting goods ;

b) Mindful of the need to modernize the economy, presently dominated by raw materials production, and to develop basic sectors conducive to building a rational structure, measures will be taken to achieve the most effective level of processing minerals as well as raw materials of animal and plant extraction and to produce that are competitive on the world market ;

c) Pursuing the policy of modernizing existing industries by re-equipping them with advanced technology and techniques, and developing export-oriented industries such as food, light, mining and chemical industries as well as biotechnology and new products on the basis of raw materials available in the country ;

d) In enhancing its export potential, Mongolia shall promote cooperation with foreign countries in the fields of processing mineral resources, including gold, copper, molybdenum, uranium, and of manufacturing finished products thereof, as well as in the area of full processing agricultural raw materials and producing goods which are capable of competing on world market ;

e) Expanding markets for Mongolia export commodities ;

f) Developing fuel, energy, transportation, communication and other necessary components of economic infrastructure and creating favorable conditions for securing access to sea ports and transit to them ;

g) Integrating in the international transportation, information and communication networks, particularly those in North-East Asia ;

h) Pursuing a policy of securing foreign assistance and technology for developing small and medium industries oriented towards the production of import substituting goods ;

i) taking advantage of Mongolia`s natural, historical and cultural heritage, international tourism will be developed by enhancing its material basis and raising its service level to world standards ;

j) Securing most favored nation treatment in foreign trade and retaining for a certain period the status which enables Mongolia to get soft loans and grants.

IV. FOREIGN POLICY IN SCIENCE AND TECHNOLOGY

21. The main objective of foreign relations in the scientific and technological fields will lie in making full use of external factors to build and enhance a modern national scientific, technical and technological potential capable of serving as a driving force for the effective development of the national economy and industry and able to be competitive at regional, continental and global levels.

22.Mongolia shall apply the principle of benefiting from world scientific and technological achievements to enrich the pool of national endowment and intellectual capacity which are congruous with the national human and natural resources, the level of social theory and thought as well as with the unique culture of its pastoral livestockbreeding economy.

23.In implementing its scientific and technological foreign policy, Mongolia shall adhere to the following basic guidelines :

a) Introduction advanced technology and methods into production and services. In doing so, priority will be given to the selective introduction of research-intensive technology. Greater attention will be paid to introducing technologies related to processing mineral resources, raw materials of animal and plant extraction, and use of renewable energy sources ;

b) Gearing the national scientific and technological information system to the international information network ;

c) Developing bilateral and multilateral cooperation in the field of intellectual property as well as science and technology.

V. CULTURAL AND HUMANITARIAN FOREIGN POLICY

24. The main objective of the cultural and humanitarian foreign relations reside in protecting the culture and the way of life of Mongols, endowing their unique cultural heritage and enriching it with the achievements of world culture, restoring national historical and cultural assets, recovering cultural and art

relics from abroad, in using cultural cooperation for the purpose of educating and training skilled personnel capable of working in new conditions,
introducing Mongolia to foreign countries, expanding the ranks of well-wishers and supporters of Mongolia, encouraging Mongolian studies in other
nations and promoting mutual understanding and trust.

25. In promoting cultural and humanitarian cooperation, Mongolia will practice both Government and people`s diplomacy, and apply the principle of
respect for human rights, freedoms, equality and mutual benefit.

26. In developing humanitarian relations with foreign countries, Mongolia shall adhere to the following guidelines :

a) safeguarding the rights, freedoms, legitimate interests and the security of Mongolian citizens residing or traveling abroad through the promotion of
broad cooperation with foreign countries in the legal sphere ;

b) enhancing contacts and cooperation with Mongolian nationals residing abroad and mutual support in preserving and developing the Mongolian
language, culture, and traditions as well as securing their contributions to Mongolia`s progress and growth ;

c) taking preventive measures to thwart the influence of reactionary movements and groups prejudicial to the national security of Mongolia and the unity
of its people ;

d) giving priority to training in developed countries of Mongolian students, managerial personnel and specialists in the field of market economy, politics,
law, management and marketing as well as in the leading areas of the country`s scientific and technological fields. In doing so, Mongolia shall seek to
benefit from specialized funds of international organizations and developed countries, scholarships of public and private universities and institutes for the
purpose of training students, upgrading specialists, arranging degree studies, training highly skilled workers as well as for using the services of foreign
lecturers and scholars of excellence ;

e) studying the advanced methods and technology of training and management of foreign countries in general education and vocational training with a
view to applying them flexibly in a way suiting the specific conditions of the country ;

f) in restoring and protecting Mongolia`s historical, cultural and natural heritage and assets and in sharing them with other nations, Mongolia shall
cooperate with Asian countries which have similar historical, religious and cultural legacies as well as with other interested countries, UNESCO and other
related international organizations ;

g) promoting active relations with international organizations, foundations and non-governmental institutions in the field of education, culture, arts, sports
and information, acceding to relevant treaties, establishing and promoting direct ties between similar organizations, encouraging the exchange of scholars,
teachers, creative workers, representatives of the media and sportsmen, taking part in international cultural, art and sport events, and organizing such
measures in the country ;

h) promoting cooperation designed to help bring about favorable external conditions for ensuring the country`s ecological security, maintaining its ecological balance and protecting nature.

DEFENSE AND FOREIGN POLICY

1. The defense set-up of Mongolia and military reform policy shall be implemented consistently in accordance with the principles of the State military policy and measures shall be taken to eradicate distortions and problems accumulated in this field in recent years. Within the framework of these aims following actions shall be taken:

- Revise and work out Defense and other laws & regulations, incorporate and enforce ways & forms of civic control over activities of Armed forces and other military organizations;
- Define priorities and implement an initial stage of upgrading weapons & armament and technical renovation of Armed forces & Border Security Force;
- Improve the organization of military, intensify the reforms, and increase the capabilities of military force;
- Upgrade qualification of personnel of professional military units through improvement of terms and conditions of voluntary military services on agreement basis;
- Revise and improve the training concept of military personnel of Armed forces in conformity with the contemporary needs and goals, conduct training in the areas different from basic responsibilities, such as natural disaster relief, rectification of damages of industrial accidents and humanitarian assistance to civilians;
- Conduct training for those of substitute military service in particular cases such as to take measures to avoid natural disaster or to prevent industrial accidents and to fight them.
- Ensure preparatory measures and undertake initial steps to participate in UN peace-keeping activities by personnel of Armed forces;

2. Independence and sovereignty of Mongolia shall be protected and conducive environment for peaceful life to its people shall be created. Within the framework of these aims following actions shall be taken:

- Evaluate implementation of the State policy on the Border of Mongolia, laws and regulations related to border and of international agreements to which Mongolia acceded and improve their legal regulation. Create an independent set-up of Border Security Forces;
- Conduct activities to stop and eliminate cross-border pilferage, intensify preventive measures against violations of State border, especially in Uvs, Zavkhan, Huvsgul, Dornod and Sukhbaatar aimags and ensure the integrity and non-violability of the borders of Mongolia;
- Improve step by step the process of renovation of communication, technical supplies and transport of the Border Security Forces;
- Improve the system of involvement of citizens, local organizations in regions in the protection of State border;
- Undertake measures to further perfecting and renewing the agreements with the Russian Federation and the People's Republic of China on border regime and border ports and cross-points;
- Develop incentives for stable and constant work by military officers and warrant officers in regions;
- Improve living conditions and social security of military officers and warrant officers, assist them in obtaining civil profession simultaneously. Support the provision of job

opportunities for family members of military officers and warrant officers serving at the border;

- Actively participate in multilateral activities on strengthening regional security and military confidence building, expand external military relations and cooperation;
- Resolve issues of creation of funds for rectification of damages caused by natural disasters and major industrial accidents;
- Ensure all aspects of national security such as political, economic, civilizational, ecological etc. and prevent internal and external factors that may adversely affect on national security;
- Create conducive environment for peaceful life of citizens and expand mutual cooperation between citizens and police;
- Create legal environment which will ensure protection of the rights of Mongolian citizens working abroad and foreign citizens living in Mongolia;

3. The Government shall thoroughly carry out, in line with the new realities at home and abroad, the principles and priority directions defined in the National Security as well as Foreign Policy Concepts of Mongolia and actively pursue an independent, open and multi-pillared foreign policy in accordance with its national interests and goals of sustainable development. The government shall uphold the continuity and integrity of foreign policy and shall continue to strengthen the independence, sovereignty and international position of Mongolia. Within the framework of this objective, the foreign policy program of the government is defined as follows:

The neighboring countries:

- Good neighborly, friendly relations and all-round cooperation with the neighboring countries shall be maintained and promoted on the basis of traditions and confidence.
- Good-neighborly, friendly relations, and equal, mutually beneficial cooperation with the Russian Federation shall be developed and expanded in all spheres and directions according to the provisions and spirit of the Treaty on Friendly Relations and Cooperation between Mongolia and the Russian Federation and all outstanding problems shall be solved in an appropriate way.
- The good-neighborly, friendly relations and equal, mutually beneficial cooperation with the People's Republic of China shall be developed in a stable manner in accordance with the provisions and spirit of the Treaty on Friendly Relations and Cooperation as well as of the Joint Declaration of 1998 signed between Mongolia and People's Republic of China.
- Cross-border pressing issues with neighboring countries shall be settled, the opportunities and potentials of economic cooperation shall be optimized, its efficiency shall be increased, cultural and humanitarian relations shall be promoted.

Relations with the countries of the Asia-Pacific region:

- An active foreign policy shall be pursued in the Asia-Pacific region, bilateral relations and cooperation with countries of this region shall be developed and expanded.
- Bearing in mind that the relations with the USA are significant in strengthening Mongolia's democracy and market economy system, the relations and cooperation with this country shall be further developed and enhanced.
- The comprehensive partnership relations and cooperation with Japan shall be further strengthened and expanded.
- Friendly relations and cooperation with countries of the Asia- Paclflc region such as the Republic of Korea and the Republic of India shall be promoted.
- Level of political relations with ASEAN member states, as well as with Australia, New Zealand and Canada shall be upgraded and the framework of cooperation with these countries shall be expanded and enhanced.

- Cherishing historical and cultural traditions, friendly relations and cooperation with Central Asian countries such as the Republic of Turkey and the Republic of Kazakhstan shall be developed.
- While promoting cooperation with Latin American countries within the framework of international organizations, efforts shall be exerted to establish trade and economic relations with influential nations of this region.
- Active bilateral dialogues and talks on Asia Pacific and North East Asia regional security issues shall be promoted on regular basis.

Relations with European countries:

- Bearing in mind the significance of relations with European countries in achieving the objectives of strengthening democracy and market economy in Mongolia, mutually beneficial cooperation shall be developed with these countries.
- Partnership relations with the European Union shall be enhanced, cooperation shall be expanded and developed with its member states, in particular with the FRG, the UK, France and Italy.
- Mutually beneficial cooperation shall be developed with other European countries.

Relations with Middle Eastern and African countries:

- Within the open foreign policy of Mongolia, relations, especially trade and economic cooperation with countries of Middle East and Africa shall be developed.

Relations with the UN and other international organizations:

- The Government shall effectively participate in the activities of the United Nations Organization, its specialized agencies and other international organizations, in an endeavour to fruitfully benefit from the potentials of these organizations for guaranteeing national security, achieving social and economic goals.
- The UN GA resolution on International security and the nuclear free status of Mongolia and the National Law on Mongolia's nuclear weapon-free status shall be implemented, and the nuclear weapon-free status of Mongolia shall be secured at the international level by an appropriate international law.
- The Government] shall actively participate in the works of the Nonaligned Movement and the Group of 77, cooperate with them on issues consistent with the common goals of developing countries and of its own national interests, and shall support to advance the North-South dialogue in order to reach an agreement.
- Duties assumed under international organizations and international treaties shall be fulfilled.
- Prospects of accession to international treaties on issues of human rights, protection of environment, improvement of situation of vulnerable strata of society, transnational issues, including combating organized crimes, terrorism, narcotics shall be explored, and Mongolia shall cooperate with international organizations in this field.

Participation in the Multilateral Processes

- Mongolia shall work in a constructive and efficient manner to have its participation in the multilateral processes and dialogues on the issues related to the Asia-Pacific, Northeast and Central Asian security and in the regional economic and political integration processes.
- Mongolia shall participate actively in the ASEAN Regional Forum /ARF/ activities and shall engage in the APEC and other multilateral dialogues aimed at developing political and economic cooperation between Asia and Europe.

Promoting External Economic Relations

- The Government shall pursue a policy aimed at ensuring the unity of political and economic facets of the Mongolian foreign policy, managing the foreign economic relations in such a manner so that it should help in solving the outstanding social and economic tasks of the country.
- While promoting close cooperation with donor countries [The Government] shall create favorable conditions for foreign trade and ensure conducive environment for attracting foreign direct investment. For these purposes the related laws and regulations shall be perfected.

Protection of Mongolian citizens' rights abroad

- The Government is committed to facilitate the external travel regime for Mongolian citizens and attaches importance to the creation of an optimal legal environment for their study and work abroad. It shall also bring the consular service quality to the international standard.

Cultural and Humanitarian Relations

- In developing humanitarian relations with foreign countries due attention shall be attached to the close cooperation with individuals, NGOs and local administrations and shall encourage their activities.
- Shall promote active relations with international educational, cultural, art, sports and information organizations and foundations and accede to relevant treaties, stimulate active engagement of Mongolia in the international humanitarian activities.
- Through promotion of Mongolian national culture abroad [The Government] shall expand the ranks of well-wishers and supporters of Mongolia.
- Through expanding ties with people of Mongolian origin abroad endeavours shall be made to employ and encourage their potentials.

POLICY OF OVERCOMING GOVERNANCE CRISIS AND STRENGTHENING ORDER AND DISCIPLINE

1. The Government shall aim at establishment of "Good Governance" that would elaborate and implement government policies, serve its people efficiently and timely, meet their basic needs and requirements, and ensure justice. Within the framework of these aims following actions shall be taken:

- Develop a unified legal framework and system on the structural and organizational set-up of the Cabinet, Ministries, agencies, state and administrative institutions and create a conducive legal environment for their activities;
- Optimize distribution of rights and responsibilities of Government and State administrative institutions at all level and their goals, duties & directions of work, perspectives, strategy & organizational set-up in order to eliminate duplication of work duties and negligence & dereliction in the Government service to the public;
- Intensify reforms of Government administration and Government service, improve the skill and knowledge of civil servants and implement in stages programs, projects and other measures to increase the capabilities of government organizations.
- Ensure quality and efficiency of State services such as taxation, finance, social insurance, civil registration, health and granting of permissions/licenses for land tenure rendered by Government administration to general public;
- Improve legal basis of management and financing of Government service and switch over to new structure with proper and cost-effective set-up;
- Eliminate duplicities in issuing licenses & permissions allowed by Law, reduce number of permissions and special licenses & permissions issued through adoption and

implementation of related legislation. Halt practices of issuing illegal licenses & permissions;

- Improve means and forms of ensuring public awareness of laws and regulations, increase participation of non-government organizations in this process and encourage informal educating practices. Define legal basis of unified state information network and adopt adequate measures to ensure its reliability and efficiency through introduction of modern technology. Define and apply standards of information exchanged among government agencies;
- Improve registration and overlook of foreigners and set up its information network ;
- Expand the opportunities for citizens to monitor and evaluate the performance of their Citizen's Representative Hural and the executive agencies nominated by the Hural;
- Support the activities of non government organizations, expand their involvement in elaborating and implementing the state policy, particularly their participation in the social sector;
- Integrate the activities of some local branches of agencies, departments and institutions under the local Governor into one set-up under the jurisdiction of the Governor;
- Expand three-party partnership and cooperation of the Government, trade unions and employers' association, adopt measures to transfer some of the state activities and services to non government organizations on the basis of concluding agreements with such organizations ;
- Elaborate a special policy towards children without proper guardianship, homeless people and alcohol addicts and organize their social rehabilitation;
- Increase traffic safety, improve means and forms of police inspection and patrolling activities, renew its transport park and equipment;
- Improve availability and timely efficiency of police patrolling and inspections in urban areas, create a conducive environment for peaceful life of citizens and expand cooperation among citizens and police;

2. Improve the accountability of Government service, raise it's reputation and strengthen its capability.

- Define the requirements for improving the qualification of the public servants, introduce new forms of training that would not require additional financing, extend systematic post-graduate training opportunities at home and abroad basing on concrete policies and purposes and upgrade their professional qualification and skills;
- Improve registration of the assets and income of all political appointees, of officials and employees of high ranking state and government positions, conclude with them an anti-corruption agreement;
- Amend the Law on Government Service, create an efficient mechanism to protect the rights of professional civil servants from political pressures clearly define job descriptions and work directions of civil servants at all level and introduce a system of their job evaluation, accountability and bonus;
- Tighten the control and improve the efficiency of such control over budget revenue collection & expenditure, utilization, preservation, protection of State property and the ethical conduct of public servants and enforce regulations on independent auditing and notarizing of financial statements and performance of organizations;
- Combat all cases of pressure and misuse of their monopolistic position on part of State administrative and State service organizations regarding citizens and consumers, introduce general agreement procedures on consideration of applications from citizens by Government organizations and their monitoring;

Intensify the pace of legal reforms and improve the implementation of laws.

- Introduce a system of research, monitoring and evaluation of the implementation and efficiency of laws;
- Improve the enforcement procedure of court decisions;
- Elaborate and submit to the State Great Hural for approval basic guidelines on revising of laws and regulations of Mongolia by the year of 2004;
- Establish a national organization on human rights, undertake measures on approximation of national legislature with international agreements and conventions on human rights to which Mongolia acceded;
- Ensure equal and fair participation of all parties involved in legal process;
- Create a reliable condition for ensuring safe storage and protection of the state archives, take measures to improve and systemize the filing of government correspondence;
- Intensify works on upgrading the regulation of intellectual property rights to the world standards and make the national legislation on intellectual property rights match with international agreements and conventions. Improve the legal environment for protection of national and traditional intellectual works and technologies;
- Improve organization and coordination of government bodies' work performance and ensure transparency of their activities;

3. Combat decisively corruption, bribery, crime and eliminate their breeding ground

- Elaborate and implement a national Program against corruption;
- Improve works on investigation and prevention of new types of hard crimes such as armed robbery, drug abuse and its sales, forgery of bank-notes and their use;
- Eliminate gratuity acceptance for rendering government services like income tax and customs evaluation, tax imposition, issuing licenses and permissions;
- Reinvestigate languishing criminal cases related to privatization, customs, taxation, banking and investigative processes, and ensure transparency of information on the outcome;
- Introduce a system of public monitoring of discipline and ethical conduct of judges, ensure a mechanism of their resignation, suspension of their service and call for responsibility.
- Implement in stages the strategic plan for court jurisdiction.

MONGOLIA: FOUR DECADES AT THE UNITED NATIONS

Immediately following World War II, Mongolia sought to play an active part in building the post-war world order. In 1946 it applied for membership of the United Nations, which had just emerged as the chief mechanism for building that new order. However, because of the clash of two differing ideologies and obstruction by some countries, Mongolia could not fulfil its desire to be an active player in the international arena. It had to work hard for 15 years before finally being admitted to the United Nations. On October 27 1961 Mongolia became a fully-fledged member of the international community, a turning point in the country's contemporary history.

THE SIGNIFICANCE OF MONGOLIA'S MEMBERSHIP OF THE UNITED NATIONS

Mongolia's membership of the United Nations brought it out of isolation and into the international community of sovereign States with equal rights. It had several invaluable consequences for Mongolia's place and role in the world.

Guarantor of Mongolia's Independence

Mongolia's membership of the United Nations has been the most viable guarantee of its independence and sovereignty. The use or threat of force against Mongolia and its territorial integrity has become impossible with the United Nations standing behind us. Mongolia in turn has reaffirmed its peaceful policy by acceding to the UN Charter and solemnly undertaking to adhere to the ideals enshrined in this most powerful international legal instrument.

Recognition of Independence
At the time of its admission to the United Nations Mongolia had diplomatic relations with only 19 socialist and developing countries. Once it had UN membership, Mongolia was given de facto recognition by 100 countries at once, and this immeasurably strengthened its independence and sovereignty.
Formal recognitions of Mongolia multiplied, and diplomatic relations were established at a great pace. The country now has diplomatic ties with over 140 others.

The opening up of Mongolia
Mongolia now became relatively open to the outside world. Once forgotten, it was finally in a position to become known to the international community, and to familiarize itself with the rest of the world.

Mongolia's membership of the United Nations and of many UN system organizations, its active participation in the work of the Organization and its substantial contribution to implementing its ideals, helped to expose the country to the world, and vice versa. This later contributed to planting the seeds of democracy and a market economy in Mongolian society.

Learning to be an Active Player
Although ideologically handicapped, Mongolia had the opportunity to be part of the international community and was able to learn how to participate in debates on issues of universal interest. It also acquired enough experience to promote its own interests through the machinery of international organizations.
Receiving Assistance

As a fully-fledged member of the international community, Mongolia now had the right to United Nations development assistance. Though modest in scale, UN development assistance helped Mongolia gain access to the most advanced technologies which the non-socialist countries could offer at that time.

EXPANSION OF MONGOLIA'S INTERNATIONAL ACCEPTANCE

Once the international community had accepted Mongolia as an equal partner, the door was open to the other UN organizations and to international treaties. Since 1961 Mongolia has become a full member of 33 multilateral intergovernmental institutions, and almost 20 regional or inter-agency bodies. There is no major international organization which Mongolia has not joined, apart from certain regional groupings.
In addition, many Mongolian non-governmental organizations have joined international associations. For example, the United Nations Association of Mongolia (UNA-Mongolia) was formed in 1957 and served as a window to the UN before Mongolia's admission to the Organization. It is an active member of the World Federation of United Nations Associations, and plays a leading role in promoting the ideals of the international community among the Mongolian public.

Mongolia has ratified or acceded to over 140 international treaties and conventions, an important sign of its place and role in the world.

Mongolia fulfils with dignity its obligations to the international organizations and conventions to which it is a party, through its various financial contributions and by reporting on its performance of its obligations.

Mongolia has opened 31 diplomatic missions abroad and more than 20 embassies and offices of international organizations are established in Ulaanbaatar.

Mongolia as an Active Player at the United Nations

During the 40 years of its membership, Mongolia has transformed itself from a passive to an active player in the various United Nations organs. It has sponsored over 50 resolutions on social and economic issues adopted by the United Nations and its various organizations. It has also co-sponsored about 500 resolutions. It has paid special attention to issues such as peace and disarmament, the right of peoples to peaceful co-existence, the principles of international negotiation, far-reaching social and economic reforms, universal literacy, the public sector and cooperatives, national personnel and rural women, land-locked countries, etc.

It is at the initiative of Mongolia that the international community observes Disarmament Week from 24 to 30 October every year. This important initiative has proved to the international public that Mongolia is an ardent promoter of peace and disarmament.

In 1984 the United Nations adopted, at the initiative of Mongolia, the "Declaration on the Right of Peoples to Peace", which was well received by the international community at that period of the cold war.

Mongolia's active participation and significant role in the United Nations is widely recognized by other member States. Its representatives have been unanimously elected to important posts in the UN General Assembly such as Vice-President (on 6 occasions), Chairman of the First Committee (Disarmament and International Security), the Fourth Committee (Special Political and Decolonization), the Sixth Committee (Legal), and the Commission on Disarmament, as well as Vice-Chairman and Rapporteur of several committees. Mongolia was also elected Chairperson of the annual session of the UN Economic and Social Commission for Asia and the Pacific in 1989 and 1999 respectively.

Mongolia was a member of the UN Economic and Social Council (ECOSOC) in 1973-1976, and has now submitted its candidature for 2003-2005. It is an active member of the ECOSOC Commission on the Status of Women (1999-2002) and the Commission on Sustainable Development (2001-2003).

Since 1999, the country has started to prepare for its participation in the peacekeeping operations of the United Nations, having signed a Memorandum of Understanding with the Organization. Mongolia's military and humanitarian personnel are now trained to take part in field operations.

Mongolia has been active in the work of UN global conferences such as the World Summit for Children (New York, 1990), the UN Conference on Environment and Development (Rio de Janeiro, 1992), the World Conference on Human Rights (Vienna, 1993), the International Conference on Population and Development (Cairo, 1994), the World Summit for Social Development (Copenhagen, 1995), the World Conference on Women (Beijing, 1995), and the World Food Summit (Rome, 1996).

Mongolia took the lead in organizing the "One World" conference series, as a follow-up to these UN global conferences. The United Nations Secretary-General, Mr. Kofi Annan, has initiated an extensive and far-reaching set of reforms intended to achieve greater unity of purpose, coherence of effort and flexibility of response within the United Nations system. This reform is designed to be a continuing process rather than a single event. It is intended to foster a new United Nations for the new century. A key rallying point for implementing the Secretary-General's desire for cohesive programming is the follow-up to summits and conferences sponsored by the United Nations. To this end, Mongolia has launched a series of national youth conferences on these international forums. These youth assemblies, known as the "One

World" United Nations Conference Series, were intended to empower Mongolia's youth, its citizens and ultimately its leaders to take action on issues of global importance in the development of their own community. The series did this by revisiting five key world conferences of the 1990s.

The participation of the President of Mongolia in the United Nations Millennium Summit in 2000 was another strong indication of Mongolia's commitment to the ideals of the United Nations. As its President observed, Mongolia viewed this unprecedented gathering of world leaders "as an event of historic importance that offers us a unique opportunity to reaffirm our faith in the United Nations..."

MONGOLIA'S VISION OF THE UNITED NATIONS IN THE 21ST CENTURY

Mongolia sees the United Nations as a powerful partner in its development and progress. It respects the Organization as "the indispensable common house of the entire human family, through which we will seek to realize our universal aspirations for peace, cooperation and development."

It will continue actively promoting the United Nations, especially its reform measures. For a small State like Mongolia, the United Nations is of special value in terms of safeguarding its interests, lending it a voice on global issues and promoting its development. Mongolia is therefore strongly in favour of further enhancing the role and credibility of the UN and democratizing its work.

Mongolia holds the view that "if the United Nations is to adequately respond to the challenges of today's increasingly interdependent and rapidly changing world, a great deal will depend on its ability to adapt itself to an environment that is markedly different from the one in which it was conceived by its founders..."

Our vision of the future of the Organization has been elaborated in the Memorandum of the Government of Mongolia on enhancing the role of the United Nations in promoting the security interests of small States, which was circulated at the United Nations in 2000 as document A/55/310.

We expect that the reformed and reinvigorated Organization can help Mongolia more in its endeavour to benefit equally from the globalization process.

The Government of Mongolia is of the view that development and progress will never be achieved unless we deal with the huge aftermath of the social crisis which has come about in the process of transition to a market economy. With this in mind, we will continue actively cooperating with the United Nations to find optimal solutions to issues such as the drastic reduction of poverty and the improvement of health care, education and living standards.

Mongolia is grateful to the United Nations for its assistance in relief efforts during the natural disasters which have afflicted the country as a result of global climate change. It will actively cooperate with the United Nations in strengthening mechanisms and institutional capacity for disaster preparedness and effective mitigation.

Information technology is a powerful means of facilitating a dynamic response to every problem of a socio-economic nature, including the participation of individuals at every level in governance, the enhancement of their knowledge, closing gaps between urban and rural development and improving people's business and earning skills, as well as effective monetary policies. We will therefore pay maximum attention to this sector as the main engine of development in the 21st century. Mongolia hopes that the United Nations will continue assisting us in the establishment of an information and communications network tailored to Mongolia's particular needs, reflected in a large land area with a sparse population.

Mongolia has developed a national policy for regional development. Through its technical assistance, the United Nations could make a major contribution to building up the regional economic development strategy, and in creating an enabling legal environment and strengthening development capacity at the local level.

There is no doubt that the United Nations will extend effective cooperation as in the past towards the achievement of our goal of nurturing a civil society that secures equality, active participation and freedom for everyone in this country.

Democracy, the promotion of human rights, and transparent and accountable governments are indispensable elements of security and development. The International Conference on Human Security, organized by the Government of Mongolia in cooperation with the UNDP in May 2000 in Ulaanbaatar, highlighted the role of an informed and mature civil society in the country as the central building block for human and national security, emphasizing that empowered and pro-active citizens have the capacity and capability to reinforce their own well-being and individual security, and accordingly their national security. The "Good Governance for Human Security" Program, initiated by the Government of Mongolia and supported by UNDP, was launched in early 2001 with a view to achieving person-centered development in each and of its aspects. Mongolia will step up its cooperation with the United Nations in this area

A REGULATION FOR RECEIVING FOREIGN CORRESPONDENTS AND JOURNALISTS IN MONGOLIA

Foreign correspondents who wish to visit Mongolia shall submit an online application in advance or upon arrival in Mongolia to the Press and Information Division, Department of Policy Planning, Information & Monitoring, Ministry of Foreign Affairs of Mongolia.

Upon arrival in Ulaanbaatar, foreign correspondents should visit the Press and Information Division and fill out an application form, if an online application was unable to send, provide with two passport size photos and $10 processing fee for each person for a Temporary Accreditation Card-TAC. The Press and Information Division issues TAC within 24 hours after it received the application. The TAC will be issued to foreign correspondent for the entire period of his/her journalistic activity.

Foreign correspondents who come to Mongolia on an agreement with other Mongolian organizations shall be issued a TAC from the Press and Information Division of the Ministry of Foreign Affairs at the official request of the host organization.

A TAC shall be issued to freelance journalists with a document notifying them as freelancer and who must have obtained a Mongolian visa.

A TAC shall be issued to foreign TV teams to cover (non-commercial) stories in Mongolia upon submission of their contract or agreement with Mongol TV or any other relevant organizations to the Division.

In all other than above cases, a correspondent who wishes to carry out his/her professional activity should apply for a TAC. A Foreign correspondent with no TAC issued shall be considered as an officially non-licensed to carry out any journalistic activity in Mongolia.

Foreign filming teams who wish to make films (documentary, TV etc.) in Mongolia on a commercial basis shall submit their request to the Ministry of Education and Science of Mongolia to obtain permission.

IMPORTANT LAWS AND REGULATIONS ON NATIONAL SECURITY

LEGAL ENVIRONMENT OF MONGOLIAN -MILITARY RELATIONS

Before 1990 the main documents which regulated Mongolian civil-military relations were the Program of the MPRP and its military policy section and legal acts such as Law on Public Military Personnel and Law on Defence. These documents reflected the contemporary ideological policy of socialism [1]

Promulgation of the Constitution of Mongolia in 1992 laid a basis for developing a humane, civil democratic society and forming a legal environment for Democratic Civil-Military relations. Article 11.1 states: 'The duty of the State is to secure the country's independence, ensure national security and public order'. Also in Article 2 of the Constitution: 'Mongolia shall have armed forces for self-defence. The rules of military service shall be determined by law'. This article became grounds to ensure the national security of Mongolia, to form a reliable system of defence and to develop patriotism in civilians as well as laying the basis for new principles of the army's mandate.

In connection with the new social relations of Mongolia, some laws were adopted which regulated and confirmed the designation and mission of the defence sector, Armed forces and relevant relations. These are as follows: The Constitution of Mongolia, National Security Concept (1994), Law on Armed forces of Mongolia (2002), Bases of State Military Policy (1994), Law on Defence of Mongolia (1993), Law on President of Mongolia (1993), Law on State Great Khural (Legislative Body) of Mongolia (1992), Law on Government of Mongolia (1993), Law on Civil Defence of Mongolia (1993), Law on Military Service Duty of Citizens and the Legal Status of Military Personnel (1992), Law on Involvement of Military and Police Personnel in UN peacekeeping operations (2002) and Law on Border of Mongolia (1993). In accordance with the adoption of these laws and regulations amendments were made to other related laws and regulations. (See Appendix one)

SECURITY SECTOR LAWS

The above-mentioned laws and regulations have contributed to legal reform, which corresponds to the new social relations of the defence sector and Armed forces which emerged over the past 10 years. Promulgated laws and regulations were processed to reflect the new process of forming international security, new defence strategy, periodic public view and demands, as well as on the basis of international practice and scientifically based research. In that law, instructions and trends towards defining basics of the country's defence system and armed forces control, and measures to be taken during the country's transfer to state of war were given. Furthermore, state administration and military governing organisation's power to provide training in peacetime, organisation, entity and citizen's duties, armed forces missions, organisational structure, personnel, legalization of military personnel status in conformity with democratic society system and market economy relations are defined. Within the framework of these activities, the power allocation for regulation of legal acts and laws of Mongolia was created. These laws are as follows:

SECURITY SECTOR LAWS

No.	Name of the law	Approved in	Amended in
	State military policy		

1.	Constitution of Mongolia	1992	-
2.	National security concept of Mongolia	1994	-
3.	Concept of foreign policy of Mongolia	1994	-
4.	Basics of the state military policy of Mongolia	1998	-
5.	Law on national security of Mongolia	2001	-
6.	Law on national security Provision	1992	-
7.	Law on national security committee of Mongolia	1992	1995, 1998, 1999
Defense			
8.	Law on defense of Mongolia	1993	2002
9.	Law on Armed forces of Mongolia	2002	-
10.	Law on State Great Khural of Mongolia	1992	2001
11.	Law on President of Mongolia	1993	1997
12.	Law on Government of Mongolia	1993	1996, 2001
13.	Law on state border of Mongolia	1993	1996,1999, 2000, 2001, 2002
14.	Law on engagement of military and police personnel in UN peace keeping and international activities	2002	-
15.	Law on state secret of Mongolia	1995	-
16.	Law on personal secret of Mongolia	1995	-

1. THE CONSTITUTION OF MONGOLIA

The Constitution declares that it is the duty of the State to secure the country's independence. Mongolia shall have armed forces for self-defence and the structure and organisation of the armed forces and rules of military service shall be determined by law. Likewise, it is the duty of the citizens of Mongolia to defend their motherland and to serve in their army. By stipulating that the President of Mongolia shall be the Commander-in-Chief of the armed forces and head the National Security Council among other duties, the constitution aims to strengthen the country's defence capabilities. The Constitution thereby laid a legal basis for the honest principle and genuine aspiration that command of the army is confined to the State and the Government elected by the people of the Mongolia.

2. Concept of National Security of Mongolia

This concept shall serve the interests of the State and the people on a long-term basis and maintain the integrity of state and hereditary qualities regardless of state, social and economic circumstances. An excerpt from the concept reads:

- 'National Security of Mongolia is aimed at safeguarding the external and internal favourable conditions for ensuring the vital national interests of Mongolia. The ideological basis of the policy ensuring national security is national patriotism.
- 'Vital national interests involve the existence of Mongolian people and its civilisation, Mongolia's national independence, sovereignty and territorial integrity, inviolability of state borders, relative self-sustainability of national economy, and development with

regard to ecological balance and national unity. Vital national interests of Mongolia shall be kept by state and public protection.'

- 'State policy as well as actions taken by the State, its agencies and functionaries and its citizens aimed at creating all-around guarantees of protecting and strengthening Mongolia's vital national interests are the main ways of ensuring national security. Those measures are both preventive and creative. Mongolia attaches importance to developing its international competitiveness in the economic, cultural, scientific and technological and educational fields. Judging from this the vital national interests shall be the object of special care and protection on the part of the State and the people. Mongolian policy for safeguarding its national security includes both domestic means and means of enhancing international cooperation, through various tools such as social, economic, political-diplomatic, military-political, intelligence and legislation. Also it became a ground of advancing civil-military relations to a greater level.

3. The Bases of the State Military Policy of Mongolia

Adoption of the document entitled 'Basics of the State military doctrine' (1994) was an important step in launching armed forces reform in state and easing the social transitions. Before, the army lacked its own military doctrine. Until the declaration of the Warsaw Pact countries, the Military doctrine was neither researched nor formalised. This was due to the fact that there was no demand to articulate a specific military doctrine and, the military policy of the Mongolian People's Republic was an inseparable part of the Soviet's Far East military strategic policy

The State of the Great Khural adopted the 'Bases of the State Military Policy of Mongolia' in 1998. In accordance with it the Mongolian President approved the adoption of the 'Doctrine of the Armed forces Engagement'. It was decided to define political and military-political policy, to be followed by the state for country defence and organisation and strengthening of the armed forces in accordance with the 'The Bases of the State Military Policy of Mongolia'. To develop concepts of the armed forces, further rationalization, development and engagement in peacetime or wartime, the 'Doctrine of the Armed forces engagement' shall be used. 'The Bases of the State Military Policy of Mongolia' are concepts based on the Concept of National security of Mongolia, a defined policy of the country's defence and armed forces reform. This policy includes state attitude towards armed aggression, averting the threat of wars and armed conflict, safeguarding the country from external armed intervention, organisational development of military, and addresses the conduct of armed struggle. The above mentioned document also defines prevention against war and armed conflict, ways of implementing military structure and conducting armed struggle. It is the foundation of the defence activities related laws and regulations as well as international treaties and concessions of Mongolia.

In the document 'The Bases of the State Military Policy of Mongolia' it is stated that 'In peacetime it shall have compact, capable and professionally-oriented Armed forces, which meets the nation's defence demands and economic ability' and according to the law, the main missions of the Armed forces are:

- To be prepared to safeguard national independence, sovereignty and territorial integrity from external armed aggression
- To protect state borders and monitor the inviolability of the country's airspace
- To guard important state objects
- To render assistance in protecting the population and other material assets from the dangers of destructive means, natural and other mass calamities, and industrial accidents;
- To set up a mobilised reserve and train the population in military matters
- To render support and assistance in humanitarian acts

- To carry out functions within the UN Peace-keeping forces and other functions as stipulated in the law
- The armed forces shall, in times of peace, ensure the preparations necessary for carrying out its duty of checking and repudiating potential armed aggression[2] (See Appendix Two)

4. Law on Defence of Mongolia

Taking political, economic, social, legal and military measures to maintain the country's secure existence in conformity with national hereditary tradition and external circumstances in peacetime is common in international practice. Our law establishes our defence system and regulates relations connected with the implementation of duties undertaken by state administration, local authority, entity, and organisation of defence and citizens. That there is little reliance to provide a national defence system by single military means in this law is determined in the following stipulation:

The defence system of Mongolia is an integral political, economic, social, legal and military measures aimed at ensuring the country's preparedness for the defence of its independence, sovereignty, and territorial integrity against external armed incursion and aggression.'

In other words, the defence measures are planned by unifying political, economic, social, legal and military measures aimed at ensuring the country's preparedness for defence of its independence, sovereignty, and territorial integrity against external armed incursion and aggression. Additionally, defence is guaranteed by providing conformation and implementation activities of these measures through an integral defence system as well as by developing political-diplomatic, military-strategic, organisational and international co-operation.

The defence management system is comprised of the State Great Khural, the President of Mongolia, the National Security Council headed by the President of Mongolia, the Government, the Central Administration Office, the General Staff of Armed forces, Military administrative organisations, aimag and capital city defence directorates, and province and district defence agencies.

The defence political system's objective is to safeguard national independence, and sovereignty from external armed incursion and aggression as a basic part of the unified system. Furthermore, the defence political system consists of foreign policy, which orients towards protecting national interests, and formation of defence legal basics at internationally accepted level in conformity with basic laws and regulations of Mongolia. Also, reflection of interests of the country's defence sector in newly issued laws, and civil control over military organisations' activities are covered in basic issues of the defence political system.

The defence legal system is whole body of laws and regulations which have been implemented upon approval of the state in order to regulate relations related to defence policy of the country and activities in conformity with tenets of the documents, such as the Constitution of Mongolia, Concept of National Security of Mongolia, Concept of Foreign policy and the Bases of the State Military Policy.

The defence social system contains a set of measures to provide for citizens' preparedness of defence educationally, by health, upbringing, ethically and psychologically. Most importantly, the social security of military servicemen is protected.

The defence economic system is an aggregate of the economic capability of defence. It is an organisational measure aimed at strengthening the national economic capability; and providing for armed forces demands by establishing a special regime in labour and material as well as allocating financial resources from all sectors of the economy and entities in peacetime and wartime.

The military defence system takes the leading position in the forefront of a unified defence system. It is a complex hybrid of issues, which do not exist independent of one another, and are interrelated with. Such issues include defending national security by military force, executing basic measures of military and armed forces organisation and defining ways and organisation to realise these goals.

5. Law on Armed Forces of Mongolia

This law is being followed upon its approval in 2002. Its objective is to define the Armed forces of Mongolia, its missions, the basics of its system, structure, organisation, civil control over armed forces, civil organisations, and officials' and professionals' military command powers of armed forces, and to regulate relations in this domain.

The Armed forces missions were defined to safeguard the national independence, sovereignty and territorial integrity from external armed incursion and aggression. Besides the above mission, the Armed forces' duties to implement in peacetime were clarified. In accordance with either the approval of the Commander-in-Chief of the Armed forces and also decisions made by the Minister of Defence, certain military units and organisations may be engaged in economic and construction activities. State laws and regulations and the State military policy shall define the Armed forces organisation. In peacetime, the structure of the Armed forces comprises the General purpose troops, border troops and Internal troops, and each of them carries out their professional duties independently. Organisationally, the Armed forces consists of the General Staff of Armed forces, service branch unit; logistic and technical units; military training, research, cultural, medical, printing and information establishments, and economic and service entities. In peacetime, a military unit has a full, under-strength or extra-under-strength structure. The Armed forces military personnel consists of military servicemen and civil personnel employed by military units and organisations on a labour contract basis. According to the law, the command of the Armed forces comprise overall leadership and professional military command. [3]

In accordance with the Law on Armed forces of Mongolia the Armed forces shall fulfil the following functions besides basic duties in peacetime.

- To provide preparation to safeguard the country from external armed incursion and aggression
- To render assistance in state border protection and supervise inviolability of the air frontier of the country
- To assist in protecting and rescuing the population and their property from afflictions caused by natural, other large-scale disasters, and the use of mass destruction weapons within the crisis area and eliminating consequences thereof
- To form, stockpile and replenish mobilisation reserves
- To support training of mobilisation reserves
- To guard important state objects
- To assist humanitarian operations
- To participate in international peacekeeping activities and to execute other duties established by law.

[3] Ibid, pp. 4-6.

Also in this law it is stated that the General Staff of the Armed forces shall define number of military personnel and organisation of the armed forces units and organisations in peacetime and wartime [4]

6. Law on Civil Military Service Duties and Legal Status of the Military Servicemen

In the Constitution of Mongolia is stated that one of the basic duties of Mongolian citizens shall be 'To defend our motherland and serve in our army according to law'. The objective of this law is to regulate relations connected with military service, basic duties to be fulfilled by the citizen and their preparedness to defend the country; to establish the legal status of military servicemen and to settle related issues within this framework. This law also regulates the implementation of military duty of the Mongolian citizens, active military service, conscription for military service military reserve service and reserve service duties, and other forms of military service,.

Delivery of military service and implementation of legal acts and regulations on legal status of military servicemen by the citizens and military personnel counted as military duty of citizens.

Mongolian citizens shall undertake military duty regardless of nationality, language, race, age, social status, origin, capital, employment, position, religion, political orientation and education.

Military service consists of active military service and reserve service. Fulfilment of military duties by the citizens of Mongolia in the Armed forces is counted as active military service. The state of being enlisted on the military reserve service, and accomplishing assigned military duties during mobilisation training and musters, as well as other missions defined in the law, by men of age defined by law, and women with military service assignments constitute the service in military reserve. The Law on Amendment to Law on Citizen's military duty and Legal status of military servicemen regulate alternate military service.

Thus, the above mentioned law stipulates that citizens shall serve alternate service:

For the reasons of religious faith or moral/ethic belief, a citizen of age between 18-25 or the one with 2nd grade military reserve duty may join an alternate form of military service in professional or specialised civil defence units and sub-units or paramilitary unit for Border troops assistance and other humanitarian organisations. Term for alternative service is 24 months. The Government shall define the rules of alternate military service and the number of persons required for the alternative form of military service.

Since it is not possible to recruit conscientious objectors or all young people of military service age a suggested form of an alternate military service could be monetary contributions.

The form of an alternate military service can be monetary contributions as a substitute for personal active service defined by law. Conditions for allowance of substitution payment are defined by the State Great Khural and the amount of payment is annually defined by the Government.'

The above-mentioned provision should be understood not as substitution payment of active military service but substitution payment of alternate service. In other words, some of them serve in active military service for 12 months duration and others could serve by monetary contributions or by alternate service for 24 months due to religious faith or ethic beliefs that run contrary to military service.

Definition of legal status of military servicemen in the 'Law on Military duty of citizens and on the Legal status of the military personnel', 'Law on public service', 'Law on allowances of military personnel' and other laws of military personnel's power and alleviation directly influence improving the difficult military civil transition period. Military serviceman enjoy common civil rights and freedoms as stated in the Constitution of Mongolia and other laws and along enjoyment of certain power and rights. In compliance with the performance of military duties also some legal limitations are given to them in connection with armed forces designation and some peculiar features of military service.

7. Law on State of War

In the Constitutions of 1924, 1940 and 1960 it was stated that the right to declare and terminate a state of war should be given to state governing authority power, since no laws to regulate multilateral relations connected with these rights were issued formerly. Particularly noticeable is the lack of a law on the High Authority of Civil Society. In Section 3 of Article 25 of the Constitution of Mongolia stated: 'it may declare a state of war if public disorders in the whole or a part of the country's territory result in armed conflict or create a real threat of an armed conflict, or if there is an armed aggression or real threat of such an aggression by a foreign state.' Though there is little possibility of occurrence of such a situation there is no guarantee of non-occurrence of that situation.

State of war shall be declared and appropriate political, economic, social, legal and military regimes in the territory of Mongolia or in certain parts of the country in case of occurrence of the situation stated in the provision of Article 25 of the Constitution by the state governing authority should be provisioned. (See Appendix three)

The State Great Khural shall decide whether to declare war or not upon submission of a decision made consultation between the National Security Committee of Mongolia upon referral of the President of Mongolia. The president shall make a decree on the state of war on the whole or part of the national territory when extraordinary circumstances arise and the State Great Khural is concurrently in recess. In case of the proclamation by the President of a state of war, the State Great Khural shall be convened for an extraordinary session without prior announcement. At its special ad hoc session the State Great Hural should decide within 7 days whether they approve the Presidential decree declaring a state of war. The State Great Khural shall make the decision to terminate the state of war made by the National Security Council of Mongolia on termination of the emergency state of war and by submitting this decree to the State Great Khural by the President of Mongolia.

The State Great Khural shall exercise its exclusive competence in a state of war, as it is the highest organ of State power. This competence should be demonstrated by establishing basis of domestic and foreign policies in conformity with circumstances of a state of war. It shall regulate relations connected to establishing military and political relations with foreign countries within the framework of the set policy, forming legal frameworks for entering into military alliances and unions, endorsing joint military treaties concluded with other country in state of war, and issuing laws on stationing and transit crossing of foreign troops through the territory of the country.

The President of Mongolia shall regulate relations such as defining duties as the Commander-in-Chief of Armed forces, approving implementation plans and providing general management of armed struggle along with the leadership of the National Security Council of Mongolia and military command. The Government of Mongolia shall regulate relations stated in the law. It has to provide regular functioning of the basic social sectors and infrastructure to organise the transfer of the country's activities to a state of war, to accept assistance from the UN, other international organisations and supporting countries, and also to provide for the stationing of foreign troops within Mongolian territory in accordance with law. Furthermore, the government is authorised to prepare and allocate financial and capital resources required for combat activity of the armed forces and consumer goods, to establish emergency regime, and to organise implementation and demand observation of the social discipline of the state of war.

8. Law on State of War with other Countries

The objective of this law is to define the basics of the declaration and annulment of the state of war, and to regulate relations related with other countries and its alliances, which threaten the independence and sovereignty of Mongolia. Any country that makes a threat to or undertakes armed incursion against the independence and sovereignty of Mongolia, and any accomplice to such an incursion shall be regarded as its enemy.

A foreign country, which threatens the sovereignty and independence of the state with armed action, and parties which ally in this armed incursion shall be defined as 'enemies' under law. A particular relationship with this enemy nation, starting from the date of the declaration of war until its annulment, shall characterised as a 'state of war' with that country.

The State Great Khural shall decide whether or not to declare a state of war only after the National Security by way of the Mongolian President declares its opinion. The State Great Khural has the right to directly declare a state of war with a foreign country in special cases. The possibility that Mongolia may be in a state of war with another country without having armed struggle is not excluded.

In case of a declaration of a state of war with other country, measures will be taken to annul and stop the function of agreement and contract concluded with enemy prior to the initiation of conflict, and to sever all types of relations set in political, economic and social sectors. At the same time, after war is declared, Mongolia is to cease from international treaties previously entered into in accordance with internationally accepted legal standard and principles.[5]

9. Law on the State Border of Mongolia

The objective of this law is to regulate relations connected with implementing international agreements on border issues of Mongolia. These agreements were concluded to provide inviolability of the state border of Mongolia, enforce the state border and border area regimes, organise passage of passengers and transportation means through the state border, define border protection organisation[6] system and powers, involve citizens and organisations in border protection and charge offenders responsible for violating the aforementioned rights[7]

The borderline regarded as the State Border of Mongolia is established by the international treaties to which Mongolia is a party, and separates the territorial borderline of Mongolia from the adjacent country's borderlines on the earth and water. Air frontier shall be considered all area above the line, and underground border shall be perpendicularly downward. To establish and amend regulation on import of passengers, transportation means, goods and animals, plants and raw materials, firstly, safeguarding of national security should be provided, secondly, mutually profitable co-operation with foreign countries should be expanded, and thirdly, principles of protection of independence, territorial integrity and inviolability of the state border should be observed.

The country's land and water borders should be monitored and protected by the Air defence forces. If necessary, some military units could be engaged in guarding the state border upon decision of the Commander-in-Chief of the Armed forces. It requires some general purpose military units, sub-units and personnel to be trained on methods and tactics of safeguarding the state borders. The border troops organisation and missions, legal guarantees of military servicemen and citizens who perform duties in the state border, should be regulated by the law. Missions of the air defence forces are also defined by the law

10. Law on Engaging Military and Police Personnel in the UN Peacekeeping and other International Activities

The objective of this law is to regulate relations connected with engaging Mongolian military and police personnel and military servicemen and policemen's team in UN peacekeeping and other international activities. This law includes provisions to regulate relations with respect to the management and organisation (Government powers, powers of the Minister of Foreign Affairs, powers of the Minister of Defence and the Minister of Justice, relations connected with professional management and preparation) as well as provisions defining the salary of military personnel and policemen who participate in such activities, and the corresponding penalties for law-breaker[8]

MILITARY RULES AND REGULATIONS

The Constitution approved in 1992 defined that judicial power shall be vested exclusively in courts. Judging and settling relations connected to military process is decided by the ways described below.

In case of violation of the Constitution, or the Law on Defence, the Law on Armed forces, or the Law on National security, and laws and regulations connected with the other laws of Mongolia, committed by the armed forces military personnel, commissioned officer, non-commissioned officer, sergeant, servicemen, other military and defence sector's servicemen, with criminal purpose, violators shall be charged with criminal responsibility in accordance with the Criminal Code of Mongolia, the Civil Code, the Criminal Procedure Law, the Law on Court of Mongolia, which were issued in correspondence with the Constitution of Mongolia. If violation of laws, regulations, procedures and rules have no criminal feature, to the charge will be administrative responsibility in accordance with related laws and regulation.[9]

There is no separate court-martial in Mongolia. Violations and criminal cases connected to the Armed forces military personnel are settled in accordance with the Civil Code of Mongolia, the Criminal Code of Mongolia and the Law on Civil Court of Mongolia. Article 10 of the Criminal Code of Mongolia contains a special clause named Military crime.

In the case that a Mongolian citizen, member of armed forces, or persons liable to military service commit any crime stated in the special clause of the stated law by violating regulations during mobilisation, military training and musters shall be defined as a military crime.[10]

Nevertheless, in the case a of crime committed during the state of war it shall be regulated in the following way: 'A crime violating any regulation of military service during a state of war or proclamation of a state of war with another country shall be regulated by the law of Mongolia approved in the stated period.' In section 11 of the Criminal Code a special clause is included: 'Crime against security and peace of human being'[11] This regulates matters related with war and military operations.

Also there are Military rules and regulations that regulate internal relations of the armed forces and other military establishments. The President of Mongolia approves general rules of armed forces in accordance with his prerogative rights. The Military rules of Mongolia relate to the internal activities, officials and personnel of the Armed forces. For this it reflects how objective civil control functions, how civil-military relations are to be conceived and whether the principle of the government division functions honestly. The Military rules of Mongolia are as follows:

1. Military Internal Service Rules

They shall define general obligations and rights, and relations of military servicemen of Mongolia, internal discipline of military units and sub-units, and high-ranking officers' duties. Internal services shall be regulated during a state of war or a state of war with another country by battle rules and present rules.

[9] The Law on the Courts of Mongolia. [10] The Criminal Code of Mongolia. [11] Ibid.

2. Military Disciplinary Rules

These rules shall define military disciplinary content, military servicemen's duties on observance of it, types of incentives and fines and rights of governors who shall implement the disciplinary measures. The present rules regulate relations connected with conferring incentives to those who successfully complete disciplinary action, and charging violators of disciplinary measures with a fine. Moreover, citizens, who are demobilized from the army but still have the right to wear uniform must comply with these rules in case of uniform usage.

3. Military Camp and Duty Service Rules

These rules determine principles of organisation of military camp and guard duty, execution, organisation of camp measures with military engagement, and rights and obligations of military officials and military servicemen.

4. Military Procession Rules

These rules regulate military personnel's conduct in armed and unarmed demonstration, including movement, unit, sub-unit parades with vehicles, salutations, performance of demonstration checks, carrying of the Battle banner and positioning and safeguarding its proper place, and performing proper parade duties[12]. If the violation of military rules is that of a criminal nature, a Mongolian citizen should accordingly be charged with criminal responsibility by applying the sections of Military Crime, Crime against security and peace of human being and other sections of the Criminal Code of Mongolia.

The final objective of civil-military relations of a democratic society are security, economical defence, and economic and business cooperation. Therefore, it is understandable that geopolitical, geo-economical, geo-strategic trends and trends of a regional nature shall be the basis of activities, legal programs and cooperation in every country. Mongolian military and legal reforms are being carried out with respect to these factors.

Regional geopolitical, geo-economical and geo-strategic trends are illustrated in documents such as the Concept of foreign policy of Mongolia, the Concept of National Security, the Law on Defence, and the Basis of the State Military Policy of Mongolia.

The legal environment for professionally oriented, compact and capable armed forces is being developed thanks to by state attention to issues of the country's security, maintenance of defence capacity and upgrading military build-up and formation and accomplishing effective harmonious civil-military relations.

For example, documents related to the intensification of measures of military reform were released three times (in 1993,1997, 2002) since 1992 and approved at the state level. The President of Mongolia (the Commander-in-Chief of the Armed forces), upon approval initiated an organisation devoted to this purpose entitled, 'Program on development of military building until 2005'.

However, much depends on our country's economic capability. It is undeniable that certain difficulties face the military building reform process due to the influence of great social and economic changes being experienced in our country. This results in the limitation of Mongolia's ability to sustain herself? In the defence sector,. Thus, measures illustrated in the above policy documents ca not always be fully implemented.

Basic issues of defence policy such as legal reform, its upgrading, Mongolia's security, reform in the defence sector, development of civil-military relations, and creation of a legal environment were strongly taken into consideration by the state. There are increasing demands to settle these comprehensive issues related to the defence sector. For example, there is still no processing of the law on legal status of the contracted workers of the Armed forces, law on usage of the airspace of the country, or the law on domestic flights in the country. It remains to be seen what the arrangements, legal status, and ultimate ramifications of such policy could have on the future of Mongolia.

LAW ON INTELLIGENCE ORGANIZATION

CHAPTER ONE GENERAL PROVISIONS

Article 1. Purpose of the Law

1.1. The purpose of this law is to determine the framework, organizational structure, and the basic principles of operation of Mongolian Intelligence Organization (hereinafter "Intelligence Organization"), and to regulate relations concerning procedures of serving in intelligence organizations and legal status of the intelligence officer.

Article 2. Legislation on Intelligence Organization

2.1. The legislation on Intelligence Organization shall constitute of the Constitution of Mongolia, Law on Intelligence Operations, Law on National Security, and other legal acts adopted in conformity with this law.

Article 3. Definitions

3.1. The following terms shall have the following meanings in this law:

3.1.1. "Foreign Intelligence activity" means an activity to ensure Mongolian national security, and gather intelligence and evidence significant for the formulation and implementation of the government policies.

3.1.2. "Counter-Intelligence activity" means an activity to uncover, thwart, and prevent activities conducted by foreign intelligence services and citizens aimed to spy and sabotage, and crimes prescribed by the law to the General Intelligence Agency.

3.1.3. "Intelligence Service" means an organization and its subdivisions and units conducting intelligence operation.

3.1.4. “Intelligence Method” means set of measures employed by intelligence service aimed to gather confidential and other information and evidences significant for implementing its objectives.

3.1.5. “Intelligence” means information and evidence gathered by intelligence service using covert means based on its objectives.

3.1.6. “Covert Means” means methods employed to gather information and evidence.

3.1.7. “Cover” means to conceal an activity to implement the objectives of the intelligence operation by using different organization, person, activity, identification, and other items.

3.1.8. “Clandestine Operative” means an officer of intelligence service working undercover in other organizations.

3.1.9. “Agent” means a person covertly working with competent organizations conducting intelligence operation.

3.1.10. “Contracted Assistant” means a person covertly working with competent organizations conducting intelligence operation based on contract and reward.

Article 4. Intelligence Organization

4.1. Intelligence Organization means an organizational framework aimed to ensure Mongolian national security by means of intelligence method.

Article 5. Principles of Operation of the Intelligence Organization

5.1. The main principles of operations of Intelligence Organization are to respect the rule of law, human rights, and freedoms, have unified and centralized leadership, ensure secrecy, combine overt and covert means of operations, and rest upon the support of organizations and citizens.

Article 6. Ensuring Human Rights and Freedoms in Activities of the Intelligence Organization

6.1. Intelligence Organization is prohibited from infringing and limiting human rights and freedoms except in cases provided in the law.

6.2. If the officer of the Intelligence Organization unlawfully violates human rights and freedoms, and legal interest of the citizen during the process of intelligence operation, Intelligence Organization or prosecutor and court shall restore victims’ rights and freedoms, compensate the damage, and impose punishments stated in the legislation upon the guilty personnel.

6.3. Personal information exposed during the process of intelligence operation that may harm person’s reputation and legal interests shall only be disclosed at the discretion of that person except in cases provided in the law.

Article 7. Budget of the Intelligence Organization

7.1. Intelligence Organization shall be financed from the state budget and the state shall ensure the economic resources for the organization’s operation. The budget of the Intelligence

Organization shall be sufficient to enable the organization to implement its objectives.

7.2. The budget for the operations of the Intelligence Organization shall be approved by the State Great Khural as a special item based on the budget review and upon the proposal by the Special Supervisory Sub-Committee.

Article 8. Assisting the Intelligence Organization

8.1. Government and non-government organizations, economic entities, and citizens shall render necessary assistance specified in the Articles 9, 10, 11, 12, 13, and 14 of the Law on National Security to the Intelligence Organization and its officers for performing its functions. Intelligence Organization shall be responsible for the expenses and property damages occurred as a result of the assistance.

CHAPTER TWO FRAMEWORK, FUNCTION AND RIGHTS OF THE INTELLIGENCE ORGANIZATION

Article 9. Framework of the Intelligence Organization

9.1. The framework of the Intelligence Organization shall be composed of General Intelligence Agency, Military Intelligence Organization, Border Intelligence Service, and its subdivisions and units.

Article 10. General Intelligence Agency and its Functions

10.1. General Intelligence Agency is central administrative organ which has an objective to coordinate operations of Intelligence Organizations, and formulate and implement policy to ensure national security by means of intelligence method.

10.2. The State Great Khural shall pass resolution to establish, alter, and dissolve the General Intelligence Agency, and its regulations shall be approved by the Government.

10.3. The subdivisions and units under the jurisdiction of the General Intelligence Agency shall be established by the Government resolution accordingly to its principles of jurisdiction and objectives.

10.4. School, training, academic research, economic entity, service organization, and security and special trained units may be established under the jurisdiction of the General Intelligence Agency.

10.5. The General Intelligence Agency shall have its own symbol. The prototype of the symbol and its procedures of use shall be approved by the Director of the General Intelligence Agency.

10.6. General Intelligence Agency shall use seal, stamp, and official form.

10.7. General Intelligence Agency shall perform the following functions:

10.7.1. Conduct Foreign Intelligence operation;
10.7.2. Conduct Counter-Intelligence operation;
10.7.3. Fight against the crimes prescribed by the law;
10.7.4. Process information related to ensuring national security and present it to the concerned organizations and officials;
10.7.5. Other functions specified in the law.

Article 11. Duties of the General Intelligence Agency

11.1. General Intelligence Agency shall carry out the following duties:

11.1.1. To protect Mongolian national interest and collect, gather, analyze, and evaluate intelligence related to ensuring national security, and inform state competent organizations and public officials specified in this law.

11.1.2. To uncover, thwart, and prevent espionage and sabotage acts conducted by foreign intelligence services, citizens, and agents.

11.1.3. To prevent, uncover, and thwart activities that endanger the national economic security.

11.1.4. To reveal and investigate crimes prescribed by the law to the General intelligence Agency, and search for its suspect.

11.1.5. To preserve the security of the Mongolian border, armed forces, and other military forces by means of intelligence operations within the limit of rights.

11.1.6. To ensure the security of the state information and communication.

11.1.7. To prevent Mongolian organizations, economic entity, and citizens abroad from being targeted by the activities of foreign intelligence services.

11.1.8. To prevent serious disruption of objects critical to the national economy and to conduct co-operation with competent organizations to determine the cause of the disruption and severe infectious diseases of humans, livestock, and plants.

11.1.9. To provide professional support to the activities of and work with the organization authorized to conduct Intelligence operations.

11.1.10. Other duties specified in the law.

Article 12. Rights of the General Intelligence Agency

12.1. General Intelligence Agency shall have the following rights:

12.1.1. To conduct surveillance and search, track postal communication, intercept communication and information network, and operate technical devices of intelligence operations in order to implement the objectives specified in the law.

12.1.2. To obtain information and evidence from government and non government organizations, economic entity, and public officials and citizens necessary for carrying out the duties specified in the law.

12.1.3. To acquire technical devices of the intelligence operations and authorize its use and transportation. To seize and confiscate technical devices of the intelligence operations used by unauthorized organizations, public officials, and citizens for private purpose.

12.1.4. To enter the buildings of organization, economic entity, and residents, question public officials and citizens, verify identification, conduct physical, property, and vehicle search accordingly to the regulations stated in the law, and withhold all evidences and properties linked to the violation of the crimes prescribed by the law to the General Intelligence Agency.

12.1.5. To search and detain persons suspected of the crimes prescribed by the law to the General Intelligence Agency.

12.1.6. To establish and operate front organization and economic entity.

12.1.7. To use address, identification, official uniform, and other items of different organization as a cover in order to conceal objects and specific activities of Intelligence Organization.

12.1.8. To conduct research and analysis, and recruit, engage, and receive support from professional organizations and experts.

12.1.9. To supervise the implementation of the legislation on the use, possession, and transportation of explosive, radioactive, toxic substances, and illegal drugs and firearms that endanger the security of the general population and ecological system.

12.1.10. To take measures to ensure the safety of the organization and the staff.

12.1.11. To work together with Foreign Intelligence services and organizations based upon the principles of equity, mutual respect, and non-intervention.

12.1.12. To ensure the safety of the organizations and economic entity without discriminating based on its forms of property, and provide professional support for the preservation of the business confidentiality.

12.1.13. To purchase information on matters relating to the functions of the Intelligence Organization.

12.1.14. To approve procedures related to the implementation of the articles relevant to the legislation on ensuring national security within the limit of rights in accordance with the law.

12.1.15. To issue warning to citizens and necessary requirements to follow for government and non-government organizations, and economic entity for the purpose of neutralizing the cause and condition of the uncovered crime and violation exposed during the process of the implementation of the intelligence operation specified in the law.

12.1.16. Other rights specified in the law.

Article 13. Military Intelligence Organization

13.1. Military Intelligence Organization is a military organization with main objective to provide the high authorities of the Mongolian Armed Forces with military-political and military-strategic intelligence.

13.2. The Government, based on the consent of the Commander-in-Chief of the Armed Forces, shall establish, alter, and dissolve Military Intelligence Organization.

13.3. The procedures of the Military Intelligence Organization shall be approved by the joint resolutions of the Chief of the General Staff of the Armed Forces and the Director of the General Intelligence Agency.

13.4. Military Intelligence Organization shall follow the respective articles in this law when performing its activities.

Article 13. Border Intelligence Service

13.1. Border Intelligence Service shall implement the main objective of providing the high authorities of Border Defense Organization with intelligence on conditions of the border area.

13.2. Minister of Justice and Internal Affairs shall approve the structure and the number of personnel of the Border Intelligence Service.

13.3. The procedures of the Border Intelligence Service shall be approved by the joint resolutions of the Director of the Border Defense Organization and the Director of the General Intelligence Agency.

13.4. Border Intelligence Service shall follow the respective articles in this law when performing its activities.

CHAPTER THREE MANAGEMENT OF THE GENERAL INTELLIGENCE AGENCY AND ITS POWERS

Article 14. Management of the General Intelligence Agency

14.1. The Prime Minister of Mongolia, with the consent of the President of Mongolia, shall appoint and dismiss the Director of the General Intelligence Agency.

14.2. The General Intelligence Agency shall be commanded by its Director based on principles of unified leadership, and the advisory council shall be employed under the Director of the General Intelligence Agency.

Article 15. Powers of the Director of the General Intelligence Agency

15.1. In addition to the powers specified in the Law on Intelligence Operations, the Director of the General Intelligence Agency shall exercise the following powers:

15.1.1. To provide the central organization with operational, and its subdivisions and units with unified authorities.

15.1.2. To determine organizational structure, staffing, salary fund, and salary system and amount of the officer, and to appropriate money within the approved budget.

15.1.3. To issue instruction of the intelligence operations in conformity with the law and organize activities to supervise the implementation.

15.1.4. To authorize the use of covert means accordingly to the Law on Intelligence Operations.

15.1.5. To make decision to acquire, possess, operate, and utilize technical devices of intelligence operation.

15.1.6. To provide the President of Mongolia, the Chairman of the State Great Khural, and the Prime Minister with information relating the matters of ensuring the national security.

15.1.7. To supervise the activities of General Intelligence Agency and Intelligence officers, and to organize activities to ensure their safety.

15.1.8. To represent General Intelligence Agency on relations with domestic and foreign organizations.

15.1.9. To appoint and dismiss Intelligence officers and to confer military rank.

15.1.10. To make decision to establish and dissolve front organization, and to direct and supervise its activities.

15.1.11. To submit proposal to the Government regarding the number of undercover personnel in the government organizations.

15.1.12. To issue resolution and instruction on internal affairs of General Intelligence Agency.

15.1.13. Other powers specified in the law.

15.2. In the absence of the Director of the General Intelligence Agency, all rights shall be vested in a Deputy Director. The Government shall appoint and dismiss the Deputy Director of the General Intelligence Agency.

Article 16. Oversight of Activities of the Intelligence Organization

16.1. The State Great Khural, through its appropriate sub-committee, shall monitor the implementation of legislation on activities of Intelligence Organization, and receive report and information from the Director of the Intelligence Organization.

16.2. The President of Mongolia, as the head of the National Security Council, shall receive report and information from the Director of the Intelligence Organization when necessary, be informed of its activities, and assign duties related to the matters of ensuring national security based on the decisions of National Security Council.

16.3. The Prime Minister of Mongolia shall receive information from the Director of the General Intelligence Agency, determine the course for ensuring national security during the fiscal year, and assign duties to gather information and evidence significant for formulating and implementing government policy, and fight against the crimes prescribed by the law.

CHAPTER FOUR LEGAL STATUS OF THE INTELLIGENCE ORGANIZATION OFFICER

Article 17. Intelligence Organization Officer

17.1. Government intelligence official who has taken an oath provided by this law and carrying out intelligence operation or equal to that is an intelligence officer.

17.2. /The provision was repealed by the law of August 2, 2007/

17.3. /The provision was repealed by the law of January 20, 2000/
/The provision was changed by the law of May 30, 2003/

17.4. Intelligence officer shall use military rank and uniform.

17.5. Presiding officers of the Intelligence Organization may be conferred high military rank.

17.6. The term of performing intelligence and identical duty shall be equated to service in the military. The Government shall approve the condition and regulation for such service.

17.7. The Government, on the recommendation of the Director the General Intelligence Agency, shall determine the list of operations and positions equal to intelligence service.

17.8. Legal status of the administration and service personnel of the Intelligence Organization shall be regulated by the law on Government Organizations, Law on Labor, and other legislative acts.

Article 18. The Oath of Intelligence Officer

18.1. Citizens of Mongolia shall swear the following oath to enter into Intelligence service:

"I, the citizen of Mongolia, am swearing to endeavor myself selflessly, will respect the State rule of law, ensure state and official secret, and fairly honor obligations and ethical norms of intelligence officer. If I welsh on this oath, I shall be held accountable under the law."

18.2. The President of Mongolia shall approve the procedures of taking oath of the intelligence officer.

Article 19. Ethical Requirements for Intelligence Officer

19.1. Intelligence officer has a duty to implement the decisions made by the authorities of the Intelligence Organization. The decisions of the authorities of the Intelligence Organization shall be in conformity with legislative acts and Provision 19.2. of this law.

19.2. In addition to the provisions specified in the Laws on Government Organization and Anti-Corruption, the following are prohibited for intelligence officer:

19.2.1. To Infringe and limit human rights and freedoms.

19.2.2. To intend to subdue and frighten using the name of the Intelligence Organization and his/her position.

19.2.3. To use his/her position and subordinates for private purpose.

19.2.4. To transmit, publicize, and inform information to others regarding his/her occupation without the special permission from the authority.

19.2.5. To carry out additional duty concurrently for salary except in cases provided in the law.

19.2.6. To strike, and to plan and organize measures directed at disturbing the normal activities of the Intelligence Organization, and to participate in such events.

19.2.7. To travel abroad without the permission of the authorized officials of the Intelligence Organization within 2 years following the discharge and dismissal from the service, or while performing his/her duty.

19.2.8. Other prohibitions provided in the law for government officials.

Article 20. Responsibility of Intelligence Officer

20.1. If the Intelligence officer violates legal and ethical requirements, he/she shall be subject to the sanctions specified in this and other laws.

Article 21. Disciplinary Punishment for Intelligence Officer

21.1. The following disciplinary punishments shall be imposed upon Intelligence Officer:

21.1.1. Warning;
21.1.2. Reduction in base salary by up to 20 percent for up to 3 months;
21.1.3. Demotion of the military rank;
21.1.4. Demotion of the employee rank;
21.1.5. Discharge from the Intelligence Service;

21.2. The Government shall approve the regulation concerning disciplinary code.

Article 22. Salary for Intelligence Officer

22.1. The salary of the Intelligence officer shall consist of base salary and bonus specified under the Provision 28.2.3 of the Law on Government Service.

22.2. The Government shall determine the special condition allowance and bonuses for the length of government service in addition to the base salary of the Intelligence officer.

Article 23. Vacation for Intelligence Officer

23.1. Intelligence Officer shall receive 15 working days of vacation every year.

23.2. Additional 2 working days shall be added to the vacation for every 5 years of government service.

Article 24. Guarantees for Intelligence Officer Conducting its Operation

24.1. Intelligence officer shall not be assigned duties not prescribed by the law.

24.2. Citizens and officials shall abide by legal and ethical requirements within the scope of rights of Intelligence officer without regarding jurisdiction.

24.3. Arresting and detaining intelligence officer while he/she is carrying out the duties of the Intelligence Organization, and conducting physical, property, and vehicle searches without the permission of the Director of the General Intelligence Agency is prohibited.

24.4. Government shall be responsible for the damages caused by the wrongdoing of intelligence officer during the process of implementing his/her duty in approved manner, organizing measures of intelligence operation, filing a crime, and conducting investigation.

24.5. Authorized officer assigned duty shall be responsible for the damages occurred due to the implementation of the duty in an approved manner by the intelligence officer.

24.6. Unauthorized organizations and officials are prohibited from interfering with the activities of intelligence officer.

24.7. Intelligence officer shall be provided with other guarantees specified in the law.

Article 25. Discount and Compensation for Intelligence Officer

25.1. Intelligence officer working on border shall be subject to the Provisions 36.4 and 36.6 of the Law on Border.

25.2. Intelligence officer unable to continue to work due to his/her identity being revealed while on duty or other reasonable excuses shall be provided with assistance on acquiring different occupation and profession, and Intelligence Organization shall render assistance to the officer relocating. The government shall be responsible for other related expenses.

25.3. Intelligence Organization shall be responsible for expenses of meal occurred during night shift and increased level of readiness, and food and supplies during the training.

25.4. The expenditures for transportation used by intelligence officer while carrying his/her duty shall be reimbursed by Intelligence Organization.

25.5. If the spouse of the Intelligence Officer is forced to resign from his/her current job as a result of Intelligence Officer being assigned to work in different location, Intelligence Organization shall provide the spouse with the benefit equal to the average monthly salary of the Intelligence Officer.

25.6. Intelligence Organization shall provide the Intelligence officer and his/her spouse with round-trip auto and train fares based on its current market prices once in every two years.

25.7. Officer of the Intelligence Organization shall receive other discounts and compensations specified in the law.

Article 26. Pension, Benefit and Assistance for Intelligence Officer

26.1. Relations concerning pension and benefit for Intelligence Officer shall be regulated according to the Law on Pension and Benefit for Military Personnel.

26.2. Regulations concerning benefit for Intelligence Officer who is performing special duty to infiltrate into foreign intelligence service and organization, and criminal organizations.

26.3. Intelligence Officer has a right to receive other assistance specified in the law.

Article 27. Use of Firearms, Special Devices and Physical Force

27.1. Intelligence Organization and Intelligence Officer may use firearms, special devices, and physical force under the conditions specified in this law.

27.2. Regulations concerning the use of firearms, special devices, and physical force shall be approved by the Director of the General Intelligence Agency with the consent of the Minister of Justice and Internal Affairs.

27.3. Intelligence Officer shall prevent crimes and other legal offenses, and to arrest and detain the offender, and use physical force and fighting techniques to carry out the duties when other means are unable.

27.4. Intelligence Organization and Intelligence Officer shall use the following special devices to fight against the crimes prescribed by the law and to carry out the duty to protect.

27.4.1. Various special devices;
27.4.2. Special devices for stopping vehicles;

27.4.3. Special devices for protection.

27.5. Intelligence Officer may use firearms in the following situation where other means are unable to be utilized to prevent criminal activities:

27.5.1. Assault by a person, which may endanger the life and cause serious damage to the health of intelligence officer, agent, and contract agent;

27.5.2. Group assault or use of weapons to break into the protected objects of the Intelligence Organization;

27.5.3. Escape of the person suspected of serious crimes prescribed by the law to the General Intelligence Agency.

27.6. The use of firearms must be preceded by a warning in any cases.

27.7. If a person is killed or injured as a result of the use of firearms by Intelligence Officer, immediate measures shall be taken to provide urgent medical care to the victim and to report to the superior who then shall report directly to the prosecutor.

27.8. List of firearms and special devices to be used by Intelligence Organization for protection shall be approved by the Director of the General Intelligence Agency.

Article 28. Intelligence Officer on Duty

28.1. In addition to the regular work hours of duty, Intelligence Officer shall be considered on duty when commuting between home and work.

CHAPTER FIVE OTHER PROVISIONS

Article 29. Legal Obligation

29.1. Those in violation of the Law on Intelligence Organization shall be subject to criminal, administrative, and disciplinary sanctions.

THE CONSTITUTION OF MONGOLIA

We, the people of Mongolia:

- Strengthening the independence and sovereignty of the nation,
- Cherishing human rights and freedoms, justice and national unity,
- Inheriting the traditions of national statehood, history and culture,
- Respecting the accomplishments of human civilization, and
- Aspiring toward the supreme objective of developing a human, civil, democratic society in the country

Hereby proclaim the Constitution of Mongolia.

CHAPTER ONE SOVEREIGNTY OF MONGOLIA

Article 1

1. Mongolia is an independent, sovereign republic.
2. The supreme principles of the activities of the State shall be ensurance of democracy, justice, freedom, equality and national unit and respect of law.

Article 2

1. By its state structure, Mongolia is a unitary State.
2. The territory of Mongolia shall be divided into administrative units only.

Article 3

1. State power shall be vested in the people of Mongolia. The people shall exercise state power through their direct participation in State affairs as well as through the representative bodies of State power elected by them.
2. Illegal seizure of State power or attempt to do so shall be prohibited.

Article 4

1. The territorial integrity and frontiers of Mongolia shall be inviolable.
2. The frontiers of Mongolia shall be safeguarded by law.
3. Stationing of foreign troops in the territory of Mongolia, allowing them to cross the State borders for the purpose of passing through the country's territory shall be prohibited unless an appropriate law is adopted.

Article 5

1. Mongolia shall have an economy based on different forms of property which takes into account universal trends of world economic development and national specifics.
2. The State recognizes all forms of both public and private property and shall protect the rights of the owner by law.
3. The owner's rights shall be limited exclusively by due process of law.
4. The State shall regulated the economy of the country with a view to ensure the nation's economic security, the development of all modes of production and social development of the population.
5. The livestock is national wealth and be protected by the State.

Article 6

1. The land, its subsoil, forests, water, fauna and flora and other natural resources in Mongolia shall belong exclusively to the people and be under the State protection.
2. The land, except those given to the citizen of Mongolia for private possession, as well as the subsoil with its mineral wealth, forest, water resources and game shall be the property of the State.
3. The State may give for private ownership plots of land, except pastures and areas under public utilization and special use, only to the citizens of Mongolia. This provision shall not apply to the ownership of the subsoil thereof. Citizens shall be prohibited to transfer the land in their possession to foreign nationals and stateless persons by way of selling, bartering, donating or pledging as well as transferring to others for exploitation without permission from competent State authorities.
4. The State shall have the right to hold responsible the land owners in connection with the manner the land is used, to exchange or take it over with compensation on the grounds of special public need, or confiscate the land if it is used in a manner adverse to the health of the

population, the interests of environmental protection and national security.
5. The State may allow foreign nationals, legal persons and stateless persons to lease land for a specified period of time under conditions and procedures as provided for by law.

Article 7

1. Historical, cultural, scientific and intellectual heritages of the Mongolian people shall be under State protection.
2. Intellectual values produced by the citizens are the property of their authors and the national wealth of Mongolia.

Article 8

1. The Mongolian language is the official language of the State.
2. Section 1 of this Article shall not affect the right of national minorities of other tongues to use their native languages in education and communication and in the pursuit of cultural, artistic and scientific activities.

Article 9

1. The State shall respect religions and religions shall honor the State.
2. State institutions shall not engage in religious activities and the Religions institutions shall not pursue political activities.
3. The relationship between the State and the Religion institutions shall be regulated by law.

Article 10

1. Mongolia shall adhere to the universally recognized norms and principles of international law and pursue a peaceful foreign policy.
2. Mongolia shall fulfil in good faith its obligations under international treaties to which it is a Party.
3. The international treaties to which Mongolia is a Party, shall become effective as domestic legislation upon the entry into force of the laws on their ratification or accession.
4. Mongolia shall not abide by any international treaty or other instruments incompatible with its Constitution.

Article 11

1. The duty of the State is to secure the country's independence, ensure national security and public order. 2. Mongolia shall have armed forces for self-defence. The structure and organization of the armed forces and the rules of military service shall be determined by law.

Article 12

1. The symbols of the independence and sovereignty of Mongolia are the State Emblem, Banner, Flag, Seal and the Anthem.
2. The State Emblem, Banner, Flag and the Anthem shall express the historical tradition, aspiration, unity, justice and the spirit of the people of Mongolia.
3. The State Emblem shall be of circular shape with the white lotus serving as its base and the "never-ending Tumen Nasan" pattern forming its outer frame. The main background is of blue color signifying the eternal blue sky, the Mongols traditional sanctity. In the center of the Emblem a combination of the Precious Steed and the Golden Soyombo sign is depicted as an

expression of the independence, sovereignty and spirit of Mongolia. In the upper part of the Emblem, the Chandmani (Wish-granting Jewel) sign symbolizes the past, the present and the future. In the lower part of the Emblem, the sign of the Wheel entwined with the silk scarf Hadag in an expression of reverence and respect, symbolizes continued prosperity. It is placed against the background of a "hill" pattern conveying the notion of "mother earth."
4. The traditional Great White Banner of the unified Mongolian State is a state ceremonial attribute.
5. The State Flag shall be a rectangle divided vertically into three equal parts colored red, blue, and red. The blue color of the center of the flag, symbolizes "the eternal blue sky" and the red color on both sides symbolizes progress and prosperity. The Golden Soyombo sign shall be depicted on the red stripe nearest to the flag pole. The ration of the width and length of the Flag shall be 1:2.
6. The State Seal having a lion-shaped handle, shall be of a square form with the State Emblem in the center and the words "Mongol Uls" (Mongolia) inscribed on both sides. The President shall be the holder of the State Seal.
7. The procedure for the ceremonial use of the State symbols and the text and melody of the State Anthem shall be prescribed by the law.

Article 13

1. The capital of the State shall be the city where the State Supreme bodies permanently sit. The capital city of Mongolia is the city of Ulaanbaatar.
2. The legal status of the capital city shall be defined by law.

CHAPTER TWO HUMAN RIGHTS AND FREEDOMS

Article 14

1. All persons lawfully residing within Mongolia are equal before the law and the court.
2. No person shall be discriminated against on the basis of ethnic origin, language, race, age, sex, social origin and status, property, occupation and post, religion, opinion or education. Everyone shall have the right to act as a legal person.

Article 15

1. The grounds and procedure for Mongolian nationality, acquisition or loss of citizenship shall be defined only by law.
2. Deprivation of Mongolian citizenship, exile and extradition of citizens of Mongolia shall be prohibited.

Article 16

The citizens of Mongolia shall be guaranteed the privilege to enjoy the following rights and freedoms:

1) Right to life. Deprivation of human life shall be strictly prohibited unless capital punishment is imposed by due judgement of the court for the most serious crimes, constructed by Mongolian Penal Law.
2) Right to healthy and safe environment, and to be protected against environmental pollution and ecological imbalance.
3) Right to fair acquisition, possession and inheritance of movable and immovable property. Illegal confiscation and requisitioning of the private property of citizens shall be prohibited. If the

State and its bodies appropriate private property on the basis of exclusive public need, they shall do so with due
compensation and payment.
4) Right to free choice of employment, favorable conditions of work, remuneration, rest and private enterprise. No one shall be unlawfully forced to work.
5) Right to material and financial assistance in old age, disability, childbirth and child care and in other circumstances as provided by law;
6) Right to the protection of health and medical care. The procedure and conditions of free medical aid shall be defined by law.
7) Right to education. The State shall provide basic general education free of charge. Citizens may establish and operate private schools if these meet he requirements of the State.
8) Right to engage in creative work in cultural, artistic and scientific fields and to benefit thereof. Copyrights and patents shall be protected by law.
9) Right to take part in the conduct of State affairs directly or through representative bodies. The right to elect and to be elected to State bodies The right to elect shall be enjoyed from the age of eighteen years and the age eligible for being elected shall be defined by law according to the requirements in respect of the bodies or posts concerned.
10) Right to form a party or other public organizations and unite voluntarily in associations according to the social and personal interests and opinion. All political parties and other public organizations shall uphold public order and State security, and abide by law. Discrimination and persecution of a person or joining a political party or other public organization or for being their member shall be prohibited. Party membership of some categories of State employees may be suspended.
11) Men and women shall have equal right in political, economic, social, cultural fields and in family affairs. Marriage shall be based on the equality and mutual consent of the spouses who have reached the age defined by law. The State shall protect the interests of the family, motherhood and the child.
12) Right to submit a petition or a complaint to State bodies and officials. The State bodies and officials shall be obliged to respond to the petitions or complaints of citizens in conformity with law.
13) Right to personal liberty and safety. No person shall be searched, arrested, detained, persecuted or deprived or liberty save in accordance with procedures and grounds determined by law. No person shall be subjected to torture, inhuman, cruel or degrading treatment. Where a person is arrested he/she, his/her family and counsel shall be notified within a period of time established by law of the reasons for and grounds of the arrest. Privacy of citizens, their families, correspondence and residence shall be protected by law.
14) Right to appeal to the court to protect his/her right if he/she considers that the right of freedoms as spelt out by the Mongolian law or an international treaty have been violated; to be compensated for the damage illegally caused by other; not to testify against himself/herself, his/her family, or parents and children; to self-defence; to receive legal assistance; to have evidence examined; to a fair trial; to be tried in his/her presence; to appeal against a court judgement, to seek pardon. Compelling to testify against himself/herself shall be prohibited. Every person shall be presumed innocent until proved guilty by a court by due process of law. Application of charges of convicted to the members his/her family and relatives shall be prohibited.
15) Freedom of conscience and religion.
16) Freedom of thought, free expression of opinion, speech, press, peaceful demonstration and meetings. Procedures for organizing demonstrations and other assemblies shall be determined by law;
17) Right to seek and receive information except that which the State and its bodies are legally bound to protect as secret. In order to protect human rights, dignity and reputation of persons and to defend the State national security and public order, secrets of the State, individuals, or organizations which are not subject disclosure shall be defined and protected by law.
18) Right to freedom of movement within the country and freedom to choose the place of one's

residence, right to travel or reside abroad, to return to home country. The right to travel and reside abroad may be limited exclusively by law in order to ensure the security of the nation and population and protect public order.

Article 17

1. Citizens of Mongolia while upholding justice and humanism, shall fulfil in good faith the following basis duties:

1) respect and abide by the Constitution and other laws;
2) respect the dignity, reputation, right and legitimate interests of other;
3) pay taxes levied by law;
4) defend motherland and serve in the army according to law.

2. It is a sacred duty for every citizen to work, protect his/her health, bring up and educate his/her children and to protect nature and the environment.

Article 18

1. The rights and duties of aliens residing in Mongolia shall be regulated by the Mongolian law and by the treaties concluded with the State of the person concerned.
2. Mongolia shall adhere to the principle of reciprocity in determining the rights and duties of foreign nationals in an international treaty being concluded with the country concerned.
3. The rights and duties of stateless persons within the territory of Mongolia shall be determined by the Mongolian law.
4. Aliens or stateless persons persecuted for their convictions, political or other activities pursuing justice, may be granted asylum in Mongolia on the basis of their well-founded requests.
5. In allowing the foreign nationals and stateless persons residing in Mongolia to exercise the basic rights and freedoms provided for in Article 16 of the Constitution, the State may establish certain limitations upon the rights other than the inalienable rights spelt out in international instruments to which Mongolia is a Party, out of the consideration of ensuring the national security, populations, and public order.

Article 19

1. The State shall be responsible to the citizens for the creation of economic, social, legal and other guarantees for ensuring human rights and freedoms, to fight against violation of human rights and freedoms and to restorate of infringed rights.
2. Human rights and freedoms as defined by the Constitution and other laws in case of a state of emergency or war shall be subject to limitation only by a law. Such a law shall not affect the right to life, the freedom of thought, conscience and religion, as well as the right not to be subjected to torture, inhuman and cruel treatment.
3. In exercising his/her rights and freedoms one shall not infringe on the national security, rights and freedoms of others and violate public order.

CHAPTER THREE THE STRUCTURE OF THE STATE

I. The State Ih Hural of Mongolia

Article 20

The State Ih Hural of Mongolia is the highest organ of State power and the supreme legislative power shall be vested only in the State Ih Hural.

Article 21

1. The State Ih Hural shall have one chamber and consist of 76 members.
2. The members of the State Ih Hural shall be elected by citizens of Mongolia entitled to vote, on the basis of universal, free, direct suffrage by secret ballot for a term of four years.
3. Citizens of Mongolia who have reached the age of 25 years and are eligible for elections shall be elected to the State Ih Hural.
4. The procedure of the election of members of the State Ih Hural shall be defined by law.

Article 22

1. If extraordinary circumstances arising from sudden calamities occurring in the whole or a part of the country, imposition of martial law or outbreak of public disorder prevent regular general elections from being held, the State Ih Hural shall retain its mandate till extraordinary circumstances cease to exist and the newly elected members of the State Ih Hural are sworn in.
2. The State Ih Hural may decide on its dissolution if not less than two thirds of its members consider that the State Ih Hural is unable to carry out its mandate, or if the President in consolidation with the Chairman of the State Ih Hural, proposes to do so for the same reason. In case of such a decision, the State Ih Hural shall exercise its powers till the newly elected members of the State Ih Hural are sworn in.

Article 23

1. A member of the State Ih Hural shall be an envoy of the people and shall represent and uphold the interests of all the citizens and the State.
2. The mandate of a member of the State Ih Hural shall begin with an oath taken before the State Emblem and expire when newly elected members of the State Ih Hural are sworn in.

Article 24

1. Chairman and Vice-Chairman of the State Ih Hural shall be nominated and elected from among the members of the State Ih Hural by secret ballot.
2. The term of office of the Chairman and Vice-Chairman of the State Ih Hural shall be four years. They can be relieved of or removed from their posts before the expiry of their terms for reasons defined by law.

Article 25

1. The State Ih Hural may consider at its initiative any issue pertaining to domestic and foreign policies of the state, and shall keep within its exclusive competence the following questions and decide thereon:

1) to enact laws, make amendments to them;
2) to define the basis of the domestic and foreign policies of the State;
3) to set and announce the date of elections of the President and the State Ih Hural and its members;
4) to determine and change the structure and composition of the Standing Committees of the State Ih Hural, the Government and other bodies directly accountable to it according to law;
5) to pass a law recognizing the full powers of the President after his/her election and to relieve

or remove the President;
6) to appoint, replace or remove the Prime Minister, members of the Government and other bodies
responsible and accountable to the State Ih Hural as provided for by law;
7) to define the State's financial, credit, tax and monetary policies; to lay own the guidelines for the country's economic and social development; to approve the Government's program of action, the State budget and the report on its execution;
8) to supervise the implementation of laws and other decisions of the State Ih Hural;
9) to define the State borders;
10) to determine the structure, composition and powers of the National Security Council of Mongolia;
11) to approve and change the administrative and territorial divisions of Mongolia at the suggestion by the Government;
12) to determine the legal basis of the system, structure and activities of local self-governing and administrative bodies;
13) to institute honorific titles, orders, medals and higher military ranks; to determine the table of ranks in some special fields of State service;
14) to issue acts of amnesty;
15) to ratify and denounce international agreements to which Mongolia is a Party; to establish and sever diplomatic relations with foreign State at the suggestion of the Government;
16) to hold national referendums. To verify the validity of a referendum in which the majority of eligible citizens has taken part, and to consider the question which has obtained majority votes as decided;
17) to declare a state of war in case the sovereignty and independence of Mongolia are threatened by armed actions on the part of a foreign Power, and to abate it;
18) to declare a state of emergency or martial law in the whole or some parts of the country in special circumstances described in Sections 2 and 3 of this Article, and to approve or nullify the President's decree to that effect.

2. Under the following extraordinary circumstances the State Ih Hural may declare a state of emergency to eliminate the consequences thereof and to restore the life of the population and society to norm:

1) natural disasters or other unforeseen dangers which have threatened or may threaten directly the life, health, well being and security of the population inhabiting in the whole or a part of the country's territory, occur;
2) state authorities are not able within legal limits to cope with public disorders caused by organized, violent, illegal actions of any organization or a group of people threatening the constitutional order and the existence of the legitimate social system.

3. The State Ih Hural may declare martial law if public disorders in the whole or a part of the country's territory result in an armed conflict or create a real threat of an armed conflict, or if there is an armed aggression or real threat of an aggression from outside.
4. The other powers, structure and the procedures of the State Ih Hural shall be defined by law.

Article 26

1. The President, members of the State Ih Hural and the Government shall have the right to legislative initiate.
2. Citizens and other organizations shall forward their suggestions on draft laws to those entitled to initiate a law.
3. The State Ih Hural shall officially promulgate national laws through publication and, if law does not provide otherwise, it shall be effective 10 days after the day of publication.

Article 27

1. The State Ih Hural shall exercise its powers through its sessions and other organizational forms.
2. Regular sessions of the State Ih Hural shall be convened once in six months and last not less than 75 working days on each occasion.
3. Extraordinary sessions may be convened at the demand of more than one third of the members of the State Ih Hural, and / or on the initiative of the President and the Chairman of the State Ih Hural.
4. The President shall convoke the first session of the State Ih Hural within 30 days following the elections. Other sessions shall be convoke by the Chairman of the State Ih Hural.
5. In case of the proclamation by the President of a state of emergency or war, the State Ih Hural shall be convened for an extraordinary session within 72 hours without prior announcement.
6. The presence of an overwhelming majority of the State Ih Hural shall be required to consider a session valid, and decisions shall be taken by a majority of all members present and voting if the Constitution and other laws do not provide otherwise.

Article 28

1. The State Ih Hural shall have Standing Committees dealing with specific fields.
2. The State Ih Hural shall determine the competence, structure and procedures of the Standing Committees.

Article 29

1. Members of the State Ih Hural shall be remunerated from the State budget during their tenure and shall not hold concurrently any posts and employment other than those assigned by law.
2. Immunity of members of the State Ih Hural shall be protected by law.
3. If a question arises that a member of the State Ih Hural is involved in a crime, it shall be considered by the session of the State Ih Hural and decide whether to suspend his/her mandate. If the court proves the member in question to be guilty of crime, the State Ih Hural shall terminate his/her membership in the legislature.

II. The President of Mongolia

Article 30

1. The President of Mongolia shall be the Head of State and embodiment of the unity of the people.
2. An indigenous citizen of Mongolia who has attained the age of forty five years and has permanently resided as a minimum for the last five years in native land, shall be eligible for election to the post of President for a term of four years.

Article 31

1. Presidential elections shall be conducted in two stages.
2. Political parties which have obtained seats in the State Ih Hural shall nominate individually or collectively Presidential candidates, one candidate per party or coalition of parties.
3. At the primary stage of the elections citizens of Mongolia eligible to vote shall participate in electing the President on the basis of universal, free direct suffrage by secret ballot.
4. The State Ih Hural shall consider the candidate who has obtained a majority of all votes cast

in the first voting as elected, the President and shall pass a law recognizing his/her mandate.
5. If none of the candidates obtains a majority vote in the first round, second voting shall take place involving the two candidates who obtains the largest number of votes in the first round. The candidate who a law recognizing his/her mandate shall be passed by the State Ih Hural.
6. If neither of the candidates wins in the second ballot, Presidential elections shall be held anew.
7. The President can be re-elected only once.
8. The President shall not be a member of the State Ih Hural or the Government and shall not concurrently hold the post of the Prime Minister or any other posts and pursue any occupation not relating to his duties assigned by law. If the President holds another office or a post he/she shall be relieved of it from the date on which he/she takes an oath.

Article 32

1. The mandate of the President shall become effective with an oath taken by him / her and shall expire with an oath taken by the newly elected President.
2. Within 30 days after the election the President shall take an oath before the State Ih Hural: " I swear that i shall guard and defend the independence and sovereignty of Mongolia, freedom of the people and national unity and shall uphold and observe the Constitution and faithfully perform the duties of the President".

Article 33

1. The President enjoys the following prerogative rights:

1) to exercise the right to veto against a part or entirety of laws and other decisions adopted by the State Ih Hural. The laws or decisions shall remain in force if a two thirds of the members participating in the session of the State Ih Hural present do not accept the President's veto;
2) to propose to the State Ih Hural the candidature for the appointment to the post of Prime Minister in consultation with the majority party or parties in the State Ih Hural if none of them has majority of seats, as well as to propose to the State Ih Hural the dissolution of the Government;
3) to instruct the Government on issues within the areas of his competence. If the President issues a decree to that effect, it shall become effective upon signature by the Prime Minister;
4) to represent the State with full power in foreign relations and, in consultation with the State Ih Hural, to conclude international treaties on behalf of Mongolia;
5) to appoint and recall heads of plenipotentiary missions of Mongolia to foreign countries in consultation with the State Ih Hural;
6) to receive the Letters of Credence or Recall of Heads of diplomatic missions of foreign states to Mongolia;
7) to confer state titles and higher military ranks and award orders and medals;
8) to grant pardon;
9) to decide matters related to granting and withdrawing Mongolian citizenship and granting asylum;
10) to head the National Security Council of Mongolia;
11) to declare general or partial conscription;
12) to declare a state of emergency or a state of war on the whole or a part of the national territory in the emergency situation described in Sections 2 and 3 of Article 25 of this Constitution under undelayable circumstances when the State Ih Hural is in recess and issue ordinances of the beginning of military operations. The State Ih Hural shall consider within 7 days the presidential decree declaring a state of emergency or a state of war and shall approve or disapprove it. If the State Ih Hural does not take decision on the matter, the Presidential decree shall be void.

2. The President shall be the Commander-in-Chief of the armed forces of Mongolia.
3. The President may address messages to the State Ih Hural and/or to the people, he may at his own discretion attend sessions of the State Ih Hural, report on and submit proposals concerning vital issues of domestic and foreign policies of the country.
4. Other specific powers may be vested in the President only by law.

Article 34

1. The President within his powers shall issue decrees in conformity with law.
2. If a Presidential decree is incompatible with law, the President himself or the State Ih Hural shall invalidate it.

Article 35

1. The President shall be responsible to the State Ih Hural.
2. In case of breach of his oath, violation of the Constitution and the President's authority, the President may be removed from his post on the basis of the finding of the Constitutional Court by an overwhelming majority of members of the State Ih Hural present and voting.

Article 36

1. The person, residence and transport of the President shall be inviolable.
2. Dignity and immunity of the President shall be protected by law.

Article 37

1. In the temporary absence of the President his full powers shall be exercised by the Chairman of the State Ih Hural.
2. In the event of the resignation, death or voluntary retirement of the President his full powers shall be exercised by the Chairman of the State Ih Hural pending the inauguration of the newly elected President. In such a case the State Ih Hural shall announce and hold Presidential elections within four months.
3. The procedure of exercising the duties of the President by the Chairman of the State Ih Hural shall be determined by law.

III. The Government of Mongolia

Article 38

1. The Government of Mongolia is the highest executive body of the State.
2. The Government shall implement the State laws and according to the duty to direct economic, social and cultural development shall exercise the following powers:

1) to organize and ensure nation-wide implementation of the Constitution and other laws;
2) to work out a comprehensive policy on science and technology, guidelines for economic and social development, and make State budget, credit and fiscal plans and to submit these to the State Ih Hural and to execute decisions taken thereon;
3) to elaborate and implement comprehensive measures on sectional, intersectoral, as well as regional development;
4) to undertake measures on the protection of the environment, rational use and restoration of natural resources;
5) to guide the Central state administrative bodies and to direct the activities of local

administrations;
6) to strengthen the country's defence capabilities and to ensure national security;
7) to take measure for the protection of human rights and freedoms, to enforce the public order and to prevent of crimes;
8) to implement the State foreign policy;
9) to conclude and implement international treaties with the consent of and subsequent ratification by the State Ih Hural as well as to conclude and abrogate intergovernmental treaties.

3. The specific powers, structure and procedure of the Government shall be determined by law.

Article 39

1. The Government shall comprise of the Prime Minister and members.
2. The Prime Minister shall, in consultation with the President, submit his/her proposals on the structure, composition and change of the Government to the State Ih Hural.
3. The State Ih Hural shall consider the candidatures proposed by the Prime Minister one by one and take decision on their appointment.

Article 40

1. The term of the mandate of the Government shall be four years.
2. The term of office of the Government shall start from the day of the appointment of the Prime Minister by the State Ih Hural and terminate upon the appointment of a new Prime Minister.

Article 41

1. The Prime Minister shall lead the Government and shall be responsible to the State Ih Hural for the implementation of State laws.
2. The Government shall be accountable for its work to the State Ih Hural.

Article 42

Personal immunity of the Prime Minister and members of the Government shall be protected by law.

Article 43

1. The Prime Minister may tender his/her resignation to the State Ih Hural before the expire of his/her term of office if he/she considers that the Government is unable to exercise its powers.
2. The Government shall step down in its entirety upon the resignation of the Prime Minister or if half of the members of the Government resign at the same time.
3. The State Ih Hural shall consider the matter and make a final decision within 15 days after taking initiative to dissolve the Government or receiving the President's proposal or the Prime Minister's statement on resignation.
4. The State Ih Hural shall consider and take decision on the dissolution of the Government if not less than one fourth of the members of the State Ih Hural formally proposes the dissolution of the Government.

Article 44

If the Government submits a draft resolution requesting a vote of confidence, the State Ih Hural shall proceed with the matter in accordance with Section 3 of Article 43.

Article 45

1. The Government shall, in conformity with legislation, issue resolutions and ordinances which shall be signed by the Prime Minister and the Minister concerned.
2. If these resolutions and ordinances are incompatible with laws and regulations, the Government itself or the State Ih Hural shall invalidate them.

Article 46

1. Ministries and other government offices of Mongolia shall be constituted in accordance with law.
2. State employees shall be Mongolian nationals. They shall strictly abide by the Constitution and other laws and work for the benefit of the people and in the interest of the State.
3. The working conditions and social guarantees of state employees shall be determined by law.

IV. THE JUDICIARY

Article 47

1. The judicial power shall be vested exclusively in courts.
2. Unlawful institution of courts under any circumstances and exercise of judicial power by any other organization but courts shall be prohibited.
3. Courts shall instituted solely under the Constitution and other laws.

Article 48

1. The judicial system shall consist of the Supreme Court, Aimag and capital city courts, Soum, intersoum and district courts. Specialized courts such as criminal, civil and administrative courts may be formed. The activities and decisions of the specialized courts shall not but be under the supervision of the Supreme Court.
2. The structure of courts and the legal basis of their activities shall be defined by law.
3. The courts shall be financed from the State budget. The State shall ensure economic guarantee of the courts activities.

Article 49

1. Judges shall be independent and subject only to law.
2. Neither a private person nor any civil officer be it the President, Prime Minister, members of the State Ih Hural or the Government, officials of political parties or other public organizations shall not interfere with the exercise by the judges of their duties.
3. A General Council of Courts shall function for the purpose of ensuring the independence of the judiciary.
4. The General Council of Courts, without interfering in the activities of courts and judges, shall deal exclusively with the selection of judges from among lawyers, protection of their rights and other matters pertaining to the ensurance of conditions guaranteeing the independence of the judiciary.
5. The structure and procedures of the General Council of Courts shall defined by law.

Article 50

1. The Supreme Court shall the highest judicial organ and shall exercise the following powers:

1) to review and take decision at first instance on criminal cases and legal disputes under its jurisdiction;
2) to examine decisions of lower-instance courts through appeal and supervision;
3) to examine and take decision on matters related to the protection of law and human rights and freedoms therein and transferred to it by the Constitutional Court and the Prosecutor General;
4) to provide official interpretations for correct application of all other laws except the Constitution;
5) to make judgements on all other matters assigned to it by law.

2. The decision made by the Supreme Court shall be a final judiciary decision and shall be binding upon all courts and other persons. If a decision made by the Supreme Court is incompatible with law, the Supreme Court itself shall have to repeal it. If an interpretation made by the Supreme Court is incompatible with a law, the latter shall have precedence.
3. The Supreme Court and other courts shall have no right to apply laws that are unconstitutional or have not been promulgated.

Article 51

1. The Supreme Court shall comprise the Chief Justice and judges.
2. The President shall appoint the judges of the Supreme Court upon their presentation to the State Ih Hural by the General Council of Courts, and appoint judges of other courts on the proposal of the General council of Courts.
3. A Mongolian national of thirty five years of age with higher legal education and experience in judicial practice of not less than 10 years, may be appointed as a judge of the Supreme Court. A Mongolian national of twenty five years of age with higher legal education and legal practice for not less than three years, may be appointed as a judge of the other courts.
4. Removal of a judge of a court of any instance shall be prohibited except in cases when he/she is relieved at his/her own request or removed on the grounds provided for in the Constitution and / or the law on the judiciary and by a valid court decision.

Article 52

1. Courts of all instances shall consider and make judgement on cases and disputes on the basis of collective decision-making.
2. In passing a collective decision on cases and disputes, the courts of first instance shall allow representatives of citizens to participate in the proceedings in accordance with the procedures prescribed by law.
3. A judge alone may take decision on some cases which are specifically singled out by law.

Article 53

1. Court trials shall be conducted in the Mongolian language.
2. A person who does not know Mongolian shall be acquainted with all facts of the case through translation and shall have the right to use his/her native language at the trial.

Article 54

Court trials shall be open to the public except in cases specifically singled out by law.

Article 55

1. The accused shall have a right to defence.
2. The accused shall be accorded legal assistance according to law and at his/her request.

Article 56

1. The Prosecutor shall exercise superve registration of cases, investigation and the execution of punishment, and participate in the court proceedings on behalf of the State.
2. The President shall appoint the State Prosecutor General and his/her deputies in consultation with the State Ih Hural for a term of six years.
3. The system, structure and legal basis of the activities of the Prosecutor's Office shall be determined by law.

CHAPTER FOUR ADMINISTRATIVE AND TERRITORIAL UNITS OF MONGOLIA AND THEIR GOVERNING BODIES

Article 57

1. The territory of Mongolia shall be divided administratively into Aimags and a capital city; Aimags shall be subdivided into Soums; Soums into Baghs; the capital city shall be divided into districts and districts into Horoos.
2. Legal status of towns and villages located on the territories of administrative divisions shall be defined by law.
3. Revision of an administrative and territorial unit shall be considered and decided by the State Ih Hural on the basis of a proposal by a respective local Hural and local population, and with account taken of the country's economic structure and the distribution of the population.

Article 58

1. Aimag, the capital city, Soum and district are administrative, territorial, economic and social complex having their own functions and administrations provided for by law.
2. Borderlines of Aimags, the capital city, Soums and districts shall be approved by the State Ih Hural at the presentation by the Government.

Article 59

1. Governance of administrative and territorial units of Mongolia shall be organized on the basis of combination of the principles of both self-government and central government.
2. The self-governing bodies in Aimag, capital city, Soum and district shall be Hurals of Representatives of the citizens of respective territories; in Bagh and Horoo- General Meetings of citizens. In between the sessions of the Hurals and General Meetings, their Presidiums shall assume administrative functions.
3. Hurals of Aimags and the capital city shall be elected for a term of four years. The memberships of these Hurals as well as those of Soums and districts, and the procedure of their election shall be determined by law.

Article 60

1. State power shall be exercised on the territories of Aimags, the capital city, Soums, districts, Baghs and horoos by their respective Governors.
2. Candidates for Governors are nominated by the Hurals of respective Aimags, the capital city, Soums, districts, Baghs and Horoos. Governors of Aimags and the capital city are appointed by the Prime Minister; Soums and district Governors by the Governors of Aimags and the capital city; Governors of Baghs and Horoos by the Governors of Soums and districts respectively for a term of four years.
3. In case the Prime Minister and Governors of higher levels refuse to appoint the gubernatorial candidates, new nominations shall be held in the manner prescribed in Section 2 of this Article. Pending the appointment of a new Governor the previously appointed Governor shall exercise his/her mandate.

Article 61

1. While working for the implementation of the decisions of a respective Hural, a Governor, as a representative of State authority, shall be responsible to the Government and the Governor of higher instance for proper observance of national laws and fulfilment of the decisions of the Government and the respective superior body in his/her territory.
2. Governor shall have a right to veto decisions of respective Aimag, capital city, Soum, district, Bagh and Horoo Hurals.
3. If a Hural by a majority vote overrides the veto, the Governor may tender his/her resignation to the Prime Minister or to the Governor of higher instance if he/she considers that he/she is not able to implement the decision concerned.
4. Governors of Aimag, the capital city, Soum and district shall have secretariats/Offices of the Seal. The Government shall determine the structure and staff limit individually or by a uniform standard.

Article 62

1. Local self-governing bodies besides making independent decisions on matters of socio-economic life
of the respective Aimag, the capital city, Soum, district, Bagh and Horoo shall organize the participation
of the population in solving problems of national scale and that of larger territorial divisions.
2. The authority of higher instance shall not take decision on matters coming under the jurisdiction of local
self-governing bodies. If law and decisions of respective superior State organs do not specifically deal with
definite local matters, local self- governing bodies can decide upon them independently incomformity with thee Constitution.
3. If the State Ih Hural and Government deem it necessary they may delegate some matters within their
competence to the Aimag and capital city Hurals Governors for their solution.

Article 63

1. Hurals of Aimag, the capital city, Soum, district, Bagh and Horoo shall adopt resolutions and Governors
shall issue ordinances within their competence.
2. Resolutions of the Hurals and Ordinances of the Governors shall be in conformity with law, Presidential
decrees and decisions of the Government and other superior bodies, and shall be binding within their
respective territories.
3. Administrative and territorial units, and the powers, structure and procedure of their governing bodies
shall be determined by law.

CHAPTER FIVE THE CONSTITUTION TSETS OF MONGOLIA

Article 64

1. The constitutional Tsets shall be an organ exercising supreme supervision over the implementation of the Constitution, making judgement on the violation of its provisions and resolving constitutional disputes.
It shall be the guarantee for the strict observance of the Constitution.
2. The Constitutional Tsets and its members in the execution of their duties shall be guided by the Constitution only and shall be independent of any organizations, officials or anybody else.
3. The independence of the members of the Constitutional Tsets shall be ensured by the guarantees set out
in the Constitution and other laws.

Article 65

1. The Constitutional Tsets shall consist of 9 members. Members of the Constitutional Tsets shall be
appointed by the State Ih Hural for a term of six years upon the nomination of three of them by the State

Ih Hural, three by the President and the remaining three by the Supreme Court.
2. A member of the Constitutional Tsets shall be a Mongolian national who has reached forty years of age
and is experienced in politics and law.
3. The Chairman of the Constitutional Tsets shall be elected from among 9 members for a term of three
years by a majority vote of the members of Constitutional Tsets. He may be re-elected once.
4. If the Chairman or a member of the Constitutional Tsets violates law, he/she may be withdrawn by the State Ih Hural on the basis of the decision of the Constitutional Tsets and on the opinion of the institution which nominated him/her.
5. The President, members of the State Ih Hural, the Prime Minister, members of the Government and members of the Supreme Court shall not be nominated to serve on the Constitutional Tsets.

Article 66

1. The Constitutional Tsets shall review and make judgement on the disputes at the request of the State Ih Hural, the President, the Prime Minister, the Supreme Court and the Prosecutor General and/or on its own initiative on the basis of petitions and information received citizens.
2. The Constitutional Tsets in accordance with Section 1 of this Article shall make and submit judgment to the State Ih Hural on:

1) the conformity of laws, decrees and other decisions by the State Ih Hural and the President, as well as Government decisions and international treaties signed by Mongolia with the Constitution;
2) the conformity of national referendums and decisions of the Central electoral authority on the elections of the State Ih Hural and its members as well as on Presidential elections with the Constitution;
3) the breach of law by the President, Chairman and members of the State Ih Hural, the Prime Minister, members of the Government, the Chief Justice and the Prosecutor General;
4) the well-foundedness of the grounds for the removal of the President, Chairman of the State Ih Hural and the Prime Minister and for the recall of members of the State Ih Hural.

3. If a decision submitted in accordance with Clauses 1 and 2 of Section 2 of this Article is not acceptable to the State Ih Hural, the Constitutional Tsets shall re- examine it and make final judgement.
4. If the Constitutional Tsets decides that the laws, decrees and other decisions of the State Ih Hural and the President as well as Government decisions and international treaties concluded by Mongolia are incongruous with the Constitution, the laws, decrees, instruments of ratification and decisions in questions shall be considered invalid.

Article 67

Decisions of the Constitutional Tsets shall immediately enter into force.

CHAPTER SIX AMENDMENTS TO THE CONSTITUTION OF MONGOLIA

Article 68

1. Amendments to the Constitution may be initiated by organizations and officials enjoying the right to legislative initiative and / or proposed by the Constitutional Court to the State Ih Hural.

2 A national referendum on constitutional amendment nay be held on the concurrence of not less than two thirds of the members of the State Ih Hural. The referendum shall be held in accordance with the provisions of Clause 16, Section 1, Article 25 of the Constitution.

Article 69

1. An amendment to the Constitution shall be adopted by not less than three fourths of votes of all members of the State Ih Hural.
2. A draft amendment to the Constitution which has twice failed to win three fourths of votes of all members of the State Ih Hural shall not be subject to consideration until the State Ih Hural sits in a new composition following general elections.
3. The State Ih Hural shall not undertake amendment of the Constitution within 6 months pending the next general elections.
4. Amendment which have been adopted shall be of the same force as the Constitution.

Article 70

1. Laws, decrees and other decisions of state bodies, and activities of all other organizations and citizens should be in full conformity with the Constitution.
2. This Constitution of Mongolia shall enter into force at 12.00 hours on the 12 the of February of 1992, or at the hour of Horse on the prime and benevolent ninth day of Yellow Horse of the first spring month of Black Tiger of the year of Water Monkey of the Seventeenth 60-year Cycle.

LAW OF MONGOLIA ON ITS NUCLEAR-WEAPON-FREE STATUS

CHAPTER ONE GENERAL PROVISIONS

Article 1. Purpose of the Law

The purpose of the present Law is to regulate relations pertaining to the preservation of the territory of Mongolia in its entirety, including its air space, land, waters and the sub-soil free from nuclear weapons, which constitutes an important factor for ensuring Mongolia's security.

Article 2. Legislation on Mongolia's nuclear-weapon-free status

2.1 The legislation on Mongolia's nuclear-weapon-free status shall consist of the Constitution of Mongolia, the present Law and other legislative acts adopted in conformity with them.

2.2 In case an international treaty to which Mongolia is a party contains provisions different from those provided for in the present Law, the provisions of the international treaty shall prevail.

Article 3. Definitions

3.1. The definitions contained in the present Law shall have the following meaning:

3.1.1 . "nuclear weapon" means any explosive device that is capable of releasing nuclear energy in an uncontrollable manner and that can be used for hostile purposes;

3.1.2. "nuclear-weapon-free status" means a legal status of being free from nuclear weapons.

Article 4. Prohibitions resulting from the nuclear-weapon-free status

4.1 An individual, legal person or any foreign State shall be prohibited on the territory of Mongolia from committing, initiating or participating in the following acts or activities relating to nuclear weapons:

4.1.1 develop, manufacture or otherwise acquire, possess or have control over nuclear weapons;
4.1.2 station or transport nuclear weapons by any means;
4.1.3 test or use nuclear weapons;
4.1.4 dump or dispose nuclear weapons grade radioactive material or nuclear waste.

4.2 Transportation through the territory of Mongolia of nuclear weapons, parts or components thereof, as well as of nuclear waste or any other nuclear material designed or produced for weapons purposes shall be prohibited.

Article 5. Uses of nuclear energy and technology

5.1 The use of nuclear energy and technology shall be permitted only by the State administrative authority in charge of nuclear energy and solely for peaceful purposes such as health care, mining, energy production and scientific research in accordance with the provisions of the international treaties to which Mongolia is a party as well as in conformity with the norms and principles of international law.

5.2 For the purpose of implementing Article 5.1 of the present Law and banning the dumping or storage in the vicinity of the borders of Mongolia of nuclear material or waste that might directly or in the long run indirectly adversely affect the safety of the population and the environment, Mongolia shall cooperate with the International Atomic Energy Agency (IAEA), other appropriate international organizations and the States that have nuclear programs.

CHAPTER TWO VERIFICATION

Article 6. National verification of the implementation of the legislation on the nuclear-weapon-free status

6.1 On the basis of the proposals of the central administrative authority in charge of foreign relations and of other organizations, the National Security Council of Mongolia shall, within its functions and competence, coordinate the following activities:

6.1.1 implementing of a single State policy concerning the prohibited and permitted activities pertaining to the nuclear-weapon-free status in Mongolia;
6.1.2 institutionalizing internationally Mongolia's nuclear-weapon-free status;
6.1.3 taking an active part in the activities of the appropriate international organizations, exchanging information on the prohibited and permitted activities in Mongolia and providing information to national organizations.

6.2 The competent authority of Mongolia shall have the right to gather information, stop, detain and search any suspected aircraft, train, vehicle, individual or group of persons.

6.3 The central administrative authority in charge of foreign relations shall be entrusted with monitoring the compliance with the present Law and the international commitments assumed by Mongolia in connection with the nuclear-weapon-free status.

6.4 Non-governmental organizations or individuals may, within the mandate provided for by the legislation, exercise public oversight of the implementation of the legislation on the nuclear-weapon-free status and submit proposals thereon to the relevant State authority.

Article 7. International verification on the implementation of the legislation on the nuclear-weapon-free status

7.1 Mongolia shall conduct international verification over the implementation of the present Law in cooperation with the relevant international organizations or by concluding special international agreements thereon.

CHAPTER THREE LIABILITY

Article 8. Liability for violation of the legislation on the nuclear-weapon-free status

8.1 An individual or legal person that violates Article 4 of the present Law shall be held liable in accordance with the Criminal Code.

8.2 The facility, equipment, material, raw material or means of transportation used for the activities prohibited by Article 4.1 of the present Law shall be expropriated by the State.

8.3 An individual or legal person that violates the present Law shall pay compensation for the damage caused to the interests of Mongolia as well as to the population, the environment and the properties in accordance with the relevant legislation of Mongolia or in conformity with the appropriate international treaty, the principles and norms of international law.

8.4 In case of violation or suspected violation of the present Law by a foreign State, Mongolia shall, within its international treaty obligations or norms and principles of international law, officially notify the State concerned of the violation or suspected violation, request explanation and peacefully resolve any question that may arise therefrom. If deemed necessary, the International Atomic Energy Agency (IAEA) and other relevant bodies could be asked for assistance. In case of a dispute of a legal mature, measures could be taken up to referring the matter to the relevant international court or arbitration.

Article 9. Amendment and termination of the Law

9.1 If the vital interests of Mongolia are affected, the present Law may be amended or terminated.

CHAIRMAN OF THE STATE
GREAT HURAL OF MONGOLIA

R. GONCHIGDORJ

RESOLUTION 19 OF THE STATE GREAT HURAL OF MONGOLIA ON MEASURES TO BE TAKEN IN CONNECTION WITH THE ADOPTION OF THE LAW ON ITS NUCLEAR-WEAPON-FREE STATUS

In its foreign policy, Mongolia sets the goal of pursuing its national interests, developing friendly cooperation with all the countries of the world as well as actively contributing, to the extent possible, to the efforts of the international community to strengthen peace and security. It is also pursuing a policy of refraining from joining any military alliance or grouping, or allowing the use of its territory against any other State as well as banning the stationing on its territory of foreign troops and weapons, including nuclear and other weapons of mass destruction. With respect to its two neighboring States, Mongolia is pursuing the policy of maintaining balanced and friendly relations and developing broad cooperation.

Mongolia consistently advocates disarmament and, on its part, is taking concrete steps to promote the goal of non-proliferation of nuclear weapons. Within the framework of this policy, in 1992 Mongolia declared its territory a nuclear-weapon-free zone and has since been pursuing the policy of and taking the measures aimed at institutionalizing and guaranteeing it. One of the results of such a policy has been the adoption by the United Nations General Assembly at it 53rd regular session on 4 December, 1998 of the resolution 53/77D entitled "Mongolia's international security and nuclear-weapon-free status".

Keeping Mongolia's territory free of nuclear weapons is fully in line with its policy aimed at strengthening its national security by political and diplomatic means.

Strengthening Mongolia's nuclear-weapon-free status at the State policy level, further clearer defining of the status and its observance would be important in strengthening mutual confidence and Mongolia's external security environment as well as in linking the country's national security to regional security and stability.

Mongolia's nuclear-weapon-free status represents a novel approach in the practice of international relations, which in its wider context could be considered as our country's concrete contribution to the policy and efforts of the international community aimed at strengthening the regime of non-proliferation of nuclear weapons.

Based on the all above and in connection with the adoption of the Law of Mongolia on nuclear-weapon-free status, the State Great Hural of Mongolia resolves:

1. To mandate the Government /R. Amarjargal/ to take the following measures:

> 1/ to actively cooperate with and acquire assistance from the relevant States, international organizations, including the International Atomic Energy Agency, in implementing the Law of Mongolia on the nuclear-weapon-free status and the United Nations General Assembly resolution entitled "Mongolia's international security and nuclear-weapon-free status";
>
> 2/ to take the necessary measures to ensure normal functioning of the stations designed to monitor nuclear weapons tests, that are situated on the territory of Mongolia;
>
> 3/ to report, as the case may be, to the Standing Committee on Security and Foreign Policy Affairs of the State Great Hural of Mongolia on the implementation of the Law of Mongolia on the nuclear-weapon-free status, of the present Resolution and other legislative acts adopted in conformity with them.

2. The present Resolution shall be implemented from the day of the entry into force of the Law of Mongolia on the nuclear-weapon-free status.

GOVERNMENT ROLE IN CONTROLLING ARMED FORCES AND NATIONAL SECUTRITY

The Mongolian Defence system and legal basis of Mongolia's armed forces structure became a political issue when Mongolia resolutely chose democracy and free market economy. Mongolian armed forces were then legalised and their functions formalised in the Constitution of Mongolia, the law on defence, and the collection of laws on the defence sector.

Politically, it can be considered that our armed forces, which developed according to the experiences and organisation theory of a socialist army Soviet army structure, are in a new period of development. This transition to a new political system and social order is markedly different from the previous socialist social structure of Mongolia and requires adjustments.

Today, for the first time in Mongolian history, the Mongolian Armed forces are legally declared in the Constitution which explicitly states that 'Mongolia shall have armed forces for self-defence.'[1]

In the Law on Defence of Mongolia, adopted in 1993, legislated the principles structuring the armed forces .This legislation provided nine provisions correlated with one another.. This illustrated a new development trend in the legal reform and structural theory of Mongolia's armed forces. Since civil-military relations and civil control are of utmost importance in the present work, the following provision is important to keep in mind: 'armed forces and other military measures shall be under civil control.'[2] This is the legal basis in Mongolia for the democratic civil control of armed forces.

In the former Soviet totalitarian regime, there existed entire control of armed forces by the communist party, which built the state as well. Control was directly implemented through the Central Committee of the Mongolian People's Revolutionary Party (MPRP), its Control Committee, the Party Commission by the Political Bureau of People's Army, the first stage party bureau, People's Monitoring Committee and other public agencies. Moreover, the control was implemented through the state administrative organisations and their representatives.

Though these controls were different in their methods and shapes, the contents and features were addressed by the highest institution of the MPRP in a wholly ideological and in some respects anarchical manner. In that time, many forms of cooperation existed between economic entities of urban and rural areas, public institutions and civilians on the one side and army units and divisions on the other. Special partnerships, with patterns of direct relation, were developed intensively.

[1] The Constitution of Mongolia, (Ulaanbaatar, 1998), p. 10. [2] The Law on Defence of Mongolia, Law Collection of the Defence Sector, (Ulaanbaatar, 1995), p. 68.

At this time, from 1925-1990, the Mongolian armed forces basically operated only according to the one party policy. with control coming from that party as well. Therefore, one could equate the control of armed forces to the internal control of the party. For this reason, the army was not willing to inform the people of failures and violations occurring within in the army, thus causing lack of information of the armed forces. The totalitarian regime considered the armed forces as the main tool of defence activity, so that military matters were highly privileged. It can be said that the issues of the defence policy were totally above criticism, even above the law.

Civilians, workers and professionals, did not have an understanding of the challenging tasks and features of armed forces, nor did they have to cooperate together with army or have a wide knowledge of the army. Likewise, the army, which was used to controlling civilians, did not have a clear idea of how democratic system addressed their relations with civilians.

More notably, civil control of armed forces was not public. The party that had the governing power over the whole state controlled everything and anybody. An active civil control could was impossible and there was little understanding among civilians as to whether the situation and principles of armed forces are proper to social interests.

Under such a regime, legal mechanisms influencing army activity in the interests of the people did not exist. People did not know at all how the measures of the constitution and other laws, provisions and requirements on the armed forces could be fulfilled. They only understood that as constituents of army, they must use weapons as dictated by the resolutions of the highest political administration. Therefore, we know that during Soviet history in some cases resolutions on army deployment without proper commands were made by the highest political administration.

In the present social transition period, however, thorough civil control of armed forces has not yet been implemented despite the wide range of social, political and legal measures, which have already taken place.

In the first years of the formation of new social relations, the aim to build a defence system and the legal basis of armed forces was set, and the Law on Defence was adopted by the Parliament. This may be considered as a revolution in development of defence sector. This law stipulated, that:

Armed forces and military general command shall be implemented and controlled by the Parliament, the President, the Government and the Cabinet Member responsible for Defence issues, within the superpower, given them by the Constitutions, this law and other laws shall be under civil control.'[3] In the law on Armed forces of Mongolia, which was adopted by the State Great Khural in 2002, it is defined that 'Armed forces shall be under civil control.'[4]

This determines the structure of Armed forces. The Law on Amendments to the Law on defence clearly defines the rights and duties of civil control subjects as follows: 'Civil control of armed forces is an open activity monitoring the implementation of the state laws and regulations, the acts of military professional administration of armed forces, and budget finance and its expenditure.'[5]

As provided in the above mentioned laws, civil control institutions of Armed forces of Mongolia are comprised of the State Great Khural, the President of Mongolia, the Government and its structural organisations, also NGOs, media, and political parties. Moreover, even ordinary people should be involved in this system.

THE STATE GREAT KHURAL (THE PARLIAMENT)

Plenary power such as to establish activities of legal basis of armed forces, to determine major trends of strengthening the basis of state policy and armed forces, to adopting the budget of defence measures shall be exercised by the State Great Khural. Therefore it directly controls armed forces.[6]

'The State Great Khural is the supreme organ of the State power, and legislative power shall be vested solely therein'[7] is defined in the article 20 of the Constitution. That means Mongolia has parliamentary governance.

Therefore the Parliament has power to discharge, abolish, and to appoint the Cabinet, lead by the Prime Minister, and moreover to pass laws on limiting Presidential Power, to relieve and to discharge the President.

According to the Article 25 of the Constitution, the State Great Khural 'may consider on its initiative any issue pertaining to domestic and foreign policies of the country' and has the authority on defence policy and national security levels. Some examples include; determining the basis of the State's domestic and foreign policies; determining and changing the structure and composition of the Standing Committees of the State Great Khural, the Government and other bodies directly accountable to it by the law; defining the state's financial, credit, tax and monetary policies, laying down basic guidelines for the country's economic and social development, approving the Government's program of action, the State budget and the report on its execution; supervising the implementation of laws and other decisions of the State Great Khural; determining the structure, composition and powers of the National Security Council of Mongolia; declaring a state of war in the event that the sovereignty and independence of the State are threatened by armed actions on the part of a foreign power, and ending it; declaring a state of emergency or martial law in the whole or some parts of the country in special circumstances and approving or nullifying the President's decree to that effect.

As provided in Article 6 of the Law on Defence, the State Great Khural is authorised 'to establish legal basis for the defence system and implement civil control over the armed forces and military activities.'[8] This was reflected in the law, adopted in 1993. This reflection gave principal significance to form a new system of civil control of armed forces. As above mentioned, being under civil control became a principle of organising the armed forces. Thus, this article changed. Moreover, the following rights are provided:

- to prevent threat of war and resolve disputes with other countries by political means,
- to determine bases of the State military policy of Mongolia, to approve the budget for defence measures and determine guidelines for strengthening defence capabilities of the country,
- to give special rights to military personnel,
- to determine the legal basis of measures of common military rules about limitation of their rights and freedom,
- to determine the basis of social security and legal guarantees for military personnel,
- to approve or terminate international treaties of Mongolia on military cooperation,
- to determine the legal circumstances of military personnel with respect to their specific duties, to establish senior military ranks,
- to carry out a decision on stationing on and passing through the territory of Mongolia of foreign troops.[9]

In 2002, the State Great Khural adopted the law on Armed forces. It was a matter of great consequence for founding the legal basis of civil control implementation and activities regulation of armed forces according. In other words, for first time the Armed forces were legalised. This is a clear example of how the State Great Khural gives its citizens power to carry out civil control.

In this way, according to the Constitution and other laws, the State Great Khural has a role in the implementation of the following rights, similar to the majority of parliaments around the world:

1) to approve the related laws and budget of defence field, 2) to control fulfilment of laws, legislation and other resolutions, 3) to appoint and replace the defence minister, and 4) to declare a state war and a state of emergency.

In the temporary absence of the President, the Chairman of the State Great Khural will exercise his power. The Government is responsible for the fulfilment of State laws, and is accountable for its duties to the State Great Khural. 'The President shall account to the State Great Khural'[10]. This indeed shows that the State Great Khural is not only the supreme institution of state power that implements civil control on armed forces, but it is also the 'state supreme body'.

THE PRESIDENT

The President of Mongolia has the power to command the Armed forces both in peacetime and wartime. According to the Constitution, '...the President shall be the Head of the State and embodiment of the unity of the Mongol people...'[11], the president, as a state supreme representative who is elected by all the people, is a subject of extreme power for implementation of civil control on armed forces. The legal fact that the President shall be the Commander-in-Chief of Armed forces of Mongolia, carries important weight in allowing him to exercise his duties. The President of Mongolia in regard to national defence possesses the following prerogative rights, described in article 35 of the Constitution;

to put a ban on the laws and other resolutions on the whole or a part of them, which are approved by the Parliament and to give directions to the Government on the issues in regard to his prerogative rights..., ...to confer state titles and higher military ranks and award orders and medals, to head the National Security Council of Mongolia, to declare general or partial conscription, ... to declare a state of emergency or martial law on the whole or a part of the national territory and to order the deployment of armed forces during extraordinary circumstances and the State Great Khural, in between two sessions, cannot be summoned at short notice...',

moreover to make a decision to mobilise the army. But in article 7 of the law on Defence of Mongolia, as the President is a Commander-in- Chief of Armed forces, his prerogative rights are clearly defined. It is more directed towards the command of the Armed forces and the implementation of civil control over it. In addition, the following powers are an important source for civil control;

to control the completeness of material sources which are necessary for ensuring the country's safety and implementation of state army policy, to put a proposal and summary on budget of defence acts to the State Great Khural, to approve the military common rules, to determine the principles of conferring military ranks to military personnel[12]

According to his prerogative rights, the President shall give a speech and express his comments while the budget of defence acts are discussed by the State Great Khural annually. It gives a stimulus and a basis upon which to approve the military budget.

According to the article 13 of the law 'on armed forces' it is described that the President is the Commander-in-Chief of Armed forces. Because of this, the President shall have rights to adopt the organisational scheme of armed forces in time of war and peace, to corroborate the plans that use the armed forces in war and to confer private to higher military ranks of the combat readiness, to make a resolution concerning the beginning of a war according to the related laws and legislation, to give a resolution to transfer the armed forces to the organisational structure of wartime, to approve the doctrine of using the armed forces, to adopt the charter of the General Staff of Armed forces, to appoint the commander of the General Staff of Armed forces on the consultation with the State Great Khural, to make a resolution to support the protection of the state border and particular objects with general use soldiers, and to determine the principles of participation of divisions and organisations of armed forces in economic activities and construction work. Also the proposal that the president of Mongolia makes a clarification of the changes in international and regional army, politics, economy, science, technology and military acts, as pointed out in the State Great Khural.[13]

Considering that, the President of Mongolia is firstly the Commander-in-Chief of the Armed forces, secondly the head of the National Security Council of Mongolia, thirdly, the subject empowered to declare conscription and a state of war upon consultation with the State Great Khural, as well as, fourthly, to transfer army and to exercise civil control in time of war and peace.

THE GOVERNMENT

According to the Constitution, the Government is 'the highest executive body of the State.'[14]. The Government shall exercise 'the following powers: carrying out State laws and directing the economic, social and cultural development of the country.'[15] Also it possesses considerable power with respect to defence. For example, to organise and ensure nationwide implementation of the Constitution and other laws, ... to work out a comprehensive policy on science and technology, basic guidelines for economic and social development, the State budget, credit and fiscal plans and to submit these to the State Great Khural and to execute decisions taken there within, to elaborate and implement comprehensive measures on sectoral and inter-sectoral development, to strengthen the country's defence capabilities and to ensure national security.

According to the article 13 of the Law on Government of Mongolia, the Government has the following power to defend the state and to ensure the national security:

to work out and implement the military policy of defending the state and ensuring the national security, to run activities to strengthen the armed forces, to give the direction in order to defend the state border, work out and implement the policy to ensure the national security, to make a fund of material sources that are required to defend the state and to provide the national security, and to run activities to supply this fund, and organise activities to defend the state secret.[16]

Also according to this law, the Government shall take measures to protect the population from natural disasters, to eliminate the consequences of natural disasters, and to manage civil defence work.

In the Law on Defence of Mongolia, the prerogative rights of the Government are indicated in detail. For instance, the Government is:

- to direct activities of the state administrative organisations, the local authority and the local authority units on the issues of defending state and local defence'[17]
- to submit a draft budget for defence measures to the State Great Khural
- to carry out decisions on establishing or dissolving military units and organisations in consultation with the Commander-in-Chief of the Armed forces
- to define locations of military units and organisations, and issue land permission for the territories to be utilized for defence needs
- to approve mobilisation plans for state administrative organisations, provinces and the capital city
- to define the size of material sources necessary for state and armed forces' mobilisation needs, and organise measures for their formation and utilization
- to provide state mobilisation readiness in peacetime, and when necessary, to switch the country to a state of war according to the decision of the State Great Khural or President of Mongolia [18]

- to instruct the activities of the NGOs and state administrations in order to educate people with patriotic ideology and to form proper civil military relations
- to determine and implement the policy that is directed towards enhancing the wishes and interests of citizens to fulfil military service duty[19]
- to determine the number of conscripts for each year, as well as the number of reservists to participate in mobilisation exercises and training, and set up a timetable for conscription in consultation with the Commander-in- Chief of the Armed forces;
- to conclude agreements on military and military technical cooperation with the governments within the competence provided by law
- to establish state administrative organisations in charge of border protection and civil defence, to appoint or dismiss their heads according to a proposal by the Member of Government in charge of defence
- to solve issues related to providing the armed forces and other troops with necessary equipment
- to define the types and volume of armament and military equipment acquisition from abroad, and upon the State Great Khural's approval, allocate necessary funding.[20]

The Government of Mongolia has the following duties: 1) to implement the State Great Khural decisions on defence policy and activities 2) to fulfil the mobilisation task of administrative units of aimag and the capital city 3) to finance the measures, which are directed to strengthen the armed forces and ensure the country.

From this, it is clear that the Government is an institution that fulfils its authority on one hand, and initiates civil control on the other hand. It accomplishes this by way of implementing the activities of the state policy on defence, regulating the adopted budget and finance, and providing the readiness of armed forces. In order to fulfil these duties, the role of the Ministry of Defence has become the leading institution which carries out administrative and democratic civil control of armed forces.

MINISTRY OF DEFENCE

Ministry of Defence, the central state administration in charge of defence, has to fulfil the following duties:

- to approve mobilisation plans and defence policy, and organise its implementation
- to submit proposals on providing the Armed forces with army techniques and other materials, and to implement the resolutions on that matter
- to educate and train personnel in defence field and to represent legal interests of military personnel
- to supply the Defence Sector with progressive technology and to work out policies on modernisation of technical equipment, and to implement and supervise resolutions in this regard
- to define policy research work and study in the defence field, and to organise its implementation;
- to determine the kind of research work and data required for defence activity plans and to make them operational;
- to determine the number of fixed-term conscripts, timetable of mobilisation each year and to put forth a proposal to the Government to determine the maximum number of professionals to be mobilised in order to work on contractual basis, on consultation with the Ministry of finance[21]

In article 1 of the Law on Amendments in the Law of Defence, it stipulated that 'the Member of the Government responsible for defence issues shall be separated from active military work,'[22], and his rights and duties are determined as follows:

- to implement defence policy
- to submit proposals on the issue of improving the national defence system to the Government and the National Security Council, and to the Commander-in-Chief of the Armed forces
- to submit general military rules to the President for approval
- to make agreements on defence cooperation with other countries within the competence provided by the Government;
- to submit a draft budget for defence measures to the Government, and to control the expenditure of the adopted budget
- to appoint and to discharge defence inspectors
- to control the implementation of defence laws and regulations, the president's command on defence issues, resolutions of the government and ministry of defence in related organisations and labour units, and to give instructions on their implementation;
- to solve the issues of eliminating, abolishing, transferring and receiving movable properties that belong to the fixed capital as well as immovable property of the legal persons of defence sectors who are subject to the Law on State Property, and to control the orders;

• to submit proposals on the privatisation of properties of legal persons who are subject to the Law on State Property in accord with the government.[23]

According to the Law on Armed forces, the member of the Government in charge of defence has the power to determine policy in reference to the social, economical and legal basis of the armed forces and to organise the implementation of proposal on strengthening the armed forces of the Government and the National Security Council, to account it to the Commander-in-Chief of Armed forces, to organise the activities to provide the armed forces with military weapons of general use, techniques, equipment, to submit a proposal on the reform of military weapons of general use and techniques, to resolve and make regulations on the budget classifications of general army use.

The Ministry of Defence is a basic institution for carrying out civil control of armed forces, managing and regulating the activities of armed forces, and to supplying it with required materials, and implementing the state defence policies within the country.

THE NATIONAL SECURITY COUNCIL OF MONGOLIA

The National Security Council of Mongolia is a State Consultation organisation which coordinates the comprehensive policy development of the state for ensuring national security and its implementation. It is also empowered to control implementation measures. This council accounts for its duties and actions to the State Great Khural. The President, the Chairman of the SGK and the Prime Minister are members of the National Security Council of Mongolia. According to the Constitution, the head of the National Security Council is the President. and he has the power to lead the Council activities in general, to determine and fix agendas, to chair meetings, to represent the council and to organise the working group.

As described in Article 4 of the Law on National Security Council, it has duties to control the implementation and regulation of policies ensuring national security such as strengthening the existing security of the State by investigating of the social and political life of the country, and safeguarding the state and social structure as defined by the Constitution. Furthermore, it can submit proposals on the basis of the state military policies to strengthen the structure and organisation of the armed forces, determining the defence policies of the State by the President of Mongolia to the State Great Khural. Finally, is has the right to determine necessary measures by making investigative work on international society, economy, science, technology, army and politics in terms of the interests of national security of the State.'[24]

The National Security Council consists of its council members, secretary, advisor, reporter and researcher. The secretary of the NSC is authorised to do research work on the matter concerning the basic rights and duties of the Council, to assess and evaluate, to justify decisions, to organise how to control implementation, to assist the council in making use of their authorization, and to inform them on studies and surveys and news about the National Security. The President appoints the secretary of the Council.

The vice chairman of the State Great Khural, the head of Standing Committee of National Security and Foreign policy, the leaders of the party represented in the State Great Khural and factions participate in meetings of the Council with advisory right.

Cabinet members of the Government, heads of special agencies and administration members of the General Staff of Armed forces shall be reporters and be responsible for investigating the issues of ensuring the vital national interests and security in the related fields, and determining necessary reports, comments and draft resolutions in order to submit them to the Council meeting, and to implement them in their units' field.

Highly-professional scientists and experts shall be nominated as specialists of the council on an honorary basis. They are responsible for making professional summaries on investigation and research into the drafts of Council resolutions and certain issues ensuring the national security.

The Council establishes working groups on vital issues such as domestic and foreign events which especially benefits national security and has a scientific division dealing with research. The Laws on the National Security Council determine these issues. As described in this law, the Council shall have the following rights:

- to 'make a summary by discussing the implementation process of the related law and ideology of the national security;
- to work out the basis of the state domestic and foreign, and the defence policies ensure the national security, give direction to decide extraordinary issue related to the implementation of it;
- to audit and to know the related organisation on the involved issues of the direction of the Council, hear their leader's report and information, give them advise, direction and teachings;
- to give the task and demand to the organisations that have a role of implementing the state policies and ensuring the national security, as described in the rights
- to take required results of the investigation and information from the related organisations in the task, advice, and agreement, fund and undertake research about important national security issues, funded as a form of scientific project'.

As described in Section 2 of Article 25 of the Constitution, the council exercises an important role in organising the resolutions about the declarations of a state emergency when extraordinary circumstances arise, or implementing the state of emergency situation, which goes into force on command of the President of Mongolia.

Although resolutions of the Council should be features of instructions, these constructions shall be verified as a solution of the central and supreme state administration bodies, and it legislated that the implementation of the solution shall be informed within a certain period. The related state administration body shall provide the National Security Council with necessary information, and the information database is established according to above-mentioned law and the internal job instructions of the National Security Council of Mongolia, which was adopted by the President of Mongolia on his command No155 of 1999.

As provided in the documents 'Basics of State Military Policies', the National Security Council shall exercise to'...regulate the implementation of the state military policies by the law and legislation, examine how the state policies are reflected in these laws'[25]

The State Great Khural also exercises the power to examine the acts of Armed forces through the central state administration body in charge of defence. As a Commander-in-Chief of Armed forces and the Head of the National Security Council, the President shall exercise prerogative rights to supply the armed forces with regular administration, define and approve legal acts necessary to the implementation of military professional administration, inform the State Great Khural, consult with the Government on defence issues and give directions. The National Security Council is a main consultation organisation, and moreover, the working unit of the council is responsible for supplying the state and the government leaders with necessary information and consultations. Thus, the policies and activities of the State Defence, and legal system of civil control on Armed forces are constituted successfully, and it may be summarised that in last 10 years, civil and military organisations have been cooperating productively on issues of the implementation of these basic legal acts. As a result, the State Great Khural is a social institution which has an important power to form civil control mechanisms of armed forces, leading and directing the defence policies and activities by implementing modern parliamentary control of the armed forces.

CONTROL SYSTEM OF THE STATE GREAT KHURAL

Civil control of the Armed forces of Mongolia is to be exercised by the President and national representatives in the State Great Khural, which were elected by the people, themselves. Civil control mechanisms implemented by the Commander-in-Chief of the Armed forces, the State Great Khural and the Government are correlated and compensate each other. The State Great Khural exercises the main control on the Armed forces without sharing it with other governing subjects. Therefore, it can be considered as the most integral part of civil control of the Armed forces of Mongolia.

In the following, the matter shall be broken down in terms of Mongolia as a leader and a representative. As a leader, the State Great Khural may exercise its power to control the Armed forces through the Government and its fully authorised members (representatives). The Standing Committees have plenipotentiary power to examine the implementation of adopted laws and resolutions of the State Great Khural, and have the power to influence policies and activities of the executive governance. But, the State Great Khural members carry out civil control of Armed forces through the Standing Committees, the Cabinet Secretariat and its members who are responsible for defence issues.

The State Great Khural has a special role for developing a control system and constituting a legal basis of the defence domain. Until 1990s, there was basically no other law or legal acts other than the 'Law on Military Service Duty of all people of the People's Republic of Mongolia' (1981) which regulated relations in the defence sector. Later, in 1990s, legal work was done with articles related to the defence field of the Constitution, security concepts, military doctrine, as well as Law on Defence, Law on Border, Law on Civil Defence, Law on Legal Condition of Military Personnel and Civil-Military Roles.

The Constitution, and the law on legal stipulations of military personnel and civil military role were adopted by the State Great Khural in 1992; the Law on Defence and the Law on Border were adopted in 1993; the Law on Civil Defence, Law on Subsidy and Pension of Military Personnel, Concepts on Securities and Foreign Policies, basic acts of military doctrine were adopted in 1994, and the law on Armed forces was adopted in 2002. With this framework, the legal basis of defence field was constituted.

STANDING COMMITTEES

The Standing Committees are special forms of organisational structure of the State Great Khural. As a common standard of the parliament, the Standing Committees perform the main part of the activities of the State Great Khural. Therefore, the main body of civil control on Armed forces is also the Standing Committee. In accordance with specific responsibility areas, the State Great Khural keeps seven Standing Committees. Within the responsibilities of the Standing Committees, issues of the Defence Sector are divided in the following way:

1) The Standing Committee on National Security and Foreign Policies,

- Policy of ensuring the national security of Mongolia
- Defence and Armed forces of Mongolia
- Saving and storing State secrets and
- Border sovereignty of Mongolia and its protection

2) Standing Committee on Social Policies:

- Social welfare of military personnel
- Labour relations, labour welfare.

3) Standing Committee on the State Structure:

- An executive supreme body, Presidential structure
- The administration units of Mongolia, ... its administration, organisation, and activities
- The public service
- Governmental organisation

4) The Standing Committee on budget:

- State budget, state income and outcome
- Budget consolidation, budget performance and budget control

5) The Standing Committee on Judiciary

• Legal policies of Mongolia.

These Committees possess the common power to 'implement the control of the State Great Khural within the related action work, determine the issues that will be discussed in the session and make preparatory proposal and summary'[26] on defence issues. This is pointed out clearly in article 13 of the Law on State Great Khural. Standing

Committees exercise certain defence related powers according to their area of responsibility.

To give an overview of SGK powers towards civil control the following examples shall be given: to keep control of the implementation of laws and other legal documents enacted by the GSK and on the work of units that report their activities directly to the State Great Khural; to hear and discuss the report of speakers of the Government, and its members, as well as of other organisations appointed by the State Great Khural; to make questions and to receive answers; to make proposals or summaries of appointing, selecting and discharging of responsible persons of the above mentioned organisations; to collect information such as research, report, news, and make conclusions about the implementation of the resolutions of the State Great Khural; to hear information on the implementation of laws and other legal gestures of the SGK as well as on issues that will be discussed in the Parliament session, and to request related organisations to issue evaluation data, report, survey results; to keep control of the SGK; to make public surveys or to ask professional institutions for a summary concerning any draft law; to appoint a working group of experts and researcher. Thus, the Standing Committees are furnished with strong power to control the implementation of laws and resolutions that are adopted by the State Great Khural and as well as to influence the activities and policies of the executive governance.

Within the power of the Standing Committee, the following procedure is used in civil control implementation: The Ministry of Defence is to request the commander of the General Staff of Armed forces to hear his reports, to receive civilian's petition and offence on armed forces and defence field, and to make a decisions in this regard. Also, reports of the Minister of Defence will be heard in the plenary sessions of the State Great Khural and in the meetings of the National Security Council meetings. Some instructions will be given to the Minster of Defence.

As for Mongolia, having parliamentary governance, it is more appropriate that the Standing Committee on Defence implements civil control on Armed forces through the Government. In addition, the State Great Khural has the opportunity to maintain control in cooperation with State Control Committee, being introduced to the results and taking measures based on the outcome of this procedure.

STATE CONTROL COMMITTEE

The State Control Committee was an organisation authorised to control the income of state, centralization of its budget, diversification and expenditure of budget properties, and monitoring controls on maintenance, expenditure, storage and protection of state properties. In addition, it examined whether civil servants and state officials abused their power in certain cases. The budget of the State Control Committee had to be enacted by the State Great Khural. The committee was financed by the state centralised budget. As indicated in section 5 of chapter 6 of the Law on State Control (no longer in force), the State Control Committee annually accounted for its activities to the State Great Khural. Therefore, it facilitated the implementation of parliamentary control.

As the Law on State Control was no longer in force, the State Control Committee was renamed the National Auditory Office, and its activities are extended. The new Laws on State Audit (2003) and State Control (2003) regulate these relations.

As indicated in the aforementioned, the 'State Control mechanism covers the control of the State Great Khural, the President, the State Auditory Office and of the control the state administrative units (hereafter referred to as 'professional control'), control of the Constitutions Court, arbitrary, prosecutors, local self-governing bodies and the control which shall be kept according to the present law' [27]. The 'System of State Auditory Office consists of the State Auditing Centre and local institutions. The State Auditing Centre shall be represented by the National Auditing Office and the local institutions shall be represented by the auditing offices of provinces and the capital city'

As indicated in the Law on State Control, the Government 'shall regulate the issues of organizing relations between professional control institutions, and make decision for building a fruitful system of administrative control.' The Ministries and agencies 'keep control over the implementation of laws and legislation, Cabinet resolutions, and decrees of the President on legal party of related organisations and legal persons having state, and to hear, if necessary, reports of the authorities of that organisation[29] The Professional Audit Control Centre 'keeps control on the implementation of principles that are legalized by the state organs on the basis of laws.'[30] In this way, the professional control system is fused and use of civil control is achieved through this system. In the Law on State Audit, 'the General Auditor of Mongolia and accredited auditor by the State Great Khural shall make an audit on the expenditure of budget properties for intelligence offices, armed forces and executive police office.'[31] 'It is prohibited that all persons other than the head of the National Security Council and the State Great Khural, other organisations and officials monitor the activities of the National Auditory office and General Auditory of Mongolia and give instruction for work performance.'[32]

To create any control process takes a lot of time and requires manpower. At the present, the State Great Khural is facing difficulties exercising efficient control of the implementation of laws. For this reason, as indicated in the Law on State Control, there is an opportunity to build a system that makes it possible to keep accountability in cooperation with the State Control Committee or to make a request on certain issues to the Central control committee for monitoring. That could be a possibility to improve results.

REALITIES OF PARLIAMENTARY CONTROL

The Members of the State Great Khural play an important role in implementing Parliamentary control, and within this practicing civil control on armed forces.

Compared to Western countries, the defence sector is not a political issue in the constituency of the members of the State Great Khural because defence industries are not developed in our country and relatively few ordinary people work in military units. Therefore, many other problems which have to be urgently solved within the four years' legislation period will decide issues in the constituency. The next election result will depend on how a Member of Parliament solved urgent problems in his constituency.

Due to this, even though it is beneficial that the micro management problem, common in parliaments of 'western countries' emerges, the Members of the State Great Khural are not interested in defence issues. There is no way to give priority to interest of time by ignoring the national security issue, for it is of significant importance to provide the members of the State Great Khural with defence information and knowledge.

There is no specific case in legislation that represents the interests of armed forces personnel and other troops. For this reason the State Great Khural faces certain problems in pursuing proper policy towards the Defence Sector. Election results in 2000 showed that military officials are able to compete in Parliamentary elections and to reach necessary results to bring military representation into the parliament. It is clear that reasons such as having served in the army and worked in military institutions provide the members of the State Great Khural with more information and advice in addition to consultation with government and non-government organisations and research institutes that are experienced in national security and defence fields.

To have military representatives in the parliament by competing in parliamentary election and to have many members that support the state military policy, defence and armed forces are essential for ensuring the integral policy in the defence field, as well as for prudent distribution of the budget and controlling the expenditure.

The Government plays a basic role in defending the country, reforming and developing the armed forces. This power is implemented through the Ministry of Defence. A referent, who is responsible for the defence field, works in the division of the centralised administrative offices of the Government, and regulates the issues related to the defence field. This referent assists the Government to formulate resolutions and to publicize data and research other important sources.

The Ministry of Defence, central administration for defence issues in civil democratic society, has an important role in civil control implementation of the Armed forces. The legal basis of this work has been already discussed above. However, in order to implement civil control of the Armed forces, the Ministry of Defence provides administration authority, trains military personnel, represents interests of military personnel, supplies people with necessary news and advertises military policy among them. He additionally publicizes 'Mongolian Defence White Paper', control training, arms-techniques, material equipment and readiness of war and mobilisation of armed forces, and makes summaries of real results of military action.

For the first time, in 1996 the Government of Mongolia appointed a person without military background as Minister of Defence. Between 1996-2000, the Coalition Government resigned three times. In that time the Minister of Defence was replaced in short periods. That did not give any opportunity to become acquainted with defence field activities or carry out steady actions and perform effective civil control. Also, it had several negative consequences. Firstly, the ordinary politician did not have a chance to get acquainted with defence policies and activities. Secondly, military personnel consider politicians as temporarily authorities, and finally, the value of democracy deteriorated. A Defence Minister without military background is an administrative person responsible for implementing civil control of state administrative units. In our country, it is considered to be important to determine the power of the defence minister by laws and to strengthen his position through support of professionals who are specialised in defence issues. The issue of having a minister of defence, who is a member of the parliament at the same time has been discussed too. On the one hand it is advantageous to have a parliament member, who is an expert on defence issues. However, on the other hand, it is a disadvantage for implementing civil control on daily activities of defence because the minister, who is a parliament member, does not have time enough to work in the Ministry of Defence.

The Administrative Control Service of Defence (ACSD), which was founded to control defence sector activities, clearly contributed to the duty fulfilment of civil control. This organisation runs activities within the authority of the Minister of Defence given to him with respect to his power to carry out civil control on armed forces. According to 'the Temporary Rules of Administrative Control Service of Defence', adopted by the order of the defence minister, the Administrative Control Service of Defence is an organisation with the goal of implementing defence objectives by way of controlling the implementation of laws and legislation of regulating defence relations, the President's decree, resolution of the Government, the order of the Defence Minister, rules and procedures adopted by high authority organisations in the field of defence and state central and local administrative units. Additionally, it has to protect against violations, investigate reasons for these infractions and recover losses. The ACSD exercises control according plans that can be developed independently and on its own initiation. The control activities shall be run within given power on request of higher authority and citizens' information. This method gives for the first time the opportunity to the civilians to take control on the defence sector activities by means of administrative control services. But responsibility areas control organisations overlapped. At the state policy development level, this issue was strongly considered. In order to improve the professional control quality and its result, the State Professional Control Office was founded with the aim to execute control according to a unified policy. Within this organisation, a state control inspector is responsible for defence issues. Due to this change, the above mentioned service was cancelled.

Although the State Great Khural is successfully fulfilling its duty of legislating laws in the defence field, it can be concluded that the system of fulfilling and implementing control is not yet fully complete. The following study shows that the Presidential Institute fulfils properly its duty of managing military activities and providing civil administration of armed forces.

P. Ochirbat, the former President of Mongolia, initiated the document entitled, 'The Bases of the State Military Policy of Mongolia'. This legal document enacted by the State Great Khural was related to defence sector . Also, he played an important role in developing foreign relations with two neighbouring countries and as well as establishing relationships with democratically developed western countries in defence field and strengthening military confidence of Mongolian Armed forces.

The second Presidential Election of Mongolia took place on the May 18, 1997, and N. Bagabandi, who was the candidate of MPRP, was elected as the second President of Mongolia. He proposed three tasks in his election agenda of 1997:

Firstly, to 'resolutely observe the policy to reform armed forces and other soldiers to be qualified and capable, give strength to more developed management system of armed forces and other soldiers from the government, provide social and legal assurance of defence activities, military service, police and frontier guards' constituents'. Then, in the 2001 Presidential election, his re-election showed a positive influence on strengthening civil control system on armed forces in the transition period. Firstly, it was a 'golden age' to fulfil the laws, adopted on defence field, security and foreign policy, legal documents, which have features of ideology and military doctrine, and to deepen modernisation of defence field. Also in this period, civil formed system of military administration requiring that the President performs the duty of a Commander-in-Chief of Armed forces, started to develop. N. Bagabandi executed resolute policies to maintain unity and cohesion in the armed forces in the period 1997-2001. It showed that he was rather qualified on issues of defence policy and armed forces. Thus on his re-election, continuity and quality of executive governance improved and it has played an important role in the development of the new structure and system of the defence field.

Secondly, the President of Mongolia established a practical system to determine issues of security and defence policy on the basis of the National Security Council, to initiate and cultivate legal documents, to separate defence policies and activities from challenging issues and political interests, and to be responsible for the issues of protecting interests of military personnel.

Thirdly, he considered important that the Armed forces receive civil democratic, and on the opposite side of the spectrum, military professional advice on civil administration. For this the president appointed created the position of private secretary of commander-inchief of armed forces and the position of a President's advisor on military issues in 2000. High-ranking military officers were appointed to hold those positions. It was significant that, firstly, the president has the possibility to receive military professional advice on issues of armed forces, and secondly, civil administration is able to pursue optimal policy towards the defence sector.

The President, as a subject that initiates law, appoints working groups for developing draft law on defence sector and introduces this document to the State Great Khural. This procedure creates a situation in which the Parliament members could be attracted to defence issues and also the interests of the defence sector armed forces and its personnel could be represented in the Parliament properly. For example, in the period 1997-2001, the President of Mongolia appointed working groups involving experts. These groups processed six draft laws, and proposed them to the State Great Khural. The president of Mongolia pursues the policy to appoint working groups on issues like military doctrine and modernisation programs in order to receive summary and proposal of them and gain wider knowledge and information on military issues. Additionally, he hears the reports of the of the Minister of Defence and the Commander of General Staff of the Armed Forces, visits units and offices of armed forces, and becomes acquainted with the overall activities. This policy has proved successful. Compared to other executive governance organisations of the country of the transition period, the President's Institute of Mongolia has had an opportunity of having power and rights that are strongly legislated by the Constitution and other laws. That gives them a chance to regulate the main issues related to armed forces independent of politics. For example, the President of Mongolia adopted 'Doctrine of using armed forces of Mongolia', 'Development Program on Military Structure until the year 2005', 'Procedures of giving military ranks' and 'Rules of participation of military units and organisations in business units'.

Compared with other institutions of the government, the President puts rather wide control on the activities of the armed forces. For example, in 2000 the President prescribed a strict deadline for submission of reports and information about the implementation of defence law and legislation, the financing of defence budget and expenditure, and the fulfilment of responsibilities of the Armed forces and other military laws. Also the President regularly receives reports on program implementation and formulates pertinent agendas as well If necessary, issues are discussed in meetings of the National Security Council. Between August 1997, and March 2001, the President was introduced to the activities of 16 units of armed forces, the National Defence University, 12 units and cartridges of border and internal troops, and also to the process of civil defence and field exercises. Then the President attended the conferences of administrative officials' of armed forces. The fact that the president is commander-inchief of the armed forces positively influences the implementation of civil control on armed forces, the separation of armed forces from politics and the protection of interests of the defence field.

As briefly summarised, Mongolia has 10 years of experience of parliamentary governance with democratic formation. Compared to Western Parliaments, it is a relatively short time. Since 1992 there have been three Parliamentary elections. Many laws and documents related to defence field were adopted during this timeframe. In other words, the parliament of our country constitutes a legal system to fulfil civil control of the armed forces. It may give the impression that the members of the State Great Khural do not pay much attention to defence policy and security issues during discussion in parliament. However, these discussions on draft laws related to the defence sector are often slowed down and postponed. Sometimes the adopted laws on defence issues are not even interrelated with one another.

Furthermore, although many laws and legal documents related to the defence field have been adopted, it can be noted that often narrow-minded interests of specific organisations work against each other and impede the legislative process. Furthermore, some organisations resolutely implemented these laws and legal documents but came from diametrically opposed interests. This ultimate success could be due to the fact that these laws were well processed.

The mechanism that gives information and advice to the Members of the State Great Khural in order to help provide them with political authority and to implement civil democratic control on armed forces is not yet fully constituted. The researcher R. Bold observed many years ago that

Today's State Great Khural which has an overwhelming tendency of adopting laws and budget on being supported by professional lobbyists who defend the interests of their field and professions, can not address defence issues in terms of being political policy. Therefore, laws that are dividing the armed forces into small parts according to professional differences, are not proper to our country which is small anyway. This shows that the State Great Khural is far from understanding military policy. In this condition, the research centre of the State Great Khural has to play an important role in providing the members with information related to defence field[33]

The Research and Investigation Unit of the State Great Khural has the basic function of providing members with required information, researching for members on law and other resolution drafts that are discussed during the session, and to prepare references using books, publications and archive materials. The Research and Investigation Unit is comprised of two parts, the library and archive. The research working group functions:

- to process draft laws to the State Great Khural, to make necessary research and investigation and to put forth proposals for fulfilment of adopted laws;
- to research Parliament and evaluate its results, exchange information with organisations of foreign parliament that have similar functions, make joint research and establish business relations;
- to gather necessary information for internal data network of Secretariat Office of the State Great Khural from foreign and domestic resources;
- to introduce information and proposals about the researching process and its results to members of the State Great Khural and the relevant expert, and to advertise it upon their approval.

The research and investigation unit has in total 15 officials, eight of whom work in the research section. In all, 75 per cent of officials of the research section are philosophers and sociologists. The remaining are lawyers and engineers.

Almost every issue the Unit deals with is related to security of the country and the defence field. It is clear that a wide range of information gathering and research on making laws and resolutions is required to regulate relations in this field. But there is not possible to hire further personnel or construct other apparatus' for procuring other essential and required information. Therefore, it is important to receive comments and results of research and investigation from other organisations, scientific researchers, and specialists of various fields. Taken as a whole, these research products can be considered to reflect a wider consensus on issues of national security and the defence sector and prove extremely useful to researchers of the unit. This research then becomes a main bridge aiding in the initiating of further research and reflecting the knowledge of outside organisations and experts on issues related to national security, defence and armed force. Moreover, it is a bridge to implement civil control and strengthen relations between the government and people.

The State Great Khural does not determine laws, but instead mainly adopts proposed laws. It has the advantage of influencing issues concerned in draft laws and resolutions. But it is disadvantaged in that it must consider regulating relations in a wide and various contexts. For example, it is required to constitute a unit, reflect the position of an official or system responsible for issues controlling the implementation of laws related to the defence field in daily life, to save continuity in policies, to protect from lawmaking that support the interests of only one ministry and agency, and to unify the overall policies and activities of all fields under the umbrella of the State Great Khural. However, the State depends on budget capability, and if the purpose of the policy is on target, the end, product could cut costs in the long term.

People's participation is essential for the successful implementation of civil control of armed forces. That will happen in the following ways: through the State Great Khural, the democratically elected, supreme state organ, through all local self-governing administrative units, people's representatives; through research on the 'Mongolian Defence White paper', and press and media efforts to receive accurate information; through active participation in all the activities of the armed forces; cooperation in the form of non-governmental organisations; and involving all related organisations in economising the defence budget.

CIVIL CONTROL

Civil control of armed forces is not a temporary action, a planned control or an examination respectively. It is a permanent and comprehensive action depending on the structure of the civil democratic society, social system, and formation of the activities of institutions that exercise state power and legal regulation. Moreover, it depends on qualification and knowledge, discipline and commitment of authorities of all administrative units and political culture, social awareness and views of organisations and civilians.

The formation of the compact, qualified and professional army depends on several factors. First, the subjective civil control system should be established in relation to the activities of the President and Parliament, who are established through a democratic election process, and its Government, the centre of executive governance and local administrative organisations. Second, budget revenues resulting from honest work of the manufacturer-producer-tax payer must be sufficient, and its distribution optimal. Finally, the army must be hardworking to be professional and prepared. The very aim of civil control on armed forces is to create Forces having high capabilities to ensure the security of the nation in any condition. In other words, civil control is wholly oriented towards having such a qualified Armed Force. This is provided by the results of above mentioned comprehensive and interrelated activities.

As indicated in the new Constitution of Mongolia, 'Our precious goal is to build a human and democratic civil society in the country', by defining the orientation of its development.

In the system of a democratic civil society, the Armed forces stay out of political activity, and shall always intensify professional capability in order to be ready for successfully fulfilling their duty of ensuring independence, territory integrity, and sovereignty.

While armed forces of totalitarian societies are under control of one party, which possesses the state power, in civil democratic societies armed forces are commanded by the state and stay under civil control, as the experience of other countries show. Professor, Sc. D, D. Myagmar noted

Civil control in democratic society is , first of all, one of the fundamental principles to implement the structures of armed forces. But some people consider it as administrative or sometimes political control formation. ...Actually, substance that we call civil control is an issue about regulating civil military relations in democratic and legal state condition by laws[34]

Therefore, in this book, civil control subjects are considered in the frame of related laws of Mongolia. This presents the challenging new task to constitute democratic civil control in our country which has not long been separated from totalitarian society.

[34] D. Myagmar, Thoughts on Modernisation of the Armed Forces and Defence Fields, (Ulaanbaatar: Defence University of Mongolia, 2002), p. 52.

According to this aforementioned goal, some goals for the implementation of civil control are considered practically as follows:

1) To correctly combine centralised and decentralised control. In other words, if the control of primary step organisations cab be combined, it will then be important to help each other find the mistakes of military and army life as well as civilian and to correct them.

2) One of the significant steps to fulfil civil control by protecting society and people under is that military armies do not rapidly fulfil the laws, decrees, legislation and guidance from the state and government. It is also important that they do not overlap with political policy from military authority. Some requirements shall be put in front of the armed forces within this frame. For instance:

a) armed forces shall directly and resolutely defend the state structure adopted by the Constitution;

b) activities of the armed forces are open to society and civilians, and people have a wide range of knowledge about it;

c) honest criticism of the armed forces by society and civilians should be correctly received, those who control the armed forces, shall duly take note of such commentary and study on ways of improving these shortcomings

d) beginning with the military, all the way up through to high authority, head and leader of units and sections; all shall have the capability of resolutely standing against any attempts organised by any political party and movement to involve armed forces to political struggles, especially attempts at challenging and subverting authority;

e) military personnel shall not give into the civil control and accept it as an efficient form of cooperation between military and civilians.

3) As seen in daily life, results of civil control depend on who leads the armed forces, more clearly, who is the head of the Defence Ministry, whether he is a civilian or a military person.

It is almost an unavoidable factor that in fulfilling civil control, the Minister of Defence shall be a civilian. So, it is of primary importance that the Minister of Defence shall be an active politician and an honourable statesman. Circumstances and lessons of past years have confirmed this. This unique feature of our country should be looked at more carefully.

Having civil authority in the Ministry of Defence provides the advantage to start democratic reform in the structure of Armed Force. It especially helps to provide society social care to military personnel, improve their intellectual life and relations among military personnel and to ensure the rights and freedom of military personnel.

Moreover, it plays an important role in strengthening relations between army and society, and opening the traditionally closed domain of the armed forces.

4) Civil control of the armed forces shall be fulfilled by the contribution of all branches of legislation, executing and judging governance, also of non-governmental pubic organisations. Above we already discussed some issues relating to this. Public organisations, activities of children, youth, women, student organisations and trade unions shall be directed towards giving patriot and civil-military education, most especially training and educating young people in the values of democracy.

Public media apparatus' also have an important role in civilising and humanizing the military service. Independent journalists equally figure in have making civil control efficient.[35] Public media equipment must pay attention to provide accurate and detailed information that can positively influence state administration units. For example, the authorised press office on Defence of Bundestag of the FRG actively monitors publications and programs of radio and television, and discussions on relevant matters; a task which highly appreciated. This method is widely used by opposition parties and movements as well as public organisations.

Despite that, the opening of all activities of armed forces to the public is one of the most disputed issues even in countries of developed democracy. In general, conflicts between opening Armed forces and striving for maintaining a level secrecy can never be resolved. Nevertheless, the Bundeswehr authority pursues the policy increasing openness.

For our country it is necessary to decide on that issue so as to enable civil and public organisations to use the media, and to take measures improving the capability of journalists, correspondents and publishers.

6) In order to carry out civil control and to be fully efficient, the following basic requirements shall be met:

a) to organise highly monitored control of all military organisations;

b) to urgently adopt and put into force legal acts oriented to the implementation of civil control in the activities of military organisations;

c) to make changes and amendments on laws and legislation, which are in force at the present time;

d) to constitute civil control systems for implementation in military organisations, and to flexibly regulate structure and organisation.

7) The civil control of armed forces must be implemented by constituents that have a close relation to military modernisation policy. In other words, in today's condition for military modernisation , the civil control of armed forces is a high priority.

STRATEGIC ECONOMIC INFORMATION

ECONOMIC OVERVIEW

The process of restructuring of the Mongolian economy started in December 1988. Since 1991, the Mongolian Government has been working toward solving fundamental economic problems: to overcome the shock derived from the abrupt end of the Soviet assistance and find new markets following the collapse of the CMEA trading block. Recovering from this crisis and determining the long term economic goals are of vital importance. The Government of Mongolia is working with IMF, IBRD, ADB, and EEC to implement a number of reform measures designed to stabilise the economy; reverse the decline in production and raise the living standard of the population.

Government procurement has been substantially reduced.The price and exchange rate were liberalised; and a new taxation system was created. Bank reserve requirements were increased. The dual exchange rate was abolished and replaced with a unified floating rate. A strong tendency towards macroeconomics stabilisation was evident in the 1994 inflation results. A significant improvement in the supply of key consumer goods, particularly foodstuffs, has been achieved since 1993. In the last year the Government has been concentrating its efforts on the implementatio of the mid-term program of restructuring of the Mongolian economy agreed to with the IMF.

The Mongolian economy has been shifting gradually from an agrarian-industrial economy to an industrial-agrarian-based one. The Mongolian economy expanded into processing of animal husbandry raw materials, garment production, building materials, food, and mining. The diversification of industry proceeded in coal, copper and molybdenum mining, grain and fodder production, consumer goods.

The law on privatisation passed in May 1991 and as subsequently amended, defines procedures and responsibilities for the privatisation process. The privatisation is being implemented in two phases. In the first "small" privatisation phase, the assets of small businesses, enterprises, shops and retail outlets with a total voucher value of Tg 5,9 billion, were auctioned to individuals. In the second big privatisation phase, the assets of large state enterprises with a total voucher value of Tg 13.9 billion are being converted into joint stock companies, with shares for sale in batches at the Mongolian Stock Exchange.

Over 3000 entities (including livestock holdings) with assets worth Tg 3.7 billion and with some 947000 shareholders have been privatised. Certain enterprises are of strategic economic importance and a state interest is retained. Secondary market tradings started in summer 1995

A two-tier banking system replaced the previous monobank in 1991 with the adoption of the Banking Law by Parliament. According to that law the Mongolbank (the Central Bank) is authorised to implement the monetary policy of the Government. Commercial activities of the former State Bank were transferred to commercial banks. The Central Bank has a supervisory role with regard to banking activities and observance of regulations by the commercial banks. Due to the tight policy pursued by the Mongolbank some positive signs appeared in the monetary sector. The slowdown in inflation led to a gradual decrease in nominal interest rates in 1994 and increase of togrog-denominated time deposits.

For up dated exchange rate of national currency (Togrog-Tg) consult the "Homepage of Mongolian Chamber of Commerce and Indusrtry"
http://www.mongoliaonline.mn/mcci

Central Bank tightened up the regulations on clearing credits. Reserve money increased due to an increased liquid ability of the banks. Foreign currency deposits rose by only 6 % in the year.

MAJOR TRENDS

Following sweeping political changes in 1990, Mongolia embarked on an ambitious program of economic reforms aimed at replacing the centrally planned economy. This goal was pursued against the background of a series of severe external shocks, notably the abrupt termination of the Soviet Union's trade support and foreign aid which comprised 37% of Mongolia's GDP.

In the years immediately after the reform program began, the economy declined. Output decreased, the balance of payments deteriorated, and inflation grew rapidly, reaching almost 400% in 1992. The Mongolian social safety net could not meet the demands placed upon it. Nonetheless, Mongolia remained committed to reform. It has closely followed the recommendations of IMF advisors and has used the IMF's enhanced structural adjustment facility to slow the decline of the economy. In 1993-94, the economy hit bottom and began to rebound. In 1994 Mongolia achieved positive growth for the first time since the reform process began, with growth of 2.4%. Since 1995 the economy has grown by 3-6% a year. Unemployment is about 20% and underemployment is higher. After the June 1996 parliamentary elections the new government accelerated the pace of reform and announced the liberalization of energy prices and its intent to increase the speed of privatization. The Ministry of Finance and central bank were committed to providing a stable macroeconomic environment. Thanks to these efforts, inflation dropped to 17% in 1997, 6% in 1998 and 10% in 1999.

Mongolia's reform government, under the Democratic Coalition, has made important economic progress. Sound macro-economic policies, supported by the donor community, have allowed Mongolia to weather the worst of the Asian financial crisis, despite several drops in world prices of Mongolia's key exports: copper, cashmere, and gold. Gross Domestic Product (GDP) grew by 2.7 percent in 1999, continuing the positive growth trend begun in 1995. Inflation was 10 percent, marking the second year in a row with moderate price increases, compared to hyper-inflationary rates earlier in the decade. Most impressive has been the growth of the private sector. The private sector share is now 72 percent. Private sector value-added grew by 12.7 percent in 1997, 15.0 percent in 1998, and 6 percent in 1999.

The total external trade turnover for 1999 equaled USD $761.4 million, of which USD $335.6 million were in exports and USD $425.8 million in imports. The total trade volume was down 10.3 percent from 1998, particularly imports, reflecting the imposition of a 5 percent import tariff in mid-1999 as required by IMF conditionality. Exports of textiles and textile articles increased by 58.7 percent or USD $45.7 million. However, mineral product exports declined by 13.2 percent, showing the effects of the gold export tax imposed in late 1998 and the low world price for copper.

New firms are emerging in Mongolia. In 1998 textile and garment exports were larger than mineral exports for the first time in Mongolian history. Due to the relative stability of Mongolia, some American firms have established operations here, using Mongolia as a base for operations in Siberia. The modest trend is expected to continue as firms begin to realize the strategic location of Mongolia. In addition, the informal sector is emerging as a major engine of growth and employment and may account for 13 percent of the GDP.

During the past four years the Mongolian economy has been transformed from a state-owned to a private one. This has been the result of three complementary trends:

- Private enterprises have performed far better than state enterprises in sector after sector, and agriculture, which is an almost entirely private sector, has been the leading growth sector.
- New private companies have been contributing more and more to economic output
- A sustained broad privatization program has shifted significant number of enterprises from state to private ownership.

PRINCIPAL GROWTH SECTORS

Mongolia's long-term growth depends principally on mineral and petroleum extraction, and value-added processing of livestock products (particularly cashmere and meat). While tourism offers some potential, it is limited by the short summer, the cost of travel to Mongolia, and lack of infrastructure (roads, hotels, etc.). For more information, see Chapter 5.

GOVERNMENT ROLE IN THE ECONOMY

Since the beginning of reform in 1990, the role of the government in the economy has been strong. Adjustments in purchase prices for grain and other commodities, wage increases for state workers, difficulty in collecting national taxes, and the decline of world market prices for Mongolia's principal exports (gold, copper, cashmere) have contributed to a decline in official government revenues. The largest state-owned enterprises (such as Erdenet copper concern) have yet to be privatized. However, the private sector now makes up over 70% of GDP and privatizations continue through sealed bid auctions.

INFRASTRUCTURE INVESTMENT

Infrastructure development is the key to Mongolia's economic development. A north-south paved road running from the Russian border to the Chinese border through the capital city is complete from Ulaanbaatar north to the Russian border. The project was financed by the Asian Development Bank. A north-south rail corridor already exists. The country lacks an east-west paved road or rail line. Without transportation infrastructure it is difficult to attract investment in the mining or petroleum sectors. However, the government does not have the resources to undertake these projects.

If the government continues with privatization of major state-owned companies, the national petroleum distribution company, NIC, will be sold within a year. NIC imports petroleum products, mainly from Russia, and distributes and sells them countrywide. A Mongolian-Chinese joint venture company, the Mongolian Refinery Company, plans to construct a refinery 45 km east of Ulaanbaatar. Several gold and coal mines have been privatized through sealed-bid auction. The embassy makes every effort to inform US businesses of these opportunities through International Market Insight (IMI) reporting and the National Trade Data Base.

KEY INDUSTRIAL SECTORS

The process of industrialisation of Mongolia began in early 1940s with construction of a power plant and some semi-processing enterprises of raw materials in Ulaanbaatar. With the membership of the country in CMEA, the process accelerated. The new industrial cities such as Darkhan and Erdenet were founded. The country received financial and technical assistance not only from former Soviet Union, but also from Eastern European countries. Gross industrial output grew significantly throughout the 1980s, averaging about 9 per cent per annum during the first half of the decade, and 5 per cent thereafter.

AGRICULTURE

Although the Mongolian economy has experienced considerable ndustrialisation for the last 3 decades, the agriculture sector remains the backbone of the economy, with about 26 per cent of GNP. Itis employing 95 percent of the rural population and 40 percent of the total labour force.It accounts for about 44 per cent of total ex-ports, mostly livestock products. 80 percent of the land is suitable mainly for ex-tensive animal husbandry. 29.3 million heads of live-stock include: 13.5 mln sheep, 9.1 mln goats, 3.5 mln cattle, 2.8 mln horses and 0.36 mln camels. Around 95 per cent of all livestock is in private possession. Agriculture has important linkages with the rest of the conomy and provides more than 75 per cent of raw materials and other inputs for leather and shoes fac-tories, wool processing mills, milk and bakery plants.

The strategy of the Government is to reduce the dependence of the economy on agriculture, in particular, animal husbandry based on traditional nomadic culture and to move to a more technologically sophisticated industry-based production structure. In this strategy, while agriculture would continue to be an important component of production, the strategic focus will be developing it as an input supplier for higher value-added and growth-leading manufacturing activities.

Crop cultivation began on a significant scale only in 1950s by developing virgin land. Most crop cultivation takes place on large state farms. Although important progress has been made towards diversifying agriculture, and, in particular, attaining self-sufficiency in cereal crops such as wheat, livestock raising continues to be the dominant subsection in agriculture, contributing over 70 per cent of the gross output in the sector. However, agricultural crops which contributed less than 1 per cent of the gross output of the sector in 1940 have improved their share to 30 per cent today. In 1996 the farmers harvested 220140 tonnes of grain and 69840 tonnes of potatoes and vegetables.

Mongolian agriculture produces the highly-valued raw materials such as cashmere, camel wool, horse tail, etc.. Herd quality improvement is sought, particularly, in such a field as colour rationalisation.

MINING

Since the first industrial exploitation of 500 deposits of 40 different minerals have been evaluated and 150 deposits have been worked on. In the 1980s, the mining industry was targeted for expansion. Mining output rose substantially during the ten-year period beginning in 1978. Assistance from CMEA was given for geological surveying activities in Mongolia through the years. Joint Soviet-Mongolian surveying activities were conducted throughout Mongolia.

In the 1970s and 1980s the main activities were focused on industrial minerals, including copper, molybdenum, fluorspar, phosphorites, gold, tin and coal. Today, nearly 200 deposits of coal, ferrous and non-ferrous metals, rare earth metals and precious stones are being mined. Mining is dominated by large-scale development of coal, copper, fluorspar and molybdenum, whereas mining of gold, tin and tungsten is primarily small scale. Mining sector accounts for a significant share of national income, and coal, copper, fluorspar and molybdenum are the most important commodities produced. Copper, molybdenumand fluorspar account for 60 per cent of export revenues of the country. Except for the Mongolian-Russian Joint Venture of copper ore-extraction in Erdenet, the mining sector has limited development, but geological surveys suggest it has an important future in foreign exchange earnings.

Nearly three quarters of the coal production of Mongolia comes from the Baganuur, Nalaykh and Sharyngol mines and is used primarily for production of electric power. Baganuur lignite supplies a thermal power station at the mine site and meets much of the energy requirements of the mining and industrial centres in Bor-Ondor, Darkhan, Erdenet and Ulaanbaatar in northern Mongolia.

Mongolia is one of the leading world producers of fluorspar, and a major producer and exporter of copper and molybdenum among the former centrally planned economies.

Fluorspar deposits being mined in east-central and south-east Mongolia include those at Berkh and Bor-Ondor (Khentiy), Khar-Ayrag (Dornogovi), Urgen (Dornogovi) and Hajuu-Ulaan (Dornogovi). Essentially all fluorspar output was traditionally exported to the former Soviet Union for use in its metallurgical industry.

The copper and molybdenum deposit at Erdenet was initially surveyed by Mongolian and Czechoslovakian scientists in the mid-1960s and subsequently investigated by Soviet and Mongolian geologists. Joint Soviet-Mongolian development of the deposit proceeded through the 1970s, and in December 1978 the Erdenet mine complex began operations. Several stages of expansion took place at Erdenet boosting concentrate production capacity to 16 million tones per year. Erdenet officials are today seeking advanced recovery technologies for the copper-molybdenum complex, in addition to financial assistance for a metal smelter facility.

Mongolia has a wide variety of mineral resources available for development. Though the minerals industry will continue to be dominated by production of coal, copper, fluorspar and molybdenum, other commodities will also be subject to new or expanded development, including gold, silver, limestone, nickel, phosphate, rare earth metals, tin, tungsten, zealots, lead and zinc. Mongolia will require continued financial and technical investment from external sources to develop its minerals base.

Given the varied geological environment of Mongolia, the long-term prospects for mining in the country are considered favourable. Efforts to attract foreign investors to the mining activities of Mongolia in the years ahead will be influenced by several factors, including the favourability of rules and regulations governing joint minerals development, and the stability of the country which will reassure investors and buyers alike of the guaranteed continuity of production.

Mongolia is uniquely situated to take advantage of minerals trade, both with its two neighbouring nations, Russia and China, and also with the rapidly developing and industrialised nations of the Asia-Pacific region. Located between Russia and China, both large mineral-consuming and producing nations, Mongolia has been and will continue to be a major supplier of minerals to these two large economies, albeit under differing arrangements.

The access of Mongolia to European markets and those of the Asia-Pacific region is also quite favourable. An obvious difficulty is the necessity to tranship ores /concentrates/ metals to these markets either through Russia to Europe or through China to the Asia-Pacific region. However, neither route presents an insurmountable barrier. Considering that Mongolia has been a supplier of ores/concentrates to Russia and Eastern Europe in the past, it has a proven means of access and known markets in that area. Continued and expanded trade with those areas is very likely.

Mongolia reached an agreement with China on the transhipment of goods, including ores/concentrates from Mongolia through China to the port facilities of Tianjin for forwarding to the Asia-Pacific region. Mongolia used this route for shipping tens of thousand tonnes of copper concentrate from the Erdenet mine to Japan. An alternate route through Russia to the port of

Nakhodka is also available and already being used by Mongolia for shipping of goods to the Asia-Pacific region.

In the near future, Mongolia's new major external markets will be within the Asia-Pacific region, specifically Japan, Republic of Korea and USA. This does not take into account existing long-term contractual arrangements with Russia. Subsequent, markets within ASEAN and Indochin may present opportunities for Mongolian mineral commodity trade. Reopening and expansion of markets with Russia and Eastern Europe will be dependent on the economic performance and political stability in these areas.

A further factor in determining the nature and extent of the minerals trade from Mongolia will be the development of a proposed copper smelter to refine copper ore produced at Erdenet. The development of a smelter now or in the future would materially facilitate copper trade by increasing the value-added to the Erdenet ore, which is now exported as a concentrate, and would reduce transportation volumes and costs and would produce a more desirable product for most of the world market. A secondary benefit of on-site smelting of Erdenet ore would be the recovery of by-product molybdenum, silver, gold and other metals for sale on the world market.

An internal market for minerals in Mongolia is very small and is primarily for iron and steel. With construction of a metal recovery facility at Darkhan, using scrap metal, domestic demand can be satisfied. Although primarily designed for domestic supply, the Darkhan plant could be expanded for the production of iron and steel for export. Additionally, an iron and steel facility is being discussed with several countries to exploit the iron ore reserves of Tumurtiin Ovoo. Discussions on how to exploit iron ore reserves at Tumurtiin Ovoo are taking place with several countries.

Though the major mining areas are all adjacent to, or connected with, the existing rail system to Russia and China, the poor transportation infrastructure of Mongolia is a main constraint for new minerals' development and trade. However development of new fields may require infrastructure investment either on roads or branch railway lines (up to a maximum of 100 km length).

Mongolian Parliament adopted in December 1994 a new law on Mineral resources which improves the legal environment for mineral exploitation. Other factors that have an impact on decisions to invest will include infrastructure and energy constraints, climate conditions and division of management control
to joint ventures.

Mongolia has many important mining projects and petroleum fields which are available for joint venture and foreign direct investment. Starting 1989, Mongolia has been negotiating with major foreign companies on prospecting for and processing of oil. Several international energy firms are already pursuing investment opportunities in Mongolia, surveying the southern, eastern and south-eastern regions of Mongolia for prospective oil deposits. Western company officials have estimated oil reserves in place at two known fields of Mongolia at 50 million barrels, of which between 10 to 30 per cent can be recovered.

Priority also is given to mining and processing of lead, zinc, silver, molybdenum, gold, copper deposits.

Gold mining is to be increased at least 4 times over the current volumc by way of establishing small and medium enterprises of all forms of ownership within the framework of the " Gold project". Placer gold production is profitable.

MANUFACTURING

Mongolia has built a significant capacity in light- and food- industry. The major enterprises of light industry are concentrated in Ulaanbaatar, Darkhan, Erdenet and Choibalsan cities. A number of enterprises have an excess capacity and are monopolist in the sector. The development of Mongolian light industry was designed to add value to the raw materials produced by animal husbandry and to create jobs for the increasing urban population mainly female residents. The developmentof Mongolian light industry began with establishment of wool washing, spinning and animal skin-processing enterprises. Also large state-owned garment factories were built. Military and other uniforms, fur and sheepskin garments have significant share in their products.

During 70s and 80s, the sector extended to the production of shoes, carpet, leather and skin garments. Three big carpet factories are situated in Ulaanbaatar, Erdenet and Choibalsan. The sector used to export its products to the CMEA member countries under fixed prices from bilateral government agreements. Until recently, the large state-owned wool- and skin-processing factories have played an important role in the national economy. In 1992-1993, all state- owned companies of light industry sector were privatised through "yellow" voucher scheme and became share-holding companies.

Wool and Cashmere Processing branch of the sector contributes over 10 per cent to the net industrial production and employs 5 per cent of workers. Only 2 out of 20 previous large state-owned companies remain as state property and the rest became share-holding companies. In recent years, a considerable amount of small and medium capacities have been introduced in the sector. Mongolia produces 20.000 m/t of sheep wool, about 2000 tons of cashmere and 1500 tons of camel wool per year. Encouragement is given to foreign investment in cashmere processing.

Skin and hide processing is traditionally known to Mongolians.Development of the hide and skin processing industry is based on the raw materials of about 8-9 million animals slaughtered yearly in Mongolia. The industry expanded rapidly with the establishment of an integrated leather garment and shoe factory for the production of domestic consumption and export. The whole sector is privatised. There are many small and medium enterprises involved in processing hides and skins and producing leather garments.

Almost all products of food industry are consumed on the domestic market. There are large-scale meat processing and flour plants in Ulaanbaatar, Darhan, Choibalsan and Suhbaatar.

Enterprises are divided into two categories by their size and significance; big enterprises with the production for the consumption of the country or to some extent for export and the local food factories with small production.

In early 1990s the sector suffered lingering stagnation and sharp decline across all areas.The light and food industry sectors of Mongolia have mainly obsolete, outdated equipment and technology except for a few cashmere processing enterprises. In the new business environment, the light and food industries are facing great difficulties concerning quality and cost of their production. Foreign investment is considered an important source for the recovery and further development of the sector.

Nowadays investors from USA, South Korea, Hong-Kong and other countries are establishing joint ventures with Mongolian partners using the existing facilities and skilled workers of the sector. They also are engaged in the production of garments for export using imported inputs.

Foreign investors are attracted by the favourable conditions set forward by Mongolian enactment concerning foreign investment and preferential tariff treatment in USA, EU and Japanese market for products of Mongolian origin. National economic development has been leading to the introduction of new manufacturing industries such as production of construction materials, assembly lines of various types based on imported spare parts, metallurgy in Mongolia.

Increasing demand for steel and iron products led Mongolia to construct its own steel mill in Darkhan city. The operation of this ill started in 1993 with annual capacity of 100.000 tons.

TOURISM AND SERVICE INDUSTRY

Although tourism in our country began to be a recognizable part of our economy 40 years ago, the Government at that time did not give proper attention to its development. Tourism policy was neglected, the material basis of tourism organization was not strengthened and infrastructure therefore remained poor. Training of personnel in the industry does not meet international standards and nothing much has been done to bring services and facilities up to the required level to satisfy sophisticated travellers.

Individual tourism and tourism originating from western countries were not encouraged, despite the fact that nowadays there are many countries which derive much of their income from tourism. We believe that tourism is an important source of foreign exchange and therefore it can become a vital part of the Mongolian economy. An important, but indirect effect of foreign tourism is the generation of foreign investment. After the political and economic changes of 1990, Mongolia opened its borders. The bases for developing tourism in Mongolia are its diverse fauna and flora, its pristine nature, fresh air, pure crystal water, rare animal kingdom, unique historical and cultural traditions, nomadic life style of Mongolian herdsmen. Particularly, in the last few years Mongolia has been more attracting foreign tourists and is becoming one of the fascinating destinations of the world. Since the transition of our country to a market oriented economy around 200 private and public entities involved in tourism have been set up within a few last years . On the one side, companies are becoming very eager to reap the benefits from tourism activity, and on the other side the state organizations are trying to determine the path of legislating and regulating the sector so that the business itself, its customers and the country's economy could all be given equal protection. Because tourism is a specific and efficient sector of the economy the Government of Mongolia has recently approved "Basic Guidelines for the Development of Tourism in 1995-2005". Subsequently, within the framework of the guidelines Programme of actions for 1995-1996 was worked out. Eco tourism has been identified as a main potential for development of the sector in the country. The most serious constraints in the development of tourism were determined as (1) the inappropriate infrastructure and tourism services; and (2) the inadequate human resource capabilities in the sector. Based on the Guidelines, the country has been divided into seven main regions, depending on their potential for attracting foreign tourists. In addition, a gradual approach towards their development has been adopted. The main regions for the development of tourism are as follows:

Ulaanbaatar - the capital of Mongolia, was founded in 1639. The centre of Buddhism in the country has grown to reflect a mix of ancient traditions and modern life style.

Khuvsgul region - Mongolia's alpine area with snow-covered mountains and crystal clear lakes. Lake Khuvsgul is one of the deepest in the world, twin of the famous Baikal Lake in Siberia.

Orkhon Valley - the site of the ancient Karakorum, or throne of the Khans. The famous Erdene Zuu Monastery, the first temple in the country, is still functioning, and has numerios monuments and historical relics.

Gobi Desert - largest and best known desert in Asia. Not a sand desert like the Sahara, it has a rich biodiversity with many fascinating plant and animal species.

Mongolian Steppes - the vast, flat, treeless plains were the site of many ancient battles, and refuge of horse thieves. In some areas, caves lead underground into huge water-filled caverns.

Hentii aimag - the birth place of Chingis Khan. Set amongst beautiful scenery are monuments to the emperor, as well as museums displaying his life history and achievements.

However, an accurate analysis of the tourism potential in these regions, cost and benefits involved has not been undertaken because of lack of basic information and data on the number and status of existing tourist facilities and visitors to the country. The Tourism Policy Department was first established in 1995 within the former Ministry of Trade and Industry with the objective implementing the Guidelines. Now this Department operating within the Ministry of Infrastructure is assigned a large number of responsibilities, including the elabration of regulations and procedures related to tourism activities. Besides, the Department coordinates the participation of the country in the activities of the world and regional tourist organizations. Mongolia became a full member of the World Tourism Organization in 1990. The number of foreign visitors in 1995 exceeded 110 thousand, from which 15% were tourists. Most of the tourists came from Japan, Western Europe & USA.

INFRASTRUCTURE. ENERGY SUPPLY

The industrialisation of the country led to the foundation of the present network of energy supply. Mongolia has developed energy production based on coal burning thermal power plants. There are 6 major thermal power plants of different capacity; three of them are situated in Ulaanbaatar with capacity of 21MW, 134MW and 560MW, and the others in Darkhan, Choibalsan and Erdenet cities with capacities of 48MW, 48MW and 36MW respectively.

The main economic region of Mongolia, and the region along the Trans-Mongolian Railroad and its spurs are connected with high power transmission lines. This network is known as Central Energy System (CES) which also is linked to the Buryat Energy System of the Russian Federation through 220KW line. The CES network consists of 1044 km of 220KV, 2100 km of 110KV and 2950 km of 35KV transmission lines, and covers the territory of Selenge, Bulgan, Darhan-Uul, Orkhon, Tov, Ovorkhangai, Arkhangai, Dornogovi and Govisumber aimags. The CES provides power supply to one third of the territory and half of the population of the country.

The headquarters of the CES is located in Ulaanbaata and responsible for import/export of electricity and its distribution. The CES is under the direct supervision of the Ministry of Agriculture and Industry. The towns and settlements beyond the CES network have their own small power stations or diesel generators.

During periods of power shortage, especially in winter, the CES buys electricity from Russia and distributes among its consumers. Thanks to the considerable Government investment, and the financial and technical assistance from the donor countries and international organizations, the power supply of the country is being improved.

There is a proposal that a hydropower station of 250 MW capacity on the river Egiin Gol will be constructed with a soft loan from the Asian Development Bank (ADB). Also other smaller ones are under construction in the different parts of the country.

TRANSPORTATION

Specific conditions of the country predetermine the development of its transportation network, dominated by the auto-transportation regarding the inland territory and by railroad. Air-transportation is vital for the remote aimags. A small fleet of cargo boats operates on the lake of Khovsgol and Selenge river. Mongolia is also seeking to establish its own ocean fleet operating from the nearest port. Legislation regarding such matters as registration and domicile is being drafted and will be enacted.

The Trans-Mongolian Railroad connecting Russian and Chinese railroad network runs through Central Mongolia from north to south. The development of the rail system of Mongolia started in the 1930s with the construction of the 238 km long broad-gauge railway linking Choibalsan with the-ex Soviet Union in the east. A 400 km long railway, linking Ulaanbaatar with the Soviet Union was completed in 1949, and subsequently extended southward an additional 700 km to the Chinese border. This 1,400 km stretch of railway today provides the major link for Mongolia with Russia and China and the rest of the world.

The main industrial and commercial centres such as Ulaanbaatar, Darkhan, Erdenet, Sainshand and Sukhbaatar are located along this railroad. The Mongolian rail system was established driven largely by an emphasis on expanding the mining industry. Since the completion of the Trans-Mongolian Railroad in 1956, spur routes have been constructed to support minerals development, including an 80 km line constructed to link with the Sharyn Gol coal mine, a 140 km line to link with Erdenet and a 96 km line to link with Bor-Ondor.

The spur railroads with length of about 45-150 km connecting the mining complexes to the Trans-Mongolian railroad have a vital role in the national economy. The city of Choibalsan, the centre of Dornod aimag, is directly connected with Russia. The total length of railroads of Mongolia is 1815 km.

The joint Mongolian-Russian concern "Ulaanbaatar railroad" operates Mongolian railroad.

The nearest Russian ports - Vladivostok, Vostochny and Nakhodka are located over 2000 km away. The route to the Chinese port of Tianjin enables much faster access to the sea and the distance is 1000 km from the Mongolian bor-der.

Mongolia and the People's Republic of China signed an agreement on transit which allows the transportation of Mongolian freight on the rail line from the Mongolia-China border through China to and from the port of Tianjin, providing Mongolia with direct access to the sea. Recently, new transhipment facilities have been put into operation in the Mongolian-Chinese border at Zamyn-Uud reducing significantly time of freight movement. (The Chinese railway gage is different from Mongolia's)

Auto-transportation is the most important mean of transport in the Mongolian conditions. Mongolia has 3076 km improved roads, out of which 1303 km are paved. There are 5 asphalt and concrete roads from Ulaanbaatar including the route to Russia through Darkhan, Sukhbaatar and to Arvaikheer, the centre of Ovorkhangai aimag.

An extensive domestic network of 42,000 km links the 21 major population centres and 160 smaller centres throughout the country. The vast majority of roads are simple dirt roads for which plans for improvements are being made.

All centres of aimags, somons and other towns have their filling stations.

Both state and private auto-transportation companies are operating in the domestic market. The introduction of the private sector has significantly improved the service. For Mongolia with its vast territory, the auto transport has a vital significance , and therefore it is important to create a reliable network of paved roads. Alongside with this, a need to build up improved railroads for international routes is emerging.

Taking into account the favourable geographical position of Mongolia located on the cross-roads linking the European continent and Pacific region it might be economically justified to develop air transport system.

The national air-transportation company (state enterprise) MIAT is the major domestic carrier. MIAT serves the regular links with Irkutsk, Moscow, Beijing and Alma-Ata. The company also operates charter flights to Seoul, Osaka, Singapore, Berlin and other cities.

Besides MIAT, three private air-transportation companies operate mainly in the domestic lines.

The main airport of Mongolia was reconstracted by ADB soft loan. According to the project, the main building of the airport is planned to be extended by 30 per cent and the runway - be reaped and lengthened. New hangars and warehouses will be added to the existing facilities.

Private Transportation Companies were established and playing the significant role in the transport industry of Mongolia.

TELECOMMUNICATIONS

The national integrated telecommunication network of the country consists of 4000 km analogue microwave and 30.000 km open wire lines connecting amigo centres and salmons. There are 325 switching systems with a capacity of 100.600 telephone lines in the network.

The establishment in 1990 of the ground station of the "Asiasat" and "Intelsat" system in Ulaanbaatar has enabled Mongolia to be connected automatically with a telex and fax network of over 190 countries. The international telecommunication services are handled through 74 channels of satellite systems including Intelsat, Intersputnik and Asiasat. In 1992-1993 a new Ulaanbaatar city digital technology telephone exchange with capacity of 40.000 lines was installed and is now in full use.

The postal service is rather inexpensive . In most cases, letters and parcels can be sent from post offices at a low cost. However, for reliable air freight service it is recommended that DHL be used.

Telegraph services are provided through teleprinters in post and telecommunications offices. The private sector has introduced telecommunications services such as E-mail and pager service.

Cellular net mobile telephone system is in place in Ulaanbaatar. Mongolia is committed to renew the whole communication system nation-wide.

Ref: http://www.magicnet.mn/datacom/"Datacom" Co., Ltd is the main service provider of world-wide Internet network communication. For average rate of international telecommunication tariffs please consult the home page of Mongolian Chamber of Comerce and Industry at http://www. Magicnet.mn/mccu.

LABOUR

High population growth rate during the 1960s and 1970s has provided an abundant labour force in the 1980s and 1990s. The developing national economy employed this labour pool. The centralised economy was providing new jobs for nearly 90.000 men and women yearly. A vast network of training and professional education was created. Graduates from secondary schools were sent to the former USSR and East European countries for higher education. Nearly 240.000 trainees completed the vocational schools between 1964-1990. New development projects had difficulties concerning shortage of labour force.

Today's labour market in Mongolia is characterised by increasing unemployment, and consequent decline in training process. The average registered unemployment is 657 per 10.000 persons. There is therefore a possibility to develop labour intensive industry.

FINANCIAL SYSTEM

The Mongolian Stock Exchange started its operations in February 1992. Now it has 29 broker firms each connected with the Stock Exchange with computer network. The national big privatisation programme is being realised through the Stock Exchange and it is planned to privatise altogether more than 400 companies with the registered capital worth 11 bln.togrog.

The main goal of the Mongolian Stock Exchange for the nearest future is to intensify capital investments into the production and service.

BANKING

The present banking system of Mongolia was formed in the beginning of 1990s when many newly founded commercial banks launched their operations along with state banking system. The transition to a two-tier banking system was completed in April 1993 when reserve management functions were moved to Mongolbank.

Until 1991, Mongolia had a monobank system, and all central and commercial banking activities were carried out by one institution. The state Bank of Mongolia functioned as a cashier, directing credit in line with the Planning Committee's instructions and handling foreign transactions in line with CMEA barter arrangements. It opened some 400 branches around the country which accepted savings deposits and disbursed credit to enterprises and government agencies.

In May 1991, a new Banking Law became effective, under which the State Bank was divided into a central bank, called the Bank of Mongolia, and a foreign trade bank called the State Bank of Mongolia /International/. The Bank of Mongolia's Chairman is responsible to the legislature /The State Great Khural/ thus making the central bank independent of the government. The Banking Law provides the framework for the development of a fully functioning central bank capable of managing money and credit using indirect instruments, leaving the allocation of resources to markets.

The Central Bank of Mongolia - Mongolbank - is responsible for the implementation of the laws and enactments concerning the banking. It also has functions to manage official foreign exchange reserves, issue bank notes, render banking service to the Government and to elaborate monetary policy. Also Mongolbank supervises the commercial banks.

The commercial activities of the former State Bank have been transferred to new commercial banks which were established in 1992. As of January 1, 1994, the commercial banks have to meetTg 400 mln paid-up capital requirement, up from the previous level of Tg 50 mln. Adoption of this rule led to the consolidation of several smaller banks and to the closure of others. Nowadays, there are operating 11 commercial banks including 1 privately owned bank. The year of 1994 had brought positive results in the monetary sector, which were early due to the strict monetary policy pursued by the Bank of Mongolia.

First year results under the new Enhanced Structural Adjustment Facility (ESAF) Program were reported in 1994. The ESAF program aims at developing the macro-economic management system which is necessary for a market economy. The successful implementation created conditions allowing the receipt of financial assistance from the International Monetary Fund (IMF) and other international financial institutions, as well as from donor countries. Thanks to IMF's assistance, the Bank of Mongolia developed a mechanism for clearing settlement at the Bank and made progress in solving the problems related to bad loans of commercial banks. Exchange Regime

There is free exchange of currency at the exchange rates determined by the floating togrog.

TAXATION

Mongolia's Parliament, the State Great Khural, has adopted ammendments to tax laws that scrap virtually all import duties, slash taxes on business , offer incentives to foreign investors and raise the income tax threshold. The radical reforms took effect from May 1, 1997.

The principal amendments to the tax laws are described below.

1. The main points of the ammendments to the Law on Individual Income Tax (1993) are given below:

The newly amended Law defines permanently residing, temporarily residing and non-residing persons as a taxpayer.

The newly amended Law points out in details the registration procedure of taxpayers. In tax calculations a camel, a cow and a horse is considered as 2 heads of animals, and a sheep and a goat is taken as 1 head of animal accordingly.

An individual with cattle in his ownership will be imposed 2-5% income tax. Income from 150-200 heads of animals is exempt from taxes.

Returns from use of copyright, programming, patents, models, trademarks, know-how, as well as cinema, video, audio and other records are subject to taxation.

Proceeds from art performance or sport awards, games of chance or lottery are levied income tax. · A permanently residing taxpayer engaged in production of crop, potatoes and vegetables is given 50% tax abatement as regards income from the above-mentioned activity.

2. The main points of the amendments to the Law on Business Entity and Organization Income Tax are given below:

Income from the sale of real estate is levied 2% tax.

The following income are exempt from taxes:
- Interest earned on Government debt;
- Membership fees and donation of non- governmental organizations;
- Monetary donation of taxpayers contributed to educational organizations;

and registered with financial and taxation authorities;
- Income from donor blood, or other blood items;

A foreign oil company operating on the principle of production sharing contract with the Mongolian Government is exempt from tax on income based on its share or repatriation of profit abroad.

Producers of crop, potatoes and vegetables is given 50% tax abatement on their income from above-mentioned activities.

The list of taxpayers is enriched by non-state organizations, religious institutions, juridical persons of state and local ownership, as well as other juridical persons conducting economic activity.

Income tax is not imposed on assets directed to health insurance, routine repairs, temporary constructions, bonus item in the construction's budget, and to compensation of possible loss from exchange rate.

Bank loan loss provisions are tax deductible.

For the list of goods and rate of excise tax imposed as well as Foreign investment policy and regulations, please refer to the "Homepage of Mongolian Chamber of Commerce and Industry" http://www. Mongoliaonline.mn/mcci/

VISA REGULATIONS

The simplification of visa procedure comes next to the liberalization of the tax legislation, as the latest effort of the Government to open up the Mongolian market and create conditions near to free trade status.

The Government is now preparing two-level measures. Softening of visa regulations is expected to instigate the growth of the number of visitors to Mongolia, including businessmen and potential investors. Firstly, the draft of supplements and amendments to the Law on Legal Status of Foreign Citizens will be submitted to the Parliament in the nearest future. Secondly, new regulations enforced from May 1 comprise the changes as follows:

Visa for a foreign visitor is issued within 24 hours, if the duration of the stay in Mongolia is 30 days or less.

No invitation is needed for applicants to get Mongolian visa.

A citizen from a country where there is no Embassy of Mongolia or where there are certain difficulties in obtaining visa can get it at the international ports of the country as Buyant-Ukhaa, Zamyn Uud, Sukhbaatar and Altanbulag.

Honorary Consuls of Mongolia have the right to issue visas to travel to Mongolia on the approval from the Ministry of External Relations.

STOCK EXCHANGE

Mongolian Stock Exchange started its activities on February 7 , 1992 . Its activities include creation of necessary conditions for implementing privatization of the state - owned enterprises , establishing brokerage firms in local areas of Mongolia , and setting up computerized network throughout the country to conduct trading of the listed stocks. Law of Securities was approved by the Great Khural , in end of 1994 . Secondary securities market has started and first secondary trading was started on August 28, 1995 . At that stage foreigners will be allowed to buy stocks.

CAN MONETARY POLICY BE EFFECTIVE DURING TRANSITION?: LESSONS FROM MONGOLIA[3]

Mongolia has undergone dramatic changes during its transition to a market economy, with fundamental restructuring in both the real economy and the financial sector. How effective is monetary policy in such a changing environment?

A key element of each former centrally planned economy's transition to a market economy has been the establishment of financial markets and institutions that can support such an economy. But introducing and, in particular, creating confidence in, such markets and institutions has been a long process. Moreover, difficulties such as banking crises, high ratios of nonperforming loans to total loans, inexperienced management, political interference, currency appreciation, and high or moderate inflation rates have posed additional challenges for monetary policy.

The policy of Mongolia's monetary authorities has been to keep the growth rate of the money supply stable while dealing with these transition-specific challenges as they occur. In addition, because of Mongolia's climate, which is characterized by extremes of temperature, the Mongolian economy is highly seasonal, and the authorities have occasionally intervened in the foreign exchange market to avoid excessive exchange rate fluctuations stemming from large, weather-related swings in exports and imports. Such a pragmatic approach to monetary policy has been necessary in many transition economies. This article discusses whether Mongolia's approach has been facilitated by a stable money demand and a predictable relationship between inflation and monetary variables.

MONGOLIA'S EXPERIENCE

Mongolia's experience has been different from that of most other transition countries in four respects. First and most important, there has been a political consensus on the need for a bold and comprehensive approach to reforms. Despite significant shifts in the governing coalitions and periods of political gridlock, national governments have pursued essentially the same objectives. Second, Mongolia did not—unlike many other transition countries—experience a prolonged period of moderate inflation. Annual inflation fell below 10 percent in the first half of 1998 and has stayed low since then. Third, unlike the Central and Eastern European transition countries, Mongolia has not been a recipient of large capital inflows and has therefore not confronted the challenges that such inflows present for the monetary authorities. Fourth, the Mongolian economy has been significantly affected by both the Asian crisis of 1997 and, in particular, the Russian crisis of 1998. Consequently, its currency has appreciated considerably (in both nominal and real terms). This appreciation has been instrumental in lowering annual inflation rates from the moderate range to single digits, although this reduction was probably achieved at some cost to output.

The table on page 45 compares real GDP in 1989 and 1998 for Mongolia with that in the other transition economies and shows that Mongolia has done better than most. Out of 27 transition countries, only Poland, Slovakia, and Slovenia have been doing significantly better than

[3] **Torsten Sløk** is an Economist in the World Economic Studies Division of the IMF's Research Department.

Mongolia, while the Czech Republic and Hungary have performed equally well. This simple measure has limitations, however, and does not reveal much about the development of institutions or the role of policies in individual transition countries. To analyze the role of policies during the transition—in particular, thes role of monetary policy—one has to examine the relationship between monetary variables and inflation and real economic activity.

Development of real GDP in transition countries
(1989 = 100)

	1989	1998
Eastern Europe	100	93.4
CIS[1] countries	100	54.0
Baltic states	100	71.4
All of the above	100	64.5
Mongolia	100	93.1

Sources: United Nations, 1999, Economic Survey for Europe, No. 2, Appendix Table B.1. Data for Mongolia are IMF staff estimates.
[1] Commonwealth of Independent States.

MONETARY POLICY IN TRANSITION

A market-based monetary policy depends on the existence of a market for money and foreign exchange. Specifically, reserve requirements, refinance windows, government and central bank bills and bonds, and credit allocation through banks or credit auctions are needed. If the institutional framework for monetary policy and these specific monetary instruments are lacking or malfunctioning, the conduct and effectiveness of monetary policy will be impeded. Most transition economies have gradually established an institutional framework and introduced instruments and financial markets that function like those in developed countries, although they are smaller and less liquid.

Mongolia enhanced the role of monetary policy in the early stages of its transition. In May 1991, a two-tier banking system was introduced to replace the previous, central bank-based system.

Directed credits, which until 1991 had been determined by the credit plan, were limited to priority sectors and oil imports and were phased out in mid-1994. Bank-by-bank ceilings and interest rate controls on commercial bank deposit and lending rates that had been imposed in the initial transition phase were also eliminated. In addition, the central bank introduced reserve requirements on business and household demand deposits in 1991, central bank bills in 1993, and a regular refinancing auction at market-determined rates in 1995. The degree of independence given to the central bank, the Bank of Mongolia, is surprisingly similar to that observed in many developed countries.

The Banking Law of Mongolia, adopted in 1996, states that the two primary objectives of the Bank of Mongolia are to ensure a stable value for the Mongolian tugrik and to act as supervisor of the financial system. In summary, the institutions and financial markets required for an effective monetary policy in Mongolia have, to a large extent, been created.

Over the transition period, Mongolia's banking sector has faced major challenges, including a high volume of nonperforming loans. To strengthen the banking system, measures have been taken, under IMF-supported programs, to reduce operating costs, resolve the financial situations of insolvent banks, and increase loan recoveries. The ratio of foreign exchange deposits to broad money has for most years been less than 20 percent, the average for all transition countries since 1991. But the interest spread, defined as the difference at the end of the year between the rates on short-term bank loans in domestic currency and rates on deposits was, over the same period, one of the highest in the transition countries. The high interest rates have been maintained throughout the transition period to preserve and restore confidence in the banking system. While progress has been made in strengthening the system, problems remain, particularly in the balance-sheet positions of several private banks.

CAN MONETARY POLICY WORK IN TRANSITION?

A key challenge for monetary policy in transition is that inflation is not just a monetary phenomenon. Apart from the usual demand-pull and cost-push pressures, at least five additional influences pose challenges for the conduct of monetary policy. First, price liberalization at the beginning of transition results in an initial price level adjustment and substantial changes in relative prices and hence also in inflation. Second, this adjustment in relative prices brings about a significant reallocation of resources, and subsequent monetary financing of rising fiscal deficits resulting from a combination of declining fiscal revenues and rigid expenditure patterns also generates inflationary pressures. Third, downward rigidities in goods and labor markets, together with the indexation of prices, generate more permanent moderate inflation (15-40 percent a year) in many transition countries. Fourth, as income grows, so does the price level of the economy (in line with the so-called Balassa-Samuelson effect), and authorities have to determine to what extent inflation comes from this source.

Finally, privatization, institution building, and the creation of competitive markets take considerable time, and the speed with which competition and efficiency are introduced in the private sector significantly affects inflation rates during the transition. Given all these transition-specific influences on inflation, the existence of predictable relationships between key economic variables, necessary for monetary policy to be conducted effectively, cannot be taken for granted. To investigate the relationships among inflation, the exchange rate, reserve money, broad money, and net credit to the government in Mongolia, a causal analysis of relationships among economic variables has been carried out. Granger-causality tests give an indication of how these variables affect each other over time. All series measure 12-month changes, beginning in December 1995 and ending in June 1999. The chart on page 45 shows the causal relationships among the variables for different time periods.

One conclusion drawn from the results of the causality tests is that net credit to the government plays a key role. In the short run, this variable does not affect inflation directly but has an effect on it through the above-mentioned monetary variables. In the longer term (five to six months), net credit to the government becomes a function of the other monetary variables and affects inflation directly. A second conclusion is that the exchange rate has a significant effect on inflation during all time periods examined. In the very short term, it is the only variable explaining inflation directly. In other words, if the exchange rate changes, businesses immediately react by adjusting domestic prices. Third, in the longer term, the money supply explains inflation directly, and this indicates that it is the money-supply rule that has brought down inflation in Mongolia.

To explore this further, a money-demand relationship has been estimated using annual data covering 1993-98 for 22 Mongolian regions (see Sløk (2000) for details). The analysis provides two key insights. First, the money-demand estimation confirms that there is a significant and stable relationship between real money and real income over the sample period.

Second, the income elasticity is approximately one-half, which suggests that a 1 percent increase in income leads to a 0.5 percent increase in the demand for money. This elasticity is significantly below that for most member countries of the Organization for Economic Cooperation and Development, which is usually close to 1. The lower elasticity in Mongolia could indicate that considerably fewer and less complex transactions are carried out by its banks and firms than by their counterparts in highly developed economies. In other words, the lower income elasticity of the demand for money suggests that, in Mongolia, money is held primarily to carry out transactions.

In sum, a stable relationship exists between the money supply and economic activity in Mongolia, which has made it possible for the monetary authorities to use a money-supply-growth rule to guide monetary policy. Furthermore, their use of such a rule has been successful in bringing down inflation.

CONCLUSION

In a transition economy with institutions as rudimentary as Mongolia's, a stable demand for money and a predictable relationship between inflation and monetary variables can be found, and a market-based monetary policy can be implemented effectively. To strengthen the effectiveness of monetary policy, however, the authorities need to continue with reforms—in particular, banking sector and public administration reforms. Looking forward, other transition countries have managed to maintain annual inflation rates in the single digits by adopting inflation-targeting frameworks.

Such a framework has the advantages of being transparent and easily monitored by the public and of allowing monetary policy to keep inflation low while policymakers cope with domestic and international shocks. Inflation targeting, however, is not suitable for countries that have not completed structural adjustment, are starting with high inflation, or are susceptible to large shocks. In the event of such large shocks, inflation targeting could have sudden, marked effects on monetary instruments that could, in turn, have severe implications for the real economy. Moreover, as a consequence of its pronounced temperature fluctuations, Mongolia experiences seasonal movements in the exchange rate, which, if left unsmoothed, could have undesirable effects on inflation. In sum, it is not clear whether it would be useful for Mongolia to adopt an inflation-targeting framework at this stage of its transition.

Reference:

Torsten Sløk, 2000, "Monetary Policy in Transition: The Case of Mongolia," IMF Working Paper 00/21 (Washington: International Monetary Fund).

MINERAL POTENTIAL OF MONGOLIA

(Main minerals)

GOLD (AU)

Gold mineralization has taken place, with various intensity, during the early and late Precambrian-early Cambrian, Paleozoic, Mesozoic and Cenozoic time however the main gold mineralization is associated with magnetic activity during Permian and Triassic - Jurassic time. Placers were formed during the Cretaceous-late Neogene and Pliocene-Holocene time.

The known gold mineralizations in Mongolia are represented by three economic types: veins, mineralized zones, and placers. Although vein occurrences are the most widely developed of all gold occurrences the bulk of proven gold reserves associated with placers and mineralized zones.

On the base of geological data (tectonic structure, mineral occurrences, age of mineralization, gold content) ten main gold metallogenic provinces within Mongolia have been defined.

It should be emphasized that because of a very low level of geological knowledge, with respect to the western and southern portion of Mongolia and an emphasis on only placers and/ or quartz vein mineralization in the studied areas, the true gold potential of these large regions is largely conjectural. Nevertheless, the number of occurrences defined based on limited data clearly suggests a high gold potential overall for the region.

Additionally, although not identified, available geologic data would indicate that occurrences of (a) gold-bearing conglomerates of Cretaceous and Tertiary age should be expected in southern and western Mongolia, (b) gold mineralization associated with ancient volcano- sedimentary areas in Central Mongolia and (c) ancient epithermal gold occurrences (island arc associations) may be expected in the Kharkhira, Ulzeet, and Southern Mongolian gold provinces.

BASE METAL (CU, MO, PB, ZN)

Copper-molybdenum (Cu-Mo) mineralization in Mongolia is primarily of three deposit types, i.e., late Paleozoic-early Mesozoic Cu-Mo porphyries, Cu-Ni magmatic segregations associated with grabbo of unknown age and Paleozoic-Mesozoic stratabound coppers.

The Cu-Mo deposits previously described occur within four main base metal provinces in Mongolia, i.e., the Altai, North Mongolian and South Mongolian provinces.

In addition to the previously described Cu-Mo deposit types and provinces, Mongolia also has a large number of middle to late Mesozoic Pb-Zn deposits of various deposit types, largely in the eastern of the country. The main deposit types, skarn, mineralized explosive pipes, vein, mineralized zones. The known base metal deposits were mainly formed in the middle-late Mesozoic. They are located in eastern part of country.

The main Pb-Zn deposits located in Central Mongolian province, and several perspective occurrences in Altai province.

The Northern Central and Southern metallogenic provinces of Mongolia have a high potential for a discovery of new deposits of Cu, Mo, Pb, Zn. In the North and South Mongolian provinces, the potential is greater for Cu-Mo porphyries, in Central Mongolian and both Pb, Zn and Cu-MO porphyry deposits.

Most perspective for the discovery of large scale copper and/or polymetallic mineralization is the Altai province in South Mongolia where there is the intersecting of three regional geologic structures (Altai metallogenic province, Beitianshan tectonostratigraphic terrane and a complex zone of faults.

Regionally the Altai metallogenic province includes areas of Russia (Gornii Altai), China (Altai), and Mongolia (Mongolian Altai). In the Gornii Altai of Russia large deposits of lead and zinc have been discovered, whereas on the Russia-Mongolian border hydrothermal Pb-Zn deposits, and volcano-clastic Fe mineralization have been identified.

In the Altai zone of China, in mid-Paleozoic sandstone, shales and volcanoclastic deposits of synorogenic-synvolcanic massive Cu-Ni sulfides occurrences indicate that at least two major synorojenic massive sulphide deposits, in addition to Kuroko-type massive sulphide deposits will be discovered. Based on the same favorably criteria as used in the China Altai region it is estimated that similar deposits would occur in the adjacent Mongolian Altai. On the base of above-mentioned data is possible to predict the presence of economic deposits of Cu, Mo, Pb, Zn, and Ni in the Mongolian Altai. Recently, in the northern part of the Altai zone Cu occurrences of stratiform type have been discovered as well as synorogenic Cu-Ni mineralization associated with gabbro bodies.

In the southern Mongolia the Altai metallogenic province intersects the Bietianshan tectono-stratigraphic terrane and at this zone of intersection both areas are in turn intersected by a late-Devonian-Carboniferous fault zone extending NW from China through Mongolia. The fault zone is approximately 850-900 km in length and 30-50 km in width and which, based on recent epicenter studies, is tectonically active. This area of complex intersection of the three zones is known to contain Pb-Zn deposits however is considered highly prospective for the occurrence of several deposits and deposit types. In particular the complex rock types present include volcano-sedimentary, sandstone-carbonate formations, small to medium sized intrusions of tonalites, leucogranites, alkalic granites, syenites, gabbro and ultramafic rocks. Additinally, numerous crosscutting faults, of different orientation provide the host environment for diverse deposit types.

FLUORITE

Fluorite mineralization is widespread throughout Mongolia in rocks of Late Paleozoic to Late Mesozoic age. The major time of economically important mineralization took place during late Mesozoic / late Jurassic-early Cretaceous epochs). The fluorite mineralization represented by two economic types: epithermal vein and metasomatic ore bodies.

Late Mesozoic fluorite mineralization is associated with rare earth and lead-zinc mineralization but not in economical quantities. Three major fluorite provinces have been defined in Mongolia, i.e., the North Mongolia, Trans-Mongolian and South Mongolian with the Trans-Mongolian province having the largest reserves and being the most actively exploited.

The major characteristics of the main provinces are shown in the Table 7. The fluorite reserves/resources of Mongolia are estimated at 18/23-33, respectively.

RARE-EARTH ELEMENTS (REE)

Rare-Earth Metals (Ta, Nb, Zr, W, Sn)--REM

Genetically and spatially REE and REMs in Mongolia are primarily felsic and alkalic rocks of late-Mesozoic, early Mesozoic and late Paleozoic age. Known deposits of REE and REM are subdivided on the following basis:

REE, REM mineralization (metasomatic zones) with alkalic granitoids and volcano-plutonic complexes.

Tungsten (W) vein and stockwork mineralization in granitoids.

Tin (Sn) vein and skarn mineralization in granites and carbonate rocks.

Within Mongolia six REE and/or REM provinces have been identified; the Altai, North Mongolian Hentii, Hangai, Southeast Mongolian, South Mongolian and the geologic attributes of these provinces are given in Table 8.

REE and REM occurrences are widely distributed throughout Mongolia with the most promising areas, based on available data, being the Altai and South Mongolian provinces for Ta, Nb, Zr, Y, W and REE, respectively.

URANIUM

Uranium exploration in Mongolia has started in 1940's by Mongolian and former Soviet Union geological organisations. Prior to1966, numerous uranium occurrences were discovered in coal deposits. In the period from 1967 to 1988 the exploration work became more systematic. As result of these exploration works, four "uranium - bearing provinces" were defined Mongol - Priargun, Gobi - Tamtsag, Hentei - Daur and Northern Mongolian. Several deposits were discovered in that time Dornod, Gurvanbulag, Mardai in eastern and Kharaat in southern Mongolia. The proven uranium resources of Mongolia occur in these deposits, which represent 62000 tonnes of entire country are estimated to amount to 1 307 000 tonnes of uranium. Uranium mining in Mongolia started in 1989 with exploration of the Mardai open pit in eastern Mongolia. The ore is processed in the Russian Priargunsky ore dressing plant. The mine was operated by a Russian - Mongolian joint venture to 1993.

US ASSISTANCE

USAID's efforts to support Mongolia's ongoing economic and political transition address key U.S. national interests, including promoting economic prosperity and broad-based growth as well as democracy and the rule of law. USAID/Mongolia's two strategic objectives are mutually reinforcing and strongly support the U.S. Government's goal of helping Mongolia transform itself into a bastion of market-oriented and democratic stability in Northeast Asia. Mongolia now stands at a critical juncture in its transition to an open market and democratic society. Despite past reform successes, neither its political nor economic transformation is complete.

Public institutions are still run in a top down fashion, with decisions being made in the capital with little feedback from local areas. Economic hardships remain for many, particularly in rural Mongolia. Existing hardships have been exacerbated by the financial crisis in Asia that has adversely affected worldwide demand for two of Mongolia's principal exports – copper and cashmere. In Mongolia's vast rural areas, economic growth is not occurring at a rate sufficient to raise living standards, extend benefits to a larger population, reduce vulnerabilities to external shocks, and ensure the consolidation of the democratic transition.

Ultimately, the long-term success of Mongolia's democratic reform depends on all segments of Mongolian society feeling they have a stake in a new economic system and are able to benefit from market reform. USAID's assistance for Mongolia has been effective in assisting the Government to adopt policies and implement reforms, which greatly spurred economic development and growth in urban areas, particularly Ulaanbaatar, as well as facilitated democratic transition at the national level. In FY 1999, USAID began working under a new five-year strategy (FY1999-2003) which marks USAID's movement toward increased attention to rural area growth and development.

DEVELOPMENT CHALLENGE

The development challenge for Mongolia remains unchanged–it is to create a stable political and economic environment that enables it to attract the domestic and foreign investment necessary for broad-based, sustainable development. Key obstacles remain to the realization of Mongolia's development potential, specifically in rural areas: (1) undeveloped and insufficient energy supplies and transportation and communication systems impede the movement of goods, people and information throughout the country; (2) inefficient state-run institutions, including banking and capital markets, make it difficult to mobilize savings and investment and limit the productivity of resources; (3) inadequately developed judicial and enforcement services are unable to ensure the rule of law; and (4) in rural areas, inexperienced civil society organizations are unable to foster economic growth and provide feedback to government at the local and national levels on policies and programs.

Despite these obstacles, Mongolia has a number of strengths which can serve as a strong foundation for sustained development, namely (1) a broad commitment to the development of democracy and a market economy; (2) strong internal social cohesion; (3) a highly literate population; and (4) a government committed to reform and development.

USAID's strategy for Mongolia is to help it establish a market-oriented and democratic society by (1) consolidating Mongolia's democratic transition and (2) accelerating and broadening environmentally sound private sector growth, with a particular focus on bringing change to rural areas. To accomplish these results, USAID will establish the foundation for an effective rural society. Rural business associations, women's groups, local chambers of commerce, herders' associations, and progressive cooperatives will benefit from USAID assistance in selected regions and serve as vehicles to demonstrate a bottom-up approach to development heretofore untried in Mongolia. USAID also seeks to improve the effectiveness of Parliament and the judiciary so they become more accountable to the people they serve.

On the economic front, assistance will help accelerate and broaden private sector growth. USAID will facilitate the transfer to the private sector of productive assets in agriculture, industry, mining and infrastructure that are now under state control. A second key area of assistance will be to increase the efficiency of Mongolia's financial markets through privatizing banks, establishing independent and transparent capital market institutions, and putting the national pension system on a sound financial footing. Improving the environment for business is also a critical aspect of enhancing private sector growth. USAID will ensure that Mongolia's accelerated growth is environmentally sustainable by addressing issues critical to pasture and crop land degradation and better resource management.

OTHER DONORS

Among bilateral donors, the United States ranks third, behind Japan and Germany, in the amount of its grant assistance to the Government of Mongolia. The International Monetary Fund (IMF), the Asian Development Bank (ADB), the World Bank, and the Government of Japan also provide substantial development-related loans to Mongolia. Donor attention to, and funding for, Mongolia diminished somewhat over the past year, due to competing demands for significant donor assistance to address the Asia financial crisis as well as due to the impact of the crisis on Japan, Mongolia's major bilateral donor. The Government of Mongolia is taking steps to establish viable donor coordination mechanisms and reacted positively to USAID's offer to help in this effort. USAID has been coordinating with the IMF and the ADB in bank restructuring and privatization and has started discussions with the World Bank on issues related to the power sector.

PROGRAM

USAID's Rural Civil Society Program (RCSP) and the Farmer to Farmer (FtF) program are the primary vehicles for USAID's rural area focus. With technical assistance and training aimed at a wide range of selected civil society organizations (e.g., women's group, business associations, cooperatives), RCSP will develop and strengthen their institutional capabilities to become effective advocates and implementers of economic and democratic reform. RCSP will also foster cooperation between local governments and these civil society organizations to create a joint agenda for policy reform that will strengthen rural economies and civil society. FtF will use experienced U.S. volunteers to assist local organizations to develop private agriculture in Mongolia, with a focus on animal health, improved animal breeding and improved efficiency of the crop sector.

At the national level, USAID will continue to provide assistance to the government and parliament that helps ensure public awareness of parliamentary actions and key reform issues as well to help with the actual drafting of critical laws. Building on its success in developing judicial benchbooks (i.e., digests of laws and precedents), USAID will begin implementation of a more comprehensive program of judicial reform and enforcement that will include training to professionalize the judiciary.

On the economic front, USAID will continue to assist in the privatization of state-owned enterprises, increase the efficiency of financial markets, and improve the business environment. USAID intends to conclude its current programs of financial sector restructuring, pension reform, and energy sector sector restructuring in FY 2000. By supporting a joint effort with the U.S. Department of the Interior and the Philadelphia Academy of Sciences in the Lake Hovsgol region, USAID will demonstrate how development and natural resource management can be effectively joined.

THE WORLD BANK AND MONGOLIA

Mongolia has made considerable progress over the past 18 months in adjusting to the huge 1998-99 external price shocks. In the run-up to the July 2000 elections, however, fiscal and monetary discipline slackened considerably, to the detriment of macroeconomic stability and the implementation of donor-supported structural reforms.

On July 2, 2000, the opposition Mongolian People's Revolution Party (MPRP, who ruled during 1920-90 and 1992-96) virtually swept the parliamentary elections, receiving 51percent of the vote and capturing 72 of the 76 parliamentary seats--the remainder of the vote was split among 16 other parties and independents. Only one member of the ex-democratic coalition, which had governed since mid-1996 with 50 parliamentary seats, was elected.

While GDP growth averaged 4 percent during 1996-1999, per capita income stagnated over the course of that period owing to the pronounced 1998-99 external shocks that cost the economy about 14 percent of GDP and the incidence of poverty remained unchanged at about 36 percent.

On top of this, the execptionally severe 1999-2000 winter weather inflicted large welfare losses on a significant share of the population.

In August, 2000, the new Government, headed by Prime Minister N. Enkbayar, restructured public administration, and adopted its 2000-04 Action Program. The Ministry of Finance has been transformed into the Ministry of Finance and Economics (MOFE) and a new Ministry of Industry and Trade (MIT) created. Establishment of the MOFE is a welcome initiative: it will take full charge of donor coordination-heretofore splintered, and hopefully provide an institutional basis for a more comprehensive and long-term approach to development policy formulation and implementation.

ECONOMIC DEVELOPMENTS

Background. During the 1990s, Mongolia made considerable progress in laying the institutional and policy foundations for a private, market-based economy, including price and trade liberalization, launching large-scale privatization, curtailing budget transfers and lending to state enterprises, and setting-up a commercial banking system. During 1995-99, Mongolia also drastically curtailed inflationary financing of the public sector and pursued tight monetary policies. In addition to the modest, but sustained recovery in Gross Domestic Product (GDP) since 1994, inflation, which had averaged more than 50 percent during 1995-96, was cut to 20 percent in 1997 and 6.5 percent in 1998, before accelerating to 10 percent in 1999 in the wake of the huge external price shocks.

In 1999, agriculture, almost exclusively livestock production, accounted for about 35 percent of GDP; commerce, 29 percent; services, 18 percent; mining, 10 percent; and industry, 7.5 percent. Mining, mainly copper and gold, generated more than 80 percent of the economy's export earnings. Industry includes wool and cashmere processing, leather goods production, food processing, construction, and, in recent years, garments. Mongolia, with a population of 2.4 million, has a labor force of 800,000, 40 percent of which is employed in livestock production.

Recent Economic Developments. During the first six months of 2000, Mongolia's GDP continued to expand, the trade deficit declined slightly and gross international reserves also increased, but annual inflation accelerated to 15.4 percent in June 2000 from 10 percent in December 1999 This mixed performance stemmed from stepped-up Government borrowing from the domestic banking system and the excessively fast growth of monetary aggregates. The exceptionally harsh winter weather also contributed to higher inflation, by causing meat prices to soar.

The liquidity, solvency and loan portfolio of the banking system all improved considerably during the first part of 2000, thanks in part to the upsurge in liquidity in the economy and in part to the commercial banks' efforts to contain their nonperforming loan portfolios by limiting new lending to the private sector.

Fiscal performance weakened during the first half of 2000. The overall fiscal deficit was only slightly above the programmed level, but net domestic bank credit to Government was 3.6 times greater than programmed as no adjustments to spending levels were made to offset lower-than-projected net donor external financing to Government. New fiscal measures generating additional revenues and/or savings of about 2.5 percent of GDP would be needed to bring the fiscal program back on track during 2000-01. Such measures, together with a significant increase in central bank bill rates, would decelerate monetary growth, putting inflation on a downward path.

POVERTY IN MONGOLIA

Like other transitional economies which lost large external subsidies from the former Soviet Union and Council for Mutual Economic Assistance (CMEA) export markets, Mongolia experienced a sharp depression and increased poverty in the first part of the 1990s. In 1995, 36.3 percent of the population lived below the weighted national average poverty line of US$17 per month, according to the 1996 Living Standards Measurement Survey (LSMS). Of these, about 18 percent were destitute with monthly incomes below US$10. In 1998, the incidence of poverty had declined somewhat, to 35.6 percent, according to a new LSMS.

While Mongolia's health and education indicators are strong compared to those in other countries at similar income levels, and the Government's expenditures for health and education are high by international standards, social indicators deteriorated during the first half of the 1990s following the abrupt loss of massive subsidies from the former Soviet Union, equivalent to about 30 percent of Mongolia's GDP in 1990. Until 1990, Mongolia had close to universal coverage of basic education. The severe depression of output and incomes and cutbacks in government expenditures after the loss of these external subsidies reduced enrollment rates sharply, especially among the poor.

Social indicators subsequently stabilized, however, as the economy began to recover and improved appreciably in the last half of the decade, although they have not yet recovered to the levels achieved in 1990.

TRANSITIONAL AND STRUCTURAL POVERTY

- As in other transitional economies, unemployment and poverty increased due to external shocks-the loss of Soviet subsidies and CMEA markets, and the resulting collapse of the centrally planned economy.
- The ensuing closure of uneconomic state enterprises and drastic downsizing of others, whether as privatize concerns or in state hands, initially led to widespread unemployment. The associated decreases in state investment and subsidies, given weak infrastructure and isolated markets, contributed to production declines and caused structural changes in the labor market.
- Privatization of herds has increased livestock numbers substantially, but the collapse of state marketing systems, shrinking state veterinary services and the uncertain state provision of emergency fodder during winter storms has affected the quality of livestock herds. Many such services were in large part uneconomic. Despite the efficiency gains associated with privatization, particularly in light of subsequent consolidation of herds, privatization has led to greater rural income inequality.
- The extensive health and education systems also deteriorated significantly due to budgetary constraints, as evidenced by increased maternal and child mortality during the first half of the 1990s.

DEVELOPMENT CHALLENGES

The main challenge facing the new Government is to progressively reduce poverty and improve living standards for all Mongolians. To achieve this, the economy must grow about 6-7 percent per annum, and the Government must concentrate its scarce resources on efficient service provision better targeted to the poor. Higher growth will require macroeconomic stability; privatization of the largest state enterprises; increasing both savings and the productivy of investment; and stable incentives for private enterprise to develop activities rooted in Mongolia's comparative advantages.

Growth alone will not alleviate poverty, however, nor sustain support for difficult policies. Mongolia will also need to invest in its people, build technical skills, and target the social safety net more efficiently. In broad policy terms, this means: (a) pursuing prudent fiscal and monetary policies; (b) promoting private sector-led growth; (c) targeting poor households more effectively; and (d) managing natural assets in a sustainable manner.

Mongolia's financial system is overbanked, fragile and state-dominated. The Government has started a comprehensive program, with the support of the World Bank, the Asian Development Bank (ADB), the International Monetary Fund (IMF) and other donors, to shore-up the banking system and enable it to play its proper role in the development process, that is, mobilizing greater domestic savings and channeling these into high-productivity investments.

A long-term program for developing domestic banking skills is also needed. A viable banking system would help to foster private sector-led growth and investment. Mongolia's growth prospects are largely determined by the soundness of domestic policies and the external environment: ability to fully integrate into international markets and attract higher levels of foreign direct investment (FDI) is crucial. The redirection of trade from the former CMEA countries and the liberalization of the trade regime are facilitating this process.

Trade data show significant penetration of new markets: over 50 percent of exports in 1997 were to Western Europe, East Asia and the United States. Source countries for FDI have become equally diverse. FDI, especially from Asia, has slowed in the wake of the regional financial crisis. Mongolia is seeking to attract FDI in oil and gas, mining, tourism and light and agro-industry.

The Government also aims to restore universal basic education and further reduce infant and maternal mortality. For this, a rationalization and reprioritization of health and education expenditures will be necessary. The Government recognizes the need for reform to ease the budgetary burden of health care by improving efficiency of public health services and introducing a new health insurance system. The Government is working to strengthen primary health care, particularly at the rural district level and below and to encourage private sector participation in health service delivery. Steps are also being taken to enhance efficiency in the education sector, including rationalization of staff.

Urban services, particularly water supply and sanitation, need to be upgraded so as to improve the living standards of the poor. Priority areas are informal housing districts of Ulaanbaatar and *Aimag* (province) centers. The Government also intends to expand water supply and sanitation services to provincial urban and peri-urban districts, based on demand and willingness to pay. A broader issue is the future of municipal finance, and thus municipal service provision and urban planning capacity, in the face of central government budget constraints and budget reforms under the public administration reform program.

THE WORLD BANK IN MONGOLIA

Mongolia became a member of the World Bank Group in February, 1991. Since that time, the International Development Association's (IDA) portfolio has developed from quick-disbursing balance of payment assistance and technical assistance to comprise operations supporting *poverty alleviation*, *rehabilitation of infrastructure*, and *structural reforms* primarily in the financial and enterprise sectors.

IDA's main objectives in Mongolia are to support the Government in completing the transition to a market-led economy, to improve living standards and reduce poverty. To this end, IDA is assisting the Government to create an environment conducive to private sector-led growth, to tackle transitional and structural poverty, and to manage the country's resources strategically to improve long-term growth. Specifically, IDA is working to:

- promote equity in development through direct poverty alleviation assistance to ensure continued support for the most vulnerable groups;
- support medium-term macroeconomic stabilization and thus lay the foundation for broad-based economic growth and improved living standards;
- facilitate private sector development and associated employment and income-generation opportunities;
- develop infrastructure to support private sector growth and market development, contribute to increased foreign investment and global integration, and;
- to improve the living conditions of the poor by improving access to services and increasing efficiency gains, particularly in energy and water supply.

Since 1997, the International Finance Corporation (IFC) has approved financing of US$1.7 million for one project (in leather garments) costing US$3.5 million. For fiscal year 2000, the IFC expects to consider investments in the agribusiness and mining sectors. The IFC may also assist the Government's privatization efforts. The Multilateral Investment Guarantee Agency (MIGA) and the Foreign Investment Advisory Service (FIAS) are also supporting investment promotion.

Or contact:
The Washington External Affairs Office
Jill Wilkins / Kimberly Versak
Tel: 202-473-1792/202-473-4919
Fax: 202-522-3405
Email: jwilkins@worldbank.org / kversak@worldbank.org

The World Bank Country Office in Mongolia
Richard Lynn Ground, Resident Representative
Tel: 961-1-312-647
Fax: 976-1-312-645

TRAVEL TO MONGOLIA

US STATE DEPARTMENT SUGGESTIONS

COUNTRY DESCRIPTION: Mongolia is a vast country of mountains, lakes, deserts and grasslands. It peacefully abandoned its communist system in 1990 and has successfully made the transition to a parliamentary democracy. Economic reforms continue. The country's development has been hampered by inadequate infrastructure, particularly in the energy, transportation, and communication sectors. Travelers to Mongolia should be aware that shortcomings in these areas might have an impact on travel plans.

ENTRY AND EXIT REQUIREMENTS: A valid passport is required for American visitors. No visa is required for Americans visiting for fewer than 90 days. Visitors planning to stay in Mongolia for more than 30 days are required to register with the Immigration, Naturalization and Foreign Citizens Agency in Ulaanbaatar during their first week of arrival. American visitors who fail to register and stay longer than 30 days may be stopped at departure, denied exit, and fined. Americans planning to work or study in Mongolia should apply for a visa at a Mongolian Embassy or Consulate overseas. Failure to do so may result in authorities denying registration, levying a fine, and requiring that the visitor leave the country. For current information visas and registration requirements travelers should contact the Embassy of Mongolia at 2833 M Street, N.W., Washington, D.C. 20007, telephone: (202) 333-7117 or http://www.mongolianembassy.mn

Travelers arriving or departing Mongolia through China or Russia should be aware of Chinese and Russian visa regulations. American citizens are not permitted to transit through China or Russia without a visa. For more information on China, see the Consular Information Sheet for China. For more information on Russia, see the Consular Information Sheet for Russia. Travelers planning travel to Russia should get visas prior to arriving in Mongolia. They are difficult to obtain in Mongolia.

In an effort to prevent international child abduction, many governments have initiated procedures at entry/exit points. These often include requiring documentary evidence of relationship and permission for the child's travel from the parent(s) or legal guardian if not present. Having such documentation on hand, even if not required, may facilitate entry/departure.

SAFETY AND SECURITY: There have been no acts of terrorism, kidnappings or incidents with organized crime or extremist groups in Mongolia. There are no regions of instability in the country. U.S. citizens are advised to avoid occasional protests and street demonstrations in Ulaanbaatar as the demonstrations may become unruly.

CRIME: Over the past few years there has been a significant rise in crime in Mongolia, particularly in Ulaanbaatar, the capital. Violent crime is increasing, and it is not advisable to walk alone through the city after dark. The most common crimes against foreigners are pickpocketing and bag snatching. Travelers should be especially cautious when taking public transportation and in crowded public areas, such as open air markets, the State Department Store, the Central Post Office, and Gandan Monastery. U.S. citizens who detect pickpocketing attempts should not confront the thieves, as they may become violent.

The loss or theft abroad of a U.S. passport should be reported immediately to the local police and the U.S. Embassy. If you are the victim of a crime while overseas, in addition to reporting to local police, please contact the nearest U.S. Embassy or Consulate for assistance. The Embassy/Consulate staff can, for example, assist you to find appropriate medical care, to contact family members or friends and to explain how funds could be transferred.

Although the investigation and prosecution of a crime is solely the responsibility of local authorities, consular officers can help you understand the local criminal justice process and find an attorney, if needed. U.S. citizens may refer to the Department of State's pamphlet, *A Safe Trip Abroad*, for ways to promote a trouble-free journey. The pamphlet is available by mail from the Superintendent of Documents, U.S. Government Printing Office, Washington, D.C. 20402, via the Internet at http://www.access.gpo.gov/su_docs, or via the Bureau of Consular Affairs home page at http://travel.state.gov.

MEDICAL FACILITIES: Medical facilities in Mongolia are limited, and some western medicines are unavailable. Infectious diseases, such as plague and meningococcal meningitis, are present at various times of the year. Serious medical problems requiring hospitalization and/or medical evacuation to the United States can cost thousands of dollars or more. Doctors and hospitals often expect immediate payment for health services. For more information, please contact the U.S. Embassy in Ulaanbaatar or the Centers for Disease Control and Prevention's international travelers hotline (see below).

MEDICAL INSURANCE: The Department of State strongly urges Americans to consult with their medical insurance company prior to traveling abroad to confirm whether their policy applies overseas and if it will cover emergency expenses such as a medical evacuation. U.S. medical insurance plans seldom cover health costs incurred outside the United States, unless supplemental coverage is purchased. Further, U.S. Medicare and Medicaid programs do not provide payment for medical services outside the United States. However, many travel agents and private companies offer insurance plans that will cover health care expenses incurred overseas, including emergency services such as medical evacuations.

When making a decision regarding health insurance, Americans should consider that many foreign doctors and hospitals require payment in cash prior to providing service and that a medical evacuation to the U.S. may cost well in excess of $50,000. Uninsured travelers who require medical care overseas often face extreme difficulties. When consulting with your insurer prior to your trip, please ascertain whether payment will be made to the overseas healthcare provider or if you will be reimbursed later for expenses you incur. Some insurance policies also include coverage for psychiatric treatment and for disposition of remains in the event of death. Useful information on medical emergencies abroad, including overseas insurance programs, is provided in the Department of State's, Bureau of Consular Affairs brochure *Medical Information for Americans Traveling Abroad*, available via the Bureau of Consular Affairs home page at http://travel.state.gov or autofax service at 1-202-647-3000.

OTHER HEALTH INFORMATION: Sanitation in some restaurants is inadequate. Stomach illnesses are frequent. Bottled water and other routine precautions are advisable. Information on vaccinations and other health precautions, such as safe food and water precautions and insect bite protection, may be obtained from the Centers for Disease Control and Prevention's hotline for international travelers at 1-877-FYI-TRIP (1-877-394-8747); fax 1-888-CDC-FAXX, (1-888-232-3299), or via the CDC's Internet site at http://www.cdc.gov/travel/. For information about outbreaks of infectious diseases abroad, consult the World Health Organization's web site at http://www.who.int/en. Further health information for travelers is available at http://www.who.int/ith.

TRAFFIC SAFETY AND ROAD CONDITIONS: While in a foreign country, U.S. citizens may encounter road conditions that differ significantly from those in the United States. The information below concerning Mongolia is provided for general reference only and may not be totally accurate in a particular location or circumstance:

Safety of Public Transportation: Poor
Urban Road Conditions/Maintenance: Poor
Rural Road Conditions/Maintenance: Poor
Availability of Roadside Assistance: Poor

Driving in the capital city of Ulaanbaatar can be extremely difficult due to poorly maintained streets, malfunctioning traffic lights, inadequate street lighting, undisciplined pedestrians, and a shortage of traffic signs. There has been a dramatic increase in the number of vehicles on the roads in recent years, but the knowledge and skills of the driving population has not kept pace with the growth of automobiles. There are many metered taxis in Ulaanbaatar. There are no car rental companies operating in Mongolia, but it is possible to hire a car and driver from tourist companies. Public transportation within the capital is extensive, cheap, and generally reliable, but it is also extremely crowded (see information on crime above). There are few paved roads outside of the capital, and driving can be hazardous, particularly after dark. For additional general information about road safety, including links to foreign government sites, see the Department of State, Bureau of Consular Affairs home page at http://travel.state.gov/road_safety.html. For specific information concerning Mongolian driver's permits, vehicle inspection, road tax and mandatory insurance, contact the Embassy of Mongolia at 2833 M Street, N.W., Washington, D.C. 20007, telephone: (202) 333-7117.

AVIATION SAFETY OVERSIGHT: As there is no direct commercial air service at present, or economic authority to operate such service, between the U.S. and Mongolia, the U.S. Federal Aviation Administration (FAA) has not assessed Mongolia's Civil Aviation Authority for compliance with international aviation safety standards for oversight of Mongolia's air carrier operations. For further information, travelers may contact the Department of Transportation within the U.S. at 1-800-322-7873, or visit the FAA's Internet web site at http://www.faa.gov/avr/iasa/.

The U.S. Department of Defense (DOD) separately assesses some foreign air carriers for suitability as official providers of air services. For information regarding the DOD policy on specific carriers, travelers may contact DOD at 1-618-229-4801.

Mongolia has upgraded its aviation facilities and communications and air traffic control capabilities. However, the American Embassy has reported some general safety and reliability concerns regarding domestic flights operated by the national airline MIAT. The Embassy does not prohibit its employees from flying on MIAT, but does encourage them to exercise prudence and good judgment when boarding domestic flights. If Embassy employees see potential hazards, such as missing safety belts or passenger overcrowding, they are advised to get off the plane and wait for another flight.

CUSTOMS REGULATIONS: Mongolian customs authorities enforce strict regulations concerning import and export of items such as firearms, ammunition and antiquities. Import of firearms or ammunition requires prior approval from the Government of Mongolia. Export of antiquities requires a special customs clearance certificate issued by authorized antique shops at the time of purchase. For additional information contact the Embassy of Mongolia at 2833 M Street, N.W., Washington, D.C. 20402, tel: (202) 333-7117.

CRIMINAL PENALTIES: While in a foreign country, an American citizen is subject to that country's laws and regulations, which sometimes differ significantly from those in the United States and may not afford the protections available to the individual under U.S. law. Penalties for breaking the law can be more severe than in the United States for similar offenses. Persons violating Mongolian law, even unknowingly, may be expelled, arrested, or imprisoned. Penalties for possession, use, or trafficking in illegal drugs in Mongolia are strict, and convicted offenders can expect jail sentences and heavy fines.

SPECIAL CIRCUMSTANCES: Traveler's checks denominated in dollars are accepted at some hotels and may be converted to dollars or Tugriks at several banks. Credit cards can be used at a variety of hotels, restaurants, and shops in Ulaanbaatar. Outside of the capital, travelers should have cash. Cash advances against credit cards are available at commercial banks such as Trade and Development Bank and Golomt Bank. International bank wire transfers are also possible. There is a handful of ATM machines in Ulaanbaatar, but none outside the capital.

CONSULAR ACCESS -- American citizens are encouraged to carry a copy of their passports with them at all times, so that, if questioned by local officials, proof of identity and citizenship are readily available.

DISASTER PREPAREDNESS - WINTER POWER SHORTAGES-- Severe fuel shortages and problems with central heating and electrical systems may cause seriously reduced heating levels and power outages in Ulaanbaatar and other cities during the winter. Smaller towns in the countryside may have no heat or electricity at all. The Embassy advises all American residents in Mongolia to be prepared to depart if there is a complete energy failure. General information about natural disaster preparedness is available via the Internet from the U.S. Federal Emergency Management Agency (FEMA) at http://www.fema.gov/.

CHILDREN'S ISSUES: For information on international adoption of children and international parental child abduction, please refer to the Department of State Internet site at http://travel.state.gov/children's_issues.html or telephone 1-888-407-4747.

REGISTRATION/EMBASSY LOCATION: Americans living in or visiting Mongolia are encouraged to register with the Consular Section of the American Embassy in Mongolia and obtain updated information on travel and security within Mongolia. The Embassy is located in Micro Region 11, Big Ring Road, Ulaanbaatar. The telephone number is (976)-11-329-095, and the Embassy web site is http://www.us-mongolia.com/

BUSINESS TRAVEL

Visas: Foreigners traveling to Mongolia must have a valid passport and entry/exit visa. Short-term visitors who plan to stay in Mongolia for less than 30 days do not need a letter of invitation when applying for a visa overseas. Those who plan to stay for more than 30 days require an invitation from a state administrative organization, political party, public organization, economic entity, Mongolian citizen, or a foreign citizen who has resided in Mongolia more than three months. Visas can be obtained from Mongolian embassies and consulates worldwide. The cost of an entry/exit visa for a US citizen is $45. Two photographs are required. US citizens can also get visas on arrival at the Ulaanbaatar airport or at the Russian or Chinese border crossings if arriving by train. The cost for this kind of visa is $50.00. A seven-day extension of the existing visa costs $15.00 plus $2.00 for each additional day of extension. Visas are issued on the next working day. Express service entails surcharges of up to 100% of the normal fee.

Residency Permits: All foreigners wishing to remain in Mongolia for more than 30 days must apply to the State Center for Civil Registration and Information (part of the police department) for a residency permit. US investors can contact the Foreign Investment and Foreign Trade Agency (FIFTA) for assistance. Permits are generally issued within a couple of days and are valid for a period from three months to one year. A temporary residency permit can be renewed an unlimited number of times. Each renewal will re-validate the permit for a period of from three months up to one year, as requested by the investor.

Chinese Visas: A US citizen traveling to Mongolia via China MUST/MUST have valid Chinese visas. A visa is required even if the traveler is only transiting Beijing airport. If you transit Beijing twice (to and from Mongolia), you must have a two-entry Chinese visa.

Health: Western standard medical care is not available in Mongolia. Travelers are encouraged to buy medical evacuation insurance.

Business Hours: The standard work week is Monday through Friday, 0900-1800, with an hour for lunch.

Holidays (on the day before an official Mongolian holiday, offices close at 1400):
January 1: New Year
February : Lunar New Year (dates vary every year)
June 1: Mother and Child Day
July 11-13: Naadam, the Mongolian national holiday
November 26: Constitution Day

In-Country Travel: There are no restrictions on in-country travel. MIAT airline offers domestic service to all provincial capitals. Jeeps are also available for hire for more remote destinations. Most of Mongolia's road network is unpaved and travel can be prolonged, tiring and adventurous.

Practical Information: There are several hotels of reasonable standard in Ulaanbaatar. Lodging in outlying towns is basic; hotels frequently do not have hot water and sometimes no water at all. Ger camps (felt tents) offer alternative accommodation. The tourist ger camps are clean and comfortable and usually have reliable plumbing. The Mongolian diet is based on dairy products and mutton. Outside Ulaanbaatar vegetables are rarely served, although root vegetables are often available at local markets. Ulaanbaatar offers a variety of restaurants offering traditional Mongolian food as well as European and Asian cuisine. The standard voltage is 220 volts/50Hz. Sockets are of the two-pronged pin type (similar to Russian). International direct dial is available in hotels. In Ulaanbaatar, internet cafes abound. Parts of Mongolia are not connected to the power grid. Outside Ulaanbaaatar few Mongolians speak a foreign language. A translator is required and can be hired in Ulaanbaatar. The cost is approximately $30 per day. Although many government officials speak English, they often prefer to conduct official meetings in Mongolian. Plan to hire a translator.

Temporary Entry: The Mongolian Chamber of Commerce and Industry can arrange for duty free import of display items for trade shows. For more information, contact the MCCI in Ulaanbaatar: Mr. S. Zorigt,, Head of Exhibitions and Trade Fair Bureau, MCCI, Sambuu Str. 11, Ulaanbaatar 38, Mongolia; fax: 987-1/324-620; email: Monchamb@magicnet.mn.

SUPPLEMENTS

US AND COUNTRY CONTACTS

A. MONGOLIAN GOVERNMENT

Ministry of Agriculture and Industry
tel: (976-1) 325-028
fax: (976-1) 323-442

Ministry of Defense
tel: (976-1) 458-755
fax: (976-1) 450-496

Ministry of External Relations
Political Department
Foreign Trade and Economic Cooperation Department
Enkh Taivny gudamj 7A
Ulaanbaatar, Mongolia
tel: (976-1) 311-311
fax: (976-1) 322-127
mongmer@magicnet.mn

Ministry of Finance
tel: (976-1) 329-070
fax: (976-1) 320-247

Ministry of Health and Social Welfare
Olympic Str.-2
Ulaanbaatar-11, Mongolia
tel: (976-1) 321-569
fax: (976-1) 327-872
mhsw@magicnet.mn

Ministry of Infrastructure Development
Government Building-2
United Nations Str-49
Ulaanbaatar 210646, Mongolia
tel: (976-1) 324-379
fax: (976-1) 311-381

Ministry of Justice
tel: (976-1) 325-225
fax: (976-1) 322-383

Ministry of Nature and Environment
tel: (976-1) 326-595
fax: (976-1) 321-401

Ministry of Science, Technology, Enlightenment and Culture
Government Building III
Ulaanbaatar, Mongolia
tel: (976-1) 327-445
fax: (976-1) 323-158
bmostec@magicnet.mn

Central Bank
The Bank of Mongolia
Commerce Str. -6
Ulaanbaatar-11, Mongolia
tel: (976-1) 322-166
fax: (976-1) 326-252
telex: BOMCB MH 79333

Civil Aviation Administration of Mongolia
Buyant-Ukhaa Airport
Ulaanbaatar-34, Mongolia
tel: (976-1) 379-888
fax: (976-1) 313-127
caamak@magicnet.mn

Coal Authority of Mongolia
Ulaanbaatar-21, Mongolia
tel: (976-1) 681-995
fax: (976-1) 681-995

Customs General Administration
Ulaanbaatar-20, Mongolia
tel: (976-1) 323-715
fax: (976-1) 329-024

Ulaanbaatar Customs Administration
PO Box 86
Ulaanbaatar-34, Mongolia
tel: (976-1) 328-473
fax: (976-1) 328-970

Foreign Investment and Foreign Trade Agency
2nd floor, Sambuu Str. 11
Ulaanbaatar 38, Mongolia
tel: (976-1) 321-438
fax: (976-1) 324-076
investboard@magicnet.mn
website: www.mol.mn

Intellectual Property Office of Mongolia
Baga toiruu-31
Ulaanbaatar-46, Mongolia
tel: (976-1) 321-323
fax: (976-1) 327-638

Minerals Resources Authority
Builders' Square 13
Ulaanbaatar 211238
tel: (976-1) 310-370
fax: (976-1) 327-307
mram@magicnet.mn

National Tourism Center of Mongolia
Ms. Haliun, General Director
Chinggis Avenue-11
Ulaanbaatar-28, Mongolia
tel: (976-1) 318-492
fax: (976-2) 318-492

National Statistical Office
Baga toiruu-44
Government Building 3
Ulaanbaatar-11, Mongolia
tel: (976-1) 320-262
fax: (976-1) 324-518

Petroleum Authority of Mongolia
PO Box 37/81
Ulaanbaatar, Mongolia
tel: (976-1) 631-176
fax: (976-1) 631-176
petromon@magicnet.mn
http://www.pam.mn

General Department of National Taxation of Mongolia
Jigjidjav Str-6
Ulaanbaatar-46, Mongolia
tel: (976-1) 321-340
fax: (976-1) 327-686

B. CHAMBERS OF COMMERCE/TRADE ASSOCIATIONS

American Mongolian Business Group
Mr. Maurice Lynch, President
Munkh-Orgil, Idesh and Lynch
International Trade Center
Baga toiruu 37 B
Suite 500/5th floor
Ulaanbaatar, Mongolia
tel: (976-1) 325-344
fax: (976-1) 325-358
mlynch@mongolialaw.com

Mongolian Association of Advocates
Ulaanbaatar-46, Mongolia
tel: (976-1) 326-861
fax: (976-1) 326-861
erdem@mtu.edu.mn

Mongolian Chamber of Commerce and Industry
Mr. S. Demberel, Chairman
Sambuu Str-11
Ulaanbaatar-38, Mongolia
tel: (976-1) 327-176
fax: (976-1) 324-620
monchamb@magicnet.mn

Mongolia Consumers' Union
Mr. Tsendbayar, Director
Room 302
Trade Unions Building
Sukhbaatar Square
Ulaanbaatar, Mongolia
tel: (976-1) 320-026

Mongolian Employers' Federation
Khudaldaanii gudamj-15
Ulaanbaatar-38, Mongolia
tel: (976-1) 325-635
fax: (976-1) 325-635
monef@magicnet.mn

Mongolian Stock Exchange
Sukhbaatar Square-14
Ulaanbaatar, Mongolia
tel: (976-1) 310-470
fax: (976-1) 325-170
msebatj@magicnet.mn

Mongolian Women Lawyers Association
PO Box 547
Ulaanbaatar 210646, Mongolia
tel: (976-1) 322-212
fax: (976-1) 322-212
mwla@magicnet.mn

C. MARKET RESEARCH FIRMS

Mongolian Advertising Association
Room 1205
Sambuu Str-11
Ulaanbaatar-38, Mongolia

tel: (976-1) 323-035
fax: (976-1) 323-035
buderdene@usa.net

Mongolian Marketing Associatioin
Mr. Dagvadorj, President (also professor at National University of Mongolia)
PO Box 20/192
Ulaanbaatar, Mongolia
tel: (976-1) 327-813
fax: (976-1) 324-385
econinst@magicnet.mn

D. BANKS

Golomt Bank
Sukhbaatar Square-3, 4th floor
Ulaanbaatar-11/20A, Mongolia
tel: (976-1) 311-530
fax: (976-1) 312-307
telex: 79247 GLMT MN
golomt@magicnet.mn

Trade And Development Bank
Khudadaalnii gudamj-7
Ulaanbaatar-11, Mongolia
tel: (976-1) 326-289
fax: (976-1) 311-618
telex: 79334 TDB MH
SWIFT Code: TDBMMNUB
TDBMGTG@magicnet.mn

Savings Bank
tel: (976-1) 312-043

E. US EMBASSY CONTACTS

US Embassy Ulaanbaatar
Big Ring Road
Ulaanbaatar
Mongolia
Tel: (976-1) 329-095
Fax: (976-1) 320-776

Mailing Address From US:
US Embassy Ulaanbaatar
4410 Ulaanbaatar Place
Department of State
Washington, DC 20521-4410

Ambassador's Office
Ambassador Alphonse F. La Porta
ambassador@usembassy.mn

DCM Mark Willis
dcm@usembassy.mn

Defense Attache Office
Maj. John Baker
Defense Attache
dao@usembassy.mn

Economic/Commercial Section
Economic/Commercial Officer Laura Byergo
econ@usembassy.mn

Commercial Assistant Allison Croft
commerce@usembassy.mn

Political Section
Political Officer Lynn Roche
pol@usembassy.mn

Consular Section
Consular Officer Tim Roche
cons@usembassy.mn

F. WASHINGTON-BASED USG MONGOLIA CONTACTS

US Department of Commerce
International Trade Administration
Mongolia Desk Officer Brenda Carter
14th And Constitution Avenue
Washington, DC 20230
Tel: (202) 482-3583
Fax: (202) 482-1576

Multilateral Development Bank Office
Tel: (2020) 482-3399
Fax: (202) 482-5179

TPCC Trade Information Center
Tel: 800-USA-Trade

US Department Of State
Office of China And Mongolia
Bureau of East Asia & Pacific Affairs
Room 4318, 2201 C Street, NW
Washington, DC 20520
Tel: (202) 647-6796
Fax: (202) 647-6820

US Department of Agriculture
International Trade Policy
Asia American Division
Foreign Agricultural Service Stop 1023
1th And Independence Ave., SW
Washington, DC 20250-1023
Tel: (202) 720-1289
Fax: (202) 690-1093
Email: deatonl@fas.usda.gov

Office of US Trade Representative
600 17th Street, NW
Washington, DC 20506

G. US BASED MULTIPLIERS
US-Mongolia Business Council
Steve Saunders, President
1015 Duke Street
Alexandria, VA 22314-3551
tel: 703/549-8444
fax: 703/549-6526
steve.saunders@us-mongolia.org

EMBASSIES, CONSULS AND HONORARY CONSULS

EMBASSIES

Bulgaria
Accredited to: Albania, Greece, Cyprus, Macedonia, Slovenia, Croatia, Yugoslavia, Bosnia-Herzegovina
Sofia 1113, ul.Frederic Jolio Curie 52, Embassy of Mongolia, Fax: 00359-2-9630745, Tel: 00359-2-9630765
E-Mail: mongemb@mbox.infotel.bg

Belgium
Accredited to: Denmark, Luxembourg, Netherlands
Ambassade de Mongolie, Avenue Besme 18, 1190, Bruxelles, Belgium, Fax: 0032-2-3443215, Tel: 0032-2-3446974
E-mail:embassymongolia@skynet.be

Canada
Consulate Genaral of Mongolia
BCE Place, Suite 1800, P.O. Box 754
181 Bay Strcct, Toronto, Canada M5J 2T9
Tel: (416) 865-7776; Fax: (416) 865-1515
E-mail: consulgen@mongolia.org

China
Accredited to: Australia, New Zealand, Pakistan, Brazil, Argentine
Embassy of Mongolia,No 2,Xiushui Beijie Jian Guo Men Wai Da Jie, Beijing, China, Fax: 0086-10-6532-5045, Tel: 0086-10-6532-1810
E-mail: monembbj@public3.bta.net.cn

Cuba
Accredited to: Mexico, Chile
Embajada de Mongolia, Calle 66 No 505 Esguina a 5 ta-A, Tel: 0053-7-242763, Fax: 0053-7-240639

Czech Republic
Accredit to: Slovakia, Romania
Velvyslanectvi Mongolska, Na Marne 5,Praha-6, 160000 Ceska Republika, Fax: 004202-24314827, Tel: 004202-24311199
E-mail:monemb@bohem-net.cz

DPRK
DPRK Pyongyang, Mansu-dong, Embassy of Mongolia, Fax: 00850-23817616, Tel: 00850-23817322

Egypt
Accredited to: Palestine, Jordan, Syria, Israel, Oman, Yemen, Kuwait, Emirates
Embassy of Mongolia, 33A Mohamed Mazhar street, Zamalek Cairo Egypt, Fax:0020-2-3414229, Tel : 0020-2-3409574
E-mail:monemby@intouch.com

France
Accredited to: Spain, Italy, Portugal
Ambassade de Mongolie, 5, Avenue Robert Schumann, 92100 Boulogne-Billancourt, Fax:0033-1-46053016, Tel: 0033-1-46052318
E-mail:106513.2672@Compuserve.com

Germany
Accredited to: Switzerland
1.Botschaft der Mongolei Siebengebirgsblick 4-6, 53844 Troisdorf Germany, Tel: 0049-2241-402727 Fax: 0049-2241-47781
E-mail: Mongolbot@aol.com
2. Gotlandstrasse 12, 10439 Berlin, Fax: 0049-30-4469321, Tel: 0049-30-4469320
E-mail: ganbat@metronet.de

Hungary
Accredited to: Austria, Moldova

Hungary 1022 Budapest, Bogar Utca 14/cMongol Nagykovetsege, Fax:00361-2125731, Tel: 0036-1-2125731
E-mail:mnk@mail.datanet.hu

India
Accredited to: Nepal, Bangladesh, Sri-Lanka
Embassy of Mongolia, 34,Archbishop Makarious Marg, New Delhi 110003 India, Fax:0091-11-4633240, Tel: 0091-11-4631728
E-mail:Embassy.mongolia@gems.vsnl.net.in

Japan
Embassy of Mongolia, 21-4 Kamiyama Cho Shibuya Ku, Tokyo 150, Fax:0081-33-469-2216, Tel: 0081-33-469-2088
E-mail:embmong@gol.com

Kazakhstan
Accredited to: Kyrgyzstan, Tajikstan, Turkmenistan
g.Almaty ul.Aubakerova 1/1, Embassy of Mongolia
Fax: 007-3272-293259, Tel: 007-3272-200865
E-mail:monkazel@kazmail.asdc.kz

Lao PDR
Accredited to: Cambodia, Thailand, Myanmar, Brunei
Embassy of Mongolia, Q. Wat Nak Km.3, P.O.Box 370, Ventiane Lao P.D.R, Fax:00856-21-315221, Tel: 00856-21-315220

Poland
Accredited to : Latvia, Lithuania, Estonia, Ukraine
Ambasada Mongolii 00478 Warszawa, Polska , ul.Rejtana 15 m.16, Fax:0048-22-484264
E-mail:mongamb@ikp.atm.com.pl

R.O.K
Embassy of Mongolia
33-5 Hannan-Dong, Vongsan-gu, Seoul, Korea Fax:0082-2-794-7605,Tel:0082-2-794-1350
E-mail: monemb@uriel.net

Russian Federation
Accredited to: Armenia, Belarus, Georgia, Iran, Finland
Moscow 121069, ul.Borisoglebovskaya 11, Embassy of Mongolia, Tel:077-095-290679 ; Fax:077-095-2916171
E-mail: mongolia@glas.apc.org
bayar@msk.tsi.ru
Website: http://www.icsti.su/mongol

Switzerland
Accredited to Holy See, Malta
Mission Permanente de la Mongolie Geneve 4, Chemin des Mollies 1293 Bellevue/GE, Fax:0041-22-7743201, Tel: 0041-22-7741974
E-mail:mission.mongolia@itu.ch

Turkey
Embassy of Mongolia, G.O.P. Koza Sokak-107, Ankara
Tel: 0090-312-4467977; Fax: 0090-312-4467791
E-mail: mogolelc@turnet.net.tr

Vietnam
Accredited to: Malaysia, Philippines, Singapore, Indonesia
Embassy of Mongolia, 39, Tran phu str.Hanoi, Vietnam, Fax: 0084-4-8454954, Tel: 0084-4-8453009
E-mail:mongembhanoi@hn.vnn.vn

UK
Accredited to: Iceland, Norway, Sweden
Mongolian Embassy, 7 Kensington Court, London W8 5DL, United Kingdom, Tel: 0044-171-937-0150 ; Fax:0044-171-9371117
E-mail: embmong@aol.com

USA
Accredited to: Canada
1. Embassy of Mongolia, 2833 M street, N.W. Washington, D.C.20007, USA
Fax:001-202-2989227; Tel: 001-202-333-7117
E-mail:monemb@aol.com

2. Permanent Representative of Mongolia to UN
not accredited to other countries but serves as point of contact with countries of Africa, Latin America and the Pacific

6 East 77th street, New-York, N.Y.10021
USA , Fax: 001-212-8619464
Tel: 001-212-4726517
E-mail:mngun@undp.org
Website:
http://www.undp.org/missions/mongolia

CONSULS

Russia
1. Irkutsk
Irkutsk, St. Lapina-11, General Consulate of Mongolia
Tel: 007-3952-342145, 007-3952-342447
2. Ulaan-Ude
Ulaan-Ude, St.Erbanova-12, "Baikal" Hotel
General Consulate of Mongolia
Tel: 007-30122-20507, Fax: 007-30122-63244
E-mail: mnc@bss.ru

China
Huh hot
Zhongguo Huhe Haote, Xincheng gu
Wulanziagu 5 hao, Lou Menggu
Lingshiguang
Tel: 0086-471-4953254, Fax: 0086-471-4953250

Singapore
100, St. Patrick Road, St. Patrick
Garden,Singapore 424191
Fax:0065-3481753, Tel: 0065-3480745

HONORARY CONSULS OF MONGOLIA

Austria
Mr.Johannes Stiedle, Honorary Consul of Mongolia in Austria, AUHOFSTRASSE 65-67, A-113-Vienna/Austria,
Fax: 431877373336

Australia
Mr. Sean Hinton, Honorary Consul of Mongolia in Australia
112/189 Phillip street, Waterloo, NSW 2017, Australia, Tel&fax: 61- 2- 93194797,
E-Mail:sean_hinton@mckinsey.com

Denmark
Mr. Anders Jungersen, Honorary Consul of Mongolia in Denmark
UNISCRAP A / S, Genvindings Industry
Fiskerihavnsgade 6, DK-2450 Kobennavn SV,
Fax: 45 33 12 03 73

Italy
Mr. Aldo Colleoni, Honorary Consul of Mongolia in Italy
Via Giulia, 10-34126 Trieste- Italy
Tel: 39 40 575422, Fax: 39 40 575431
E-mail: consmong@tin.it

Israel
Dr. Jacques Leventhal, Honorary Consul of Mongolia in Isreal
9 Frishman Street. TelAviv 63578. Isreal
Tel: 972 35 243 929, Fax:972 35 272 361
E-Mail:clascard@netvision.net.il

The Netherlands
Mr. J. G. Brummeihuis, Honorary Consul of Mongolia in the Netherlands
Notarissen De Cuserstraat 5, 1081CK
Amsterdam-Buitenveldert, Postbus 71094,
1008 88 Amsterdam, Fax: 020 644 96 38

Sweden
Mrs. Anita Gerdne, Honorary Consul of Mongolia in Sweden
Gotabergsgatan 34, S-411 34 Gothenburg,
Fax: 46 31 160770

Thailand
Dr. Supong Limtanakool, Honorary Consul of Mongolia in Thailand
94 Rimklongprapa road Banksue,Bangkok
10800, Thailand, Fax: 662 259 03 59

USA
Mr.Edward T. Story, Honorary Consul of Mongolia in USA
1221 Lamar Suite 1201, Houston, Texas
77010 USA
Tel: 713-759-2922, Fax: 713-646-6666

Germany
1. Mr. Dirk Pfeil, Honorary Consul of Mongolia in Main, Germany
Eshersheimer Landstr.62-60, 60322
Frankfurt am Main
Fax: 069 153 096 66, Tel: 069 153 096 10
2. Mr. Bernd Klingsohr, Honorary Consul of Mongolia in Bavaria, Germany
Automag Bushner & Linse GmbH & Co KG
Postfanch 12 01 09, 80030 Munchen, Fax:

089 510 22 02, Tel: 089 510 22 66
E-mail: Hon_consul@mongolei.de

Korea
Mr. Zeon Beyon-Kuk, Honorary Consul of Mongolia in The Republic of Korea
189-17, Onchon 1-Dong, Dongrae-Gu, Pusan, Korea, Postal Code No. 607-061,
Tel: 8251 555-8182, 558-3891, Fax: 8251 555-4715

Malaysia
Mr. Datuk Syed Abdul Rahman Alhabshi, Honorary Consul of Mongolia in Malaysia
45th floor Empire Tower, City Sq. Center, 182 Jalan Tun Razak, 50400, Kuala-Lumpur, Malaysia
Tel: 03-2621933, Fax: 6032620933

FOREIGN EMBASSIES & REPRESENTATIVES OF INTERNATIONAL ORGANIZATIONS IN MONGOLIA

FOREIGN EMBASSIES

Bulgaria
POB 702, Olympiin Gudamj 8, Ulaanbaatar
Tel: 329721, Telex 220 BGTIS
Ambassador H.E. Mr. EDVIN SUGAREV
E-mail: posolstvo.bg@magicnet.mn

China People's Republic
C.P.O. Box 672, Zaluuchuudyn Urgun Chuluu 5, Ulaanbaatar 13, Mongolia
Tel. 320955, 323940, Fax 311943
Ambassador H.E.Mr. QI CHIJIA

Cuba
C.P.O.Box 710, Negdsen Undestnii Gudamj 5 ,Ulaanbaatar 13, Mongolia
Tel. 327709, 327708, Telex 79228
Ambassador H.E. Mr. ESTEBAN LOBAINO ROMERO

Czech Republic
C.P.O.Box 665, Diplomatic Apartments 95, Ulaanbaatar 13, Mongolia
Tel. 321886, 326661, Fax. 323791, Telex 255 OBZA MH
Ambassador H.E. Mr. JOSEF FASS (res. in Beijing)
Charge d` Affaires Mr. ZDENEK OKUNEK
E-mail: czechemb@magicnet.mn

Democratic People's Republic of Korea
C.P.O.Box 671, Negdsen Undestnii gudamj 12, Ulaanbaatar 13, Mongolia
Tel. 322795, 323458, Telex 250
Ambassador H.E. Mr. JONG JANG HYON

France
B.P.687, 13 Ulaanbaatar Mongolia
Tel.312118, 99114424, Fax.324519
Ambassador H.E.Mr. JACQUES-OLIVIER MANENT
AmbaFrance@magicnet.mn

Germany
C.P.O.Box 708, Negdsen Undestnii gudamj 7, Ulaanbaatar 13, Mongolia
Tel. 323325, 323915, Fax. 323905
Ambassador H.E.Mr. JURGEN ELIAS
E-mail:uz1@magicnet.mn

Hungary
C.P.O.Box 668, Enkhtaivany gudamj 1, Ulaanbaatar, Mongolia
Tel. 323973, 320972, Fax. 311793, Telex 79322
Ambassador H.E. Mr.BELA TOROCSIK
E-mail:Hunamb@magicnet.mn

India
C.P.O. Box 691, Zaluuchuudyn Urgun Chuluu 10, 11th Micro District, Ulaanbaatar, Mongolia
Tel. 329522, 329524, Fax. 329532,
Ambassador H.E. Mr. KUSHOK BAKULA
indembmongolia@magicnet.mn

Japan
C.P.O. Box 1011, Olympiin gudamj 6, Ulaanbaatar, Mongolia
Tel. 320777, Fax. 313332
Ambassador H.E. Mr. SHINJI KUBOTA
E-mail:eojmongol@magicnet.mn

Korea
C.P.O. Box 1039, Olympiin gudamj 10, Ulaanbaatar, Mongolia
Tel. 321548, 310153, Fax. 311157
Ambassador H.E. Mr. HWANG KIL SHIN

Lao P.D.R
C.P.O. Box 1030, Ihk Toiruu 59,
Ulaanbaatar 13, Mongolia
Tel. 326440, 329898, Telex 79251
Ambassador H.E.Mr. VANHEUANG VONGVICHIT

Russia
C.P.O. Box 661, Enkhtaivany gudamj A-6,
Ulaanbaatar, Mongolia
Tel. 326836, 327071, Fax. 327018, Telex 251 UB
Ambassador H.E. Mr. NIKOLAI VICTOROVICH PAVLOV

Turkey
Enkh Taivny gudamj 5,Ulaanbaatar, Mongolia
Te: 313992
Ambassador H.E. Mr. VAROL OZKOCAK
E-mail:turkemb@magicnet.mn

United Kingdom
C.P.O. Box 703, Enkh taivany gudamj 30,
Ulaanbaatar 13, Mongolia
Tel. 358133, 358238, Fax. 358036, Telex 79261
Ambassador H.E. Mr. JOHN CLIVE DURHAM
E-mail:britemb@magicnet.mn

USA
C.P.O. Box 1021, Ikh Toiruu 59/1,
Ulaanbaatar 13, Mongolia
Tel. 329095,329606, Fax. 320776
Ambassador H.E. Mr. ALPHONSE LA PORTA
E-mail:aeub@magicnet.mn

Viet Nam
Enkhtaivany Urgun Chuluu 47, Ulaanbaatar, Mongolia
Tel. 358923, 358917, Telex 249
Ambassador H.E. Mr. VU VAN VACH

Yuqoslavia
C.P.O. Box 700, Diplomatic Apartment 95,
Ulaanbaatar, Mongolia
Tel. 322380, Fax. 325597, Telex 259Yu amb
Charge d` Affaires Mr. RAIKO GRIGICH

Finland
Ministry of Foreign Affairs of Finland
P.O. Box 176, Fin-00161, Helsinki
Tel. (358-9) 134151, Fax. 13415798
Ambassador H.E. Mr. TAISTO Tolvanen

Kazakhstan
District Chingeltei, 6th MicroDistrict,
Diplomatic Building 95, Apartment 11, P.O. 38, Box 291, Tel: 312240
Charge d` Affaires Mr. VALIKHAN KONURBAYEV
Representatives of International Organizations

UNDP
Resident Representative Mr.Douglas GARDNER
Mailing Address: UNDP, C.P.O. 49/207,
Ulaanbaatar, Mongolia
Street Address: 7 Erhuu Street, Ulaanbaatar
Tel. 327585, 321539 Fax. 326221
E-mail: registry@undp.org.mn
Website: http://www.un-mongolia.mn

UNFPA
Resident Representative Mr.Douglas GARDNER
Mailing Address: UNFPA Representative,
P.O.Box 49/207
Ulaanbaatar, Mongolia
Street Address: Enh-Taivan Street-13B
Research and Training Centre of Health Management, National Institute of Medical Science Ulaanbaatar, Mongolia

WHO
Resident Representative Mr. U.H. Susantha de SILVA
WHO Representative,Post Box 663,
Ulaanbaatar, Mongolia
Tel. 327870 Fax. 327870
Street Address: Government Building No.8
3rd Floor, 3 Karl Marx Street , Ulaanbaatar, Mongolia
E-mail:wrmog@magicnet.mn

IMF
Resident Representative Mr. Geoffrey OESTREICHER
Room 257, Government House,
Ulaanbaatar
Tel. 329153, 323802 Fax. 312181

UNICEF

Asst.Representative Ms. Katherine HINTON
Ulaanbaatar-46, Government Building ? 2
Rooms 402-414
Tel. 312201, 312183 Fax. 327313
Mailing Address: UNICEF Assistant Representative Sukhbaatar Duureg, Ulaanbaatar-46, Mongolia
E-mail:unicef@magicnet.mn

UNCHR
Street Address: Trade Union`s Building, 2nd Floor, Room 214 Sukhbaatar Square 3, Ulaanbaatar-11, Mongolia
Mailing Address: C/o UNDP Resident Representative P.O. Box 49/207, Ulaanbaatar, Mongolia
E-mail:unchrmon@magicnet.mn

SELECTED BUSINESS CONTACTS

MAJOR NEWSPAPERS

Business Times - a weekly business paper, in Mongolian, published by the Mongolian Chamber of Commerce and Industry
Mongol Messenger - weekly English language paper published by the Mongolian news agency MONTSAME (the Mongolian national news agency)
Mongolyn Medee - (News of Mongolia) daily newspaper of the Erel Company
Odriin Sonin - (Daily News) daily newspaper
UB Post - weekly English-language newspaper published by Mongol News Group
Unoodor - (Today) independent daily newspaper published by Mongol News Group
Zuuny Medee - (Century News) daily newspaper

TELEVISION STATIONS

Channel 25, owned by the Mongol News Group
Eagle TV - independent station operated by a US-Mongolian joint venture
Mongol TV - state-owned broadcaster
RGB - independent television station in Darhan
UBS - (Ulaanbaatar Broadcasting System) citizens representative board

ADVERTISING ASSOCIATION:

Mongolian Advertising Association
Room 1205
Sambuu Str-11
Ulaanbaatar 38, Mongolia
tel: (976-1) 323-035
fax: (976-1) 323-035
buderdene@usa.net

MULTILATERAL AGREEMENTS

1.	Geneva Convention for the Amelioration of the Condition of the Wounded and Sick in Armed Forces in the Field, 1949	1958
2.	Geneva Convention for the Amelioration of the Condition of Wounded, Sick and Shipwrecked Members of Armed Forces at Sea, 1949	1958
3.	Geneva Convention relative to the treatment of prisoners of war, 1949	1958
4.	Geneva Convention relative to the protection of civilian persons in time of war, 1949	1958

5.	Charter of the United Nations, 1945	1961
6.	Convention on the privileges and immunities of the United Nations, 1946	1962
7.	Constitution of the World Health Organization, 1946	1962
8.	Constitution of the United Nations Educational, Scientific and Cultural Organization, 1945	1962
9.	Convention for the Unification of Certain Rules Relating to International Carriage by Air, 1929	1962
10.	Treaty banning nuclear weapon tests in the atmosphere, in outer space and under water,1963	
11.	Convention of the World Meterological Organization, 1947	1963
12.	Convention against discrinimation in education, 1960	1964
13.	Convention for the Protection of Cultural Property in the Event of Armed Conflict, 1954	1964
14.	Convention on the Political Rights of Women, 1953	1965
15.	Convention on Transit Trade of Land-locked States, 1965	1966
16.	Vienna Convention on Diplomatic Relations,1961	1967
17.	Treaty on principles governing the activities of States in the exploration and use of outer space, including the moon and other celestial bodies, 1967	
18.	Constitution of the International Labour Organizations, 1919	1968
19.	Constitution of the United Nations Industrial Development Organization, 1966	1968
20.	Protocol for the Prohibition of the Use in War of Asphyxiating, Poisonous or Other Gases, and of Bacteriological Methods of Warfare, 1925	
21.	Slavery Convention,1926	1968
22.	Supplementary Convention on the Abolition of Slavery, the Slave Trade, and Institutions and Practices Similar to Slaver,1956	1968
23.	Treaty for the Non-Proliferation of Nuclear Weapons, 1968	1969
24.	Convention on the Prevention and Punishment of the Crime of Genocide, 1948	
25.	International Convention on the Elimination of All Forms of Racial Discrimination, 1966	1969
26.	Convention (No. 103) concerning maternity protection, 1951	1969
27.	Convention (No. 59) , fixing the minimum age for admission of children to industrial employment, 1937	1969

28.	Convention (No. 100) concerning equal remuneration for men and women workers for work of equal value, 1951	1969
29.	Convention (No. 111) concerning discrimination in respect of employment and occupation, 1958	1969
30.	Convention (No. 87) concerning freedom of association and protection of the right to organize, 1948	
31.	Agreement on the rescue of astronauts, the return of astronauts and the return of objects launched into outer space,1963	1969
32.	Convention on the privileges and immunities of the specialized agencies of the United Nations , 1947	1970
33.	Treaty on the prohibition of the emplacement of nuclear weapons and other weapons of mass destruction on the sea-bed and the ocean floor and in the subsoil thereof, 1971	1971
34.	Convention for the Suppression of unlawful seizure of aircraft, 1970	1971
35.	Montreal Convention against unlawful actions against security of civil aviation, 1971	
36.	Convention on the prohibition of the development, production and stockpiling of bacteriological (biological) and toxin weapons and on their destruction, 1972	
37.	Convention on the international liability for damage caused by space objects, 1972	1972
38.	Constitution of the Universal Postal Union, 1874	1973
39.	Statute of the International Atomic EnergyAgency, 1956	1973
40.	International Covenant on Economic, Social and Cultural Rights, 1966	1974
41.	International Covenant on Civil and Political Rights, 1966	1974
42.	Constitution of the United Nations Food and Agricultural Organization 1974	
43.	International Convention on the Suppression and Punishment of the Crime of Apartheid, 1973	1975
44.	Convention on the prevention and punishment of crimes against internationally protected persons, including diplomatic agents, 1973	1975
45.	Convention on the Representation of States in International Organizations, 1975	1976
46.	Convention (No. 122) concerning employment policy, 1964	1976
47.	Convention on the High Seas, 1958	1976
48.	Barselona Declaration recognizing the Right to a Flag of States having no Sea-coast, 1921	
49.	Convention on the prohibition of military or any other hostile use of environmental modification techniques, 1976	1978
50.	Convention on the prohibition of military or any other hostile use of environmental modification techniques, 1976	1978
51.	Convention establishing the World Intellectual Property Organization, 1967	1979
52.	Convention on the Elimination of All Forms of Discrimination against Women, 1979	1981
53.	Convention concerning the minimum age for admission to employment underground in mines, 1967	1981
54.	Convention on prohibitions or restrictions on the use of certain conventional weapons which may be deemed to be excessively injurious or to have indiscriminate effects, 1980	
55.	Convention concerning the Use of Broadcasting for the Cause of Peace, 1936	1985

56.	Convention of Paris for the Protection of Industrial Property, 1883	1985
57.	Madrid Agreement concerning the International Registration of Marks, 1891	1985
58.	Convention on registration of objects launched into outer space, 1974	1985
59.	Chicago Convention on International Civil Aviation, 1944	1986
60.	Vienna Convention on the Physical Potection of Nuclear Materials, 1979	1986
61.	International Telecommunication Convention,1865	1986
62.	Convention Against Apartheid in Sports, 1985	1987
63.	Vienna Convention on the Law of Treaties, 1969	1988
64.	Constitution of the International Civil Aviation Organization 1944	1989
65.	Vienna Convention on Consular Relations, 1963	1989
66.	Convention on the Rights of Child , 1989	1990
67.	Convention on Offences and Certain Other Acts Committed on Board Aircraft, 1963	
68.	Articles of Agreement of the Internal Monetary Fund (IMF), 1945	1991
69.	Articles of Agreement of the International Bank for Reconstruction and Development (World Bank), 1946	1991
70.	Constitution of the Asia Pacific Telecommunity, 1976	1991
71.	Supplementary Protocol to the International Covenant on Civil and Political Rights, 1966	
72.	Convention on Consent to Marriage, Minimum Age for Marriage and Regsitration of Marriages, 1962	1991
73.	New York Single Convention on Narcotic Drugs, 1961	1991
74.	Patent Cooperation Treaty, 1970	1991
75.	New York International Convention against the taking of hostages, 1979	1992
76.	United Nations Framework Convention on Climate Change, 1992	1993
77.	Rio de Janeiro Convention on Biological Diversity, 1992	1993
78.	United Nations Convention to Combat Desertification in those countries Experiencing Serious Drought and/or Desertification, particularly in Africa,1993	1993
79.	Convention on the Prohibition of the Development, Production, Stockpiling and Use of Chemical Weapons and Their Destructions 1993	1994
80.	Convention on International Trade in Endangered Species of Wild Fauna and Flora, 1973	
81.	Vienna Convention for the Protection of the Ozone Layer, 1985	1995
82.	Protocol Additional to the Geneva Convention relating to the protection of victims of armed conflicts, 1977	1995
83.	Convention on the Settlement of investment disputes between states and nationals of other states, 1965	
84.	Agreement on the Establishment of World Trade Organization, 1994	1996
85.	General Agreement on Tariff and Trade, 1994	1996
86.	Convention on the International Maritime Organization, 1948	1996

87.	Convention on Maritime Transportation, 1958	1996
88.	United Nations Convention on the Law of the Sea, 1982	1996
89.	Convention on Contract for the International Sale of Goods,1980	1997
90.	The Comprehensive Nuclear Test-Ban Treaty, 1996	1997
91.	Basel Convention on the Control of Transboundary Movement of Hazardous Wastes and Their Disposal, 1989	1997
92.	Berne Convention for the Protection of Literary and Artistic Works, 1886	1997
93.	Convention on Road Traffic, 1968	1997
94.	Convention on Road Signs and Signals, 1968	1997

BASIC TITLES FOR MONGOLIA

IMPORTANT!
All publications are updated annually!
Please contact IBP, Inc. at ibpusa3@gmail.com for the latest ISBNs and additional information
Global Business and Investment Info Databank: www.ibpus.com

title
Mongolia A "Spy" Guide
Mongolia Air Force Handbook
Mongolia Banking & Financial Market Handbook
Mongolia Business and Investment Opportunities Yearbook
Mongolia Business and Investment Opportunities Yearbook
Mongolia Business and Investment Opportunities Yearbook Volume 1 Strategic Information and Opportunities
Mongolia Business and Investment Opportunities Yearbook Volume 1 Strategic Information and Opportunities
Mongolia Business Intelligence Report
Mongolia Business Law Handbook
Mongolia Business Law Handbook
Mongolia Business Law Handbook
Mongolia Business Law Handbook
Mongolia Central Bank and Financial Policy Handbook
Mongolia Company Laws and Regulations Handbook
Mongolia Constitution and Citizenship Laws Handbook - Strategic Information and Basic Laws
Mongolia Constitution and Citizenship Laws Handbook - Strategic Information and Basic Laws
Mongolia Country Study Guide
Mongolia Country Study Guide Volume 1 Strategic Information and Developments
Mongolia Country Study Guide Volume 1 Strategic Information and Developments
Mongolia Customs, Trade Regulations and Procedures Handbook
Mongolia Diplomatic Handbook
Mongolia Ecology & Nature Protection Handbook
Mongolia Ecology & Nature Protection Laws and Regulation Handbook
Mongolia Economic & Development Strategy Handbook

title
Mongolia Energy Policy, Laws and Regulation Handbook
Mongolia Export-Import Trade and Business Directory
Mongolia Foreign Policy and Government Guide
Mongolia Foreign Policy and Government Guide
Mongolia Free Trade and Industrial Zones Handbook
Mongolia Immigration Laws and Regulations Handbook - Strategic Information and Basic Laws
Mongolia Immigration Laws and Regulations Handbook - Strategic Information and Basic Laws
Mongolia Industrial and Business Directory
Mongolia Industrial and Business Directory
Mongolia Internet and E-Commerce Investment and Business Guide: Regulations and Opportunities
Mongolia Investment and Business Guide
Mongolia Investment and Business Guide
Mongolia Investment and Business Guide
Mongolia Investment and Trade Laws and Regulations Handbook
Mongolia Labor Laws and Regulations Handbook - Strategic Information and Basic Laws
Mongolia Labor Laws and Regulations Handbook - Strategic Information and Basic Laws
Mongolia Land Ownership and Agriculture Laws Handbook
Mongolia Land Ownership and Agriculture Laws Handbook
Mongolia Land Ownership and Agriculture Laws Handbook
Mongolia Mineral & Mining Sector Investment and Business Guide
Mongolia Mineral & Mining Sector Investment and Business Guide
Mongolia Mining Laws and Regulations Handbook
Mongolia National Security and Defense Policy Handbook
Mongolia National Security and Defense Policy Handbook
Mongolia Recent Economic and Political Developments Yearbook
Mongolia Recent Economic and Political Developments Yearbook
Mongolia Recent Economic and Political Developments Yearbook
Mongolia Starting Business (Incorporating) in....Guide
Mongolia Tax Guide
Mongolia Tax Guide
Mongolia Taxation Laws and Regulations Handbook
Mongolia Telecom Laws and Regulations Handbook
Mongolia Telecommunication Industry Business Opportunities Handbook
Mongolia Traders and Investors Handbook
Mongolia Traders Manual: Export-Import, Trade, Investment
Mongolia Transportation Policy and Regulations Handbook

WORLD COUNTRY STUDY GUIDES LIBRARY

Strategic political, geographic, economic, business information, contacts and important developments

Price: $99.95 each

1.	Abkhazia (Republic of Abkhazia) Volume 1 Strategic Information and Developments
2.	Afghanistan Country Study Guide Volume 1 Strategic Information and Developments
3.	Aland Country Study Guide Volume 1 Strategic Information and Developments
4.	Albania Country Study Guide Volume 1 Strategic Information and Developments
5.	Algeria Country Study Guide Volume 1 Strategic Information and Developments
6.	Andorra Country Study Guide Volume 1 Strategic Information and Developments
7.	Angola Country Study Guide Volume 1 Strategic Information and Developments
8.	Anguilla Country Study Guide Volume 1 Strategic Information and Developments
9.	Antigua and Barbuda Country Study Guide Volume 1 Strategic Information and Developments
10.	Antilles (Netherlands) Country Study Guide Volume 1 Strategic Information and Developments
11.	Argentina Country Study Guide Volume 1 Strategic Information and Developments
12.	Armenia Country Study Guide Volume 1 Strategic Information and Developments
13.	Aruba Country Study Guide Volume 1 Strategic Information and Developments
14.	Australia Country Study Guide Volume 1 Strategic Information and Developments
15.	Austria Country Study Guide Volume 1 Strategic Information and Developments
16.	Azerbaijan Country Study Guide Volume 1 Strategic Information and Developments
17.	Bahamas Country Study Guide Volume 1 Strategic Information and Developments
18.	Bahrain Country Study Guide Volume 1 Strategic Information and Developments
19.	Bangladesh Country Study Guide Volume 1 Strategic Information and Developments
20.	Barbados Country Study Guide Volume 1 Strategic Information and Developments
21.	Belarus Country Study Guide Volume 1 Strategic Information and Developments
22.	Belgium Country Study Guide Volume 1 Strategic Information and Developments
23.	Belize Country Study Guide Volume 1 Strategic Information and Developments
24.	Benin Country Study Guide Volume 1 Strategic Information and Developments
25.	Bermuda Country Study Guide Volume 1 Strategic Information and Developments
26.	Bhutan Country Study Guide Volume 1 Strategic Information and Developments
27.	Bolivia Country Study Guide Volume 1 Strategic Information and Developments
28.	Bosnia and Herzegovina Country Study Guide Volume 1 Strategic Information and Developments
29.	Botswana Country Study Guide Volume 1 Strategic Information and Developments
30.	Brazil Country Study Guide Volume 1 Strategic Information and Developments
31.	Brunei Country Study Guide Volume 1 Strategic Information and Developments
32.	Bulgaria Country Study Guide Volume 1 Strategic Information and Developments
33.	Burkina Faso Country Study Guide Volume 1 Strategic Information and Developments
34.	Burundi Country Study Guide Volume 1 Strategic Information and Developments
35.	Cambodia Country Study Guide Volume 1 Strategic Information and Developments
36.	Cameroon Country Study Guide Volume 1 Strategic Information and Developments
37.	Canada Country Study Guide Volume 1 Strategic Information and Developments

38.	Cape Verde Country Study Guide Volume 1 Strategic Information and Developments
39.	Cayman Islands Country Study Guide Volume 1 Strategic Information and Developments
40.	Central African Republic Country Study Guide Volume 1 Strategic Information and Developments
41.	Chad Country Study Guide Volume 1 Strategic Information and Developments
42.	Chile Country Study Guide Volume 1 Strategic Information and Developments
43.	China Country Study Guide Volume 1 Strategic Information and Developments
44.	Colombia Country Study Guide Volume 1 Strategic Information and Developments
45.	Comoros Country Study Guide Volume 1 Strategic Information and Developments
46.	Congo Country Study Guide Volume 1 Strategic Information and Developments
47.	Congo, Democratic Republic Country Study Guide Volume 1 Strategic Information and Developments
48.	Cook Islands Country Study Guide Volume 1 Strategic Information and Developments
49.	Costa Rica Country Study Guide Volume 1 Strategic Information and Developments
50.	Cote d'Ivoire Country Study Guide Volume 1 Strategic Information and Developments
51.	Croatia Country Study Guide Volume 1 Strategic Information and Developments
52.	Cuba Country Study Guide Volume 1 Strategic Information and Developments
53.	Cyprus Country Study Guide Volume 1 Strategic Information and Developments
54.	Czech Republic Country Study Guide Volume 1 Strategic Information and Developments
55.	Denmark Country Study Guide Volume 1 Strategic Information and Developments
56.	Djibouti Country Study Guide Volume 1 Strategic Information and Developments
57.	Dominica Country Study Guide Volume 1 Strategic Information and Developments
58.	Dominican Republic Country Study Guide Volume 1 Strategic Information and Developments
59.	Ecuador Country Study Guide Volume 1 Strategic Information and Developments
60.	Egypt Country Study Guide Volume 1 Strategic Information and Developments
61.	El Salvador Country Study Guide Volume 1 Strategic Information and Developments
62.	Equatorial Guinea Country Study Guide Volume 1 Strategic Information and Developments
63.	Eritrea Country Study Guide Volume 1 Strategic Information and Developments
64.	Estonia Country Study Guide Volume 1 Strategic Information and Developments
65.	Ethiopia Country Study Guide Volume 1 Strategic Information and Developments
66.	Falkland Islands Country Study Guide Volume 1 Strategic Information and Developments
67.	Faroes Islands Country Study Guide Volume 1 Strategic Information and Developments
68.	Fiji Country Study Guide Volume 1 Strategic Information and Developments
69.	Finland Country Study Guide Volume 1 Strategic Information and Developments
70.	France Country Study Guide Volume 1 Strategic Information and Developments
71.	Gabon Country Study Guide Volume 1 Strategic Information and Developments
72.	Gambia Country Study Guide Volume 1 Strategic Information and Developments
73.	Georgia Country Study Guide Volume 1 Strategic Information and Developments
74.	Germany Country Study Guide Volume 1 Strategic Information and Developments
75.	Ghana Country Study Guide Volume 1 Strategic Information and Developments
76.	Gibraltar Country Study Guide Volume 1 Strategic Information and Developments
77.	Greece Country Study Guide Volume 1 Strategic Information and Developments
78.	Greenland Country Study Guide Volume 1 Strategic Information and Developments
79.	Grenada Country Study Guide Volume 1 Strategic Information and Developments
80.	Guam Country Study Guide Volume 1 Strategic Information and Developments
81.	Guatemala Country Study Guide Volume 1 Strategic Information and Developments
82.	Guernsey Country Study Guide Volume 1 Strategic Information and Developments
83.	Guinea Country Study Guide Volume 1 Strategic Information and Developments
84.	Guinea-Bissau Country Study Guide Volume 1 Strategic Information and Developments
85.	Guyana Country Study Guide Volume 1 Strategic Information and Developments
86.	Haiti Country Study Guide Volume 1 Strategic Information and Developments
87.	Honduras Country Study Guide Volume 1 Strategic Information and Developments
88.	Hungary Country Study Guide Volume 1 Strategic Information and Developments
89.	Iceland Country Study Guide Volume 1 Strategic Information and Developments
90.	India Country Study Guide Volume 1 Strategic Information and Developments

91.	Indonesia Country Study Guide Volume 1 Strategic Information and Developments
92.	Iran Country Study Guide Volume 1 Strategic Information and Developments
93.	Iraq Country Study Guide Volume 1 Strategic Information and Developments
94.	Ireland Country Study Guide Volume 1 Strategic Information and Developments
95.	Israel Country Study Guide Volume 1 Strategic Information and Developments
96.	Italy Country Study Guide Volume 1 Strategic Information and Developments
97.	Jamaica Country Study Guide Volume 1 Strategic Information and Developments
98.	Japan Country Study Guide Volume 1 Strategic Information and Developments
99.	Jersey Country Study Guide Volume 1 Strategic Information and Developments
100.	Jordan Country Study Guide Volume 1 Strategic Information and Developments
101.	Kazakhstan Country Study Guide Volume 1 Strategic Information and Developments
102.	Kenya Country Study Guide Volume 1 Strategic Information and Developments
103.	Kiribati Country Study Guide Volume 1 Strategic Information and Developments
104.	Korea, North Country Study Guide Volume 1 Strategic Information and Developments
105.	Korea, South Country Study Guide Volume 1 Strategic Information and Developments
106.	Kosovo Country Study Guide Volume 1 Strategic Information and Developments
107.	Kurdistan Country Study Guide Volume 1 Strategic Information and Developments
108.	Kuwait Country Study Guide Volume 1 Strategic Information and Developments
109.	Kyrgyzstan Country Study Guide Volume 1 Strategic Information and Developments
110.	Laos Country Study Guide Volume 1 Strategic Information and Developments
111.	Latvia Country Study Guide Volume 1 Strategic Information and Developments
112.	Lebanon Country Study Guide Volume 1 Strategic Information and Developments
113.	Lesotho Country Study Guide Volume 1 Strategic Information and Developments
114.	Liberia Country Study Guide Volume 1 Strategic Information and Developments
115.	Libya Country Study Guide Volume 1 Strategic Information and Developments
116.	Liechtenstein Country Study Guide Volume 1 Strategic Information and Developments
117.	Lithuania Country Study Guide Volume 1 Strategic Information and Developments
118.	Luxembourg Country Study Guide Volume 1 Strategic Information and Developments
119.	Macao Country Study Guide Volume 1 Strategic Information and Developments
120.	Macedonia,Country Study Guide Volume 1 Strategic Information and Developments
121.	Madagascar Country Study Guide Volume 1 Strategic Information and Developments
122.	MadeiraCountry Study Guide Volume 1 Strategic Information and Developments
123.	Malawi Country Study Guide Volume 1 Strategic Information and Developments
124.	Malaysia Country Study Guide Volume 1 Strategic Information and Developments
125.	Maldives Country Study Guide Volume 1 Strategic Information and Developments
126.	Mali Country Study Guide Volume 1 Strategic Information and Developments
127.	Malta Country Study Guide Volume 1 Strategic Information and Developments
128.	Man Country Study Guide Volume 1 Strategic Information and Developments
129.	Marshall Islands Country Study Guide Volume 1 Strategic Information and Developments
130.	Mauritania Country Study Guide Volume 1 Strategic Information and Developments
131.	Mauritius Country Study Guide Volume 1 Strategic Information and Developments
132.	Mayotte Country Study Guide Volume 1 Strategic Information and Developments
133.	Mexico Country Study Guide Volume 1 Strategic Information and Developments
134.	Micronesia Country Study Guide Volume 1 Strategic Information and Developments
135.	Moldova Country Study Guide Volume 1 Strategic Information and Developments
136.	Monaco Country Study Guide Volume 1 Strategic Information and Developments
137.	Mongolia Country Study Guide Volume 1 Strategic Information and Developments
138.	Monserrat Country Study Guide Volume 1 Strategic Information and Developments
139.	Montenegro Country Study Guide Volume 1 Strategic Information and Developments
140.	Morocco Country Study Guide Volume 1 Strategic Information and Developments
141.	Mozambique Country Study Guide Volume 1 Strategic Information and Developments
142.	Myanmar Country Study Guide Volume 1 Strategic Information and Developments
143.	Nagorno-Karabakh Republic Country Study Guide Volume 1 Strategic Information and Developments

144. Namibia Country Study Guide Volume 1 Strategic Information and Developments
145. Nauru Country Study Guide Volume 1 Strategic Information and Developments
146. Nepal Country Study Guide Volume 1 Strategic Information and Developments
147. Netherlands Country Study Guide Volume 1 Strategic Information and Developments
148. New Caledonia Country Study Guide Volume 1 Strategic Information and Developments
149. New Zealand Country Study Guide Volume 1 Strategic Information and Developments
150. Nicaragua Country Study Guide Volume 1 Strategic Information and Developments
151. Niger Country Study Guide Volume 1 Strategic Information and Developments
152. Nigeria Country Study Guide Volume 1 Strategic Information and Developments
153. Niue Country Study Guide Volume 1 Strategic Information and Developments
154. Northern Cyprus (Turkish Republic of Northern Cyprus)
155. Northern Mariana Islands Country Study Guide Volume 1 Strategic Information and Developments
156. Norway Country Study Guide Volume 1 Strategic Information and Developments
157. Oman Country Study Guide Volume 1 Strategic Information and Developments
158. Pakistan Country Study Guide Volume 1 Strategic Information and Developments
159. Palau Country Study Guide Volume 1 Strategic Information and Developments
160. Palestine (West Bank & Gaza) Country Study Guide Volume 1 Strategic Information and Developments
161. Panama Country Study Guide Volume 1 Strategic Information and Developments
162. Papua New Guinea Country Study Guide Volume 1 Strategic Information and Developments
163. Paraguay Country Study Guide Volume 1 Strategic Information and Developments
164. Peru Country Study Guide Volume 1 Strategic Information and Developments
165. Philippines Country Study Guide Volume 1 Strategic Information and Developments
166. Pitcairn Islands Country Study Guide Volume 1 Strategic Information and Developments
167. Poland Country Study Guide Volume 1 Strategic Information and Developments
168. Polynesia French Country Study Guide Volume 1 Strategic Information and Developments
169. Portugal Country Study Guide Volume 1 Strategic Information and Developments
170. Qatar Country Study Guide Volume 1 Strategic Information and Developments
171. Romania Country Study Guide Volume 1 Strategic Information and Developments
172. Russia Country Study Guide Volume 1 Strategic Information and Developments
173. Rwanda Country Study Guide Volume 1 Strategic Information and Developments
174. Sahrawi Arab Democratic Republic Volume 1 Strategic Information and Developments
175. Saint Kitts and Nevis Country Study Guide Volume 1 Strategic Information and Developments
176. Saint Lucia Country Study Guide Volume 1 Strategic Information and Developments
177. Saint Vincent and The Grenadines Country Study Guide Volume 1 Strategic Information and Developments
178. Samoa (American) A Country Study Guide Volume 1 Strategic Information and Developments
179. Samoa (Western) Country Study Guide Volume 1 Strategic Information and Developments
180. San Marino Country Study Guide Volume 1 Strategic Information and Developments
181. Sao Tome and Principe Country Study Guide Volume 1 Strategic Information and Developments
182. Saudi Arabia Country Study Guide Volume 1 Strategic Information and Developments
183. Scotland Country Study Guide Volume 1 Strategic Information and Developments
184. Senegal Country Study Guide Volume 1 Strategic Information and Developments
185. Serbia Country Study Guide Volume 1 Strategic Information and Developments
186. Seychelles Country Study Guide Volume 1 Strategic Information and Developments
187. Sierra Leone Country Study Guide Volume 1 Strategic Information and Developments
188. Singapore Country Study Guide Volume 1 Strategic Information and Developments
189. Slovakia Country Study Guide Volume 1 Strategic Information and Developments
190. Slovenia Country Study Guide Volume 1 Strategic Information and Developments
191. Solomon Islands Country Study Guide Volume 1 Strategic Information and Developments
192. Somalia Country Study Guide Volume 1 Strategic Information and Developments
193. South Africa Country Study Guide Volume 1 Strategic Information and Developments
194. Spain Country Study Guide Volume 1 Strategic Information and Developments
195. Sri Lanka Country Study Guide Volume 1 Strategic Information and Developments

196. St. Helena Country Study Guide Volume 1 Strategic Information and Developments
197. St. Pierre & Miquelon Country Study Guide Volume 1 Strategic Information and Developments
198. Sudan (Republic of the Sudan) Country Study Guide Volume 1 Strategic Information and Developments
199. Sudan South Country Study Guide Volume 1 Strategic Information and Developments
200. Suriname Country Study Guide Volume 1 Strategic Information and Developments
201. Swaziland Country Study Guide Volume 1 Strategic Information and Developments
202. Sweden Country Study Guide Volume 1 Strategic Information and Developments
203. Switzerland Country Study Guide Volume 1 Strategic Information and Developments
204. Syria Country Study Guide Volume 1 Strategic Information and Developments
205. Taiwan Country Study Guide Volume 1 Strategic Information and Developments
206. Tajikistan Country Study Guide Volume 1 Strategic Information and Developments
207. Tanzania Country Study Guide Volume 1 Strategic Information and Developments
208. Thailand Country Study Guide Volume 1 Strategic Information and Developments
209. Timor Leste (Democratic Republic of Timor-Leste) Country Study Guide Volume 1 Strategic Information and Developments
210. Togo Country Study Guide Volume 1 Strategic Information and Developments
211. Tonga Country Study Guide Volume 1 Strategic Information and Developments
212. Trinidad and Tobago Country Study Guide Volume 1 Strategic Information and Developments
213. Tunisia Country Study Guide Volume 1 Strategic Information and Developments
214. Turkey Country Study Guide Volume 1 Strategic Information and Developments
215. Turkmenistan Country Study Guide Volume 1 Strategic Information and Developments
216. Turks & Caicos Country Study Guide Volume 1 Strategic Information and Developments
217. Tuvalu Country Study Guide Volume 1 Strategic Information and Developments
218. Uganda Country Study Guide Volume 1 Strategic Information and Developments
219. Ukraine Country Study Guide Volume 1 Strategic Information and Developments
220. United Arab Emirates Country Study Guide Volume 1 Strategic Information and Developments
221. United Kingdom Country Study Guide Volume 1 Strategic Information and Developments
222. United States Country Study Guide Volume 1 Strategic Information and Developments
223. Uruguay Country Study Guide Volume 1 Strategic Information and Developments
224. Uzbekistan Country Study Guide Volume 1 Strategic Information and Developments
225. Vanuatu Country Study Guide Volume 1 Strategic Information and Developments
226. Vatican City (Holy See) Country Study Guide Volume 1 Strategic Information and Developments
227. Venezuela Country Study Guide Volume 1 Strategic Information and Developments
228. Vietnam Country Study Guide Volume 1 Strategic Information and Developments
229. Virgin Islands, British Country Study Guide Volume 1 Strategic Information and Developments
230. Wake Atoll Country Study Guide Volume 1 Strategic Information and Developments
231. Wallis & Futuna Country Study Guide Volume 1 Strategic Information and Developments
232. Western Sahara Country Study Guide Volume 1 Strategic Information and Developments
233. Yemen Country Study Guide Volume 1 Strategic Information and Developments
234. Zambia Country Study Guide Volume 1 Strategic Information and Developments
235. Zimbabwe Country Study Guide Volume 1 Strategic Information and Developments

Made in United States
Orlando, FL
04 November 2026

90207782R00181